ART AND POLITICS IN
EARLY MODERN GERMANY

STUDIES
IN MEDIEVAL AND
REFORMATION THOUGHT

EDITED BY

HEIKO A. OBERMAN, Tucson, Arizona

IN COOPERATION WITH

THOMAS A. BRADY, Jr., Berkeley, California
E. JANE DEMPSEY DOUGLASS, Princeton, New Jersey
JÜRGEN MIETHKE, Heidelberg
M. E. H. NICOLETTE MOUT, Leiden
ANDREW PETTEGREE, St. Andrews
MANFRED SCHULZE, Wuppertal
DAVID C. STEINMETZ, Durham, North Carolina

VOLUME LXVII

PIA F. CUNEO

ART AND POLITICS IN
EARLY MODERN GERMANY

ART AND POLITICS IN EARLY MODERN GERMANY

JÖRG BREU THE ELDER AND
THE FASHIONING OF POLITICAL IDENTITY
CA. 1475-1536

BY

PIA F. CUNEO

BRILL
LEIDEN · BOSTON · KÖLN
1998

This book is printed on acid-free paper.

Library of Congress Cataloging-in-Publication Data

Cuneo, Pia F.
    Art and politics in early modern Germany : Jörg Breu the Elder and
the fashioning of political identity, ca. 1475–1536 / by Pia F.
Cuneo.
        p.   cm. — (Studies in medieval and Reformation thought, ISSN
0585-6914 ; v. 67)
    Includes bibliographical references and index.
    ISBN 9004111840 (cloth : alk. paper)
    1. Breu, Jörg, ca. 1480–1537—Criticsim and interpretation.
2. Politics in art.   3. Art and state—Germany.   I. Title.
II. Series.
N6888.B6957C86   1998
769.92—dc21   98–25296
                                                                              CIP

Die Deutsche Bibliothek - CIP-Einheitsaufnahme

Cuneo, Pia F.:
Art and politics in early modern Germany : Jörg Breu the elder and
the fashioning of polkitical identity, ca. 1475 - 1536 / by Pia F.
Cuneo. – Leiden ; Boston ; Köln : Brill, 1998
    (Studies in medieval and reformation thought ; Vol. 67)
    ISBN 90–04–11184–0

ISSN   0585-6914
ISBN   90 04 11184 0

PRINTED IN THE NETHERLANDS

CONTENTS

Indices

ACKNOWLEDGMENTS

My thanks are due to those generous colleagues who took the time to read various versions of my manuscript and comment on it: Corine Schleif, Keith Moxey, Jane Williams and the two anonymous readers for the series "Studies in Medieval and Reformation Thought." I would also like to thank the series editor, Heiko Oberman, for his perspicacious commentary and the inspiration he and his work provide.

I was assisted financially by several grants which aided my research in Germany, primarily in Augsburg and in Munich: the Deutsche Akademische Austauschdienst; the Samuel H. Kress Foundation; the Office of the Vice-President for Research at the University of Arizona; and the Dean's Small Grant Fund from the College of Fine Arts at the University of Arizona.

On the production end of the manuscript, Cheryl and Terry Smart, and my copy-editor Ken Plax rendered invaluable assistance for which I am very grateful. I am also very grateful to those at Brill who carefully and competently guided my work through the publication process: Theo Joppe, Elizabeth Venekamp, Marit Alberts and Gera van Bedaf.

On a general but nonetheless vital level, I would like to thank Sheila Pitt, Suds, and Beatrix for teaching me, in so many arenas of life, the value of "getting on the bit" metaphorically speaking, and going forward. I owe a profound debt of gratitude to my husband, Peter Foley. As this book could never have been written without his help and encouragement, it is lovingly dedicated to him.

P.F.C.
Tucson, Arizona
May, 1998

LIST OF ILLUSTRATIONS

Plate 1: Breu, *Battle of Pavia*, woodcut, c. 1525, Copyright © The British Museum.

(*Plates 2–11:* Copyright © Herzog Anton Ulrich-Museum, Braunschweig)

Plate 2: Breu, *Trumpeter and Six Crossbowmen*, woodcut from the adventus series, c. 1530.

Plate 3: Breu, *Captain and Six Crossbowmen*, woodcut from the adventus series, c. 1530.

Plate 4: Breu, *Knights of Spanish Orders*, woodcut from the adventus series, c. 1530.

Plate 5: Breu, *Pageboys on Stallions*, woodcut from the adventus series, c. 1530.

Plate 6: Breu, *Court Chamberlains Count Adrian von Rois and Wilhelm Freiherr von Roggendorf-Möllenburg*, woodcut from the adventus series, c. 1530.

Plate 7: Breu, *Four Princes* (here identified from left to right as Wilhelm IV of Bavaria, Count Palatine Ottheinrich, Count Palatine Philip, Ludwig X of Bavaria), woodcut from the adventus series, c. 1530.

Plate 8: Breu, *Supreme Marshall of the Empire, Elector John the Steadfast*, woodcut from the adventus series, c. 1530.

Plate 9: Breu, *Ferdinand, Charles V, Count Palatine Friedrich and Cardinal Campeggio*, woodcut from the adventus series, c. 1530.

Plate 10: Breu, *Hungarian Lancers*, woodcut from the adventus series, c. 1530.

Plate 11: Breu, *Two Groups of Lancers*, woodcut from the adventus series, c. 1530.

Plate 12: Breu, *Suicide of Lucretia*, 1528. Alte Pinakothek, Munich. © Artothek, Spezialarchiv für Gemäldefotografie, Peissenberg, Germany.

Plate 13: Breu, *Battle of Zama*, c. 1530. Alte Pinakothek, Munich. © Artothek, Spezialarchiv für Gemäldefotografie, Peissenberg, Germany.

PLATES

Plate 1: Breu, *Battle of Pavia*, woodcut, c. 1525. Copyright © The British Museum.

Plate 2: Breu, *Trumpeter and Six Crossbowmen*, woodcut from the adventus series, c. 1530. © Herzog Anton Ulrich-Museum. Braunschweig.

Plate 3: Breu, *Captain and Six Crossbowmen*, woodcut from the adventus series, c. 1530. © Herzog Anton Ulrich-Museum, Braunschweig.

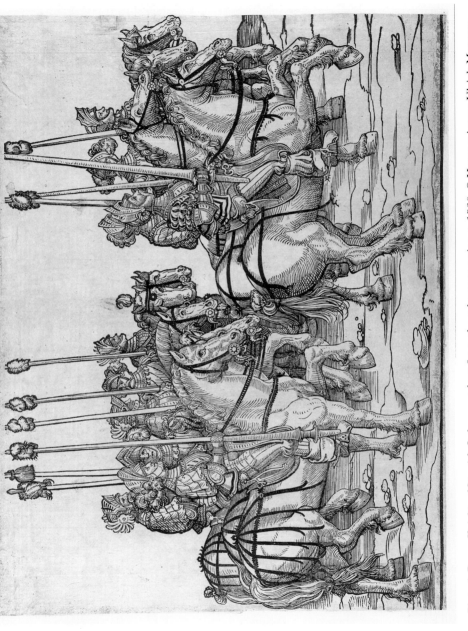

Plate 4: Breu, *Knights of Spanish Orders*, woodcut from the adventus series, c. 1530. © Herzog Anton Ulrich-Museum, Braunschweig.

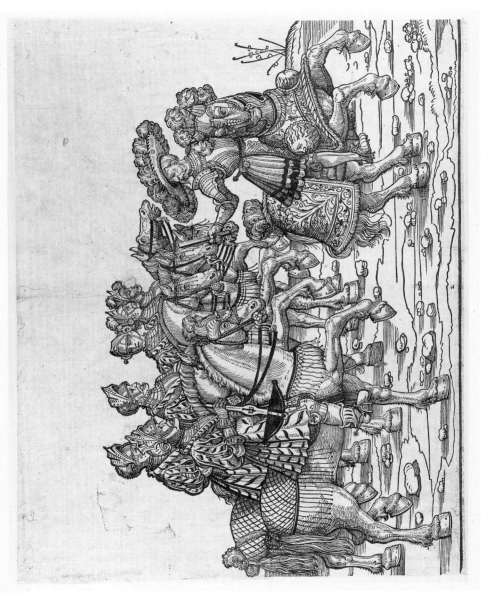

Plate 5: Breu, *Pageboys on Stallions*, woodcut from the adventus series, c. 1530. © Herzog Anton Ulrich-Museum, Braunschweig.

Plate 6: Breu, *Court Chamberlains Count Adrian von Rois and Wilhelm Freiherr von Roggendorf-Möllenburg*, woodcut from the adventus series, c. 1530. © Herzog Anton Ulrich-Museum, Braunschweig.

Plate 7: Breu, *Four Princes* (here identified from left to right as Wilhelm IV of Bavaria, Count Palatine Ottheinrich, Count Palatine Philip, Ludwig X of Bavaria), woodcut from the adventus series, c. 1530. © Herzog Anton Ulrich-Museum, Braunschweig.

Plate 8: Breu, *Supreme Marshall of the Empire, Elector John the Steadfast*, woodcut from the adventus series, c. 1530. © Herzog Anton Ulrich-Museum, Braunschweig.

Plate 9: Breu, *Ferdinand, Charles V, Count Palatine Friedrich and Cardinal Campeggio*, woodcut from the adventus series, c. 1530. © Herzog Anton Ulrich-Museum, Braunschweig.

Plate 10: Breu, *Hungarian Lancers*, woodcut from the adventus series, c. 1530. © Herzog Anton Ulrich-Museum, Braunschweig.

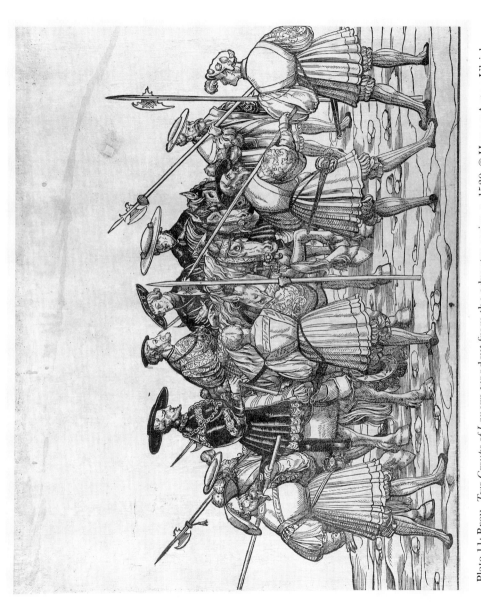

Plate 11: Breu, *Two Groups of Lancers*, woodcut from the adventus series, c. 1530. © Herzog Anton Ulrich-Museum, Braunschweig.

Plate 12: Breu, *Suicide of Lucretia*, 1528. Alte Pinakothek, Munich.
© Artothek, Spezialarchiv für Gemäldefotografie, Peissenberg, Germany.

Plate 13: Breu, *Battle of Zama*, c. 1530. Alte Pinakothek, Munich.
© Artothek, Spezialarchiv für Gemäldefotografie, Peissenberg, Germany.

CHAPTER ONE

THE ISSUES

On June 15, 1530, the Emperor Charles V of Habsburg rode into the German Free Imperial city of Augsburg on a white stallion, accompanied by a vast entourage of soldiers, clerics, and courtiers. The emperor's entrance into the city marked the initiation of an Imperial Diet that would prove uniquely important in the religious and political history of Germany. The *confessio augustana*, which had been drafted by Melanchthon for the occasion and was presented to Charles for his consideration, comprised one of the earliest and most fundamental articulations of Lutheran theology. In addition, the issue of who would become the next Roman king was settled during the course of the Diet in favor of the emperor's brother Ferdinand, thus consolidating the increasingly hegemonic (yet consistently contested) claims of Habsburg rule.

Expectations for the 1530 Diet were running high when Charles made his dramatic appearance in Augsburg. According to contemporaneous ballads and broadsheets composed in anticipation of the event, many hoped that the meeting of the emperor and his estates would bring an end to the increasingly acute confessional confusion and political factionalism which defined the entire preceding decade. Catholics hoped that Charles would demand cessation of theological and liturgical change until a papal council would decide an appropriate course of action. With equal fervor, reformers hoped that the emperor might come to understand their objections to current papal policies and allow reform to continue. Germans on both sides of the yet ill-defined confessional divide hoped that the emperor and his estates would agree to implement procedures advantageous to social and economic stability, such as standardizing weights and measures, and maintaining peaceable relationships throughout the land (*ewige Landfriede*). In short, the Diet of Augsburg was seen as an opportunity, desperately needed, to return peace and prosperity to the German territories of the Holy Roman Empire.

Such high expectations for an event occurring at what seems to have been perceived as a precarious and as a propitious moment in German history no doubt account for the extensive degree of documentation surrounding the 1530 Diet. Poems and ballads were composed, pamphlets and broadsheets were written and illustrated. Belonging to this persistent commemoration of events associated with the Diet is a woodcut series, consisting of ten sheets, which illustrate Charles V's ceremonial entrance (adventus) into Augsburg. The woodcuts have been convincingly attributed to the local artist Jörg Breu the Elder. Breu depicts various members of the emperor's entourage, including flamboyant page boys riding some of the emperor's finest horses, sturdy soldiers laden with fearsome weapons, and distinguished courtiers belonging to the local and foreign aristocracy. Charles himself is represented, wearing a brocaded doublet, riding his white stallion, and accompanied by his brother and members of the clerical and national nobility.

Such a work as Breu's is, at first glance, easily dismissed from serious historical and/or art historical analysis. The woodcuts are certainly superior in the quality of execution yet cannot be compared with the detailed naturalism and embrace of Italian Renaissance aesthetics characterizing the graphic work of Breu's contemporary, Albrecht Dürer of Nuremberg—characteristics that are enshrined within the art historical canon as the touchstones of artistic genius. In this canon, art of Early Modern Germany is allowed only two options for aesthetic significance: as positively responsive to the idealizing and classicizing art of the Renaissance (read Italian), embodied in the works of Dürer and Hans Holbein, or as seminal examples of a raw expressionism touted as characteristically German, exemplified in the works of Matthias Grünewald and Albrecht Altdorfer. Historically, Breu's woodcut series may be passed off as a mere illustration of an historic event, as simply transparent, the kind of picture one might reproduce in a history textbook in order to reinforce the textual description with an easily readable visual one: this is what happened that day, and here is a picture of it.

Upon closer examination, however, Breu's series—both its production and its viewing—is richly complicated and historically revealing. That Breu should have been chosen to commemorate Charles's adventus makes sense on a number of levels. The artist had contributed to Habsburg imagery on several occasions in the past, including painting frescoes depicting Habsburg genealogy and warfare (for the Augsburg city hall), and providing designs for glass rondelles illustrating Maximilian I engaged in battle and at the hunt (for Maximilian's hunting lodge in Lermos). In addition, it would seem reasonable to engage a local artist to commemorate a local event. But Breu was not just any local artist. He was also the author of a city chronicle describing events in his native city of Augsburg. Such texts were written rather frequently during the fifteenth and sixteenth centuries, yet the authorship of an artist, and the consistent critique of the powerful combined with sympathy for the poor in Breu's text, are highly unusual. From Breu's chronicle, we know that he appeared to embrace the reform movement already in 1524 and seemed to have expressed particular engagement with Zwingli's teachings. Breu's pro-reformational sympathies thus placed him in direct opposition to Charles V, who viewed his own role as Holy Roman Emperor traditionally—that is, as the defender of the Holy Church of Rome against all forms of challenge. Thus, artist and subject differed according to their confessional loyalties.

The patronage of the project adds another level of complexity. In chapter 4, I argue that the Wittelsbach duke of Bavaria, Wilhelm IV, commissioned Breu to carry out the woodcut series. Wilhelm, his brother, and their two Wittelsbach cousins all solemnly process together on one sheet of Breu's woodcut series. The duke had worked with Breu on a previous occasion, commissioning the artist to contribute two panels to Wilhelm's cycle of history paintings. The Wittelsbachs, like the Habsburgs, remained staunch supporters of the old faith. Wilhelm IV in fact vigorously and successfully defended his territories against any ideological incursions of reformational forces. Here we should note that artist and also patron differed in their confessional alignments. Breu in fact singled Wilhelm out in his chronicle several times for harsh critique, referring to the duke as cruel and arrogant. Wilhelm was also ambitious, and one of his goals was to wrest power from his Habsburg cousins in order to play the leading role in German politics himself. Toward this end, he entered into a complicated variety of diplomatic alliances (including ones with Protestant princes) and vied with Ferdinand of Habsburg for the position of Roman king. Thus, although Charles and Wilhelm both supported the Church of Rome, they nonetheless were political adversaries.

How odd then that Wilhelm should commission a work ostensibly glorifying Habsburg splendor and ceremony at a time when he actively sought to undermine Habsburg authority and power. And how odd that Breu should execute that commission for a man he obviously disliked for personal as well as ideological reasons. Yet this strange state of affairs is not only fascinating in the twists and turns involved in its narrative, it is also highly informative. It reveals the complexity involved in Early Modern German politics and it demonstrates the crucial role of art therein. As I argue later on in the book, the woodcuts produced at the nexus of these competing political and confessional relationships in fact accomodate a range of readings, both then and now. Both the patron (Wilhelm IV and his family) and the subject (Charles V) are glorified and yet at the same time, certain subtle visual cues are given that could serve to detract attention from the Habsburg emperor. The woodcuts could be read as presenting the Wittelsbachs, dutifully marching along in the adventus procession, as loyal servants of the Habsburgs, as indeed owing to their rank and position they were meant to be. Or they can be seen as an impressive force unto themselves, quite independent of their relationship to Habsburg. Charles can be viewed as both the ultimate authority as well as a preoccupied and rather ordinary man, upstaged in fact by some of his courtiers. The woodcut series would thus generate meaning as successfully for a Habsburg-loyal audience as for a Wittelsbach-loyal one.

Because they seem able to accomodate these various readings, Breu's woodcuts could be faulted for ambiguity, for failing to create a clear-cut and definitive political position for their viewers to adopt. Yet it is wrong to fault these images for lack of clarity when political identity and networks of loyalty and alliance were equally ambiguous and in a state of flux.[1] It is precisely the images' ability to address multiple subject positions that makes them so consummately useful as political art.

This book focuses on the complex relationship between art and politics in Early Modern Germany, of which Breu's woodcuts commemorating Charles V's 1530 adventus are an illustrative example. It will be specifically argued that a crucial function of art was to fashion political identity, and that this process, involving artist, patron, audience, and historical context, is as complicated as it is historically illuminating. In considering this particular intersection be-

---

[1] Ronald F. E. Weissman, "Reconstructing Renaissance Sociology: The Chicago School and the Study of Renaissance Society," in *Persons in Groups: Social Behavior as Identity Formation in Medieval and Renaissance Europe*, ed. Richard Trexler (Binghamton: Medieval and Renaissance Texts and Studies, 1985), 39–46. Weissman argues for the complexity of social relationships and the importance therein of "significant symbols," which I have interpreted to include cultural phenomena such as art.

tween art and politics, three themes emerge from the realm of contemporaneous cultural production. Narratives (both textual and visual) of warfare, ceremony, and history serve as particularly potent
vehicles for articulating political identity. This is so because such
narratives, by dint of their subject matter, sort out who has power
and who does not. in narratives of warfare, who wins and who loses;
in ceremony, who is more important and who is less so; and in
history, who is judged favorably and who is condemned. Sometimes
these projected relationships of power to powerlessness correspond
closely to historical fact, other times they are pure constructs, and
most times, they are somewhere in between. Whatever their relationship to reality, these textual and visual narratives function to display
power in a way that encourages the reader/viewer to respond
affirmatively to the individual or group who wields that power. This
viewing process is an important activity that creates and mobilizes
political consensus. Consequently, this book is organized around
narratives of warfare, ceremony, and history in Breu's art in order to
understand how the artist's works articulate and promote particular
political identities in response to specific historical events and conditions. How this ideological work is performed in Breu's art is compared to similar configurations involving contemporaneous texts and
images produced both north and south of the Alps so as to underline
the broad scope of concern about political identity in Early Modern
Europe.

A central tenet of my argument is the assumption that art does
not merely passively reflect social, political, and historical conditions.
Instead, art is viewed as actively performing ideological work by
offering positions for its audience to identify with and to embrace. In
this process, by identifying themselves with a certain position that is
represented visually as favorable, the viewers align themselves with
specific attendant ideologies. Articulation of identity along political
lines can thus aid in creating political consensus as well as in gener-
ating political critique. In commissioning or buying, displaying or
viewing a work of art affirmatively, one can shape or express political identity. In this way, art functions as a powerful political instrument. For the subsequent historian, art also functions as a kind of
sensitive seismic register, visualizing the traces of ideological shifts
and political tremors.

Focusing on the process through which art fashions political identity is an interpretive strategy particularly well suited for the study of

Early Modern Germany. In the fifteenth and sixteenth centuries, Germany consisted of a mosaic of cities and territories, either semi-independent and self-governing, such as in the case of the Free Imperial Cities, or controlled in varying degrees by secular and religious overlords.[2] All cities and territories, all principalities and estates, however, were ultimately answerable to their nominal head, the Holy Roman Emperor. In theory the political power structure characterizing Early Modern Germany would seem to be clearly defined, arranged hierarchically with the emperor at the top, from whom power and authority disseminated downward through the ranks of secular and ecclesiastical nobility to the citizens of the Free Imperial Cities, with the peasants and the urban poor, as usual, at the bottom of the social and political pyramid. In practice, however, the actual relationship between the emperor and his subjects was anything but clear-cut.[3] Despite the Emperor Maximilian I's (1459-1519) continued efforts to consolidate his authority in the German territories through various legislation proposed during the Imperial Diets, he was continually opposed. Viewed from the perspective of the German cities and nobility, complete submission to Habsburg authority was not necessarily in their own best self-interest. For example, Maximilian's war against Venice (1508-16) severely hampered economically vital trading between the Italian republic and German mercantile centers such as Augsburg.

The emperor's power was far from absolute owing to two basic conditions, one structural, the other economic. In Early Modern Germany, the emperor achieved his rank through election by vote of the electoral dukes. This meant he needed to gain their support by whatever means possible, which often included making concessions to their desire to exert substantial influence on the course of and conditions within the German territories. The emperor was also dependent on wealthy merchants such as the Fuggers and Hoechstetters (both Augsburg families) in order to finance one of the main activities

---

[2] For a general discussion of political and social structures of Early Modern Germany, see Bernd Moeller, *Deutschland im Zeitalter der Reformation* (Göttingen: Vandenhoeck und Ruprecht, 1977).

[3] For discussion of the political tensions in Germany between the emperor and his subjects, see Hanns Gross, "The Holy Roman Empire in Modern Times: Constitutional Reality and Legal Theory," in *The Old Reich: Essays on German Political Institutions 1495–1806*, eds. James A. Vann and Steven W. Rowan (Brussels: Les editions de la librarie encyclopedique, 1974), 3–29.

through which he could actually defend and possibly even expand his power: warfare. In this relationship as well, the emperor needed to be prepared to make compromises with the self-interest of these men. The extent of the emperor's actual political impotence is especially apparent in the election of Maximilian's grandson and successor, Charles V in 1519. In order to be elected, Charles had to swear to abide by a charter drawn up by the electoral dukes that curtailed decisively the extent of his authority over them (the so-called *Wahlkapitulation* [election agreement, literally capitulation]).[4] In addition, Charles had to borrow an enormous sum of money from the Fuggers to buy electoral votes in exchange for valuable mining and trading rights.[5]

As a result of this rather nebulous power structure, authority and control were consistently contested. Indeed, the history of Early Modern Germany can be conceptualized as a constant struggle between the Habsburg emperors, their nobility, and their citizenry, all vying with one another for power. Indeed, it has been argued that the Reformation was so successful precisely because those involved were able to take advantage of the political fragmentation already in place.[6]

Political identity, in this state of affairs, was likewise an area of contest and constantly in flux. It seems that there were available three possibilities for political identification, which correspond to the basic sources of political power in the Empire: imperial, civic/local, and national. In other words, a German could place his political loyalty and support with the emperor (as certain members of the social and educated elite did), or with his city government or local overlord (this group might include citizens of the Free Imperial cities or subjects of particular princes), or he might consider his political loyalties to lie within more of a national framework. Referring to Early Modern Germany as a nation is in some sense anachronistic since nationhood in the modern sense was not officially achieved

---

[4] Fritz Hartung, "Die Wahlkapitulationen der deutschen Kaiser und Könige," *Historische Zeitschrift* 3. Folge, 11 (1911): 306–44, especially 321–30.

[5] A copy of the "bill" for this can be found in the Staats- und Stadtbibliothek Augsburg, 2° Cod Aug 126. See *Welt im Umbruch: Augsburg zwischen Renaissance und Barock* (Augsburg: Augsburger Druck- und Verlagshaus, 1980), no. 30, 140.

[6] Robert W. Scribner, "Germany," in *The Reformation in National Context*, eds. Bob Scribner, Roy Porter and Mikulá Teich (Cambridge: Cambridge University Press, 1994), 4–29, especially 5–6.

until 1871. In the works of the German humanists, and in the epithet "of the German nation" which Maximilian attached in 1486 to the designation "Holy Roman Empire," however, there is sufficient evidence that some Germans did conceive of their land as constituting a larger state, transcending local boundaries, and characterized by a kind of national identity.[7]

These imperial, civic/local, and national sites for political identity were not necessarily mutually exclusive. For example, just because a person thought of himself as a loyal subject of the emperor, who was after all a ruler of international scope, did not mean that he could not think of himself also as proud member of the German nation. Such indeed was the case for many of the German humanists working in the opening decades of the sixteenth century. And yet, the very permeability of these political categories necessitated their fixation and clarification as the competition for power between imperial, local, and national forces became increasingly acute during the first half of the sixteenth century.

In such a situation, art and other modes of cultural production can play essential roles in helping to shape, define, and stabilize political identities. This indeed is often the main intended function of art commissioned by any patron, institutional or individual, who wishes to persuade a public to adopt a favorable stance vis-à-vis particular issues or situations. Early portraiture of Luther, for example, shows him to be learned and divinely inspired, no doubt serving to encourage confidence in the wisdom and legitimacy of his views, and thus increasing the number of his followers.[8] Art did in fact function in this way, on one level. But intended functionality does not foreclose the possiblity of other meanings generated by the interaction between work and audience, meanings that could lead in quite different directions than those primarily intended by the patron and/or even the artist. Leonardo's *Mona Lisa* is a prime example. For Francesco Giocondo, the painting was to have functioned as a portrait of his substantially younger wife, Lisa. For Vasari, writing about it in his *Lives of the Artists* (1550 and 1568), the portrait was a triumph of "modern" naturalism and artistic genius, a brilliant refu-

---

[7] James Overfield, "Germany," in *The Renaissance in National Context*, eds. Roy Porter and Mikulá Teich (Cambridge: Cambridge University Press, 1992), 92–122.

[8] Martin Warnke, *Cranachs Luther: Entwürfe für ein Image* (Frankfurt am Main: Fischer Taschenbuch Verlag, 1984).

tation of the art that had preceded it.[9] For Marcel Duchamp, who in 1919 painted a moustache on a postcard reproduction of the painting and entitled it *LHOOQ*, the *Mona Lisa* had now become the art of the past which he, through his bold gesture, claimed to refute; the portrait became the vehicle through which, by negation, the Modernists could proclaim their identity. For Sigmund Freud, the painting was evidence of its creator's particular "neurosis."[10] For the numerous companies who use the *Mona Lisa* to advertise a bewildering array of goods and services, ranging from toothpaste to tatoo removal, the painting functions as an easily identifiable yet readily mutable icon through which to promote various commodities. In this way, it functions as a triumph of consumerism.

My contention is that political art of Early Modern Germany functioned to shape political identity as intended by its patrons but also that this art accommodated readings and generated meanings other than those that may have been primarily intended. In other words, the process by which political identity is fashioned in art is complex and sometimes even contradictory. This is an important point because attending to this process in the fullness of its rich complexity also reveals a great deal about the culture producing and using these images. To understand why Vasari praised the *Mona Lisa* in terms of naturalism and as a manifestation of Leonardo's artistic genius is to understand the changing social, professional, and ideological status of the artist (and, by association, the changing role of the guilds and the marketplace) in sixteenth-century Italy. To understand how Breu's adventus woodcuts generated equally affirmative meanings for politically opposite audiences is to understand the competition for power between the emperor and the German nobility, and also how carefully masked that competition had to be. The traces of such delicate duplicity are rarely sustained in other forms of documentation.

Although the relationship between art and politics in Early Modern Germany provides many insights into history and culture, particularly through the process of political identity formation, it is mainly explored within the realm of studies dealing with the Protes-

---

[9] Giorgio Vasari, *Lives of the Artists* (1550; reprint London: Penguin Books, 1965), 1: 266–67.

[10] Sigmund Freud, *Leonardo da Vinci and a Memory of his Childhood*, ed. Peter Gay (New York: Norton, 1989).

tant Reformation. In such studies, political configurations and actions, as well as art, are predominantly assumed to be the by-product of theological debates.[11] In more nuanced studies dealing with the nexus of art, politics, and the Reformation, social issues are allowed influence on political maneuverings and artistic production.[12] Yet even these social-historical analyses remain confined within basically theological parameters.

This theological predominance undergirding the existing literature has definite consequences for the ways in which contemporaneous art is treated. Works chosen for consideration are themselves predominantly theological in orientation, be they Lutheran alternatives to Catholic altarpieces or pre-Reformation illustrated broadsheets. As a result, one is struck by the monotonous and predictable recurrence of the same art works and artists dealt with in the literature. Works such as Albrecht Dürer's *Four Holy Men* (1526; Munich, Alte Pinakothek) and Lucas Cranach the Elder's *Law and Grace* (1529; Gotha, Schlossmuseum), among others, have thus assumed canonical status. As a result, attention remains fixed for the most part upon art production in Dürer's Nuremberg and Cranach's Wittenberg. In addition, these art works are interrogated almost exclusively according to their relationship to contemporaneous theological debates, which the visual image is assumed to reveal in a transparent and easily accessible fashion.

While it is impossible even to speak about the sixteenth century without reference to the tremendous impact of the Reformation in its theological dimension on Early Modern history and culture, it is

---

[11] Literature on art and the Reformation is extensive, although only a few studies consider extratheological issues in any sustained manner. Typical examples of theologically dominated studies (all of which contain thorough and useful bibliographies) are: Carl Christensen, *Art and the Reformation in Germany* (Athens, Ohio: Ohio University Press, 1979); *Kunst der Reformationszeit* (Berlin: Elefanten Press, 1983); *Martin Luther und die Reformation in Deutschland* (Frankfurt am Main: Prestel Verlag, 1983); Werner Hofmann, Gisela Hopp and Eckhard Scherer, eds., *Köpfe der Lutherzeit*, exhibition catalogue (Munich: Prestel Verlag, 1983).

[12] See especially Robert Scribner, *For the Sake of Simple Folk: Popular Propaganda for the German Reformation* (Cambridge: Cambridge University Press, 1981); and Ernst Ullmann, *Kunst und Reformation* (Leipzig: VEB E. A. Seemann Verlag, 1983). Other authors also attend to the complex interplay between social issues and the Reformation but do not consider art: for example: Peter Blickle, *Communal Reformation: The Quest for Salvation in Sixteenth Century Germany* (New Jersey: Humanities Press, 1992), and Philip Broadhead, "International Politics and Civic Society in Augsburg During the Era of the Early Reformation 1518–1537," (Ph.D. diss., University of Kent, 1981).

important to remember that confessional politics were not then, and should not be now, separated from secular politics and vice-versa.[13] The construction of ruler ideology constitutes a particularly fruitful intersection between art and politics, one allowing for (and even necessitating) the discussion of the dynamic interaction between confessional and secular politics. Since the emperor as well as the German territorial princes enjoyed both confessional and secular authority within their respective dominions, positions of power were fashioned and refashioned out of political priorities and exigencies necessarily formed in response to the full panoply of confessional and secular issues. Since the legitimization and exercise of power were at stake, ruler imagery that communicated on a number of levels and addressed a number of concerns was created. The construction of ruler ideology in art thus constitutes a rich field of study in which to analyze the process of political identity formation.

Despite this potential richness, the literature that actually deals with ruler ideology is surprisingly scant. Carl Christensen's recent study, *Princes and Propaganda: Electoral Saxon Art of the Reformation*, focuses specifically on art produced under the Saxon princes that functioned as Reformation propaganda.[14] Although Christensen does include mention of possible secular political functions of Saxon art, his remarks on this topic come in summary fashion in the book's insightful but brief conclusion.[15] Christensen's book thus falls within the category of literature dealing mostly with confessional issues, although here he makes important contributions by focusing on little-discussed images in the noncanonical media of graphics and numismatics.

Several fine studies exist which examine political art commissioned specifically by the Habsburg rulers, although in the most recent treatment of this dynasty, Andrew Wheatcroft singles out the

---

[13] Robert W. Scribner in particular attends to the complex interaction between secular and confessional politics in *The German Reformation* (London: Macmillan, 1986), as does Philip Broadhead in "International Politics and Civic Society."

[14] Carl Christensen, *Princes and Propaganda: Electoral Saxon Art of the Reformation* (Kirksville: Sixteenth Century Journal Publishers, 1992).

[15] Christensen, *Princes*, 124–32. In this brief but interesting chapter, Christensen mentions how the images he discussed in the body of the book, particularly portraiture, "contributed to the development and perpetuation of a dynastic myth" (p. 127). He also rightly cautions that one should not read the art works' function as either religious or secular: "What we are faced with here is not an either/or choice between piety and politics; almost always it is some mixture of the two" (p. 125).

area of Habsburg imagery as needing further study.[16] Hugh Trevor-Roper,[17] Larry Silver,[18] Thomas DaCosta Kaufmann[19] and Marie Tanner[20] have all carefully considered works commissioned under the Habsburg aegis in the Early Modern period. Visual and ideological elements woven into the images are identified and explained according to their potential for political signification. These studies, however, tend to view the art primarily from the perspective of the Habsburg rulers themselves, rather than from that of the intended audience. They sometimes assume a straightforward relationship between art and ideology in which the role of art consists of passively reflecting ideologies produced at court and faithfully disseminated by the artist. History and art, form and content, artist and patron, enjoy harmonious and unproblematic relationships with one another.

This book, which also deals largely with Habsburg imagery, posits instead a less tidy relationship between art and politics by calling attention to the potential contradiction and instability involved in the production and interpretation of political meaning in a work of art. Attending to an image's potential for multivalence encourages the historian to embrace the complexity involved in the relationship between image and audience, and image and historical context. Asking how art helps to fashion identity also constitutes a new approach for the study of Early Modern German art. This has the distinct advantage of positing an active, dynamic role for the production and viewing of art, rather than a merely reflective and passive one. We need

---

[16] Andrew Wheatcroft, *The Habsburgs: Embodying Empire* (London: Penguin Books, 1996), xxviii.

[17] Hugh Trevor-Roper, *Princes and Artists: Patronage and Ideology at Four Habsburg Courts 1517–1633* (New York: Harper and Row, 1976).

[18] See the following articles by Silver: "Forest Primeval: Albrecht Altdorfer and the German Wilderness Landscape," *Simiolus* 13 (1983): 4–43; "'Die guten alten history': Maximilian I, Teuerdank and the Heldenbuch Tradition," *Jahrbuch des Zentralinstituts für Kunstgeschichte* (1986) 71–106; "Prints for a Prince: Maximilian, Nuremberg and the Woodcut," in *New Perspectives on the Art of Renaissance Nuremberg*, ed. Jeffrey Chipps Smith (Austin: The Archer M. Huntington Art Gallery, 1985), 6–21; "Shining Armor: Maximilian as Holy Roman Emperor," *Museum Studies: The Art Institute of Chicago* 12 (1985): 8–29; "Paper Pageants: The Triumphs of Emperor Maximilian I," in *Triumphal Celebrations and the Rituals of Statecraft*, eds. Barbara Wisch and Susan Scott Munshower (University Park: Penn State University Press, 1990), 292–331.

[19] Thomas DaKosta Kaufmann, *Court, Cloister and City: The Art and Culture of Central Europe 1450–1800* (Chicago: University of Chicago Press, 1995).

[20] Marie Tanner, *The Last Descendant of Aeneas: The Hapsburgs and the Mythic Image of the Emperor* (New Haven, Yale University Press, 1993).

to consider not just how politics influenced art but also how art influenced politics.

In Early Modern Germany, no other artist responded as vigorously and as frequently to political conditions in the Holy Roman Empire as did Jörg Breu the Elder of Augsburg. His city chronicle brims with political commentary, so much so that the early twentieth-century historian who edited the text felt compelled to caution the reader about the artist's volatility.[21] Like all European artists of his time, Breu produced works of art depicting religious subject matter. Many of his works, however, represent secular subjects. Most of these deal primarily with the politically potent issue of leadership and how that leadership can be justified and legitimized through warfare, ceremony, and history. Breu's art responds to this issue as it surfaced in Maximilian's and in Charles's reigns, and in Ferdinand I's tenure as his brother's viceroy in the German territories. Breu produced these works in a variety of media: frescoes on the exterior of Augsburg's town hall, woodcuts with Latin and with German inscriptions, and panel paintings for a duke's audience hall. These works thus give us an opportunity to explore not only how messages might be articulated differently in various media, but also how those messages were addressed to different audiences. Breu's activity in this realm spans the years from 1516 to the 1530s, a period that coincides with crucial events in Early Modern German history: the rise, challenge, and institutionalization of the Protestant Reformation; the transition from Maximilian's continental reign to Charles's almost global one; and the entrance of Ferdinand I onto the European political stage. These factors make Breu and his art an ideal choice for exploring the relationship between art and politics in Early Modern Germany.

It comes perhaps as a surprise, then, to learn that Breu has been all but neglected by art historical scholarship. Articles concerning the artist have appeared sporadically and almost exclusively in German scholarly journals, particularly during periods of intensified nationalistic sentiments: at the turn of the century, in the 1920s and 1930s, and briefly in the 1950s and 1960s.[22] These articles, all primarily

---

21 Friedrich Roth, introduction to Jörg Breu, *Die Chronik des Augsburger Malers Georg Preu des Älteren* Die Chroniken der deutschen Städte vom 14. bis ins 16. Jahrhundert, ed. Friedrich Roth, vol. 29 (Leipzig: S. Hirzel Verlag, 1906), 1–17, especially 11–13.

22 See bibliography in Pia Cuneo, "Art and Power in Augsburg: The Art Production of Jörg Breu the Elder," (Ph.D. diss., Northwestern University, 1991).

influenced by the formalist method of art history, seek to set the
parameters of Breu's oeuvre on the basis of stylistic criteria. In Eng-
lish-speaking domains of the discipline, the artist remains practically
unkown. This is all the more surprising in light of the fact that Breu
seems to have been highly regarded as an artist in his own day. In
addition, his city chronicle is unique as a document written by an
artist of this period and providing very detailed information about
his social and political context. Although the reasons for this exclusion will be explored in greater detail in the next chapter, let it
suffice to note here that the study of Breu's art undertaken in this
book represents the first major attempt to understand the historical
significance of this fascinating but neglected artist's work. Consequently, Breu's role as one of the most important political artists of
his day will be newly appreciated. Examining Breu's art in the chapters that follow will reveal much not only about the complexity of
Early Modern German politics, but also about the limitations of
modern art historical discourse.

CHAPTER TWO

FASHIONING THE ARTIST'S IDENTITY: BREU'S CHRONICLE AND CAREER

Before we consider how the narratives of warfare, ceremony, and history are constructed in Breu's work in order to fashion political identity, we first need to become familiar with the artist and his immediate context of the city of Augsburg. Looking at Breu within his artistic and social context will point to the artist's own conflicted and shifting identity as he seeks to negotiate the politics of his own production as well as of his position within the civic community. The fundamental assumption in dealing with Breu in this book will be to recognize the artist's agency in the production of his art, but also to recognize that that agency is sometimes deeply conflicted (in terms of the person and artist Breu) as well as productively contaminated by competing agencies of patron and viewers. It will be argued here that the very multivalence implicit in these available and competing interpretations of a work's meaning lends Breu's art its particular historical and hermeneutic richness.

First we will analyze Renaissance Augsburg's political, confessional, and economic makeup since these are the main areas of contest both for Breu's own subject positions as well as for his politically oriented work. Next, we will turn to Breu's chronicle, in which he constructs these subject positions precisely by critiquing political, confessional, and economic conditions in the city. Last, we will sketch out Breu's biography, paying particular attention to the artist's career in terms of his art production and his social connections. Breu's work for the Habsburgs and Wittelsbachs can thus be placed within the context of the artist's production whereas his multiple and varied social connections help explain the radical social and confessional positions he embraced that placed the artist in direct ideological opposition to his patrons.

Secular and Religious Politics[1]

When one considers Augsburg's political and confessional makeup during the years of Breu's production of political art, one is struck both by the basic consistency of the political framework and of the social background of those in power, as well as by the fluidity of confessional interaction. Whereas the basic political parameters of government remained constant, political decisions regarding confessional policies as well as confessional identities seem to have been pragmatically flexible. This is an important insight as it corrects a view of the Reformation that, through historical hindsight, sees the demarcations between the various confessional groups as absolute, firm and clear-cut. It seems to have been instead the case that confessional identities were in a constant state of flux during these early years of the Reformation, and that people both moved in and out of these groups fairly easily as well as understood a group's identity to mean a wide variety of things. This flexibility of identification helps to explain the basic stability of Augsburg's government during the 1520s, which actively accommodated different confessions unless they directly threatened the already pliant status quo. Jörg Breu's own adoption of different confessional identities is a prime example of that flexibility.

Renaissance Augsburg belonged to that category of cities known as the Free Imperial City (*freie Reichsstadt*).[2] This designation indicated that Augsburg, and other such economically and politically important cities including Nuremberg, was free to govern itself; it was not under the jurisdiction of any territorial lord but answered only to the emperor. Although a mark of distinction, Augsburg's status as a Free Imperial City would prove problematic after 1517 since its gradual embrace of the Reformation constituted a profound

---

[1] This section is especially indebted to the work of Katarina Sieh-Burens, whose careful analysis of Augsburg's city government during the sixteenth century is truly exemplary. Her work is indeed the exception to the stated tendency of scholars toward treating secular and religious politics separately. In her book *Oligarchie, Konfession und Politik im 16. Jahrhundert: Zur sozialen Verflechtung der Augsburger Bürgermeister und Stadtpfleger 1518–1618* (Munich: E. Vogel Verlag, 1986), Sieh-Burens analyzes the interaction between social and religious networks and what effects that interaction had on civic government.

[2] For general information on the history of Augsburg, see Wolfgang Zorn, *Augsburg: Geschichte einer deutschen Stadt*, 2nd ed. (Augsburg, Hieronymus Mühlberger Verlag, 1972); and Gunther Gottlieb, *et al.*, eds., *Geschichte der Stadt Augsburg: 2000 Jahre von der Römerzeit bis zur Gegenwart*, 2nd ed. (Stuttgart: Konrad Theiss Verlag, 1985).

act of disobedience to the city's ultimate and Catholic head, the Habsburg emperor.

Like most of the German Free Imperial Cities in the early sixteenth century, Augsburg's government was basically oligarchic, its form founded on privileges and parameters already granted and set during the Middle Ages. Political power was institutionalized within three major structures,[3] which can be seen as a series of concentric and increasingly narrow circles of influence. The Large Council (*großer Rat*) consisted of 255 annually elected members whose main duty consisted of dealing with financial matters such as taxation. The membership was made up of 12 patricians and each of the city's seventeen guilds' 12 administrators (*Zwölfer*). The Small Council (*kleiner Rat*) consisted of 42 members: each of the guilds' outgoing and incoming directors (*Zunftmeister*) as well as 8 patrician councillors (*Ratsherren*). The Small Council was mainly responsible for legislation and administration, as well as for electing men to the different Council Offices (*Ratsämter*) and to posts in the judiciary. The Council Offices were of fundamental political importance, including positions ranging from city food inspectors to the mayors. To aid their deliberations, the Small Council could avail themselves of 27 members of the Large Council personally chosen by the former. Practical political power was concentrated, however, in the hands of the Thirteen (*Dreizehner*), consisting of the two mayors (*Bürgermeister*), three city construction inspectors (*Baumeister*), three revenue collectors (*Einnehmer*), two seal masters (*Siegler*), and three councillors.

In good oligarchic fashion, this political structure ensured that political power was exercised by a sharply limited number of men; out of a population of about thirty thousand,[4] thirteen were ultimately in charge. In addition, when one looks at the individuals who held these positions, one notices two things: first, that they all came from similar (although not the same) social backgrounds; and second, that the same men kept circulating around the government, holding the same office numerous times and/or moving to different offices.

---

[3] For information on the structure of Augsburg's government, see Katarina Sieh-Burens, *Oligarchie*, 29–31; K. Sieh-Burens, "Die Augsburger Stadtverfassung um 1500," *Zeitschrift des historischen Vereins für Schwaben und Neuburg* 77 (1983): 125–49; and Wolfgang Zorn, *Augsburg: Geschichte einer deutschen Stadt*, 132–34.

[4] This is the number cited by Sieh-Burens for the beginning of the sixteenth century (*Oligarchie*, 23). See also Barbara Rajkay, "Die Bevölkerungsentwicklung von 1500 bis 1648" in Gunther Gottlieb *et al.*, eds., *Geschichte der Stadt Augsburg: 2000 Jahre von der Römerzeit bis zur Gegenwart*, 252–57.

Katarina Sieh-Burens has carefully studied the political and confessional makeup of Augsburg's government. In her examination of the city's annually elected mayors who served between 1518 and 1548 (a time span that basically overlaps with that of Breu's art production under examination),[5] she notes that within this thirty-year period only sixteen different men were elected (if two new mayors were elected each year, this would entail a group of sixty men). All sixteen came from either the patriciate or from the more prestigious guilds, especially the socially and economically privileged merchants' guild. Indeed, the elevated economic status of these men was a necessity since one received no official salary for serving as mayor.[6]

Augsburg's civic government, in terms of both its structure and the identity of its members, remained stable and even fairly static during the period in question. Also consistent was the conservative influence of the patrician and merchant interests, continually guarded by their representatives at the highest level of government. Sieh-Burens has demonstrated that the sixteen men elected mayor between 1518 and 1548 not only shared a similar socioeconomic background, they also belonged to overlapping social networks centered especially around two powerful merchant families, the Fuggers and the Welsers.[7] These networks of social and economic loyalties and interdependence ensured that the men in charge of government shared similar political concerns and interests and thus would govern in a way that would benefit themselves and each other as well as the city's economic dynamos.

When we turn to consider the effect of the Reformation on Augsburg's government, we will notice that the protection and advancement of patrician and merchant interests remained constant despite the changing patterns of confessional identity. Sieh-Burens's work indicates in fact that confessional loyalties acted only as a secondary overlay on top of the fundamentally social and economic networks. It is indeed this state of affairs that Breu repeatedly castigates in his chronicle.

The history of the Reformation in Augsburg is, of course, a complex and fascinating story of challenge, resistance and accommoda-

---

[5] The following information regarding the mayors is taken from Sieh-Burens, *Oligarchie*, 39.

[6] Ibid., 40.

[7] Ibid., 75–76; 91–103.

tion.[8] For our purposes, however, it will be sufficient to sketch the broad outlines of the groups competing for power and official sanction, and some of the issues involved. This information is crucial for understanding positions that Breu adopted in his chronicle and that potentially problematize the artist's relation to his Habsburg and Wittelsbach patrons.

Reformational ideas caught on very quickly in Augsburg, although it took a long time before the Reformation was a civic-sanctioned institution: Nuremberg became officially evangelical (meaning, in this case, Lutheran) in 1525, whereas Augsburg did not forbid the practice of Catholic ritual (and thus did not officially institutionalize the Reformation) until around the mid 1530s.[9] By this time, Augsburg had placed itself firmly within the Lutheran camp. In 1535, the city preachers publicly proclaimed their adherence to Lutheran doctrine, which greatly facilitated Augsburg's inclusion in the Schmalkaldic League of Protestant cities and princes in 1536.[10] The city clearly needed to ally itself with other Protestants as its institutionalization of the Reformation was in direct opposition to the 1530 Imperial Diet's decree demanding that Catholicism remain (or be reinstated as) the official confession in all cities.

Augsburg's path to the primarily Lutheran camp and to its rejection of Catholicism was, however, a long and tortuous one. The city was almost immediately involved in Luther's initial protest. The Church, alarmed by Luther's critique, insisted that the Augustinian monk be interviewed and persuaded to recant his ideas presented in the 95 Theses of 1517. Between October 12 and 14, 1518, Luther was interrogated by the papal legate Cardinal Cajetan; however, to no avail. The meetings took place in the Fuggers' residence in Augsburg.[11]

Even before Luther's interrogation, however, his writings were

---

[8] The literature on this subject is extensive. For a sustained look at the history of the Reformation as it pertains specifically to Augsburg, Friedrich Roth's work, although undertaken at the beginning of the century, is indispensable, based as it is on a thorough familiarity with primary documents: Friedrich Roth, *Augsburgs Reformationsgeschichte*, 2 vols. (Munich: Theodor Ackermann, 1901 and 1904).

[9] The two crucial decisions came in 1534 and 1537 when the city government first forbid Catholic preaching in all churches except those under episcopal jurisdiction (July 29, 1534) and then forbid all Catholic rituals in the entire city (January 17, 1537). See *Freiheit und Ordnung: Reformation in Augsburg* (Augsburg: Selbstverlag der Evang.-Luth. Gesamtkirchengemeinde Augsburg, 1987), 42–45.

[10] Ibid., 43–44; Friedrich Roth, *Augsburgs Reformationsgeschichte*, 2: 282–88.

[11] See Klaus-Peter Schmid, *Luthers Acta Augustana 1518* (Augsburg: FDL-Verlag, 1982).

printed in the city, thus indicating that his ideas were readily available to the Augsburg community.[12] That these ideas were not only
available but were also increasingly embraced is indicated by the city
council's decree attempting to control the printers as early as August
1520 and then again in 1523, here also to no avail.[13]

Luther's ideas were spread throughout the city in the late 1510s
and early 1520s not only by printed pamphlets but also by certain
members of the Catholic clergy sympathetic to Luther's call to reform. These included Johannes Oecolampadius (cathedral preacher
from 1518 to 1520, later a follower of Zwingli), Urbanus Rhegius
(cathedral preacher between 1520 and 1521; later preacher at St.
Anna between 1524 and 1530), and Johannes Frosch (received his
doctorate in theology under Luther in 1518; 1517 to 1523 prior of
the Carmelite monastery in Augsburg, remained at St. Anna until
1531).[14] In response to Lutheran preaching, the city council again
moved to insure that it retained control by issuing a nonetheless
ambiguous admonition to all preachers that they must preach only
the word of God.[15]

Frosch and Rhegius were also the first performers of specifically
Lutheran rituals to be documented: in 1525, Frosch broke with the
Catholic doctrine of compulsory celibacy for the clergy by marrying
Anna Schmid. The ceremony was performed by Urbanus Rhegius at
St. Anna. Later on in that same year, Frosch and Rhegius held com-
munion at St. Anna for the first time in Augsburg in both forms, that
is, offering both the bread and wine as Luther advocated.[16]

Already by 1525, sporadic events within the city marked the increasingly public acting-out of anticlerical attitudes which most times
overlapped with the espousal of Reformational ideas. The year 1524

---

[12]   Luther's commentary on the Psalm 108 was already printed in Augsburg on
September 7, 1518: *Freiheit und Ordnung*, 28; see also *Welt im Umbruch: Augsburg zwischen
Renaissance und Barock* (Augsburg: Augsburger Druck- und Verlagshaus, 1980), 1: 153–
54; and Roth, *Augsburgs Reformationsgeschichte*, 1: 61–62.

[13]   Roth, *Augsburgs Reformationsgeschichte*, 1: 62; and Phillip Broadhead, "International Politics and Civic Society in Augsburg During the Era of the Early Reformation 1518–1537" (Ph.D. diss., University of Kent), 96–97. Broadhead's meticulous
work, like Katarina Sieh-Burens's, includes a careful analysis of how secular and
confessional politics were interwoven.

[14]   *Welt im Umbruch*, 1: 147–51.

[15]   Broadhead, "International Politics and Civic Society," 97.

[16]   *Freiheit und Ordnung*, 32; *Welt im Umbruch*, 1: 147; M. Simon, "Johannes Frosch,"
in *Lebensbilder aus dem Bayerischen Schwaben*, ed. Götz Freiherr von Pölnitz (Munich: M
Hueber, 1953), 2: 181ff.

seems to have been critical in this regard. In May of that year, a
cobbler smeared cows' blood on epitaphs standing in the cathedral
yard, and a group of craftsmen threatened a monk who tried to bless
holy water in the Franciscan church after he refused to say the
prayer in German.[17] Both of these incidents can be seen as influenced by Reformational ideas. The attack on the epitaphs can be
seen as a response to criticism of the use of images by Luther's Wittenberg competitor, Karlstadt,[18] whereas the insistence on prayers
being said in German so that all could understand them was strongly
advocated by Luther. One must remain attentive to the fact that
these actions also have an important social element in that by their
acts of destruction urban laborers challenged those who enjoyed
greater social privilege. The Reformation indeed seems to have been
embraced especially by groups situated lower down in the social hierarchy in its early stages.[19] Its call for reform of both religious and
social practices was no doubt especially attractive to these groups, as
can also be seen in the case of the Peasants' War.[20]

Another serious incident occurring in 1524 is an excellent example of how social, political, and confessional issues were all mutually
inflected. In response to the preaching of Johann Schilling, who was
radically critical of social conditions within the city, the council

[17] These events are cited by Broadhead, "International Politics and Civic Society," 116 and 120; he also includes reference to their appearance in the Council's
criminal records (Urgichten). They are also described in various chronicles: Jörg
Breu, *Die Chronik des Augsburger Malers Georg Preu des Älteren 1512–1537*, Die Chroniken
der schwäbischen Städte, ed. F. Roth, Augsburg, vol. 6 (Leipzig: S. Hirzel Verlag,
1906), 24–25; Clemens Sender, *Die Chronik von Clemens Sender*, Die Chroniken der
schwäbischen Städte, ed. F. Roth, Augsburg, vol. 4 (Leipzig: S. Hirzel Verlag, 1894),
155.

[18] Broadhead states that Karlstadt had in fact been in Augsburg (101). Karlstadt's
iconoclastic treatise *Von Abtuhung der Bilder* had been published in 1522. For Karlstadt's theory of iconoclasm, see Carl Christensen, *Art and the Reformation in Germany*
(Athens, Ohio: Ohio University Press, 1979), 23–35; Serge Michalski, *The Reformation
and the Visual Arts: The Protestant Image Question in Western and Eastern Europe* (London:
Routledge, 1993), 43–50 and P.-K. Schuster, "Bilderkult und Bildersturm: refor-
matorische Ablehnung der Bilder," in *Luther und die Folgen für die Kunst*, ed. Werner
Hofmann (Munich: Prestel Verlag, 1983), cat. no. 2, 127. For iconoclasm in Augs-
burg, see Pia Cuneo, "Propriety, Property and Politics: Jörg Breu the Elder and
Issues of Iconoclasm in Reformation Augsburg," *German History* 14 (1996): 1–20; and
Jörg Rasmussen, "Bildersturm und Restauratio," in *Welt im Umbruch*, (Augsburg:
Augsburger Druck- und Verlagshaus, 1981), 3: 95–114.

[19] Broadhead, "International Politics and Civic Society," especially 108–11.

[20] Peter Blickle, *The Revolution of 1525: The German Peasants' War from a New Perspective*, trans. Thomas A. Brady Jr. and H. C. Erik Midelfort (Baltimore: Johns Hopkins
University Press, 1981).

worked behind the scenes to have Schilling removed by his order (the Franciscans) from Augsburg.[21] The council's manipulations were somehow made public, and a large-scale riot ensued during which the angry crowd held the City Council essentially hostage inside city hall. The council promised to arrange for another preacher who would meet public approval and not to prosecute anyone involved in the insurrection. The crowd dispersed, and although the council did fulfill its first promise, it later arrested and executed two weavers. According to the official record, their previous interrogation had indicated that they and others involved had been primarily concerned with toppling Augsburg's oligarchy and reinstating a more democratic rule by the guilds. The riot was thus cast as a political protest, engineered by members of the less prestigious guilds (tailors' and weavers'), whereby religious issues seemed to have played a secondary part at best.[22] Breu's narrative of this event will be particularly crucial for our understanding of his social and religious critique because he constructs the event with decidedly different and revealing accents.

Although Luther's influence in these early stages of the Reformation in Augsburg seems to have been dominant, other Evangelical groups soon vied for influence in the city. Schilling's eventual replacement at the Franciscan church was Michael Keller, an ardent supporter of Zwingli and a popular preacher.[23] Breu's positive comments about Keller beginning in entries dating from 1524 in the artist's chronicle indicate Breu's sympathy for Zwinglian ideas. Also in 1524, a pamphlet written by Zwingli about the education of boys was printed in Augsburg. Its frontispiece has been attributed to Breu, suggesting that the artist had come in contact with Zwingli's writings.[24]

Keller and other Zwinglian preachers were so successful that

---

[21] The event is described in a number of secondary and primary sources. Wilhelm Vogt, "Johann Schilling der Barfüßermönch und der Aufstand in Augsburg im Jahre 1524," *Zeitschrift des historischen Vereins für Schwaben und Neuburg* 6 (1879): 1–32; Broadhead, "International Politics and Civic Society," 124–49; see also Breu, *Chronik*, 28–33; Sender, *Chronik*, 155–59; Wilhelm Rem, *Cronica newer Geschichten von Wilhelm Räm*, Die Chroniken der Schwäbischen Städten, ed. F. Roth, Augsburg, vol. 5 (Leipzig: S. Hirzel, 1986), 204–9.

[22] Broadhead, "International Politics and Civic Society," 127–49.

[23] Wolfgang Zorn, "Michael Keller," *Lebensbilder aus dem Bayerischen Schwaben*, vol. 7 (Munich: M. Hueber, 1959), 161–72; *Welt Im Umbruch*, 1: 162.

[24] *Welt im Umbruch*, 1: 164–65; F.W.H. Hollstein, German Engravings, Etchings,

Zwinglianism became the dominant confession in Augsburg from around 1527.[25] The high point of official sanction of Zwinglianism came in 1531 when the City Council forbade communion to be carried out according to Lutheran tenets.[26] But Zwinglian dominance did not last long; as stated earlier, in 1535, all official preachers publicly proclaimed their adherence to Luther's teachings in order to end Augsburg's dangerous political and confessional isolation and to allow the city to seek allegiance with the powerful Protestant Schmalkaldic league.

Even before 1535, however, Zwinglians faced further confessional competition. Not only did they need to assert themselves against Catholics and Lutherans, but in 1526, the Anabaptists became increasingly popular.[27] In an uncharacteristic show of unity, Lutherans and Zwinglians joined together to denounce the Anabaptists, who were systematically persecuted by the authorities. By 1528 the Anabaptists no longer constituted a threat to any of the other confessions, which were once again free to compete against one another. It was particularly the interference from more radical sects that profoundly disturbed the more mainline reform movements, especially in their bid for social and political acceptability. We see this process at work on numerous occasions, for example, when Luther immediately distanced himself from the radical action of the peasants in 1524–25 as well as from the teachings of Karlstadt and Müntzer.[28]

and Woodcuts ca. 1400–1700 (Amsterdam: M. Hertzberger Verlag, 1954) vol. 4: no. 190, 178; Heinrich Röttinger, "Zum Holzschnittwerk Jörg Breu des Älteren," *Repertorium für Kunstwissenschaft* 31 (1908): 50. Exemplars of the pamphlet *Herr Ulrich Zwingli leerbiechlein wie man die knaben christlich unterweysen und erziehen soll/ mit kurtzer anzayge aines gantzen christlichen lebens M D XX IIII* can be found in Vienna, Österreichische Nationalbibliothek +35 R.58 and Augsburg, Staats- und Stadtbibliothek, 4° Th H 2995.

[25] For the development of Zwinglianism in the city, and its battle with Lutheranism for popular and official support, see Broadhead's chapter "Polemics, Pastors and the People," in "International Politics and Civic Society," 199–234 and Roth, *Augsburgs Reformationsgeschichte*, 1: 199–210

[26] *Freiheit und Ordnung*, cat. no. 22, 43–44.

[27] Roth, *Augsburgs Reformationsgeschichte*, 1: 218–74; Broadhead, "International Politics and Civic Society," 235–69; Claus-Peter Clasen, *Anabaptism: A Social History* (Ithaca: Cornell University Press, 1972); *Freiheit und Ordnung*, cat. no. 9, 32–33; *Welt im Umbruch*, vol. 1, cat nos. 81–86, 165–68.

[28] See Luther's (in)famous sermons: "Ein Brief an die Fürsten zu Sachsen von dem aufruhrischen Geist" (1524; against Thomas Müntzer and also condemning iconoclasm, which Karlstadt had advocated in 1522); and "Wider die räuberischen und mörderischen Rotten der Bauer" (1525; in response to the Peasants' War).

The inscriptions beneath Dürer's depiction of the *Four Holy Men* given to the evangelical Nuremberg City Council in 1526 include warnings against false prophets and admonitions not to stray from the true path, in this case, constructed as that defined by Luther.[29]

From the above narrative of the Reformation in Augsburg during the years of Breu's political art production, it should be clear that the Reformation did not simply "develop" in the city in any linear, progressive fashion. Instead, the 1520s seem to be characterized by constant, ongoing competition between the various confessions, as each sought to define itself in response to rapidly changing events. From the plethora of pamphlets produced by the various groups responding to one another, one clearly has the sense that the 1520s was a time in which definitions of what it meant to be Protestant, evangelical, Lutheran, Zwinglian, and even Catholic were actively in the process of being worked out.[30] This should not be surprising, as none of these confessional systems sprang fully formed from the head of respective reformers, but were rather shaped by the necessities of existing out there in the real world.

Thus, confessional identities were in a state of creative flux during the 1520s. Because those identities were also new, or in terms of the Catholics, newly justified in the face of confessional threat, they had to respond to already existing social, economic, and political identities. If we now consider the response of the City Council negotiating between the call for reform within the city and the imperial mandates to keep reform at bay, we can see just how flexible those confessional identities could be.

If we look at the list of the city's mayors between 1518 and 1536 (from the beginning of the Reformation until Breu's death), we note that the office was consistently held by Lutherans and Zwinglians; only Ulrich Arzt, who served in 1523, 1525, and 1527, was a Catho-

---

[29] Carl Christensen, "Excursus: Dürer's *Four Apostles*–A Reformation Painting," in *Art and the Reformation in Germany* (Athens, Ohio: Ohio University Press, 1979), 181–206

[30] The meaning of Eucharistic communion, for example, became one of the leading criteria for confessional identity. The Zwinglians insisted that the bread and wine represented the body and blood of Christ in the symbolic sense, while Luther maintained that transubstantiation actually and physically transformed the bread and wine into the body and blood. The meaning of communion was also hotly debated in a series of pamphlets published by theologians from both sides throughout the second half of the 1520s: see Roth, *Augsburgs Reformationsgeschichte*, 1: 197–217.

lic.[31] From this perspective, it might indeed seem surprising that the Reformation was not immediately instituted. But the mayors were not "just" Lutheran or Zwinglian. They were also closely allied with either the Fugger or Welser family, both of which remained essentially Catholic. Thus, although some of the men making up the oligarchic city government might have been personally sympathetic to the Reformation, they were wary not to compromise the interests of the powerful Catholic merchants. They also had to take into account the anti-Reformation stance of the Catholic Habsburg rulers. Whereas a weakening of the Catholic Church in Augsburg strengthened their own power and control of the city, instituting the Reformation too quickly might give the impression of caving in to popular demand, which would in turn weaken the council's authority.

When all of these factors are taken into account, it is obvious that the council had to move carefully in whatever decision it made. In fact, many of its actions seem to have been deliberately ambiguous, as in the censoring of printed pamphlets, which the council, however, never seems to have really enforced.[32] In the case of the weavers executed after the 1524 uprising, in itself hardly an ambiguous action, the motivation seems to have been less persecution of any one confession rather than a message sent regarding intolerance of any breach of the council's authority.

---

[31] The following is a chronological list of the men who were elected mayor in Augsburg from 1518 to 1536 followed by a description of each man in terms of his confessional identity, social network, and social background (this is according to Sieh-Burens, *Oligarchie*, 132). The list dramatically demonstrates how power remained in the hands of a few and delineates the important connections between these men. 1518: Hieronymus Imhof; 1519: Ludwig Hoser; 1520: H. Imhof and Georg Vetter; 1521: Ludwig Hoser, Georg Langenmantel von Sparren (who died that year) and Ulrich Rehlinger; 1522: H. Imhof and G. Vetter; 1523: Ulrich Arzt and U. Rehlinger; 1524: H. Imhof and G. Vetter; 1525: U. Arzt and U. Rehlinger; 1526: H. Imhof and G. Vetter; 1527: U. Arzt and U. Rehlinger; 1528: H. Imhof and G. Vetter; 1529: Anthony Bimmel and U. Rehlinger; 1530: H. Imhof and G. Vetter; 1531: A. Bimmel and U. Rehlinger; 1532: H. Imhof and G. Vetter; 1533: Mang Seitz and U. Rehlinger; 1534: H. Imhof and Wolfgang Rehlinger; 1535: M. Seitz and U. Rehlinger; 1536: Hans Haintzel and W. Rehlinger. Hieronymus Imhof: Lutheran, from the merchants' guild and the Welser network; Ludwig Hoser: no denomination or network, from the salters' guild; Georg Vetter: Lutheran, patrician, from the Welser network; Georg Langenmantel: no denomination or network, patrician; Ulrich Rehlinger: Zwinglian, patrician, from the Fugger network; Ulrich Arzt: Catholic, from the merchants' guild and the Fugger network; Anthony Bimmel: Zwinglian, from the weavers' guild and the Welser network; Wolfgang Rehlinger: Lutheran, patrician, from the Fugger network; Hans Haintzel: Zwinglian, from the merchants' guild and Welser network.

[32] Broadhead, "International Politics and Civic Society," 96–97.

With regard to the council's actions vis-à-vis resolutions issued at Imperial Diets, a great deal of hesitation can be observed. For example, the 1521 Edict of Worms outlawing Luther and his teachings was received by Augsburg's City Council in mid August 1521, along with an imperial mandate stating that the edict must be enforced. A month later, the council finally got around to posting a copy of the Edict on the doors of City Hall, but did little to enforce it.[33]

Augsburg was not alone in ignoring the Edict of Worms; it continued in fact to be debated at Imperial Diets throughout the 1520s. At the Imperial Diet held in Speyer in 1526, it was even agreed upon that the Edict could not be enforced on a national level and that it was up to each city/territory to act according to what its rulers felt was right before God and the emperor.[34] Another Imperial Diet was convened at Speyer three years later during which Archduke Ferdinand (Charles V's brother) revoked the resolutions of 1526 in the Diet's formal concluding document (*Reichstagsabschied*). However, a group of Lutheran princes and cities refused to sign the document as a protest against the illegal nullification of a law that had been passed by the majority. Augsburg, however, was not among the protesting parties, but instead dutifully signed the clearly anti-Reformational document.[35] The mayors that year were two Zwinglians, Anton Bimmel and Ulrich Rehlinger. In his chronicle, Breu sharply criticized the council for its action.

From this cursory view of religion and politics in Augsburg, it can be seen that they were mutually inflected to a fundamental degree: political decisions were sometimes made on a confessional basis, and even more often vice-versa. It is also evident that confessional identities were in a constant state of flux during the 1520s, as social, political, economic, and religious identities sometimes clashed and at other times meshed as groups struggled to define themselves. These shifting and complex identities are important with regard to Breu's continuing attempt to position himself vis-à-vis social, political, and religious issues in his chronicle, as well as to the pro-evangelical artist's work for the Catholic Habsburgs and Wittelsbachs.

---

[33] Roth, *Augsburgs Reformationsgeschichte*, 1: 66.

[34] Hajo Holborn, *A History of Modern Germany: The Reformation* (Princeton: Princeton University Press, 1982), 205.

[35] Ibid., 208–9. Holborn notes that the Lutherans' 1529 protest is the source of the designation "Protestant."

The Economics of Augsburg

In the second and third decades of the sixteenth century, Augsburg was not only a richly diverse community in terms of religious confessions, it was also diverse in terms of avenues of economic activity and levels of economic prosperity. The economics of Augsburg provides another important contextual level to Breu's work as it helps situate the artist's own economic position within this flourishing Renaissance city as well as further emphasizes the close financial ties between the Habsburg emperors and the merchants of Augsburg.

During the years of Breu's production of Habsburg propaganda, Augsburg's economic position in comparison to other Free Imperial Cities was very strong. The two motors that drove the city's economy were its craft production and its merchant activities. The crafts were contained within seventeen guilds, the largest of which was the weavers'.[36] Augsburg's situation with respect to guilds was decidedly different from that of Nuremberg, where the formation of guilds was strictly forbidden. Out of all the crafts practiced in Augsburg, those involved in the textile sector were the most economically significant, as the production of linen and fustian (a combination of imported cotton and indigenous flax) was Augsburg's single most important industry.[37] Breu's father was involved in the cloth industry, and there is one reference in Breu's chronicle that perhaps points to the artist's own involvement as well.[38] Of course, many other crafts were practiced in Augsburg, including the casting of armaments and the production of armor, both of which were patronized by the Habsburgs.[39] The Augsburg armorer Lorenz Helmenschmied

---

[36] Hermann Kellenbenz, "Augsburger Wirtschaft 1530 bis 1620," in *Welt Im Umbruch*, 1: 50. See also Claus-Peter Clasen, *Die Augsburger Weber* (Augsburg: H. Mühlberger Verlag, 1981).

[37] Kellenbenz, "Augsburger Wirtschaft," 50.

[38] Friedrich Roth, introduction to Breu, *Chronik*, 1; Cäsar Menz, *Das Frühwerk Jörg Breus des Älteren* (Augsburg: Kommissionsverlag Bücher Seitz, 1982), 9. The reference made in Breu's chronicle (48) has already been noted by Menz (his footnote 18). Interestingly, Breu makes this comment apparently to juxtapose his own hard work with the accumulation of wealth by unscrupulous means, such as the artificial markup of prices, a practice which was brought to light in 1531 by a scandal involving the price of *Schmalz*. The main culprit was Anthony Bimmel, a Zwinglian member of the Weavers' guild and twice elected mayor. Breu bitterly protests against Bimmel's wealth, which he claims was built up by taking from the weavers and the poor.

[39] Hermann Kellenbenz, "Wirtschaftsleben der Blütezeit," in *Geschichte der Stadt Augsburg*, 2nd ed., ed. Günther Gottlieb et al. (Stuttgart: Konrad Theiss Verlag), 262–63.

(1440–1516), and then his son Coloman (1471–1532), received important commissions from the Habsburgs (both armorers produced
for Maximilian, Coloman also worked for Charles V).[40] Circumstan-
tial evidence indicates that Breu and the Helmenschmieds might
have been well acquainted.[41]

In addition to craft production, the trading and banking enterprises of the city's merchants provided another highly significant
sphere of economic activity.[42] Augsburg was the home of many of
the most powerful south German merchants whose trading networks
extended to the very borders of the world as it was then known; the
Fugger, Welser, and Hoechstetter companies were all involved in the
East Indian spice trade, and the Welsers were even involved in the
colonization of Venezuela.[43] The Fugger company, first under the
leadership of Jakob Fugger (1459–1525) and then his nephew Anthony (1493–1560), was also involved in mining and trading metals,
especially copper.[44] Access to the mines, mostly in the eastern territories of the Holy Roman Empire, usually was acquired through
privileges granted by the Habsburgs in return for cash or credit.
Ambrosius Hoechstetter (1463–1534) was one of the Fuggers' most
formidable competitors in the mining and metals sector.[45] All three
companies of the Fuggers, Welsers, and Hoechstetters were also
deeply involved in imperial finance. As was usual for large merchant
companies, the Fugger, Welser, and Hoechstetter enterprises all

---

[40] Alexander von Reitzenstein, "Die Plattner von Augsburg," in *Augusta 955-
1955: Forschungen und Studien zur Kultur- und Wirtschaftsgeschichte Augsburgs*, ed. Hermann
Rinn (Munich: n.p., 1955), 266–67 and Ortwin Gamber, "Ersteller, Erzeuger und
Liefernormen des Augsburger Harnisches," *Welt im Umbruch*, 3: 172.
[41] Between 1502 and 1507, Breu was a neighbor of the Helmenschmieds in the
quarter of Augsburg known as the Horbruck. One of his first apprentices, Christoph
Zwingenstein, is listed in the 1506 tax records as a member of Helmenschmieds'
household. We also know from a 1520 document that Breu owned three suits of
armor, which seems to be an unusually high number (Stadtsarchiv Augsburg, Sammlung Nachtrag I, 1519–1525, and F. Roth, introduction to Breu *Chronik*, 9). Lastly,
there are a pair of portraits in the Thyssen collection that have traditionally been
identified as Agnes Breu and Coloman Helmenschmied.
[42] For general information on Augsburg merchants, see Götz Freiherr von Pölnitz, "Augsburger Kaufleute und Bankherren der Renaissance" in *Augusta*, 187–218;
and Friedrich Blendinger and Wolfgang Zorn eds., *Augsburg: Geschichte in Bilddokumente*
(Munich: C. H. Becksche Verlag, 1976), 51–59.
[43] Kellenbenz, "Blütezeit," 278–89.
[44] Götz Freiherr von Pölnitz, *Jakob Fugger, Kaiser, Kirche und Kapital in der oberdeutschen Renaissance*, 2 vols. (Tübingen: Mohr Verlag, 1949).
[45] E. Kern, "Studien zur Geschichte des Augsburger Kaufmannshauses der
Hoechstetter," *Archiv für Kulturgeschichte* 26 (1936): 162–98.

combined trade with banking and currency exchange. All three functioned as highly significant moneylenders and creditors to the House of Habsburg. For example, Ambrosius Hoechstetter's funds paid Maximilian's ransom when he was ignominiously held hostage by the city of Bruges in 1488,[46] whereas Jakob Fugger and Bartholomäus Welser provided most of the funds for the election in 1519 of Maximilian's grandson, Charles V, as Roman King.[47]

Jakob and Anthony Fugger, Bartholomäus Welser (1484–1561), and Ambrosius Hoechstetter belonged to the most economically powerful merchants in Augsburg. All remained Catholic, and all had interests inextricably bound up with the fate of the Habsburgs. Their economic importance and their close ties with the Habsburgs constituted a force against which pro-Reformation factions in the city repeatedly and only partially successfully battled. Breu worked for both Jakob and Anthony Fugger, and for Ambrosius's nephew, Georg Hoechstetter the Younger.

Despite Augsburg's steady industrial production and its importance as a center for international trade and finance, the first four decades of the sixteenth century were nonetheless economically precarious. Prices in Augsburg were continually on the rise throughout the century, beginning already around 1510, when the price of grain began to increase. The price of other staples such as beef, fat, salt, and beer followed the same basic trend, namely, upward.[48] In addition to the steadily continuing rise in prices throughout the century, certain natural disasters or market conditions caused prices in some years to jump dramatically. During the period in question, this happened in 1517, 1529, and intermittently from 1531 to 1534.[49]

Wages also increased throughout the sixteenth century, but the rate of increase did not keep pace with the rise in prices.[50] For example, in the first decade of the sixteenth century, 78 percent of a construction worker's (*Bauarbeiter*) salary was spent on food; by the end of the century, 86 percent was needed.[51] This statistic indicates

---

[46] Kellenbenz, "Blütezeit," 286.

[47] *Welt im Umbruch*, vol. 1, cat. no. 30, 140.

[48] Kellenbenz, "Blütezeit," 293–94.

[49] M. J. Elsas, *Umriss einer Geschichte der Preise und Löhne in Deutschland vom ausgehenden Mittelalter bis zum Beginn des neunzehnten Jahrhunderts*, (Leiden: A. W. Sijthoff, 1936), 186–87.

[50] Kellenbenz, "Blütezeit," 296.

[51] Kellenbenz, "Augsburger Wirtschaft," 64.

that an already large amount of an average laborer's wage was spent on food alone, and that that amount even increased.

Another concordant socioeconomic trend resulting from the discrepancy between prices and wages is the large increase in the number of poor in the city, while the growth of the middle class was much slower.[52] Between 1498 and 1554, the number of people who did not own enough personal property to tax (these people appear as *Habnits* in the tax records) increased by 88 percent while the number of those who were worth between two and four thousand gulden (which would correspond to a kind of middle class) increased by only 17.3 percent.[53] More and more people were dropping out of the middle class into poverty.

If the first half of the sixteenth century was not a good time for the middle and lower classes, it was, however, a good time for the very wealthy. Their number increased between 1498 and 1554 by 94 percent. Yet local Augsburgers took note of the corrupt practices of some of these wealthy men, actions that sometimes led to dramatic downfalls. These high-profile scandals seem to have given the impression that even life at the top had its own kind of instabilities.

In 1519, the merchant Wilhelm Rem and the Benedictine monk Clemens Sender reported in their respective chronicles on the legal battle between Ambrosius Hoechstetter and Bartolomäus Rem, who had invested money with Hoechstetter, over three thousand gulden pure profit.[54] Bartolomäus Rem had insisted that Hoechstetter owed him thirty-three thousand gulden on his investment, which the latter contested. In an out-of-court settlement, Hoechstetter was ordered to pay Rem thirty thousand gulden which he agreed to do. But because the sum was three thousand gulden short of what Rem had calculated he was owed, Rem refused to accept the settlement and began to harass Hoechstetter. Rem was placed in prison and died there in 1525. Both chroniclers interpreted this incident as an illustration of corrupt practices of the wealthy merchants.[55]

Although Ambrosius Hoechstetter got out of paying Rem the

---

[52] Kellenbenz, "Blütezeit," 290; and Julius Hartung, "Die augsburgische Vermögenssteuer und die Entwicklung der Besitzverhältnisse im 16. Jahrhundert," *Jahrbuch für Gesetzgebung, Verwaltung und Volkswirtschaft im deutschen Reich* 19 (1895): 875–76.

[53] Kellenbenz, "Blütezeit," 290; and J. Hartung, "Die augsburgische Vermögenssteuer," 875–76.

[54] Rem, *Cronica*, 116–17; Sender, *Chronik*, 146–49.

[55] Rem prefaces his account by noting how rich merchants cheated one another

money he claimed he was owed, Hoechstetter's day of reckoning came in 1529. Because he had overextended his company in a bid for a monopoly on the supply of mercury, Hoechstetter's company, one of the Fuggers' main economic competitors, went bankrupt. Despite legal and financial advisors sent by Ferdinand of Habsburg to bail out one of his family's most important creditors, Ambrosius was sent to debtors' prison, where he died in 1534.

Another financial scandal rocked Augsburg in early 1531. One of the mayors for that year, Anthony Bimmel, who belonged to the weavers' guild but was also involved in merchant activities, died suddenly on January 14. After his death, it was revealed that Bimmel had been hoarding fifteen hundred small barrels of clarified butter *(Milchschmalz)* in order to artificially create a shortage so that he could then sell the butter at vastly inflated prices and make a killing on the market.[56] But the butter had become so sour that it could not even be used as axle grease or shoe-leather oil. Eventually, it was dumped into the river Lech. The year 1531, we remember, was one characterized by highly inflated prices and food shortages, so that the waste of this foodstuff, all on account of one man's greed, must have seemed especially disturbing. Breu bitterly castigated the Zwinglian mayor's actions.[57] The artist accused Bimmel of hypocrisy and even went so far as to assert that Bimmel's death was God's way of revealing the corruption of those who should be in charge of the

---

out of large sums of money and calls them thieves: "Es waren vil reicher burger, die kafleut waren, die hetten gros geselschaften mit ainander und waren reich; aber ettlich waren unter ainander untreu, sie beschissend ainander umb vil tausent guldin . . . die also reich wurden, die hies man geschickt leutt, man sagt nicht, daß sie so gros dieb weren (there were many wealthy citizens who were merchants and who established corporations amongst each other; they were rich. But several of them were corrupt and they cheated each other out of many thousands of gulden . . . They called those who became rich clever people; they didn't say that they were big thieves); " Rem, *Cronica,* 116. Sender seems to accept Bartolomäus Rem's intimations that the profits Hoechstetter accumulated were not honestly won ("da hab ich offt von im [i.e., Rem] gehört, wie es ist zugangen, daß so in kurtzer zeit die Hechsteter so groß gut gewunen haben (I often heard from Rem how it happened that the Hoechstetter acquired so much property in such a short time);" Sender, *Chronik,* 148).

[56] Sender, *Chronik,* 328–29; and Breu, *Chronik,* 48.

[57] Breu, *Chronik,* 48. Interestingly, the Benedictine monk Sender does not overtly criticize the Zwinglian Bimmel in the same moral tones as Breu, which seems unusual since the monk could have used the opportunity to further discredit those in favor of the Reformation.

common good (i.e., those in government) yet whose only concern was for their own profit.

During the first half of the sixteenth century, then, Augsburg's society was in the process of polarization between the poor and wealthy. As we will see, however, Breu's economic position during the twenty-year period of his work on Habsburg propaganda remained absolutely stable, a testimony to the success of his financial affairs. Nonetheless, because of the general social mobility in both directions, on the basis of fluctuating economic conditions at both the top and the bottom, one gets a sense of social identities in a state of flux, a state quite similar in fact to that of confessional identities. This is an important point because it indicates the indeterminacy of group demarcations and the slippage between groups. Social meaning, that is, what and how social groups signify, thus becomes complicated, open to competitive interpretation, and so constantly in need of reconstruction and redefinition. The production and reception of art plays a crucial role in (re)defining boundaries and constructing meanings. We will see how Breu's art constructs a pro-Habsburg community in response to shifting alliances and to social and political indeterminacies. But we will also see how that response is contaminated by the artist's, the patrons', and the audiences' varied subject positions.

Jörg Breu's Chronicle of Augsburg

In his chronicle of the city of Augsburg, written sporadically between 1512 and 1536,[58] Jörg Breu commented upon the political, confessional, and socioeconomic events and conditions in his native city.

---

[58] The chronicle also contains several entries from 1537 and one from 1542. These, however, must have been added later by the copyist, as the year of Breu's death is recorded in the guild book as 1536 (Stadtsarchiv Augsburg, Reichsstadt Schätze 72b, fol. 4v). Although this date is somewhat problematic, especially as the last entry for 1536 is from December 28 and the first entry for 1537 is January 8, the entries for 1537, particularly those from February on, are nonetheless entirely different in character and reference from the rest of the preceding chronicle entries; see Cuneo, *Art and Power*, 64–68. It is most likely that Breu died fairly suddenly at the end of 1536, a year in which the plague claimed many lives in Augsburg (Claus-Peter Clasen, *Die Augsburger Steuerbücher um 1600* [Augsburg: H. Mühlberger Verlag, 1976], 18), or right at the beginning of 1537. Breu is still mentioned in the tax

Although the autograph original is no longer extant, the chronicle is available to us in a mid-sixteenth-century, handwritten copy, now preserved in the Bayerische Staatsbibliothek in Munich.[59] Because of the frank nature of the political commentary, which would certainly have proven dangerous to its author, the chronicle was most likely not meant to have been published or read in a public format.[60]

Breu's text was written at a time when the writing of civic chronicles was an established practice. Thus, Breu's chronicle is in some ways clearly representative of a particular genre of literature that presents in a chronological manner such information as the price of foodstuffs, public executions, scandals, weather conditions, crop harvests, civic construction projects, and such local goings-on.[61] From the fifteenth century alone, at least eight chronicles of Augsburg are extant, and the intense interest in civic history carried on into the

---

records for 1536, which would have been compiled in October of that year, (Roth, introduction to Breu, *Chronik*, 16) while Breu's widow is mentioned in the tax records of 1537 (Johannes Wilhelm, *Augsburger Wandmalerei: Künstler, Handwerker und Zunft 1368–1530* [Augsburg: H. Mühlberger Verlag, 1983], 422).

[59] Cod. Oef. 214. The manuscript entered the collection of A. F. Oefele in the eighteenth century; its provenance before then is unfortunately unknown (Josef Bellot's assertion in *Welt im Umbruch*, 1: 200, that the manuscript first belonged to Paul Hektor Mair is only an assumption, based on Friedrich Roth's speculations in his introduction to Breu, *Chronik*, 14. Breu's chronicle does not appear in the inventory of Mair's library from 1579; *Die Chroniken der deutschen Städte*, vol. 32, Leipzig: S. Hirzel Verlag, 1917, cff). The manuscript was given to the Bayerische Staatsbibliothek in Munich in 1902 (see F. Roth, introduction to Breu, *Chronik*, 14–15). There are no illustrations, glosses, or commentaries on the unbound paper manuscript pages.

[60] From the preface of another contemporaneous chronicle, we know that sometimes chronicles were written for private, familial circles, especially when the commentary therein contained was especially truthful. See the preface to Rem's chronicle, written between 1512 and 1527, 1–2.

[61] For general information on the production of late-medieval chronicles in the German speaking lands, see Heinrich Schmidt, *Die deutschen Städtechroniken als Spiegel des bürgerlichen Selbstverständnisses im Spätmittelalter* (Göttingen: Vandenhoeck und Ruprecht, 1958); Karl Czok, "Bürgerkämpfe und Chronistik im deutschen Spätmittelalter: Ein Beitrag zur Herausbildung bürgerlicher Geschichtsschreibung," *Zeitschrift für Geschichtswissenschaft* 10 (1962): 637–43; J. P. Bodmer, *Chroniken und Chronisten im Spätmittelalter* (Bern: Francke Verlag, 1976); Ursula Peters, *Literatur in der Stadt: Studien zu den sozialen Voraussetzungen und kulturellen Organisationsformen städtischer Literatur im 13. und 14. Jahrhundert* (Tübingen: Mohr Verlag, 1983); E. Schwab, "Einiges über das Wesen der Städtechronik," *Archiv für Kulturgeschichte* 18 (1928): 258–86; J. B. Mencke, "Geschichtsschreibung und Politik in den deutschen Städten des Spätmittelalters," *Jahrbuch des kölnischen Geschichtsvereins* 33 (1958): 1–84 and 34/5 (1960): 85–194.

sixteenth century.[62] A number of texts written in the first half of the sixteenth century cover roughly the same period that Breu's does. These texts range from guild chronicles to officially produced city government chronicles, to private texts containing politically sensitive material. The authors of these texts range from monks and humanists, to merchants, guildmasters, and civic bureaucrats.[63]

If Breu's text is unremarkable for its participation in a well-established literary genre, it is nonetheless entirely unique both in that its author is an artist and in its acerbic and perspicacious social and political commentary which consistently takes the side of the poor and the disadvantaged. Other German artists of course did produce texts, most notably Albrecht Dürer and the Augsburg printer Erhard Ratdolt for whom Breu provided religious woodcuts in the early stages of the artist's career.[64] But these other texts deal mostly with

---

[62] Fifteenth century chronicle production is discussed in Dieter Weber's excellent study, *Geschichtsschreibung in Augsburg: Hektor Mülich und die reichsstädtische Chronistik des Spätmittelalters* (Augsburg: H. Mühlberger, 1983). See also P. Joachimson, "Zur städtischen und klösterlichen Geschichtsschreibung Augsburgs im 15. Jahrhundert" *Alemania* 22 (1894): 1–32 and 123–59 and F. Frensdorff, introduction to *Chroniken der deutschen Städten*, vol. 4 (Leipzig: S. Hirzel Verlag, 1865), xxxv–xliii. The eight different chronicles are listed in Frensdorff, introduction to *Chroniken*, xxxviii–xli and Weber, *Geschichtsschreibung*, 32–45. The most well known of these include the *Chronographia Augustensium*, commissioned by the wealthy Augsburg merchant Sigmund Gossembrot and written first in Latin (1456) and then in German (1457) by the monk Sigmund Meisterlin, later printed in 1522 by Melchior Ramminger, and the chronicles written by the Augsburg merchants Burkhard Zink and Hektor Mülich.

[63] Unfortunately, there is no comprehensive study of chronicle writing in the sixteenth century as there is for the fifteenth. The chronicles that come closest to the period covered by Breu are: 1. The Langenmantel chronicle, written by the *Ratsherren* Matthäus Langenmantel, Stadt- und Staatsbibliothek Augsburg, Cod. Aug. 88. This chronicle was later copied by the *Ratsdiener* Paul Hektor Mair (Stadtarchiv Augsburg, Reichsschätze 129). Its report of the 1530 Imperial Diet held in Augsburg has been published in *Chronik der deutschen Städte*, vol. 25 (Leipzig: S. Hirzel Verlag, 1896); 2. The *Weberchronik* (Stadt- und Staatsbibliothek Augsburg, Cod. Aug. 90) and the *Chronik der Augsburger Schusterzunft*, both written by the build master and *Ratsdiener* Clemens Jäger (published in *Die Chroniken der deutschen Städte*, vol. 34 (Stuttgart and Gotha, 1929); 3. The official *Ratsbücher*, written by the city's *Stadtschreiber* and which chronicle the Council's decisions and actions (Stadtarchiv Augsburg, Reichsstadt Ratsbücher). Conrad Peutinger was *Stadtschreiber* during most of the first four decades of the sixteenth century ,and he was also a humanist; 4. The chronicle of the Benedictine monk and humanist Clemens Sender (*Die Chroniken der deutschen Städte*, vol. 23 [Leipzig: S. Hirzel Verlag, 1894]); and 5. The chronicle of the merchant Wilhelm Rem (*Die Chroniken der deutschen Städte*, vol. 25 [Leipzig: S. Hirzel Verlag, 1896]).

[64] Albrecht Dürer, *Schriften und Briefen*, ed. Ernst Ullmann (West Berlin: Verlag das europäische Buch, 1978); Erhard Ratdolt, *Die autobiographische Aufzeichnungen Erhard Ratdolts 1462–1523*, ed. H. Reicher (Vienna: n.p., 1932). Ratdolt's original manuscript is in the Österreichische Nationalbibliothek in Vienna, codex 15473.

personal family and business affairs (and in Dürer's case, also his theoretical and practical studies), and none of them engage in the impassioned political and social commentary on a civic context as does Breu's. Even the other contemporaneous chronicles written in Augsburg do not share Breu's critical view of persons in power, regardless of the authors' confessions, or the artist's sympathetic view of the poor as religiously pure and simultaneously as politically disenfranchised.

Despite the uniqueness of Breu's text, the artist's chronicle has received little attention. Those scholars that have dealt with the text do so in a disparaging manner. Their criticism centers around the personal, partisan nature of his commentary, as well as the absence of references to Breu's art. This latter criterion also explains why art historians have all but totally ignored the artist's chronicle. Even Friedrich Roth, who edited and published Breu's text in 1906, has little positive to say about the document. Roth complains about Breu's poor prose, which he describes as "lacking in art, one would almost say raw (kunstlos, fast möchte man sagen roh)," the chronicle's unkind tone ("lieblos"), the artist's inaccurate dates, and his silence about his art and his fellow artists. Roth also accuses Breu of exaggeration, lack of understanding, and the inclusion of unimportant matters which in reality reflect the bitterness of the common man in relation to the powerful and wealthy.[65]

If one looks carefully at Roth's criticism, it becomes clear that what Roth objects to has to do with notions of class and of historical objectivity, issues that are for Roth interrelated. Breu is positioned in Roth's narrative as one of the common men, a craftsman who lacks the intelligence to see beyond his own self-interest to the real issues, whose writing is raw and whose speech is coarse ("His language is that of the common man, full of coarse words and expressions [Seine Sprache ist die des gemeinen Mannes, voll von derben Worten und Redensarten].""). Instead of writing about things he understands, that is, making art, he attempts to write about history and politics and, according to Roth, necessarily gets it wrong. Instead of valuing the alternative perspective which Breu's passionately partisan chronicle offers, Roth faults it for its lack of objectivity. The assumption here is that other documents from the time were more objective and re-

---

[65] Roth, introduction to Breu, *Chronik,* 11–14.

mained untainted by personal agendas. Furthermore, Roth implies
that it is Breu's lack of understanding, which also seems to be tied in
to his status as common man, that explains the artist's inability to
remain objective. The conclusion at which Roth would like his readers to arrive is that Breu was totally out of his league when he attempted to write his chronicle. Still, Roth condescendingly asserts,
we wouldn't want to miss this document, as it portrays the individuality of the artist and provides an interesting alternative ("ein [. . .]
interessantes Gegenstück") to other chronicles.[66]

Roth's assessment of Breu's chronicle has remained for the most
part unchallenged and the same kinds of attitudes determine its continued but sporadic reception.[67] In 1970, Carla Kramer-Schlette
analyzed four contemporary Augsburg chronicles, including Breu's.[68]
She repeats the chronicles' contents and uses these as the basis for
reconstructing, in the book's entire third section, each of the writers'
personalities. Basically the same criticism as found in Roth, Kramer-
Schlette's main source, appears in her assessment. According to Kramer-Schlette, Breu had absolutely no sense for or understanding of
politics, his written account was biased and unfair, and the fact that
he appears not to have spread revolutionary ideas himself had to do
with the possibility that he simply lacked the intellectual capacity to
do so.[69] Breu is here again constructed as the wildly prejudiced, bit-

---

[66] "aber doch möchten wir diese [i.e., Breu 's chronicle] nicht missen, da sie uns
einerseits die Individualität des Mannes, die bis jetzt nur in schwachen Schatten-
rissen erschienen ist, etwas sichtbarer macht, anderseits ein in vielen Beziehungen
interessantes Gegenstück zu dem Augsburger Reformationsgeschichte behandelnden
Teil der Senderschen Chronik bildet (and yet we would not want to be without it; on
the one hand, the chronicle makes more visible the individuality of a man who has
remained until now as a vague silhouette; on the other hand, it provides an interesting alternative to the part of Sender's chronicle which deals with the Reformation
era)" Roth, introduction to Breu *Chronik*, 14. All translations into English from German texts throughout this book are mine.

[67] The following discussion focuses on the reception of Breu's chronicle which
shares the same negative assumptions with Roth. However, there is one exception to
this tendency. Gode Krämer's essay on "Jörg Breu als Maler und Protestant" (in
Welt im Umbruch, 3: 115–33) uses the chronicle to establish Breu's increasing sympathy for the Reformation. Krämer's nuanced argument and judicious and sensitive
use of the chronicle provides a valuable contribution to scholarship on Breu, especially in terms of religious issues.

[68] C. Kramer-Schlette, *Vier Augsburger Chronisten der Reformationszeit: Die Behandlung
und Deutung der Zeitgeschichte bei Clemens Sender, Wilhelm Rem, Georg Preu und Paul Hektor
Mair* (Lübeck: Matthiesen Verlag, 1970).

[69] Ibid., especially 78–83.

ter man who fails to grasp the political situations and who is even too stupid to be a revolutionary.

Ten years later, Breu's chronicle was featured in the ambitious exhibition held in Augsburg: *Welt im Umbruch: Augsburg zwischen Renaissance und Barock*. The catalogue entry regarding the chronicle contains the now familiar criticism. Breu is again the emotionally volatile and unreflective man who includes in his chronicle mention of events that are of personal interest to him (the intimation here being that this personal focus makes the chronicle less objective and thus less valuable as a historical document) and who unfortunately gives little information about his own work and none about other artists' activities. Right from the beginning, the catalogue asserts that "The chronicle of Jörg Breu is not an important contemporaneous document (Die Chronik des Jörg Breus ist kein wichtiges zeitgenössisches Dokement [. . .])."[70]

But Jörg Breu's chronicle is a tremendously important document provided we ask of it the appropriate questions. If the question—what can this text tell me about what really happened in Augsburg between 1512 and 1536—is posed, then one must admit the chronicle's limitations. There are, for example, many gaps in the narrative: there are no entries for the years 1517, 1518, 1519, 1521, 1522, 1526, and 1530. Yet even if the text was complete in terms of the years covered, would this make it any less problematic as a window onto the world of sixteenth-century Augsburg reality?

New Historicism has rightly cautioned us against using any document, no matter how detailed and "complete," too naively.[71] The

---

[70] Josef Bellot, *Welt im Umbruch*, vol. 1, cat. no. 126, 200: "Die Chronik des Jörg Breu ist kein wichtiges zeitgenössisches Dokument und kann gegenüber anderen Zeugnissen der Reformationszeit nur als Ergänzung gelten (The chronicle of Jörg Breu is not an important contemporaneous document and can only be regarded as supplementary in regard to other documents [literally witnesses] of the Reformation era)." Bellot further notes: "Breu, offenbar sehr seinen Emotionen nachgebend, nur bestimmte, ihm bemerkenswert erscheinende Ereignisse aufschrieb. Sie sind meist an Personen und Menschenschicksale gebunden. . . . [S]eine Abneigung gegen die Geistlichen der altkirchlichen Richtung ist unreflektiert. . . . Leider gibt es wenig Nachrichten über die eigene künstlerische Tätigkeit und den Kunstbetrieb in der Stadt (apparently very much giving in to his emotions, Breu wrote down only certain things which appeared remarkable to him. These things are mostly connected with people and with human destiny. . . . [H]is animosity toward the Catholic clergy is ill considered. . . . Unfortunately, there are only a few mentions of his own artistic activities or of artistic production in the city)."

[71] A model of the sensitive use of historical documents with regard to their narra-

historian's access to the past occurs only via the mediation of texts, even the most mundane of which was written by a specific person in a particular context, responding to a specific situation. Texts, then, are never totally objective but are always narrative constructions of one sort or another. The historian thus needs to think carefully about using texts as evidence and, in turn, about what that evidence is supposed to prove. If all documents are narrative constructions, then they will not function reliably as evidence of *wie es eigentlich gewesen ist* (how it really was). We therefore need to change the nature of the questions asked of the texts. If objectivity cannot be the issue, then subjectivity can. A far more suitable question to pose of a text like Breu's chronicle is: what does this document tell me about the perception of what happened and how can I as an historian understand and make sense of that perception? Two levels (at least!) of subjectivity need to be reckoned with in such an enterprise: the subjectivity of the source and that of the historian.

Breu's chronicle is loaded with subjectivity. This is precisely, in fact, what historians, operating within the paradigm of objectivity, have found so disturbing and indeed so unenlightened in the artist's text. But if the paradigm has shifted to foreground subjectivity, then Breu's chronicle has much to tell us. The artist's passionate espousal of certain causes, his vitriolic critiques, his personal focus, his readiness to interpret, even his folksy formulations, all condemned as elements that taint and distort the historical record, can now provide vital information about the artist's subjectivity and his response to events around him, a response that will complicate his work for and his relationship with his patrons.

In other words, we will not be using Breu's chronicle to get at the truth of religious, social, and political events in Augsburg during the second, third, and fourth decades of the sixteenth century. Instead, our assumption will be that these events and conditions provided the raw materials for Breu's continued self-fashioning as he positioned himself in response to them. In our analysis of Breu's chronicle, we will notice that his construction of good and evil in the city are mutually inflected by both social and confessional group identity. However, although the poor are consistently portrayed from a sympa-

---

tive and constructed quality is Natalie Zemon Davis, *Fiction in the Archives: Pardon Tales and Their Tellers in Sixteenth-Century France* (Stanford, Calif.: Stanford University Press, 1987).

thetic viewpoint in the chronicle, the good or evil of any confessional identity is entirely unstable. Whereas sometimes it is the Catholics who stand in the way of living a truly Christian life as God intended, a way of life promoted by the Lutherans and the Zwinglians, it is sometimes other Lutherans and Zwinglians who are even more of an obstruction. A far more consistent criterion for identifying good and evil than confessional identity is a group's or individual's relationship and access to structures of political and economic power. The closer the relationship and the easier the access, the more likely the group or individual will be seen as corrupt, which is why the poor always come out morally on top in Breu's chronicle, albeit almost always as victims. It is Breu's outright hostility to institutions of power and his deep sympathy for the Reformation that make his work for the Catholic Habsburgs and Wittelsbachs appear conflicted, and which, in some cases, will open his work up to possible subversive readings.

This analysis of the chronicle undertaken here in no way claims to exhaust the interpretive possibilities of Breu's fascinating text, nor to provide all information pertinent to the production and the content of the chronicle. As tempting as it is to offer one, this section will still less provide a retelling of Breu's compelling narratives. Instead, we will focus specifically on points in the artist's narrative that reveal his assumptions about confession, class, and power, and especially how these three categories intertwine.

We will start with the theological underpinning of events in Reformation Augsburg, namely, the critique of Catholicism. Right from the beginning, Breu's text is full of surprises. The artist mentions Catholics only rarely, and his critique of the old faith is fairly mild. We certainly cannot identify a sustained, pervasive critique of Catholicism in the chronicle entries written by Breu.[72] Nonetheless, when he does mention Catholics, it is almost always in a negative manner.

The first direct criticism of Catholicism comes in the chronicle entries of 1524. The artist describes the reaction of the Augsburg government to mandates issued in favor of the old faith during the Imperial Diet of 1524 held in Nuremberg. The City Council was not in agreement about whether to accept the mandates because of the

---

[72] The entries from 1537, however, are suddenly and rabidly anti-Catholic. This abrupt and unmediated change of tone is one of the reasons for being suspicious about Breu's authorship of them.

confessional split between the council's members. At this point in his narrative, Breu especially notes the clerical opposition to challenges to Catholic ritual: "So then the clerics and the devilish ones wanted to go crazy since no one wanted to obey their human, papal laws anymore."[73] Although this is strong criticism, placing the raging clerics in league with the devil and referring to papal laws as merely human constructs, Breu's remarks about Catholics, here and throughout the chronicle, remain at the level of casual asides, added commentary, and do not make up the bulk of any entry.

In the following year, 1525, Breu levels an oblique charge at the Catholic clergy regarding sexual promiscuity. Breu's praise of the marriage of Johannes Frosch, former abbot of the Carmelites and follower of Luther, seems genuine. He notes, however, that the Catholic clergy was violently opposed to this action, and then adds that it would have been an especially fine thing if Frosch had taken one of the clerics' wives or daughters as his wife.[74] Later on, in 1531, Breu names idol worshipers, the rich, and the clerics in one breath.[75] Then, in Breu's 1532 entries, the artist states that the emperor had commanded that Catholicism be reinstated, but instead of using its

---

[73] Breu, *Chronik*, 27: "da wollten die geistlichen und teuflischen also wietig werden daß man nichts von iren menschlichen, bapstlichen gesatzen mehr wollt halten [. . .]" The point Breu is making here rests on the opposition between laws that are man-made, coming from the pope (and thus open to corruption and question), and those that are divine in origin, coming from God. This opposition was a standard element in Reformation critique of Roman Catholicism. A wonderful example of this in an Augsburg context from the same year, 1524, is a printed pamphlet by the Protestant Augsburg weaver Utz Reichsner entitled: *Ayn außzug / auß der Cronicka der Bapst un iren gesatze / wie gleych förmig sy de gsatze gots un leer der apostel seyen züvergleichen* . . . ("an excerpt from the chronicle of the popes and their laws, to be compared in terms of how similar they are to the laws of God and the teachings of the apostles"), Stadt- und Staatsbibliothek Augsburg, 4 Aug. 1132. In his forward, Reichsner states that he has written this excerpt so that people can compare the pope's man-made laws with God's divine laws and see how different they are. The pamphlet describes things that have been invented by the popes for their own physical and social benefit and which have nothing to do with the teachings of Christ. Interestingly, Reichsner includes in his list prohibitions limiting women's physical involvement in ritual and ceremony. Reichsner constructs theses papal inventions as fantastic and ridiculous, and he occasionally provides dryly humorous commentary: for example, when he mentions that the lives of the saints have been written in a book, he gives the text's reference as "das ist das buch der schmalen warhait (it is [called] the book of skimpy truth)."

[74] Breu, *Chronik*, 33–34.

[75] Breu, *Chronik*, 50: "aber es [i.e., Michael Keller's preaching] hat nichts wollen helfen an den großen götzenknechten, reichen und pfaffen (but it didn't help against the big idol-worshipers, rich and clerics)."

confessional designation, Breu refers to the old faith as "the life and law of the Anti-Christ (des entecristen leben und pot)."[76]

These brief statements make up the entirety of Breu's general critique of Catholicism. At one point in his chronicle, he singles out a Catholic individual for criticism. In 1533, Anthony Fugger had a statue of Christ made that was then hoisted up to the church ceiling of St. Moritz on Ascension Day in accordance with the Catholic ritual, despite the fact that such rituals had been forbidden in the city. Breu censures his action by saying that Fugger commissioned the statue "in opposition to the entire council and community (aim gantzen rath und gemeiner stat zuwider)."[77] Two years later, however, in 1535, Breu eulogizes Anthony's brother Raymund in extremely positive terms, singling out Raymund's fairness to his laborers and kindness and generosity to the poor.[78] Breu's use of the treatment of the poor as the touchstone for establishing what is good and what is bad is typical of the artist throughout the chronicle.

If Breu's critique of Catholics in general was sporadic, and of Catholics in specific was measured, both hardly constitute a fanatic anti-Catholic platform. Breu's response to iconoclastic incidents in the city also sends mixed signals. The artist reports on four incidents occurring respectively in 1524, 1529, 1531, and 1533 (the latter when Anthony Fugger's figure of the ascending Christ was destroyed).[79] In all cases but the first, Breu refers to the religious artwork in question as an idol ("götzn") but while he does not condemn

---

[76] Roth notes that Breu is making reference to something which actually happened in 1534 (Breu, *Chronik*, n. 2, 52). Breu's entire quote reads: "Wie der kaiser auf ain abent ain post geschickt, daß man kurtz des entecristen leben und pot widerumb sollt annemen. da saß man von sechs uhr bis neun uhr in die nacht im rath (When the emperor sent the post one evening that one should quickly reinstate the life and law of the anti-Christ, then the council sat between 6:00 and 9:00 p.m.)" (52).

[77] Breu, *Chronik*, 53.

[78] Breu, *Chronik*, 69: "er ist gewesen ain mechtiger, milter mann, sonderlich den armen zu geben, niemant von im leer geen lassen. ain tugenthaftiger herr, hat seinen handtwercksleuten essen und trincken geben und an seinen tisch geladen. [. . .] hat arm leut und jederman redlich bezalt, niemant nichts abprochen (He was a mighty, mild man, especially inclined to giving to the poor; no one left him empty-handed. He was a virtuous man; he gave his laborers food and drink and invited them to his table. [. . .] He paid poor people and every person fairly, he never broke his promise to anybody)."

[79] The incidents involved a cobbler smearing cows' blood on the cathedral epitaphs (1524; Breu, *Chronik*, 25), a large crucifix and some panels dismantled and then accidentally broken at the Franciscan church by Michael Keller, the Zwinglian preacher, and Sigmund Welser, patrician and original patron of the panels (1529;

the actions, he also definitely does not condone them. In fact, he is
in two instances (1529 and 1533) at pains to describe the destruction
as accidental, although this was also no doubt a strategy to defend
the evangelical protagonists.

From the chronicle, then, we learn that Breu positioned himself
consistently in opposition to the Catholics and presented them as an
inhibiting force to the Reformation. But already in his treatment of
the Catholics, we note that Breu was not fanatically dogmatic in
terms of confessional identity. This is also most likely the case because of the lack of clear confessional identity, as discussed earlier in
this chapter. Breu's most vitriolic and sustained critique is not
leveled at the Catholics but, as we will see, at those in power, even
when they are evangelical. And Breu does not shy away from extol-
ling the virtues of Raymund Fugger, even though Fugger was Catholic.[80] Nonetheless, when Breu does make remarks about the Catholics during the period that he was working for the Habsburgs and
Wittelsbachs, those remarks are negative.

By contrast, during the same time, Breu makes mostly positive
remarks about the Evangelicals in the city. We will see that these
positive remarks begin in 1524, which also seems to mark the beginning of Breu's sympathy with the Reformation.[81] In his remarks
about Evangelicals, Breu does not differentiate between Zwinglians

Breu, *Chronik*, 43–44), assorted sculpture, panels, and a crucifix taken from inside the
Church of the Holy Cross and some partially destroyed (1531; Breu, *Chronik*, 50),
and the destruction of Anthony Fugger's figure of the ascending Christ in St. Moritz
when the Zwinglian church warden tried to take it down and it fell (1533; Breu,
Chronik, 53–54). For a social and political analysis of these events, see Cuneo, "Propriety, Property and Politics."

[80] Breu's positive remarks about Raymund come late in the chronicle, occasioned
by Fugger's death in 1535. There is some suggestion in fact that Breu became increasingly disillusioned with the course of the Reformation and those who were in
charge of carrying it out throughout the course of the 1530s. During these years,
references to the Reformation become increasingly rare, and Breu's focus becomes
almost exclusively social. Perhaps this condition of disillusionment on Breu's part
also made him more positively inclined towards Fugger, who, despite his confessional
identity, fulfilled Breu's criterion of generosity toward the poor.

[81] Breu does discuss people and events relating to the Reformation in his chronicle first in entries from 1523. Here he notes that Caspar Adler had been banned
from Augsburg. Although Breu does not specifically designate Adler as Protestant, he
writes that Adler's books were taken from him, and that these consisted of the Bible,
the Gospels and the letters of St. Paul. Breu also mentions that many people ate
meat on the fast days and broke many other religious rules. None of these remarks,
however, betrays any sympathy on Breu's part and instead seem to be written in a
neutral but curious tone (Breu, *Chronik*, 24). This changes in the entries from the
following year.

and Lutherans.[82] The artist's failure to do so reinforces the idea that there was considerable slippage and lack of clearly demarcated identity among the confessions during the 1520s. Breu's praise remains mostly in the realm of lauding or defending certain actions undertaken by the men in question. In their brevity, these remarks are similar to the artist's critique of Catholicism, yet here the focus is entirely upon individuals rather than upon blanket statements about the reformed movements in general.

Breu's clear sympathy with the Reformation is first revealed in his chronicle entries from 1524. He describes the martyrdom of an evangelical court clerk (*Gerichtsschreiber*) who dies bravely for his faith, despite that fact that he is first offered his life if he would agree to recant. We are clued in that the clerk is evangelical because Breu states that he had taken communion in both forms "as Christ commanded us (wie uns Cristus hat aufgesetzt)."[83] Breu's use of the first person plural reveals that he has included himself in those who have received Christ's commandment and who are called upon to respond. One year later, in 1525, Breu comments positively upon Frosch's marriage by saying that Frosch had only done what God had commanded ("da hat er tun, was Got geboten hat").[84]

The next phase of Breu's praise of Evangelicals occurs between 1527 and 1531. Here his praise is reserved for Zwinglians, although he never designates them as such in his entries. He seems especially fond of Michael Keller, the Zwinglian preacher at the Franciscan church. Breu describes how Keller escaped capture by Wilhelm IV

---

[82] This lack of differentiation between Lutherans and Zwinglians remains consistent throughout the chronicle. In fact, Breu later refers to Anthony Bimmel, who had Zwinglian sympathies, as "evangelisch" and even "lutterisch" (Breu, *Chronik*, 46 and 48). When Breu does make specific references to reformed confessions, he mostly uses the adjective "evangelisch" (32, 44, 46). More often than not, however, Breu avoids using confessional labels, which is also true of his references to Catholics. The one group for which this does not hold true is the Anabaptists, which Breu describes, as "widertäufer," at length in his 1527 entries (Breu, *Chronik*, 36–42).

[83] Breu, *Chronik*, 27–28.

[84] Breu, Chronik, 33–34: "Item im jar 1525 auf den 13. tag marcii hat doctor Frosch zun weissen bruedern ain junckfrau genomen zu der ehe, hat von im thon sein orden; da haben die pfaffen das verfluchtest geredt darzu. wann er sunst hett ainem sein weib oder tochter genomen, so wers ain köstlich stuck gewesen. da hat er tun, was Got geboten hat und geprediget, das hat er gehalten (On the 13th of March, Dr. Frosch, from the Carmelites, took a virgin as his wife; he rejected his vows [of celibacy]. The clerics said the most damning things about it. If he had just married one of their wives or daughters, it would have been a fine thing. He did what God commanded, and he was true to what he preached)."

of Bavaria in 1527 specifically with the help of God,[85] defends
Keller's breaking of a crucifix in 1529 as purely accidental,[86] and
maintains in 1531 that when Keller preached, the word of God was
spoken with a clear voice, despite the great opposition from those in
the City Council, described as the godless and usurers.[87] Breu also
praised the newly elected Zwinglian mayor Mang Seitz as "a Christian layman and useful to the poor (christlicher lai und den armen
dienlich)" (1531)[88] and the Strasbourg preacher Wolfgang Capito as
a "a true follower of Paul (rechter nachgeender Paulus)" who clearly
showed the people of Augsburg the folly of their ways (1532).[89]

These remarks of Breu's outlined above are brief yet positive and

---

[85] Breu, *Chronik*, 35: "sie [Wilhelm's troops] wolten suchen des fürsten feind, das
was maister Michl, der prediger zun Parfuesen hie. dannocht half im Got darvon
. . . (They sought the Prince's enemy, and that was Master Michael, the preacher at
the Franciscans here. But God helped him escape . . .)." Breu notes the opposition
between Keller, who was Zwinglian, and Wilhelm, who, like his Habsburg cousins,
remained staunchly Catholic and who actively persecuted Protestants and Anabaptists. Breu also actively constructs Wilhelm as the enemy, describing his cruelty in the
duke's search for Keller, as we will note later.

[86] Breu, *Chronik*, 43–44. The artist in fact defends Keller's actions by saying that
the large crucifix had become loose and that Keller was concerned that it might fall
and injure someone. As he and several others tried to take it down, it became too
heavy for them and it fell and broke. Clemens Sender also describes the incident,
which the Benedictine monk believed was an act of religious defilement (Sender,
Chronik, 214–17). Sender reports on Keller's sermon after the incident, in which
Keller sought to defend his actions (falsely, according to Sender) on the very same
grounds brought forward in Breu's narrative. This narrative overlap might indicate
that Breu attended Keller's sermons.

[87] Breu, *Chronik*, 50: "Item adj. 7 heumonat hat meister Michl angefangen zu
predigen, hat ain mechtigen widerstandt gehabt im rath an den gottlosen, den grossen wucherern. da ist das wort Gottes mit heller stimm geredt und gepredigt worden,
wie die propheten geschriben haben. aber es hat nichts wollen halfen an den großen
götzenknechten, reichen und pfaffen (On the seventh of June, Master Michael began
to preach and experienced mighty opposition from the godless and the big usurers in
the City Council. God's word was spoken and preached [by Keller] with a clear
voice, as the prophets had written. But it didn't help against the idol-worshipers, the
rich, and the clerics)."

[88] Breu, *Chronik*, 47: "Item adj. 24. jenner at man ain burgermeister gewelt an des
Pimmels stat [Bimmel had just died 10 days earlier] mit namen Mang Seitz, ain
weber, ain schlechter man, was aber ain cristlicher lai und den armen dienlich (On
the 24th of January, Mang Seitz was elected mayor to replace Bimmel. Seitz was a
weaver, a simple man, but he was also a member of the Christian laity and was
helpful to the poor)." Again we note Breu's emphasis on relationship to the poor as
an important criterion for the judgment of character. Nonetheless, Breu would
change his mind dramatically about Seitz, who is described in 1536 in scathing
terms, as will be discussed below.

[89] Breu, *Chronik*, 51: "Item adj. 15. hornung 1532 ist kumen Capito, ain prediger
von Straspurg, ain rechter, nachgeender Paulus, [sich] uber die prediger des evan-

are sufficient to point to the artist's sympathy for specific evangelical men and issues (e.g., communion in both forms and married clergy), although he does not seem to align himself or others with specific evangelical factions. Taken together with the brief negative comments about the Catholics, his comments indicate Breu's interest in and favoring of Reformation ideals and his critical attitudes toward the Catholic clergy.

However, Breu's subject position as evangelical is not that simple. We will see, for example, that the artist was also deeply critical of other evangelicals, especially in the later chronicle entries. His embrace of the Reformation is also inflected by social and political issues. This is especially evident in Breu's descriptions of three events from 1524. We will analyze these in some detail because they reveal how social, confessional, and political issues all coalesce. In the artist's narrative of all three events, he notes how people who tried to act upon evangelical tenets were punished. In addition, the proevangelical protagonists are either craftsmen or poor, and their punishment, which is basically unfair, is carried out at the hands of the City Council, which at that time already included evangelicals in important positions of power.[90] Breu thus sets up a dichotomy between humble people who react to the Reformation, and those in power, who try to suppress it, sometimes despite their own sympathies.

On May 8, 1524, Breu reports that several craftsmen were thrown into jail without a hearing because of their involvement in anti-Catholic activities. Two weavers, a painter, and two other craftsmen cut up a monk's parchment book of prayers after the monk referred to Lutherans as "sows and knaves (seuen und buben)" and refused to read the prayers in German.[91] A cobbler, who had smeared the ca-

---

gelion zu erkundigen in der leer und hat uns acht predig thun von unserm wesen, das wir hie treiben mit solcher grossen hochfart, neid und haß (On the 15th of February, Capito arrived, a preacher from Strasbourg, a true follower of St. Paul, in order to inquire about the preachers of the gospels and their teachings; he preached eight sermons regarding our character, which is constructed here [in Augsburg] with such extensive pride, envy and hate)."

[90] The mayors for the year 1524 were Hieronymus Imhoff, from the merchants' guild, and Georg Vetter, a patrician. Both men belonged to the Welser network, and both men were Lutheran sympathizers.

[91] Breu, *Chronik*, 25–26. The men involved were the painter Bartholomäus Duchheffter (also called Nußfelder), the weavers Hans Perringer and Ulrich Richsner, who also wrote pamphlets, and the craftsmen Franz Laminit and Sixt Sauer. The cobbler was Jörg Neßli. See Roth's annotations to Breu, *Chronik*, 25. A Bartholomäus

thedral epitaphs with cows' blood on the night of April 12 to 13, and
who had fled to St. Ulrich's, was extradited that day and also thrown
into jail with the others. Although carried to an extreme, these men
were responding to evangelical issues: the inclusion of the laity by
using German, instead of Latin, in rituals and ceremonies, and the
debate about the status of images.

Breu immediately interprets this incident according not only to
confessional but also to political and social issues. By incarcerating
the men without a hearing, the council made a show of supporting
the Catholic clergy, according to Breu, even though there had already been some official commitment to instituting some evangelical
rituals, like eating meat on fast days.[92] Already Breu points to the
inconsistencies of those in power who, in the artist's narrative, did
not seem genuine in their support of the Reformation, and who instead were constantly maneuvering between Catholic and other interests. Breu interprets this maneuvering here and in other places in
his chronicle as hypocrisy.

Breu is not fooled by the council's wavering, and neither, according to Breu's text, is the common man. In fact, Breu says that members of the community became unsettled and were highly critical of
the council's action. He implies that the men's imprisonment was
unfair by stating that they were not guilty of any crime, and then
makes a comment that expresses a sentiment that comprises a leit-
motiv of Breu's entire chronicle: "Yet the poor must bear the brunt
of it, as the kingdom of heaven is not of this world. But a powerful
man said he could give a shit about the Gospels etc." [93] For Breu, it
was always the poor who accept the true teachings of Christ and
suffer, whereas the rich and powerful, who reject Christ, are left
unpunished and continue to enjoy and abuse their wealth and
power.

A similar comment is made by Breu in his narrative regarding the

---

Nußhardt is listed in the guild book in an entry from 1505 as an apprentice of Ulrich
Maurmüller. Both Maurmüller and Breu apprenticed with Ulrich Apt and worked
together with their former teacher on the city hall frescoes. Perhaps through this
social network, Breu might have known Nußfelder (if Nußfelder and Nußhardt are
indeed one and the same person).

[92] Breu, *Chronik*, 25. In this passage, Breu refers to the City Council and to Sauer
and Richsner as "evangelisch."

[93] Breu, *Chronik*, 25: "doch die armen miessen vornen dran, wann das reich der
himel ist nit von diser welt. aber ain gewaltiger hat gesagt, er schieß in das evangeli
etc."

1524 Imperial Diet mandates, already discussed briefly earlier. Breu notes that Ulrich Rehlinger, the mayor from the previous year (and who was Zwinglian), began the trend toward accepting the antievangelical mandates. This was in opposition to the community ("die gemain") who sought the good and wanted to accept only God's commandments and reject man-made laws. As usual, Breu notes, it is only the poor who truly follow Christ, and it is the true followers who are degraded and punished ("allein der arm hauf volgt nach, wie Cristo geschach in seinem leben auf erden [...] also geschicht noch denen, die Cristum nachvolgen, die veracht und stöckt man").[94]

Even more forceful is Breu's commentary on the punishment of the two evangelical weavers because of their involvement in the 1524 August insurrection. He describes their execution in the early hours of September 15 as done quickly and furtively, without the customary tolling of bells and even without informing the men that they were going to their death. The two men were simply led out, one by one, to the door of St. Peter's (opposite the city hall) and beheaded. They were dispatched, Breu says, "without more ado than one would slaughter an animal (minder dann ainem viech)."[95]

Breu's narrative carefully constructs a hideous sequence of events that seeks to inspire contempt for the authorities. This goal is furthered by Breu's description of the two weavers as old, poor, and pious. He also notes that they were evangelical ("evangelisch") and proclaims them to be the first new Christian martyrs of Augsburg.[96] Instead of the official version of the event, which constructed the weavers as interested primarily in overthrowing the oligarchy, Breu's narrative shifts the focus to include the confessional element as significant while it constructs the weavers as victims of the council's own political treachery.

In Breu's narrative, the weavers' execution is politically motivated.

---

[94] Breu, *Chronik*, 26–27: "Only the mass of the poor follow [Christ], just as it happened to Christ during his life on earth; so it happens to those who follow Christ; they are despised and punished."

[95] Breu, *Chronik*, 32.

[96] Breu, *Chronik*, 32: "Sind zwen man gewesen, der Speiser 57 jar und ain elendt, armselig mensch, frum und evangelisch; hat kaum 6 fl werth im haus und ain alte frau, kain kindt gehabt. der Karg, ob 68 jar und auch kaum über 10 fl werth. sie sindt die ersten neuen cristen zu Augspurg gewesen zu der entlichen verfolgung des jungsten tag."

The artist notes that the charges brought against the men included blasphemy. Yet this charge rings hollow because, as Breu notes, the big bosses in town, who literally say they could give a shit about the Gospels and who ridicule the New Testament, can say what they want and are left untouched ("aber der großen heupter, die ins evangelion schissen und ins testament und Paulum verspotten, der hat mugen reden was er will"). Instead, it is only the small fry that get caught ("es faren kleine micklin [dahin]").[97] The only conclusion one can come to is that the execution was meant as a warning that the council would brook no further insubordination, no matter if that insubordination was tied to the Reformation. But this warning was made at the expense of the poor and the evangelical. Breu's pithy conclusion to his narrative is "man wollt nit das gottes wort verbieten, aber da leit der has im pfeffer."[98] This no doubt is one of those phrases which offended Roth's sense of literary savoir faire; we can perhaps best translate it as: "they [i.e., the City Council] didn't want to forbid the word of God, but therein lay the crux of the matter (literally: but the hare lies in pepper)."

Breu's interest in and sympathetic portrayal of the poor runs consistently throughout the chronicle. In some of his earliest entries, from 1513 and 1514, Breu describes the false prophetess Anna Laminit, an Augsburg woman who claimed to receive sustenance from the Eucharist alone, but who, it was subsequently discovered, actually kept a goodly supply of sausages and spice cookies underneath her cloak.[99] Breu insists that only the rich and powerful, including the emperor, believed her, whereas none of the poor paid much attention to her. Even before the onset of the Reformation then, Breu credits the poor with a kind of religious purity which enabled

---

[97] Breu, *Chronik*, 32.

[98] Breu, *Chronik*, 33.

[99] Breu, *Chronik*, 20–22. The other chroniclers Sender and Rem both report on Anna Laminit (116–17 and 11–20 respectively) but neither one makes the distinction between the wealthy, who believed in her, and the poor, who did not. "... auch ir so groß guet zugeschickt haben kaiser, könig, fürsten und herren, edlen und unedlen burger und die mechtigisten zu Augspurg, die solch groß glauben und hoffnung zu ir gehabt haben, daß man die für heilig geacht und geschetzt hat; doch kain armer nit vil auf sie geacht hat oder gehalten (she was richly endowed by emperors, kings, princes, noble and common citizens, and the most powerful people in Augsburg, who believed in her so strongly that they venerated and regarded her as a saint; yet not a single poor person paid her much attention or regarded her very highly)" (20) and "Solcher stuck braucht sie sich mit den reichen, die hetten glauben an sie (such tricks she played on the rich, who believed in her)." (21).

them to spot false religious claims long before the rich and powerful ever caught on.

Some of the latest chronicle entries, particularly from 1533 and 1536, depict the poor as victims of an unfair legal system that favored the rich. In noting the light sentence Anthony Fugger received in 1533 in connection with the Ascension Day incident at St. Moritz, Breu comments: "that was the punishment, just like the proverb goes: treat the rich as the rich, and the poor so that even God is moved to pity (das ist die straff gewesen, wie ain sprichwort ist: dem reichen als dem reichen, dem armen, daß got erbarmen)."[100] In the same year, when eating and drinking on credit was forbidden, Breu maintained that this was a law enforced mainly when the poor were involved: "Large penalties were announced but they were only aimed at the poor. Item: when Sunday came, the place was full of people who had to pay fines—there were hardly any rich people to be seen there." [101] And in one of his last entries, from 1536, Breu notes that the council forbade door-to-door singing for tips at New Year. They did so, he says, "so that poverty has no place and so that they [the council members] will not be distracted from their guzzling, gorging and whoring (damit daß die armuet kain platz hab und [. . .] daß mans nit von irem saufen, fressen und hurerei irr mach)."[102]

If the poor were the victims in Augsburg, they suffered particularly at the hands of the wealthy and powerful. It is this group of people that is the object of Breu's consistent censure, no matter what the confessional identity might be. This group is constructed in Breu's narrative not only as mistreating the poor, as we have seen, but also as engaging in unethical business practices, arrogant behavior, and hypocritical actions. Some of Breu's critiques are simply directed at the City Council in general, where confession of the perpetrators is not an issue. Instead, the issue is the abuse of power. In

---

[100] Breu, *Chronik*, 54.

[101] Breu, *Chronik*, 58: "Es war alles mit grossen straffen aufgesetzt und alles nur uber den armen gericht. item wann der suntag kam, da was das haus vol volcks mit straffen umb gelt. da sach man selten ain reichen."

[102] Breu, *Chronik*, 73. In another late entry, from 1535, Breu criticizes the ostentatious display of wealth on the occasion of a wedding, a display which he interprets as a slap in the face of the poor: the wedding was celebrated "mit solcher hochfart und bracht, aim furstenstandt gleich, und die armut gantz veracht und verschmecht (with such arrogance and pomp, like in aristocratic circles, and poverty was held in contempt and scorned)," Breu, *Chronik*, 62.

most cases, the council is also noted as acting against the wishes of the community it is supposed to represent.

Several of such incidents involved decisions regarding the implementation or hindrance of the Reformation in Augsburg. For example, Breu castigates the council's acceptance of the 1529 Speyer *Reichstagsabschied* and states that its acceptance was in opposition to the wishes of the entire community. The Council sold out on God, according to Breu, in order to protect merchant interests.[103] Again in 1532, Breu points to a split between the community, who want the Reformation implemented, and the men in power, who resist because of the effect it would have on the relationship between the city and the emperor: "The community was almost settled, it would have been glad to do the best thing, to have seen the word of God in charge, but we powerful men were even more set against that. The emperor was nearby. God have mercy on us!"[104] Similarly, in 1535, Breu notes that city workers were informed that because of the presence of a high imperial official in town, they were not allowed to work on a Catholic feast day.[105]

These incidents are reported by Breu in a manner that highlights the hypocrisy of the government as it changes its course out of deference to merchant and imperial interests. Breu also criticizes the government for its own involvement in these interests, stating in 1533

---

[103] Breu, *Chronik*, 45: "da haben unsere herren hie zu Augspurg bald haimlich in der still, außerhalb einer gantzen gemain, umb das sigel gebeten und an iren gotlosen, mörderischen, tyrannischen brief gehenckt[. . .]. ja, die ballen, saffran, goldt und silber auf wasser und landt hetten, da war es umb Got aus (then our councilors here in Augsburg secretly asked for the seal and placed it on their godless, murderous, tyrannical document [referring to the document, bearing the official city seal, stating their acceptance of the *Reichstagsabschied*]. Yes, [because of] those who had loads of wares, saffron, gold and silver [and who were trading these] by land and sea, God was sold out on)."

[104] Breu, *Chronik*, 52: "Die gemain war fast still, hett gern das best getan und hett [gern] das wort des herren gewaltig [gesehen]; aber wir groß herren [waren desto] erger dawider. der kaiser war nahent umb uns. got erbarms!" Breu's use of the first second person plural with reference to the powerful men is curious. Although to my knowledge Breu was not a member of the City Council, he perhaps counted himself amongst those who, despite his sympathy, was worried about the consequences of the city's going against the emperor's authority.

[105] Breu, *Chronik*, 65: "Adj. 1535, 5. mai, schickt man die statknecht zu den werckleuten der stat, daß sie sollten am affertag nit arbaiten, daß wir nit versundigten am götzn, wann es was des keisers stathalter hie auf, der die pfaffen aufhelt (On the 5th of May, 1535, the city servant was sent to the city workers [to tell them] that they should not work on Ascension Day, so that we shouldn't sin against the idols; the emperor's viceroy was here and he supported the clerics)."

that certain council members were buying up grain and sending it off to Venice, creating a scarcity and profiting from a resultant mark-up of prices. Breu wants his readers to feel the full force of this despicable action by adding that a poor woman was laid in chains for one night, presumably as a punishment for revealing something about the incident.[106] In other places, and particularly in the later chronicle entries, Breu comments on similar economic conditions in the city, especially those having to do with the fluctuation of grain and meat prices and the inflation of coinage value.[107] Although the government is not always made responsible for these conditions, the entries show that Breu was attentive to and critical of these market forces.

The entries just discussed are all critical of institutions of political and economic power. Names of individual men are not given. Instead, Breu's narrative finger points at the City Council in general. Certainly a confessional element must have been involved in the situations Breu describes. Many members of the council, described in general by Breu as obstructive and hypocritical, were evangelical. Yet in the entries discussed above, he does not designate any confessional identity nor emphasize the fact that his criticism involved the actions of evangelical men.[108] In other entries, however, Breu very specifically targets certain evangelical men for scathing critique, and in two further entries comments on the hypocrisy of unnamed Evan-

---

106 Breu, *Chronik*, 57: "Item adj. 21. wintermonat da schlueg das koren alle freitag hinauf umb 2ß und umb 2 1/2ß, und alle ding, nichts ausgenomen. da was kain einsehen. ein rath solts thuen, aber er thets selb und straffet kain parthei die ander. [. . .] etlich im rath dazumal, die kauften das korn auf und schicktens gen Venedig.[. . .] die schickten das in pallen wegk und in vassen, welchs auf der straß gefunden wurd; da leget man ein arms weib ubernacht in die eisen, damit das nit war sollt sein (On the 21st of September, grain prices increased by 2 and by 2½ kr, and everything, with no exception [was more expensive?]. No one could agree on anything. The City Council should have done something, but it was also involved, and one guilty party would not punish the other. Some in the Council bought up all the grain and sent it off to Venice. [. . .] They sent it off in pallets and barrels which were found en route; they clapped a poor woman in chains for a night so that word wouldn't get out [literally: so that it wouldn't be true]."

107 Breu, *Chronik*, 19 (1514); 52–53 (1532); 58 (1533); 59 (1534); 67 (1535); and 67–68 (1535).

108 This is also the case regarding two incidents discussed earlier, namely, the unfair arrest of the craftsmen in 1524 for anti-Catholic activities, and Ulrich Rehlinger's lobbying to accept the anti-Reformational final document from the 1524 Nuremberg Imperial Diet.

gelicals. We will notice again here that Breu does not categorize them as either Lutherans or Zwinglians.

Breu's criticism of certain evangelical individuals begins in 1529. Objects of his scorn in this year are the (Zwinglian) mayor Anthony Bimmel and the (Lutheran) mayor Hieronymus Imhoff. Breu refers to Bimmel as "evangelisch" but says nothing about Imhoff's confessional identity. He criticizes both of them for their hypocrisy, saying that they could play both sides of the fence, evangelical and Catholic/Imperial.[109] Bimmel comes under attack again in 1531 for his unethical business practices (regarding the butter scandal) and is brought into association with the "lutterisch."[110] A year later, it is Imhoff who comes under extended fire for his arrogance and godlessness. Breu also calls attention to Imhoff's prohibition of carnival festivities (*Fastnacht*), which was already bad enough. But when Imhoff also insisted that the annual dance of the patricians should take place during Carnival while simultaneously forbidding the popular festival, Breu specifically points out that Imhoff made the community very angry.[111] Late in the chronicle, in 1536, Breu criticizes

---

[109] Breu, *Chronik*, 46: "Es waren drei man, die regnierten die gantze stat: war doctor Beyttinger, statschreiber, und Jeronimus Imhoff, auch Anthoni Bimel, ward erst neuer burgermeister worden; er suchet schlüßl und fandts. da wenet die gantz gmain, Got und sie hetten ain evangelischen mann, da ward er noch teuflischer dann der Imhoff und waren die größten heuchler, die kain mann erkennt hat. sie konten auf baiden tailen tragen, [auf evangelisch und] auf gaistlich und kais.mt. (There were three men who controlled the whole city: they were Dr. Peutinger, city scribe, and Hieronymus Imhoff, also Anthony Bimmel–he was just newly elected mayor; he looked for a way and found it [literally: he looked for the key and found it]. The whole community thought that they and God had an evangelical man [with Bimmel], but he became even more devilish than Imhoff. They were both the biggest hypocrites that a man could ever recognize. They could play both sides of the fence [literally: they could carry both parts], the evangelical and the clerical/imperial side)."

[110] Breu, *Chronik*, 48. After describing the butter scandal, Breu remarks: "wann im zunftmeisteramt suechet er die schlüssel, wie der abbt im closter thet, wann er kunt wol auf baiden achslen trage. das sein unsere vorgeer hie gewesen und sein gut lutterisch auf unser seiten. und in 36 jarn haben sie geschunden und zesamen tragen ab den webern und dem armen mann ob den zwaimal hunderttausent gulden. und ich hab im spuelen in die dunck tragen (When he was guild administrator [of the weavers], he looked for the key, like an abbot in a monastery, because he could very well carry the load on both axles [in other words, he looked for a way in which he could accommodate all interests for his own benefit]. Those were our predecessors here, and they were good Lutherans and on our side. In 36 years, they scraped and accumulated 200,000 fl. from the weavers and the poor; and I worked in the underground weavers' workshop)."

[111] Breu, *Chronik*, 51: "sonderlich was ainer, ain aufgeblasener, hoffertiger, reicher, gotloser, deuflischer und geitziger mann [. . .] mit namen Hieronimus Im-

Wolfgang Rehlinger (Lutheran) and Mang Seitz (Zwinglian) for their excess of power and of arrogance.[112] Evidently, Breu must have changed his mind about Seitz, whom he had praised in 1531 as being helpful to the poor, but who now, according to Breu, was so swollen with power and conceit that he would hardly give his former fellow-weavers the time of day.

In two other entries, Breu comments on the hypocrisy of some who profess to be evangelical ("evangelisch") but who remain unnamed. In these entries, he speaks more generally than in the others just discussed in which he targets certain individuals. In 1529, Breu asserts that the reason the council is so upset about the crucifixion incident at the Franciscan church, is that they are afraid the emperor will take their power away from them. He then points out that while certain evangelical rituals have been implemented in the city, there is still concern that one should be on good terms with the clerics and the emperor. Breu is thus very aware of the coalescence between confessional and political issues.[113] Later on, in 1536, he draws attention to economic issues, relating how the City Council

---

hoff, der do war mit allen listen umgeben. [. . .] Item derselb mann, vorbenannt, richtet und regniret die gantze stat, hoch und nider, und was kain mensch da, wann es nit bei im war, der im guts redet oder gunnet, auch ein gantze gmain durchaus. er war [es] auch, der die fasnachtspil alle jar verpot. aber das jar 1532, da wir mainten, daß wir gantz reuwig sollten gewaidet sein, do fieng er an, daß man mueßt den herren tantz zur fasnacht haben und begeen. da waren die würfl gelegt und der gemain ain grosser stoß geben und ergernus angericht (There was especially one [of the patricians], a puffed-up, arrogant, wealthy, godless, devilish and miserly man by the name of Hieronymus Imhoff, who was completely fitted out with every kind of trick. [. . .] This same previously mentioned man judged and controlled the whole city, high and low, and nobody who had experience of him had anything good to say about him or wished him well; the whole community especially didn't either. It was also he who forbid the Carnival play every year. But in 1532, just when we thought we [the flock] would be put peacefully out to pasture, he started it up that the patrician dance should be held and celebrated during Carnival. Therewith the die was cast; the community was given a slap in the face and the damage was done)."

112 Breu, *Chronik*, 72: "Item zu der zeit ist in ainem rath alhie ain solche hochbrächtigkeit gewesen, voran in den burgermeistern Wolfen Rechlinger und Mang Seitzen, gar aufblasen und geschwollen mit macht, nichts, das nit adelich zugieng [. . .] und [der Rat] macht in [Seitz] so aufblasen, daß er kaum weßt, ob er sein weber sollt ansehen oder nit (At this time there was such pomp/luxury here in the City Council; in the first place were the mayors, Wolf Rehlinger and Mang Seitz; they were really pumped up and swollen with power. They did nothing that was not like in aristocratic circles [. . .] and the council made him [Seitz] so puffed up that he hardly knew whether or not to give his weavers the time of day [literally: to look upon them or not])."

113 Breu, *Chronik*, 44: "da hat ein rath gefurcht, man lauf über sie, und sie werden von irn eren entsetzt [. . .]. ei wir seien gut evangelisch im protkorb; wir essen fleisch,

foreclosed the sale of a particular house, an action which, for some reason Breu does not explain, went against the common good. Breu comments: "da hat niemant kain gwissen seinem brueder zum gue-ten zu helfen, nur zu verhindern, und waren sie mechtig guet evan-gelisch."[114]

In his chronicle, Breu consistently positions himself in opposition to the City Council, no matter what the confessional makeup of that body might have been. With his clearly antiauthoritarian stance, it might perhaps seem at first surprising that Breu does not take on the ultimate authority, the Habsburg emperors, in his text. However, the emphasis of Breu's chronicle is decidedly on local events and per-sons, which might explain the artist's scarce and also rather imper-sonal references to the Habsburgs.

A comparison with two other contemporary chronicles demon-strates that the lack of detailed information regarding the Habsburgs in Breu's entries is not unusual. References made in Clemens Send-er's and Wilhelm Rem's chronicles are also largely occasional, gen-eral and uncritical. An exception to this general trend is Sender's enthusiastic and detailed description of the ceremonies during the 1530 Imperial Diet held in Augsburg, which are used to construct Charles's presence there as glorious, pious and powerful.[115] By con-trast, Rem's assessment of the Habsburgs in 1519 is more critical

---

wir geen in predig, wir thuns alls, [aber] wir pieten die feirtag zu halten, wir muessen darob halten, daß wir dannest mit pfaffen, munch und dem keiser besteen. wa woll-ten wir handeln? [. . .] wir wollen dannocht wol evangelisch leren; man soll uns nit ansehen, wie wir steen (Then the council became afraid that they would be overrun and that they would be deposed of their honors [. . .]. Oh we're good evangelicals alright–as far as our breadbasket is concerned [in other words, in a superficial sense]. We eat meat, we go to the sermons, we do everything, but we mandate that the feast days must be observed, we must see to it that we are on good footing with the clerics, monks, and the emperor. How should we act? [. . .] We still want to be evangelical; one shouldn't be able to see where we stand [in other words, it shouldn't be obvious that they are evangelical because it is too dangerous. Breu is being ironic here.]."

[114] Breu, *Chronik*, 70: "Item meine herren haben vor verkauft der von Argew haus [. . .]. da hat der gemain nutz ain grossen anstoß gehabt [. . .]. o we, we, nu hindurch mit haut und har. da hat niemant kain gwissen seinem brueder zum gueten zu helfen, nur zu verhindern, und waren sie mechtig guet evangelisch (The councillors forestalled the purchase of the Argew house [. . .]. This was a real blow to the common good [. . .]. Oh dear, oh dear, they are fleecing us [? literally: just go through with skin and hair] Nobody has any conscience anymore to help his brother for the better, only for the worse [literally: to hinder him]; and they were mighty fine Protestants)."

[115] Sender, *Chronik*, 256–321.

than Sender's exuberant and superficial celebration of ceremonial appearances. The death of Maximilian and the election of his grandson Charles as Roman King in 1519 provoked Rem's reaction. He described Maximilian as a pious Austrian who lacked wits as well as capital. Because of these deficiencies, the emperor was easily taken advantage of and duped by scheming advisers and clever merchants who often collaborated for mutual profit at Maximilian's expense.[116] That Charles bought his way into power was no secret to Rem, who complained bitterly about such practices.[117] These passages, however, are exceptions. On the whole, Rem's and Sender's mention of the Habsburgs are as incidental as Breu's, which highlights the fact that the focus of these chronicles was mainly local and personal.

Breu's mention of the Habsburgs is so sporadic that it is impossible to extract from them any change of position on the artist's part. Breu's increasing involvement with the Reformation and his gradual disillusionment with the efficacy of religious reform thus find no parallel in the artist's response to the Habsburgs. Instead, the rulers are rather anonymously referred to almost as a kind of force consistently blocking the path of the Reformation. Although the Habsburgs are rarely the personal targets of Breu's frustration, Breu's entries demonstrate that he clearly recognized their goals and political maneuvering.

Maximilian appears only once in Breu's chronicle. He is mentioned not by name but simply as "kaiser" amidst an anonymous list of other powerful people who were fooled by Anna Laminit and who gave her many great gifts.[118] Later in the entry, Breu states that Maximilian's wife ("kaiser Maximilians hausfrau") participated in a procession held in Augsburg and instigated by Anna Laminit, and that it was Maximilian's sister Kunigunde of Bavaria who sent for Laminit to test her miracles and thus unmasked her as a fraud. Breu's mention of Maximilian as having been fooled by Anna Laminit seems to suggest that he concurred with Rem's assessment of the emperor as very pious but not very clever. Maximilian's gullibility, however, also functions in Breu's narrative as a foil for the discerning poor, as we have seen.

This is the only reference to Maximilian in Breu's text. He is not

---

[116] Rem, *Cronica*, 99–101.
[117] Rem, *Cronica*, 107–9.
[118] Breu, *Chronik*, 20–21.

mentioned in 1516 in conjunction with Breu's work on the Augsburg
city hall, which was carried out with the emperor's consent, and
there are no entries at all from 1518–19 when the Imperial Diet was
held in Augsburg, the last time Maximilian resided in the city.

The next mention of a Habsburg ruler appears after a twelve-year
gap, in 1525. Here the reference is to Charles's brother, the Archduke Ferdinand, who was the emperor's viceroy in the German and
Austrian territories. Breu relates how Gabriel Salamanca, Ferdinand's treasurer and advisor, had to flee for his life from the Tyrol
because he was so hated. His flight brought him to Augsburg, where
he took refuge with Jakob Fugger. When Ferdinand came to Augsburg, he reinstated the unpopular Salamanca as his treasurer: "The
prince of Austria came and again made Salamanca his treasurer—
for how long?"[119] Breu's terse question seems to express disapproval
of, if not aggravation with, this situation in which a man provoking
such violent popular rejection should be allowed to hold a position
of such responsibility and power. Ferdinand's decision is not expressly criticized in the chronicle, but its wisdom is implicitly questioned.
Ferdinand, like Maximilian, is thus constructed in Breu's text as a
man of authority but not necessarily of perspicacity.

Several references to the Habsburgs are made in Breu's entries
from 1529 and one in 1532.[120] We have already discussed these entries in terms of Breu's critique of the Augsburg authorities and their
resistance to the progress of the Reformation in order to stay in the
good graces of the emperor. These references concern the iconoclastic incident of 1529, the deliberations on the Speyer *Reichstagsabschied*
(also 1529), and a 1532/34 imperial mandate to reinstate Catholicism. In these entries, Charles is never referred to by name, only as
"kaiser," although his brother's name, "Ferdinandus" is given. The
Habsburgs are present in Breu's narrative at these points as a threatening force in the background but one to which the City Council
consistently defers, even if it meant harm to the Reformation process.

As Breu's references to the Habsburgs are so occasional and brief,
they can offer us only limited information on the artist's position vis-
à-vis these rulers. We can conclude, however, that Breu was aware

---

[119] Breu, *Chronik*, 33; "da ist komen der fürst von Österreich [Ferdinand], hat in
[Salamanca] widerumb angenomen zum schatzmaister: wie lang?"
[120] Breu, *Chronik*, 44–45 and 52.

of their goals and strategies, and that he perceived these as clearly directed against the Reformation. That Breu at least at some point strongly rejected imperial policy is indicated by his outburst in 1529 when he refers to Charles's "grausame Lügen (horrific lies)" in connection to the emperor's threat to advance into German lands and forcibly drive out all "heresy."[121] Certainly Breu's religious ideals as formulated in the chronicle and the goals of the Habsburgs as he perceived them were mutually exclusive. Nonetheless, the chronicle most clearly indicates Breu's perception that it was less the Habsburgs who posed the real threat to the Reformation than it was the weak and hypocritical Augsburg City Council.

The sparsity of Breu's commentary on the Habsburgs seems unusual in light of the artist's work for them. Breu does mention two of his patrons in the chronicle. In 1529, he names Conrad Peutinger as one of the three men who controlled the city, along with Imhoff and Bimmel, whom he then went on to criticize, as we have seen. However, Breu does not say anything specific about Peutinger.[122] From primary documentation, it is evident that Peutinger was in contact with Maximilian regarding the frescoes painted on the exterior of Augsburg's city hall. Breu was the artist who executed those frescoes as he himself mentions in an earlier chronicle entry (1516), but here without reference to either Peutinger, who must have been acting as the middle man between the emperor and the local artisans, or to Maximilian.[123] In 1536, Breu mentions his fresco work for Anthony Fugger.[124] We have seen from a previous entry that Breu was not overly fond of Anthony, whose actions in 1533 at St. Moritz, and then his subsequent light punishment, angered the artist. Working for Anthony is described by Breu in negative terms; the artist lost money, and wasted time and material on a project that Breu implies was ill conceived by its patron. Nonetheless, Breu does not mention his other Augsburg patrons: Jakob Fugger, Georg Hoechstetter, or the Meiting family. The fact that Breu chronicles only his fresco work perhaps attests to the perceived importance this medium enjoyed during the Renaissance.

Breu's discussion of the city hall frescoes in 1516 and those for

---

121 Breu, *Chronik*, 45–46.
122 Breu, *Chronik*, 46.
123 Breu, *Chronik*, 22; this will be further discussed later.
124 Breu, *Chronik*, 71–72; this also will be further discussed later.

Anthony Fugger in 1536 are the only references in the chronicle to his work. Neither of these frescoes are still extant. The information that he includes in these discussions is brief and businesslike. Although the frescoes' content and appearance are not mentioned, remuneration seems to provide the focus.

In narrating his work on city hall, Breu's account states the amount of money paid for the project and stresses that although he worked in conjunction with other artists, it was Breu himself who was in charge of the project:

> In the year of our lord 1516, I, Jörg Breu, began to paint the city hall with Ulrich Apt and Ulrich Maurmüller, and I, Jörg Breu, was the first master and I had to be in charge of all things from first to last. I provided all materials and covered the costs. In addition, I had four journeymen and two apprentices; Ulrich Apt had one son, Michael, and Ulrich Maurmüller had one apprentice. We painted from the Friday after Corpus Christi until 8 days before St. Michael's. I was given an advance of 150 gulden; thereafter, I negotiated with them [i.e., with those officials of the *Baumeisteramt*] and was given 900 gulden and 20 gulden in tips for the journeymen.[125]

Breu's pride in the role he played is obvious. According to his narrative, it was his workshop that provided materials; he covered the costs and negotiated the final and hefty sum of nine hundred gulden. Breu's leading role is also signaled in the narrative by the fact that he had a total of six assistants, whereas the other artists each had only one.

Interestingly, Breu's account does not at first appear to tally with that found in the official documents. Two entries in the *Baumeisterrechnungen* for 1516 note payments for the city hall project. According to these entries, the total cost of the project was indeed nine hundred gulden plus an additional twenty for the assistants. But there seems to be a discrepancy between Breu's leading role, as constructed in his chronicle, and the information in the documents of

---

[125] Breu, *Chronik*, 22: "Anno domini 1516 jar fieng ich, Georg Prew, an zu malen mit sampt Ulrich Abbt und Ulrich Maurmüller das rathhaus, und ich, Jorg Prew, was maister darüber und muest allen sachen vorstan und der erst und letzt sein darvon. und gab allen zeug darzu und costung. darob hett ich vier gesellen und zwen knaben, und Ulrich Apt ain sun, Michl, und Ulrich Maurmüller ain knaben. daran maleten wir am freitag nach corporis Cristi [May 23] bis acht tag vor Michaelis [Sept. 22]. also wardt mir geben zum voraus hundert und fünftzigk gulden; darnach stunde ich mit inen an, und gab man darvon neunhundert gulden und zwaintzig gulden den gesellen zu trinckgelt."

payment. According to these, Ulrich Apt seems to have been quite clearly the painter in charge. In the first document, dated January 8 1516, Apt is given an advance of three hundred gulden which he is to distribute among the other two artists, referred to literally as "his": "Item: three hundred gulden given to Ulrich Apt, painter, for his [painters] Georg Brew and Ulrich Maurmüller, in advance, for painting the city hall."[126] In the second document, dated October 4, 1516, the additional six hundred gulden are paid to the artists, with Ulrich Apt's name appearing first.[127]

It is possible that Breu's version was a fabrication and that his leading role in the project was the artist's own narrative construction, created to enhance his own standing and prestige for posterity. It is also possible, however, that Ulrich Apt was, at least on paper and for the purposes of the *Baumeisteramt* (Office of Construction), in charge of the project owing to seniority and prestige. Both Breu and Maurmüller had in fact apprenticed with Apt, who held an administrative post in the guild and also belonged to the Large Council.[128] The designation of Breu and Maurmüller as "his" in the documents may in fact refer to their former apprentice-master relationship and perhaps indicates that such relationships continued, in some form or other, even after completion of the apprenticeship and after the former pupil had become an independent master. Apt's primary placement on paper does not preclude the possibility, however, that in actual fact, Breu's workshop did carry the brunt of the work. Nonetheless, the discrepancy again cautions us in our use of Breu's chronicle. We need to attend to its narrative function as a space for the artist's self-fashioning, whether it accords with the actual situation or

---

[126] Stadtarchiv Augsburg, Reichsstadt, Baumeisterrechnungsbücher 1516, fol. 69r. Published in Wilhelm, *Augsburger Wandmalerei*, 677: "It. iiiC guldin Vlrichen Abbt maler von sein Georgen Brewen und ulrich mawrmüllers wegen auff gut Rechnung des malens am Rathaws."

[127] Stadtarchiv Augsburg, Reichsstadt, Baumeisterrechnungsbücher, 1516, fol. 60r, published in Wilhelm, *Augsburger Wandmalerei*, 678: "It. viC guldin vlrichen Abbt Jörgen Brewen und vlrichen mawrmüllern vff iiiC guldin vormals eingenomen damit sind sie alles malwercks am Rathauws gar bezahlt. [. . .] Mer xx guldin Jrn 7 knechten und 6 Buben fur ain Eerung vund trinckgelt (Item: 600 gulden given to Ulrich Abt, Jörg Breu and Ulrich Maurmüller, in addition to the advance of 300 gulden already received; therewith they are completely paid for all painting done on city hall. [. . .] In addition, 20 gulden extra for their 7 assistants and 6 boys as tip)." This last part of the entry points to another discrepancy: Breu had indicated that the artists were assisted by 8 young men, whereas the notice of payment tallies 13.

[128] Wilhelm, *Augsburger Wandmalerei*, 392–95.

not. No matter what its relationship to reality, something which we will never be able to know, Breu's 1516 entry functions to highlight his role in a financially and publicly important project.

Breu's 1536 entry, the second and last one to discuss his work, functions in a different way. Payment is also discussed here, but in the negative; there is reference to payment not received. If Breu was the star of the 1516 entry, Anthony Fugger is the villain of the 1536 entry:

> Item: on the 23rd of June I painted the back areas of Mr. Anthony Fugger's house; I worked for four summers and for half a winter. Such a lot of extensive, unnecessary construction and tearing down was done there. I was reimbursed late, and for ruined materials and delayed starts not at all; I had to let everything stand [it is unclear whether or not this means that Breu had to put all his other work aside while working for Fugger, or whether he simply had to give up the Fugger project]. [129]

Fugger seems to have commissioned an ostentatiously extensive project for his own home, and thus for personal aggrandizement. The project was poorly managed and Breu's labor was not remunerated fairly, according to the artist. Again, as with his entry describing the city hall project, there is no indication of the frescoes' subject matter or content; only the very workmanlike aspects are commented on.

I believe that Breu's focus on the financial and noncreative aspects of his work is another reason why subsequent historians have been so critical of the artist's chronicle. Not only is there almost no information provided about his art, the information that is relayed is not the kind traditional art historians want. In his entries, Breu clearly conceives of his art as a business, not as an expression of transcendental philosophical or aesthetic truths. In many ways, Breu does not fit the mold of the Renaissance artist as constructed by art historians from Vasari on; he seems to think more about money and politics than he does about art, and he is not very successful in incorporating Italianate aesthetics in his work. He is not a learned gentleman, but a local craftsman with a big mouth and an eye for money, and his work does not bow before Italian influence. Measured

---

[129] Breu, *Chronik*, 71–72: "Item adj. 23. brachmonat hab ich herrn Anthoni Fuggers hinderhaus ausgemalt und hab daran 4 summer und ein halben winter gemalt. Solche grosse, unnutzte bauung und abprechen ist da geschehen. ist mir die costung mit saumnus, verdorben zeug, aufhörung und anfang der zeit auf ein neues nit bezalt worden, hab alle ding sten miessen lassen."

against the social and aesthetic constructs that Leonardo da Vinci, Michelangelo, and Albrecht Dürer have become, Breu must fail dismally, and thus, he has fallen into art historical neglect.

Breu's Career and Social Identity

Yet if we turn to consider the artist's career and social identity in contemporary rather than modern terms, quite a different Breu emerges. Documents, commissions, and other historical evidence point to an artist who was well thought of in the local community and who must have enjoyed a certain social and artistic standing. In this section, we will consider this evidence as it allows us to place Breu's work for the Habsburgs and Wittelsbachs in the context of the artist's overall production. We will also see that the artist's social standing and social connections might help explain the high-level commissions he received. At the same time, however, Breu's social interaction was decidedly mixed, so that his social identity, in some ways like his confessional identity discussed earlier, was flexible and complex. The artist's sympathetic position toward the poor as constructed in his chronicle might have been informed by the broad spectrum of Breu's own social interaction.

Acknowledging the fact of Breu's importance in the civic and artistic community must not be mistaken for a desire to insert Breu into the canon, to find him a supposedly rightful place next to Dürer, Cranach, and other canonical artists of that problematic category designated as the Northern Renaissance. Instead, studying Breu helps us to challenge these constructs of canonicity and categorization. Breu's exclusion from the canon despite his contemporary success reveals the biased nature of the process by which artists have been selected for placement within and exclusion from the canon. This process of selection is supposedly based on assumptions about aesthetic quality; either an artist produces great art (definable by its ability to be recognized as such by audiences around the world and from all different periods) and thus deserves a place in the canon, or he is incapable of producing great art and is thus rejected. As the cases of Hans Memling and Piero della Francesca have shown, however, aesthetic quality is hardly a universally recognizable and stable criterion; what counts as great art is actually enormously mutable and is inflected by other factors, such as class and gender.

As an artist who enjoyed important local and national patronage but who has been consistently ignored by art historians, Breu is a fly in the traditional art historical ointment. He assumes similar dimensions with regard to the category of "Northern Renaissance." Here he is not alone. How is art history supposed to categorize Breu and many other successful sixteenth-century German artists, like Albrecht Altdorfer, for example, who have very little to do with Italianate aesthetics and/or an interest in classical antiquity? This awkward situation points to the fact that the vast majority of art produced in Germany during the fifteenth and sixteenth centuries does not fit into the category "Northern Renaissance," a category meant to define the art production of two centuries but which instead defines only a handful of art works produced by only a few artists. This category is flawed by the absence of presence: most artists do not fit the mold.

The category "Northern Renaissance" does not even exist in art history as it is practiced in Germany.[130] Here the constructed alternative category is, however, no less problematic, although the problems are of a different resonance; Breu and his ilk are referred to as belonging to the "Late Middle Ages" (*Spätmittelalter*). This category serves only to indicate the perceived retrograde nature of this art production, and it is thus the presence of absence (the lack of Renaissance presence) that defines German art. Coming to terms with Breu's art serves to remind us of how ill-fitting and ideologically freighted such art historical categories are.

Breu's career also helps us deconstruct another notion, one that is indeed attendant to that of the art historical canon: the individual genius. Many of Breu's works were the result of collaborative efforts, not of isolated work undertaken in the solitude of an empty workshop. Nor is this collaborative method novel in Breu's case but instead seems to have been the accepted norm in Augsburg as well as in other German cities. The collaborative nature of Breu's work will also allow us in this section to use Breu's career as a lens through which to focus on artistic production in Augsburg.

That Breu's career as an artist was successful is indicated by documents relating to his work. These fall into two categories: informa-

---

[130] This is a point Corine Schleif made to me in a recent conversation. I am grateful that she has allowed me to use her interesting and intellectually revealing observation here.

tion from the guild records regarding his apprentices, and information from expense records of various institutions and from the works themselves regarding commissions. In this section, we will consider only documented and securely attributable works. All of the information gleaned therefrom points to an artist who produced works in a variety of media for local, national, and international patrons/institutions and whose reputation must have been well established and highly regarded.

The list of Breu's apprentices whom he registered with the guild is somewhat sparse yet intriguing in terms of its potential significance, which, however, can only be gotten at through speculative interpretation. During a thirty-four-year-long career as a master artist in Augsburg, Breu registered only nine apprentices.[131] Of these nine apprentices, five were not local lads but instead came from as far away as Venice to enter Breu's workshop. The guild records also show that Breu's registration of the apprentices was erratic; in 1502 he registered two, in 1505 one, in 1507 two, in 1514 two, in 1516 one, and in 1520, the very last time Breu registers an apprentice, one.

What are we to make of this information? Some art historians have interpreted the lack of apprentices during certain years as evidence that Breu was traveling.[132] In some cases, a work commis-

---

[131] The apprentices were: 1502: his brother Klaus and Cristof Zwingenstein, son of a beltmaker; 1505: Mathias Schmid; 1507: Gall Schemel and Hans Hass from Friedberg; 1514: Hans Hassen from Füssen and Matheis Mang from Weissenhorn; 1516: Hans Stedlin from Memmingen; and 1520: Bernhart Koch from Venice. This information is found in the guild books Stadtarchiv Augsburg, Reichsstadt, Schätze, 72b, fols. 81r, 81v, 82v, 83v, 84r, 88v, 89r, 93r and Stadtarchiv Augsburg, Reichsstadt, Schätze, 72c, fols. 38v, 39r, 40r, 41v, 46v, 47r, 48,r, 52r; see also Wilhelm, *Augsburger Wandmalerei*, 422. The career of Breu's brother Klaus is sketched out by Fritz Dworschak, "Der Meister der Historia (Niclas Preu)," in *Kunst der Donauschule 1490–1540: Malerei, Graphik, Plastik, Architektur* (Linz: Landesverlag, 1965), 96–103.

[132] This theory has been put forward by several art historians, all of whom speculate that Breu's travels took him to Italy; none of these art historians consider travel to any other place. This is, I believe, not accidental, as a trip to Italy would help to legitimate Breu's status as a Renaissance artist, especially when the Renaissance is defined by its Italian paradigm. See for example: W. Schmid, "Notizen zu deutschen Malern," *Repertorium für Kunstwissenschaft* 14 (1896): 285 (he argues for two trips to Venice, one before 1512 and another before 1528); Hermann Beenken, "Beiträge zu Jörg Breu und Hans Dürer," *Jahrbuch der preußischen Kunstsammlungen* 56 (1935): 61–63 (he argues that a 1508 drawing, which he attributes to Breu, proves that he was in Italy around this time); Heinrich Röttinger, "Breu-Studien," *Jahrbuch der kunsthistorischen Sammlungen des allerhöchsten Kaiserhauses*, 28 (1909): 42, n. 1 (argues for a trip to Italy between 1512 and 1515); Campbell Dodgson, "Beiträge zur Kenntnis des

sioned by an out-of-town patron/institution, or a work that betrays
foreign influence is produced during those years and thus would
seem to substantiate those hypotheses. Works such as the *Coronation of
Mary* (destroyed in 1945), done in 1512 for Castle Reichenstein in
Upper Austria; the *Adoration of the Magi*, done in 1518 for a hospital
in Koblenz (Landesmuseum, Koblenz); the Fugger organ shutters
(Fugger chapel, St. Anna in Augsburg) from circa 1520, and a signed
and dated *Madonna and Child* (Vienna, Kunsthistorisches Museum)
from 1523, both somewhat Italianate, were all produced during or
immediately after years in which Breu did not register any apprentices.

But the traveling hypothesis surely cannot explain why Breu did
not register any apprentices during the last fifteen years (i.e., from
1521 to his death in 1536, which makes up almost an entire half) of
his career. Breu's steady and annual tax payments indicate that if the
artist was traveling, it was never for an extended period (otherwise,
his tax payments would have either ceased or substantially dropped
in value), and it hardly seems likely that the artist would have kept
up a continually peripatetic existence for fifteen straight years. The
lack of apprentices during the last fifteen years also cannot mean
that the Breu workshop was inactive since there are a number of
documented and securely attributable works produced after 1520.[133]

We are left to draw the conclusion, I believe, that either Breu did
not need apprentices because he might have had other means of
supporting himself (for which we have no documentary evidence), or
that he did not always register his apprentices with the guild.[134] In

---

Holzschnittwerks Jörg Breus," *Jahrbuch der preußischen Kunstsammlungen*, 21 (1900): 214
(he argues for three trips to Venice, one around 1512, a second around 1525 and a
third around 1535); E. Kroher, "Breu d. Ä, Jörg," in *Kindlers Malerei Lexikon* (Cologne:
Lingen Verlag, 1979), 2: 531 (he notes only one trip to Italy, around 1514/15);
Bruno Bushart, *Die Fuggerkapelle bei St. Anna in Augsburg*, (Munich: Deutscher Kunstverlag, 1994), 262 (he argues for one trip to Rome in 1520). Beenken and Kroher
maintain that the Italian influence was not wholesome for Breu's work; for Beenken,
because it ruined Breu's inherent Germanness; for Kroher, because the artist
couldn't handle it.

[133] These include: 1521 *Madonna and Child* (panel painting, Berlin), 1522 *Death of
Lucretia* (drawing, Berlin), 1523 *Madonna and Child* (panel painting, Vienna), 1524
Raising of the Cross (panel painting, Budapest), ca. 1525 *Battle of Pavia* (woodcut), 1528
Death of Lucretia (panel painting, Munich), ca. 1530 *Battle of Zama* (panel painting,
Munich), 1532–36 frescoes for the house of Anthony Fugger, 1536 *Investiture of Fer-
dinand* (woodcut).

[134] The Augsburg guild books (72b fol. 70r–v; 54a fols. 155r–v) stipulate that a
master could have a two-week period to try out a new apprentice or a journeyman,

one instance we know that this was most likely the case: in 1534, Jörg Breu the Younger was registered as a member of the guild, yet there is no previous record of his training as an apprentice with his father (or with any other artist).[135] Breu thus seems to have stood outside guild regulations either because he did not need to heed them, or because he simply did not bother to. In either case, Breu seems to have maintained a certain independence vis-à-vis the guild, an independence that, along with his out-of-town apprentices, indicates a firmly established reputation and perhaps even a kind of privileged status.

Breu's success as an artist seems substantiated when we look at the variety of commissions he received. Breu was very active on the local art scene in Augsburg, working for several printers, religious and civic institutions, and merchants/patricians within the city. For the printers Erhardt Ratdolt and Johannes Schönsperger, Breu provided illustrations for texts that ranged from the religious to the courtly epic. A crucifixion scene as well as a depiction of Mary flanked by the patron saints of Constance (both woodcuts) appear in the *Missale Constantiense* printed by Erhardt Ratdolt in 1504 and bear Breu's monogram.[136] Further illustrations for several other liturgical books printed by Ratdolt have been attributed to Breu by Dodgson.[137] Although Breu is working with a local printer, the book produced is not meant for local use, which already indicates a larger audience for Breu's images.

Around the middle of the second decade, Breu was especially involved with the Augsburg printer Johann Schönsperger, who had

---

after which he was then obliged to officially hire him. This involved registering the young man's name with the guild officials. If the youth already had guild status, the registration fee cost less than if he didn't (half a gulden and one pound of wax versus one gulden and 2 pounds of wax). This indicates that both apprentices and journeymen were hired. The guild books, however, do not mention any fines for not registering apprentices/journeymen, nor is Breu ever mentioned in the section where fines are noted (72b fol. 194r–196v). For general information on German guilds, see Hans Huth, *Künstler und Werkstatt der Spätgotik*, 4th ed. (Darmstadt: Wissenschaftliche Buchgesellschaft, 1981).

[135] *Einschreibebuch der Maler*, Stadtarchiv Augsburg, Reichsstadt, Schätze 72b, fol. 38v; 72c, fol. 65r; 54a, fol. 55r.

[136] Hollstein, *German Engravings, Etchings and Woodcuts*, 160–61.

[137] Campbell Dodgson, "Beiträge zur Kenntnis des Holzschnittwerks Jörg Breus," 192–210; idem, *Catalogue of Early German and Flemish Woodcuts Preserved in the Department of Prints and Drawings in the British Museum*, (1911; reprint, Liechtenstein: Quarto Press in association with the British Museum Production, 1980), 2: 108–19 and 423–32.

already been printing books for Maximilian since 1508.[138] Breu was involved in the production of three of these luxury books, all printed on parchment, and all involving other artists as well. In 1515, Schönsperger printed *Das Leiden Jesu Christi unsers Erlösers*, a book written by Maximilian's chaplain, Wolfgang von Maen, and dedicated to the emperor.[139] The book is a compilation of texts from the Old and New Testaments as well as from medieval sources and thus belongs to the genre of spiritually edifying texts.[140] The woodcut illustrating the torment of Christ bears Breu's monogram in the lower right-hand corner, and Dodgson attributes two other illustrations to Breu.[141] The bulk of the thirty illustrations were provided however by Hans Schäufelein and Hans Burgkmair.

In 1517, *Der Theuerdank* was printed by Schönsperger, a major undertaking involving the work of several court secretaries, editors, artists, and block cutters.[142] The work, commissioned by Maximilian, and for which its very own typeface was developed, was supervised by the Augsburg city secretary, Conrad Peutinger. Rooted in the medieval tradition of courtly epic, *Der Theuerdank* tells the story, in allegorical form, of Maximilian's travels to Burgundy to claim Princess Mary as his wife, and the adventures that befall him along the way.[143] Most of the woodcut illustrations were done by Leonhard Beck, with Burgkmair and Schäufelein providing others. Breu's involvement in this project, however, seems to have been minimal; only one of the 118 woodcut illustrations has been attributed to him.[144]

In comparison with the two books described above, Breu's involvement with Maximilian's prayer book, commissioned by the em-

---

[138] For information on Schönsperger, see Carl Wehmer, "Ne Italo Cedere Videamur: Augsburger Buchdrucker und Schreiber um 1500," in *Augusta*, 162–64.

[139] *450 Jahre Staats- und Stadtbibliothek Augsburg: kostbare Handschriften und alte Drucke*, ex. cat., Augsburg, 1987, cat. no. 135, 53. An exemplar of the book is in the Augsburg Staats- und Stadtbibliothek: 4° ThEx.240.

[140] Ibid., 53.

[141] Dodgson, *German and Flemish Woodcuts*, 109; Hollstein, *German Engravings, Etchings, and Woodcuts*, 159.

[142] Horst Appuhn, ed., *Der Theuerdank* (Dortmund: Harenberg Kommunikation, 1979); *450 Jahre Staats- und Stadtbibliothek Augsburg*, cat. no. 137, 53–54.

[143] For the production of literature at Maximilian's court and how it was meant to function, see Jan-Dirk Müller, *Gedechtnus: Literatur und Hofgesellschaft um Maximilian I* (Munich: W. Fink Verlag, 1982).

[144] Dodgson, *German and Flemish Woodcuts*, 109. Karl Giehlow asserts that shortly before going to press, it was suddenly realized that there was no illustration to chapter 31, so Peutinger quickly arranged for Breu to make one ("Beiträge zur Ent-

peror in 1508 and printed by Schönsperger in 1514, was substantial.[145] Although most of the pen-and-ink marginalia were done by Albrecht Dürer, twenty-three drawings have been attributed to Breu, along with others by Lucas Cranach, Hans Baldung Grien, Hans Burgkmair, and Albrecht Altdorfer. One of the ten copies printed on parchment was given to Conrad Peutinger.

Breu's participation in the Schönsperger projects reveals that the artist was working on commissions from Maximilian, and that these commissions were collaborative. Breu was thus working along with some of the most important artists of his day, including Albrecht Dürer. Breu also seems to have been in contact with Conrad Peutinger, who acted as the middleman between the emperor and the Augsburg artists on several projects, including as we will see, the city hall frescoes from 1516. Peutinger was a man of enormous influence in Augsburg as well as beyond the civic confines. An internationally educated lawyer and humanist, Peutinger played crucial roles in the formulation of economic and political policies and in the stimulation of humanism in Augsburg.[146]

On the basis of attribution, Breu also seems to have provided many illustrations especially for the Augsburg presses of Heinrich Steiner.[147] Books illustrated by Breu and printed by Steiner range from entertaining travel and adventure texts, like *Von Fortunato und seynem Seckel* (1530), to humanist texts, like Alciatus's *Emblematum Liber* (1531), dedicated to Conrad Peutinger, to translations of Thucydides (*Von dem Peloponneser Krieg*, 1533), Cicero (1535) and Boccaccio (*Ein schöne Cronica oder Hystori Buch, von den fürnämlichsten Weybern*, 1541).

In addition to his work for local printers, Breu was also commis-

---

stehungsgeschichte des Gebetbuches Kaiser Maximilians I," *Jahrbuch der kunsthistorischen Sammlungen des allerhöchsten Kaiserhauses* 20 [1899]: 97).

[145] Giehlow, "Beiträge zur Entstehungsgeschichte," 30–112 and Walter Strauss, ed., *The Book of Hours of the Emperor Maximilian the First* (New York: Abaris Books, 1974). The marginalia have been attributed to Breu on stylistic grounds by Giehlow.

[146] For information on Conrad Peutinger, see Christine, Horn, "Conrad Peutingers Beziehung zu Kaiser Maximilian I," (Ph.D. diss., University of Graz, 1977); Heinrich Lutz, *Conrad Peutinger: Eine politische Biographie* (Augsburg: Verlag die Brigg, 1958); Clemens Bauer, "Conrad Peutingers Gutachten zur Monopolfrage," *Archiv für Reformationsgeschichte* 45 (1945): 1–43 and 145–96; Rudolf Pfeiffer, "Conrad Peutinger und die humanistische Welt," in H. Rinn, ed., *Augusta*, 179–86. Christoph Amberger painted Peutinger's portrait in 1543 (Augsburg, Schätzlerpalais, Städtische Kunstsammlungen inv. no. 3612; see *Welt im Umbruch*, vol. 2, cat. no. 458, 107–8).

[147] Hollstein, *German Engravings, Etchings, and Woodcuts*, 4: 157–82. For information on Steiner, see *Augsburger Buchholzschnitt der Frühdruckzeit: aus der Sammlung Kurt Bösch*, (Augsburg: H. Mühlberger, 1986), 21.

sioned by local religious and civic institutions. Several entries from
the *Zechpflegerrechnungen* (church-warden expense accounts) of St. Moritz in Augsburg from 1505–7 record payments made to Breu.[148]
The entries refer to painting done behind the tabernacle ("sacrament
hauss"), for which Breu received a total of forty gulden. Because no
other artist is mentioned in the entries relating to Breu's work, as for
example, a carpenter would have been had the painting been an
altarpiece, and because the record's designation of "behind the tabernacle" seems to indicate a wall, we can assume that Breu's work
was probably a fresco, which is, however, no longer extant.

The accounts also reveal that many other artists were at work at
St. Moritz at the same time, including the painters Hans Holbein the
Elder and Ulrich Apt (Breu's former teacher), the goldsmith Jörg
Seld, and "Gregori Bildschnitzler," the sculptor Gregor Erhart.[149]
Although these other artists were working on specific projects other
than Breu's, all were hired by the same institution to work in the
same general space (the church interior), so that we might think of
St. Moritz as a kind of *Gesamtkunstwerk* to which Breu and other art-
ists mutually contributed.

Another fresco that Breu painted for a further Augsburg church
was a depiction of St. Christopher, on the North facade of the
Church of the Holy Cross. The reconstruction of the church was
completed in 1508. Both Breu and Hans Holbein the Elder were
commissioned to work on projects at the newly reconstructed site.
An early seventeenth-century chronicle records the 1509 commission
for Breu's fresco. Apparently, the fresco was made in exchange for
the artist's burial right at the church, to the parish of which Breu
belonged since purchasing a house "in der Grottenau" in 1509 and
in which he lived from 1510 until his death. The fresco was destroyed in 1926.[150]

Local civic institutions also commissioned Breu. We have already
mentioned Breu's work on the city hall in 1516, which he carried

---

[148] Stadtarchiv Augsburg, Reichsstadt, Schätze 11.I, Zechpflegerechnungen, St.
Moritz. Entries regarding Breu's work are dated December 4, 1505; October 14,
1506; March 1, 1506; and April 4, 1507. Wilhelm, *Augsburger Wandmalerei*, 423, postulates that the reference to "plab in plab" in the October 14 entry indicates that
Breu was painting *en grisaille*.

[149] Erhard was also consequently involved in Habsburg patronage; in 1509 he
executed an equestrian statue in stone of Maximilian after a design by Hans Burgkmair which was placed in front of SS. Ulrich and Afra in Augsburg. It is no longer
extant.

out in conjunction with Ulrich Apt and Ulrich Maurmüller. These frescoes will be discussed in detail in chapter 3, but for the present discussion, the important point is that the commission was an official civic one. We know this for certain because Breu's payments, as we have seen, are noted in the official *Baumeisterrechnungen*. Breu's name appears again in these accounts in 1522, when it is noted that the artist has been sent to Strasbourg to study and draw that city's defensive bastions to bring back to the Augsburg City Council.[151]

Breu also found patrons among the city's most wealthy and prestigious merchants and patricians. He provided designs for a cycle of twelve glass rondels for Georg Hoechstetter in 1520, a cycle that must have been immensely popular since a significant number of copies were made after it.[152] Breu also worked on several occasions for the Fugger family. Already before his frescoes for Anthony Fugger, done between 1532 and 1536 as noted in his chronicle, Breu had been in the employ of Jakob Fugger himself and had worked on one of the most famous and ambitious early-sixteenth-century projects in Germany: the Fugger chapel at St. Anna in Augsburg.[153] Hans and Adolf Daucher contributed sculptural work to the project, and Albrecht Dürer provided designs for two of the four epitaphs. Breu was responsible for painting the organ's two sets of wings with depictions of the *Assumption of Mary and Ascension of Christ* and the *Invention of Music*. In addition, the Langenmantel coat of arms on Breu's woodcut illustrating the *Battle of Pavia* of 1525 (plate 1) indi-

---

[150] L. Riedmüller, "Ein vergessenes Freskobild des älteren Jörg Breu," *Archiv für die Geschichte des Hochstifts Augsburg* 5 (1916-9): 629–31; and Wilhelm, *Augsburger Wandmalerei*, 423.

[151] Wilhelm, *Augsburger Wandmalerei*, 423. Breu received a little over 6 fl. for traveling from Baden (which means he must have already been out of town) to Strasbourg and for drawing the city's "basteyen." Breu's drawing has never been identified.

[152] Wolfgang Wegener, "Die Scheibenrisse für die Familie Hoechstetter von Jörg Breu dem Älteren und deren Nachfolge," *Zeitschrift für Kunstgeschichte* 22 (1959): 17–34; Julius Baum, *Altschwäbische Kunst* (Augsburg: B. Filser Verlag, 1923), 111–20; *Welt im Umbruch*, vol. 1, 116–20; see also Pia Maria Grüber (ed.), *"Kurzweil viel ohn' Maß und Ziel: Augsburger Patrizier und ihre Feste zwischen Mittelalter und Neuzeit* (Munich: Hirmer Verlag, 1994). One extant glass rondel remains and is currently housed in Augsburg (Städtische Kunstsammlungen, inv. no. 3493). The rondel bears Breu's monogram.

[153] For the latest study on the Fugger chapel, and extensive bibliography on the subject, see Bruno Bushart, *Die Fuggerkapelle bei St. Anna in Augsburg* (Munich: Deutscher Kunstverlag, 1994). The wings, currently in situ in the chapel at St. Anna, have been attributed to Breu on stylistic grounds.

cates that the work glorifying Charles V's victory over the French
was done on commission from the patrician Augsburg family.[154]

In addition to these local patrons, Breu also received a number of
out-of-town commissions, several of which came from the Austro-
German nobility. After his return from Austria to Augsburg in 1502,
where he had executed three different altarpieces for monasteries,[155]
Breu seems to have retained connections with Austria. In 1512, he
finished a panel painting of Mary surrounded by saints for the
chapel dedicated to Mary at Castle Reichenstein in Upper Austria.
His patron for this work was the nobleman Erasmus von Leich-
tenstein zu Nikolsburg.[156] Four years later, in 1516, Maximilian
commissioned a cycle of hunting and warfare scenes for his hunting
lodge in Lermos. Breu provided the designs, which were carried out
by Maximilian's court glazier and Augsburg resident Hans Knoder.[157] Maximilian's nephew, Duke Wilhelm IV (Wittelsbach) of Bavaria also called on Breu's services. Breu contributed two panel
paintings (*The Death of Lucretia*, 1528 [plate 12], and *Battle of Zama*, ca.
1529 [plate 13]) to Wilhelm's growing history cycle which included
works by Albrecht Altdorfer, Hans Burgkmair, Barthel Beham and
others.[158]

Other German institutions outside Augsburg also commissioned
Breu. In 1518, the artist completed a panel painting of the Adoration of the Magi for a hospital in Koblenz.[159] In 1536, a composite
woodcut depicting the investiture of Ferdinand and designed by

---

[154] Hollstein, *German Engravings, Etchings and Woodcuts*, 4: 174; copies in London
and Stuttgart. The woodcut is monogrammed.

[155] For Breu's brief but productive Austrian career, see Cäsar Menz, *Das Frühwerk
Jörg Breus*.

[156] W. H. von Schmelzing, "Geschichtliche Beiträge zu Kunstwerken des
deutschen Museums in Berlin," *Jahrbuch der preußischen Kunstsammlungen* 57 (1936): 10–
14. The painting, which was monogrammed by Breu, was destroyed in 1945. Luck-
ily, reproductions were made before its destruction.

[157] Friedrich Dörnhöffer, "Ein Cyclus von Federzeichnungen mit Darstellungen
von Kriegen und Jagden Maximilians I," *Jahrbuch der kunsthistorischen Sammlungen des
allerhöchsten Kaiserhauses* 18 (1897): 1–55. The drawings have been attributed to Breu.

[158] Both paintings are signed, but only *Death of Lucretia* is dated. Both panels are
located in the Alte Pinakothek in Munich, inv. nos. 7969 (Lucretia) and 8 (Zama).
See Gisela Goldberg and Christian zu Salm, *Altdeutsche Malerei: Alte Pinakothek
München, Katalog II* (Munich: F. Bruckmann, 1963), 202–17; G. Goldberg, *Die 'Alexanderschlacht' und die Historienbilder Herzog Wilhelms IV* (Munich: Hirmer Verlag, 1983);
and Barbara Eschenburg, "Altdorfers *Alexanderschlacht* und ihr Verhältnis zum Historienzyklus Wilhelms IV," *Zeitschrift des deutschen Vereins für Kunstwissenschaft* 33 (1979):
36–67.

[159] Thieme-Becker, *Allgemeines Lexikon der bildenden Künstler*, (Leipzig: E. A. See-

Breu was published by his son-in-law Hans Tirol and printed by Heinrich Steiner, evidently on commission from the Nuremberg City Council.[160]

These local and national commissions reveal Breu as an immensely versatile artist working in various media (panel paintings, manuscript marginalia, and designs for glass rondels and woodcuts), for different kinds of patrons (civic and religious institutions, nobility, merchants, patricians), dealing with a wide range of subject matter (from hunting and warfare scenes, religious themes, episodes from Classical history, to Habsburg propaganda).

Nor is this list exhaustive. The above mentioned works are those for which we know at least something about the circumstances of commission. There are, however, other securely attributable works for which we do not have any information. These include the *St. Ursula Altar* (ca. 1520s, Gemäldegalerie, Dresden; attributed), a glass rondel cycle depicting the *Story of Jacob* (ca. 1520s, Bayerisches Nationalmuseum in Munich; monogrammed), two panel paintings depicting the *Madonna and Child* (1521, Berlin and 1523, kunsthistorisches Museum, Vienna; both signed and dated), a panel painting *Raising of the Cross* (1524, Magyar Szepmüveszeti Muzeum, Budapest; signed and dated), and a woodcut cycle illustrating the *Adventus of Charles V* to the 1530 Imperial Diet at Augsburg (Herzog Anton Ulrich Museum, Braunschweig; attributed; plates 2–11).[161]

When we consider Breu's art production, we are clearly confronted by an artist whose work was consistently sought after on the local and national level by a variety of patrons, including the Habs-

---

mann Verlag, 1910), 4: 594. The painting, now in the Mittelrhein-Museum in Koblenz, is signed and dated.

[160] A. Essenwein, "Hans Tirols Darstellung der Belehnung Ferdinands I," *Mitteilungen aus dem Germanischen Nationalmuseum* 2 (1897-9): 1–22; A. Essenwein, *Hans Tirols Holzschnitt darstellend die Belehnung König Ferdinands mit den österreichischen Erblanden durch Kaiser Karl V auf dem Reichstag zu Augsburg am 5. September 1530* (Frankfurt/Main: Heinrich Keller, 1887); R. Stiassny, "Ein monumentaler Holzschnitt," *Kunstchronik* (NF), 2, no. 3, 23. Oktober (1890/1): 34–35; R. Aulinger, "Augsburg und die Reichstage," in *Welt im Umbruch* (Augsburg: Augsburg Druck- und Verlagshaus, 1981), 3: 14–15. One of the eighteen blocks bears Breu's monogram. A complete set is located at the municipal library in Nuremberg.

[161] The most extensive work on reconstructing Breu's *oeuvre* has been done by Ernst Buchner, "Der ältere Breu als Maler," in *Beiträge zur Geschichte der deutschen Kunst*, eds. Ernst Buchner and Karl Feuchtmayr (Augsburg: B. Filsner Verlag, 1928), 2: 273ff. Unfortunately, in his efforts to flesh out Breu's production, Buchner attributes many works to the artist on stylistic grounds that are highly dubious. These works have not been considered in my text.

burgs and their allies. Thus, Breu must have been a well-known and
successful artist, by contemporary standards.

Breu's attendant economic and social success is borne out by
other documents relating to Breu's tax payments, his neighborhood,
and his positions of authority. These documents indicate that Breu's
social and economic standing was relatively high, in comparison
with that of other artists, but that he was also in contact with a wide
range of people.

We will begin with Breu's tax payments, which can be found in
the Augsburg tax records *(Steuerbücher)*.[162] In the early years of Breu's
activities in Augsburg as a master painter, from 1502 to 1509, his tax
payments were very small.[163] From 1510 to 1515, however, he paid
four gulden in tax, and from 1516 to 1534, the period roughly coin-
ciding with his work for the Habsburgs and their allies, he paid at
least five gulden. In the last two years of his life, his tax payments
returned to four gulden per annum.

What do these tax payments tell us? Because the payments recorded in the tax books were extracted for taxable property, not
income, it is not possible to calculate from them Breu's exact wealth
or how much money he earned from his art production.[164] Furthermore, citizens themselves declared under oath how much tax they
had to pay on the basis of their own personal inventories.[165] Thus,
the possibility exists that some citizens estimated their own value as
lower than it actually was in order to pay less tax. In addition, savings up to five hundred gulden were tax free and therefore would
not show up in the payments.[166]

Nevertheless, it is possible to calculate the range of property value
from the tax payments. Taxable property was divided into two

---

[162] Stadtsarchiv Augsburg, Reichsstadt Steuerbücher; for Breu, the entries are in
the books from 1502 to 1536. Johannes Wilhelm has published this information,
Augsburger Wandmalerei, 422.

[163] 1502: no tax payment; 1503: basic minimal tax payment ("Kopfsteuer");
1504: 33 kr. and 2 dn.; 1505 to 1508: 25 kr. and 1 dn.; 1509: 16 kr. and 3 dn. The
reason for the sudden jump in Breu's tax payments in the next year, 1510, to 4 fl. is
not known. Since Breu would have had to have been married in 1502 when he
became an independent master, his rise in fortunes might be tied to marrying up
only if he remarried in 1510.

[164] Claus-Peter Clasen, *Die Augsburger Steuerbücher*, 7. See also Wilhelm, *Augsburger
Wandmalerei*, 382–85.

[165] Clasen, *Steuerbücher*, 24; and Anton Mayr, *Die großen Augsburger Vermögen in der
Zeit um 1618 bis 1717* (Augsburg: Selbstverlag der Stadt Augsburg, 1931), 6.

[166] Clasen, *Steuerbücher*, 9.

classes: chattels ("Barschaft"), which included such things as horses, cows, grain, tools, and cash, was taxed at one-half the total value; and property ("liegende Güter"), taxed at one-fourth of the total value.[167] If we take the two extremes of possibility—that either all of Breu's property was in chattels or all was in property—we can calculate the two poles between which the value of his possessions fell. From 1516 to 1534, Breu paid at least five gulden in tax. This means that he was worth between one and two thousand gulden and possibly up to five hundred more in savings.

When these numbers are considered with other statistics, it becomes clear that Breu's financial situation was unusually stable, and compared to that of other artists, unusually favorable. According to J. Hartung, the percentage of the populace that paid under ten gulden per annum in tax, although large, diminished dramatically between 1498 (53.2 percent) and 1526 (41.6 percent).[168] Contrary to this development, the percentage of propertyless citizens was on the rise for the same time span, increasing from 43.6 percent to 52.4 percent, which is an 88 percent increase. An even more dramatic development is noticeable with regard to the wealthiest citizens, as indicated earlier in this chapter; their percentage of the total population increased by 94 percent. Thus, in a situation in which the difference between rich and poor was increasingly drastic, and members of Breu's own financial stratum were on the decrease, Breu's financial situation seems to have been relatively stable. This indicates that he was able to maintain his position despite times of financial precariousness.

In relation to those of other artists, Breu's tax payments were higher, indicating that he was, at least in terms of property, worth more than most of his contemporaries. At the height of his tax payments, Hans Burgkmair, for example, possessed property worth between four hundred and eight hundred gulden. Some artists did pay more tax than Breu, notably, his teacher, Ulrich Apt.[169] The vast majority of painters compiled by Wilhelm, however, including Hans

---

[167] Ibid., 8.

[168] J. Hartung, "Die Augsburger Vermögenssteuer und die Entwicklung der Besitzverhältnisse im 16. Jahrhundert," Jahrbuch für Gesetzgebung, Verwaltung und Volkswirtschaft im deutschen Reich 19 (1895): 875–76.

[169] Apt's highest payment was just over 6 fl. in 1504, which then gradually sank to 3 fl. (Wilhelm, *Augsburger Wandmalerei*, 392).

Holbein the Elder and the third artist of the city hall project, Ulrich Maurmüller, were literally paying only pennies in tax.[170]

Another indicator of Breu's solid social standing is the neighborhood in which he lived from 1510 until his death,[171] and the tenants that resided in the Breu household. This information is also found in the *Steuerbücher*. The wealthy merchants Matthias Mannlich and Wilhelm Merz lived in Breu's neighborhood "in der krotenaw (Grottenau)" from the late 1520s throughout the 1530s. Mannlich was paying 130 fl. in taxes, Merz 101 fl. Also from the tax records we know that Breu's household harbored tenants with important civic connections, including the *Gerichtsschreiber* (court clerk) Franz Kotzler (1525–1528) and the syndic Caspar Tradl (1536–37). In 1531, the city physician and active Zwinglian Gereon Sailer lived in Breu's house.[172] Besides performing his duties as a physician, which included ministering to the mayor, Wolfgang Rehlinger, Sailer also undertook diplomatic missions in the employ of the City Council. In 1530 and 1531, just at the time that he was living in Breu's house, Sailer was involved in advising the City Council as to which evangelical preachers it should employ. His colleague in this advisory capacity, Balthasar Langnauer, a lawyer employed by the City Council, also lived in Breu's house from 1533–34. From 1531 onwards, Breu's son-in-law, Hans Tirol, also belonged to the household. Tirol later became *Bauvogt* (chief city architect/inspector), and an official of the important *Proviantamt* (Provisions Office).[173]

Breu seems to have held an official civic position himself. A document dated 1520 is signed by Breu as "maller [painter] und underhauptman."[174] The designation *Unterhauptmann* (a rank roughly equivalent to a second lieutenant) points to the fact that Breu held a certain supervisory role in the Augsburg civic militia. A look at the

---

[170] Wilhelm, *Augsburger Wandmalerei*, 503–4 and 525.

[171] For information on using neighborhoods as indicators of social standing, see Ernst Piper, *Der Stadtplan als Grundriß der Gesellschaft* (Frankfurt am Main: Campus Verlag, 1982). For a much older study which contains information about the situation in Augsburg, see W. Riehl, "Augsburger Studien 1857: Der Stadtplan als Grundriß der Gesellschaft," in *Kulturstudien aus drei Jahrhunderten*, 5th ed. (Stuttgart: Cotta Verlag, 1896), 313–29.

[172] For information on Sailer, see F. Roth, *Reformationsgeschichte*, 1: 360–61, n. 71, and Sieh-Burens, *Oligarchie*, 145–46 and 160.

[173] Sieh-Burens, *Oligarchie*, 161–63; and Campbell Dodgson, "Ein Miniaturwerk Jörg Breus d. J.," *Münchner Jahrbuch der bildenden Kunst* 11, N.F. (1934): 198–200.

[174] Stadtarchiv Augsburg, Sammlung Nachtrag I, 1519–1525; also cited in Roth, introduction to Breu, *Chronik*, 5.

duties of the *Unterhauptmann* will indicate that the artist must have enjoyed the trust of the City Council and a certain standing within the civic community.

As was the case in the other Free Imperial Cities of this time, the citizens of Augsburg were responsible for defending their city in case of attack or of adversity such as fire. Since mercenary soldiers were hired only in extenuating circumstances, such as the occurrence of an Imperial Diet hosted by the city, this responsibility was carried out almost exclusively by the citizens.[175] In fact, civil defense was such an important part of citizenship that, in 1520, the City Council decided to deny anyone citizenship who refused to promise to accept and carry out this duty.[176]

The civic militia was hierarchically organized, maintained and controlled by the City Council through a series of intermediary groups. The penultimate body of supervision was the *Hauptmänner* (captains), who in turn delegated responsibility to the *Unterhauptmänner*. In a 1542 civic proclamation, the *Hauptmänner* were instructed to make their *Unterhauptmänner* swear an oath to carry out their duties faithfully and in accordance with the City Council.[177] The oath makes clear that the *Unterhauptmänner* were acting on authority of the City Council and answerable to it.

The duties of the *Unterhauptmänner* reveal that they were essentially used by the council as a source of certain information about citizens at the grassroots level. Each *Unterhauptmann* was responsible for checking up on ten households. He was to insure that each male citizen within these households owned a suit of armor (and had not just borrowed it from someone else), and that it was in appropriate condition. The names of those citizens without armor were to be written down by the *Unterhauptmann* and passed on to the City Council. If no armor was purchased by those who could afford it within the allotted time limit, the council threatened the offenders with ex-

---

[175] J. Kraus, *Das Militärwesen der Reichsstadt Augsburg* (Augsburg: H Mühlberger, 1980), 74.

[176] Stadtarchiv Augsburg, Reichsstadt, *Ratsbücher*, 1520, no. 15, fol. 3r.

[177] Staat- und Stadtbibliothek Augsburg, Anschläge, "Ordnung und befelch ains ersamen Rats wie sich gemaine Burgerschafft mit harnisch und woehr vorsehen soll," September 28, 1542, 2° Aug. 10, no. 83. According to this document, the purpose of the oath was "damit er [each *Unterhauptmann*] ainem ersamen Rath verwandt ist," literally "so that he is related to the honorable City Council," or in other words, that there should be complete accord between the *Unterhauptmann's* actions and the Council.

pulsion from guild and city until the armor was obtained. Those who could not afford to purchase a suit of armor quickly were given more time to obtain one but were warned to avoid inns and drinking parties in the meantime. The council promised to keep this group under careful surveillance.[178]

In addition to information about armor, the *Unterhauptmann* was also to provide the council with information about each person's citizen status.[179] He was to keep accurate and updated lists of all persons under his jurisdiction, whereby he should differentiate between citizens (those who officially possessed the *Bürgerrecht*) and residents (those living in the city without *Bürgerrecht*). He was obligated to inform the mayor about anyone he knew or heard of without citizenship.

The 1520 document that Breu signed consists of a list of names beside each of which is written a number. The list of names most likely designates the citizens under Breu's supervision, while the number opposite indicates the number of suits of armor in the household.[180] Breu has not differentiated who had citizenship and who did not.

According to the list, Breu himself owned three suits of armor, not just the obligatory one, as stipulated in the 1542 ordinance. Perhaps this plethora of armor also further indicates Breu's relative prosperity. In a later survey, done in 1610, there were only thirty suits of armor to 353 able-bodied men in Breu's former neighborhood, thus indicating that by no means everyone could afford even one suit of armor.[181]

Thus, Breu's function as *Unterhauptmann* indicates that the artist held an important position within the civic militia. He also seems to have held a position of authority within the guild. Unfortunately, the guild books do not include lists of the guild officers, so that it is not possible to know who the officers were.[182] However, a document

---

178 J. Kraus, *Das Militärwesen*, 115 and Anschlag September 28, 1542.

179 Staats- and Stadtbibliothek Augsburg, Undated Anschlag, "Außzug der Kriegsordnung . . .," no. 25; and Anschlag, September 11, 1537, no. 81.

180 This is also what Roth surmised in his introduction to Breu, *Chronik*, 5.

181 J. Kraus, *Das Militärwesen*, 84. Breu's stock of armor could also indicate his further connections with the Helmenschmied armorers, as mentioned earlier. Perhaps this connection was strengthened by the fact that both Breu and the Helmenschmieds worked for the Habsburgs.

182 There are three extant guild books: (1) Stadtarchiv Augsburg, Reichsstadt, Schätze 72c, *Einschreibebuch der Maler, Bildhauer, Goldschläger und Glaser 1480–1542*; (2)

dated May 15, 1540, mentions Breu as treasurer (*Büchsenmeister*) of the guild along with Hans Sibenaich.[183] Since the artist had died already in 1536, the mention must have been meant posthumously. Although it is not possible to confirm this with the guild books, Breu's position as guild treasurer does not seem inconsistent with his social standing as discussed earlier.

Breu's relatively high and consistently stable tax payments, his neighborhood, and his positions as *Unterhauptmann* and guild treasurer all indicate that the artist enjoyed financial stability as well as a position of authority and good standing within the community. Even his ambitions as a chronicle writer place him among the intellectually ambitious and the historically minded. He was clearly allied with institutions of power (the City Council and the guild), and the prestigious commissions he received would seem to substantiate a fine reputation in both civic and artistic spheres.

But other documents indicate that Breu's social identity was not so one-dimensional and straightforwardly acceptable as it first may seem. Breu was by no means a wholly exemplary fellow. We have seen, for example, his vitriolic criticism of the City Council, despite his association with it. The artist's financial and social successes seem somewhat at odds with his family background, which would place him roughly within the realm of a lower middle class. His father, Georg Breu, was a cloth finisher (*Tuchscherer*) and thus a member of the weavers' guild.[184] Nothing is known about Georg Breu, who must have belonged to the number of small craftsmen. Nonetheless, Breu's family background and his possible involvement in the cloth

---

Stadtarchiv Augsburg, Reichsstadt, Schätze 72b, *Einschreibebuch der Maler etc.* This is a copy of 72c made in 1542; (3) Stadtarchiv Augsburg, Archiv des historischen Vereins, H nr. 54a, *Malerbuch.* This is a copy of 72b made in 1548/9 and continued until 1624.

[183] The original document, which concerns a *Rentenkauf*, is no longer extant, but its contents were copied later into a *Kopialbuch* (FA 6.I.3., fol. 350r) now in the Fürstlich und Gräflich Fuggersches Familien- und Stiftungsarchiv (Dillingen an der Donau). The relevant passage lists the following names: "Hans Lutzen des Rats, Hansen Braun Glaser, beide Zwölfer, Jörgen Prewen dem eltern, maler und Hansen Sibenaich glaser, baid puchsenmaister, all vier burger und gwalthaber gemainer handtwerckh der maler und glaser zu Augspurg (Hans Lutzen of the City Council, Hans Braun the glazier, both members of the Zwölfer; Jörg Breu the Elder the painter, and Hans Sibenaich, both treasurers; all four are citizens and practicing members of the painters' and glaziers' guild of Augsburg)." My thanks to Mag. F. Karg at the Fugger Archiv for his assistance.

[184] Menz, *Das Frühwerk*, 9.

industry demonstrate that the artist's social contacts were not limited to prestigious patrons and civic authorities.

In addition, Breu seems to have been periodically involved in financial litigation during the first two decades of his work in Augsburg. Entries from the court records (*Gerichtsbücher*) of 1502, 1510, 1513, and 1520 contain references to litigation involving Breu.[185] In most cases, it appears that Breu is in the position of creditor rather than debtor, in other cases one cannot determine his position. Some of these records might perhaps indicate that Breu occasionally lent money to individuals, which would again indicate his own financial security, as did his contemporary Hans Baldung Grien in Strasbourg.[186] One entry does record Breu's maid as owing one fl. and thirty-five kr. to a local tailor. The *Gerichtsbücher* records show that Breu's financial affairs were not without complication.

Although we have seen that Breu's neighborhoods "in der krotenaw" included wealthy merchants and other citizens who paid large amounts of tax, there remained a proportion of local residents who evidently possessed little. Although this proportion declined in the course of the 1500s and the neighborhood apparently became more affluent, the residents remained a heterogeneous group in terms of wealth.[187] In addition, "in der krotenaw" belonged to neighborhoods around the Church of the Holy Cross, all of which were known as bastions of radical Zwinglianism and had the reputation of being socially and politically volatile.[188] Thus, Breu's immediate surroundings must have given him the opportunity to interact with a number of individuals from a variety of social levels.

Breu had further opportunity to interact with mixed social groups at the bordello that he seems to have frequented. The institution was run by the artists Sigmund Guttermann and his wife, Elisabeth, and

---

[185] Stadtarchiv Augsburg, Reichsstadt, *Gerichtsbücher*, 1502: 183a, 245a and 326a; 1510: 49b, 189a, 199a; 1513: 7b; 1520: 57b, 59b. See also Wilhelm, *Augsburger Wandmalerei*, 424–25.

[186] Thomas A. Brady Jr., "The Social Place of a German Renaissance Artist: Hans Baldung Grien (1484/85–1545) at Strasbourg," *Central European History* 8 (1975): 295–315.

[187] In 1519, out of a total of 35 registered tax payers, 15 paid less than 1 fl. (=43%) and 27 paid less tax than Breu (=77%). In contrast, in 1536, the year of Breu's death, out of 30 registered tax payers, only 11 paid less than 1 fl. (=37%) and 15 paid less tax than Breu (=50%). Regarded in another way, the highest tax payments made in the neighborhood in 1519 were 15 fl. and 9 fl. In 1536, however, the highest payments were 130 fl. and 101 fl.

[188] Broadhead, "International Politics and Civic Society," 34–39.

seemed to enjoy a wide range of clientele.[189] In the interrogation records of several Augsburg women accused in 1533 and 1534 of prostitution at the Guttermanns, Breu's name, as well as his son's, appear repeatedly among the lists of the women's clients.[190] One woman described Breu's practice of visiting the women on Sundays and locking himself inside the house with them.[191] Some of Breu's artistic colleagues, such as the illuminator Narziß Renner, a sculptor named Gregor (Erhart?), and a painter referred to as "Georig mit dem Hasen" were clients as well. Men of many other trades came to the Guttermann's, including several innkeepers, a cutler, a goldsmith, a piper, a farmer and a clergyman. In addition to these men of more humble trades, employees of Anthony Fugger and Bartholomäus Welser as well as members of the Hanolt, Welser, Rem, and Rehlinger families also were named as clients. Thus, the Guttermann *etablisement* catered to the sexual appetites of a wide variety of men and can perhaps be viewed as a kind of local institution frequented by men of very different social and economic backgrounds.

Prior to the introduction of the Reformation in Augsburg, prosti-

---

[189] Guttermann received entrance into the guild through his wife in 1522. This is one of the several examples on record in the guild books where a male artist received guild status through marriage: *Malerbuch*, Stadtarchiv Augsburg, Archiv des historischen Vereins, H. nr. 54a, fol. 64r. See also Wilhelm, *Augsburger Wandmalerei*, 483–84.

[190] The discovery of Breu's name in the interrogation records was made by Lyndal Roper while she was researching her dissertation: "Work, Marriage and Sexuality: Women in Reformation Augsburg," (Ph.D. diss., University of London, 1985). The relevant records are: Stadtarchiv Augsburg, Reichsstadt, Urgichten, (1) Sigmund Guttermann, 29.I.1534; (2) Sigmund Guttermann, 6.II.1534; (3) Elisabeth Guttermann, 3.II.1534; (4) Elisabeth Guttermann, 6.II.1534; (5) Ursula Weißkopf, 2.VIII.1534; (6) Katherina Schwegglin, 2.II.1534; (7) Magdalena Boglerin, 1.II.1534. Breu's name appears in records 1, 5, and 6 of the above list. The women were tortured with thumbscrews to obtain testimony. Guttermann and his wife were put in the stocks and then publicly run out of town on February 7, 1534. As far as I know, none of the clients were ever punished. In 1533, a year before Breu's implication in the Guttermann prostitution ring, he commented on the punishment of a woman accused of prostitution, which was to be burnt through both cheeks: "Armut mueß blagt sein (poverty is always plagued)" (Breu, *Chronik*, 1533, 55). In 1537, Breu's former tenant and important Zwinglian citizen Dr. Gereon Sailer was fined 200 fl. for relations with a prostitute (Roth, *Reformationsgeschichte*, 2: 335 and Sender, *Chronik*, 404).

[191] "wann der maler [i.e., Sigmund Guttermann] zu predig seie komme der allt Georig prew in das haus speret es zu seie wol zu gedencken was zehandlt werde (when the painter went to the service, Jörg Breu the Elder came into the house and locked it up; one can just imagine what went on)," Stadtarchiv Augsburg, Reichsstadt, Urgicht, Ursula Weißkopf, 2.VIII.1534

tution had received considerable sanction from the Catholic Church, and the city brothel had been an important public institution. The Lutheran and Zwinglian reformers, however, were actively opposed to this practice; under their influence, several brothels in Augsburg were closed in 1532, and their campaign against prostitution continued on into the 1540s.[192] The interrogation records of the accused women who implicated Breu make plain that they continued their activities because of financial necessity.[193] Their procurer, Sigmund Guttermann, also maintained that financial difficulty motivated his action. During his interrogation, Guttermann stated that "den handl hab er bei zway jar ein getrieben, die groß Armut hab in darzu triben dan er hab nit allweg arbait gehabt."[194]

By patronizing the Guttermann *etablisement*, Breu was thus involved in an activity condemned by the religious movement that he champions in his chronicle. By having sex with the prostitutes, he was also taking advantage of the women's poverty, a practice that he so sharply condemns in his chronicle. Finally, by belonging to the circle of clientele, Breu was also breaking the law, as it was forbidden that married men visit brothels.[195]

The extant documents regarding Breu's life will never tell us exactly what sort of person he was. Nor should they provide the basis for either vilifying Breu as a law-breaking, coarse man, or for alternatively heroizing him as a kind of sixteenth-century precursor to the rebellious modern artist who flaunts middle-class sexual mores and notions of respectability. What these documents can tell us is that Breu's social identity was complex and sometimes even contradictory. He enjoyed positions of prestige and authority, but he was also engaged in activities regarded as dubious; he had contact with im-

---

[192] Lyndal Roper, "Discipline and Respectability: Prostitution and the Reformation in Augsburg," *History Workshop* 19 (1985): esp. 3–10. For further information on prostitution in Augsburg, also see L. Roper, "Mothers of Debauchery: Procuresses in Reformation Augsburg," *German History* 6 (1988): 1–19.

[193] *Urgichten*, Ursula Weißkopf, and Magdalena Boglerin.

[194] *Urgicht*, Sigmund Guttermann, January 29, 1534: "he was active in the trade for two years; great poverty had made him do it since he didn't always have work." Guttermann's case could be used to support the thesis of some historians, like Carl Christiansen, *Art and the Reformation in Germany*, that the Reformation caused many German artists' businesses to suffer.

[195] Roper, "Discipline and Respectability," 5. In Sigmund Guttermann's interrogation record of 29 January, the clients are listed in two categories: "Ledigßstand (single)" and "Eeleut (married)." In the first category we find: "Georg prew der jung weil er ledig waas" and in the second we find "allt Georg prew."

portant men in Augsburg society, as we will see especially in terms of his patrons, but he also had contact with people living on the margins of that society. Some of Breu's actions contradict positions that he constructs in the chronicle. These discrepancies point to the chronicle as a document of self-fashioning, rather than as a completely trustworthy reflection of the artist's inner and outer self.

Breu's complicated social identity, especially when taken into consideration with his equally complex confessional identity, is significant for our interpretation of the production and reception of art. It reveals the fragmentary nature of artistic agency as well as the complexity of a work's meaning. Breu constructs himself as pro-Reformational and antiauthoritarian, yet works for Catholic emperors, merchants, and nobility. He holds positions of power, yet castigates the abuse of power of which he nonetheless is also guilty in connection with prostitution (and also perhaps in moneylending). He is supportive of the Reformation, yet mostly criticizes Lutherans and Zwinglians; he is not in favor of Catholicism yet many of his patrons belong to this confession. Breu's life certainly does not provide us with an example of an artist who responds to his historical context in a consistent and straightforward manner. And this fact, just as certainly, has consequences for his artistic agency. The contradictions involved in his art production indicate that this is not an activity in which the end product, the work of art, mirrors history and/or the artist's own personal convictions. Rather, it is an activity fraught with conflict. This conflict, inherent in the inception of the art work, is also present in its reception. Works of art can be interpreted differently, and conflict arises over which interpretation best captures (or really, constructs) the work's meaning(s).

As we will see in the case studies, to which we now turn, this potential for multivalence in Breu's political works supports their function of shaping political identity by addressing a variety of audiences and concerns.

CHAPTER THREE

WARFARE

I hold that the principal and true profession of the courtier must be that of arms, which I wish him to exercise with vigor . . .   Castiglione, *The Courtier*, 1528

The principal study and care and the especial profession of a prince should be warfare. . . . It is an art of such value that not only does it preserve those who were born princes, but often enables men of private station to reach that rank.
Machiavelli, *The Prince*, 1513

If it is the special ambition of the good prince to rule over the best possible subjects, he should detest war, which is the cesspool of all vice.
Erasmus, *The Complaint of Peace*, 1517

War or battle as a thing very beastly . . . they do detest and abhor.
Thomas More, describing the inhabitants of *Utopia*, 1515–16

Krieg verzehrt leib, er und guet (War devours the body, honor, and property).
Inscription on Maximilian's *Raitpfennig* (tallying coin), minted at Hall.

Warfare in the Fifteenth and Sixteenth Centuries

Most historians agree that the period roughly between the mid-fifteenth and the mid-sixteenth centuries constituted an important time of transition between medieval and early modern warfare.[1] During these years, the use of firearms (primarily cannon and arquebuses) was gradually implemented, while the emphasis in battle was mainly on the infantry, with cavalry playing a supportive but no longer a dominant role, as it had in the Middle Ages. These changes were already clearly perceived by contemporaneous observers such as Francesco Guicciardini (1483–1540). In his *History of Italy* written be-

---

[1] See Charles Oman, *A History of the Art of War in the Sixteenth Century* (New York: E. P. Dutton, 1937); Hans Delbrück, *History of the Art of War within the Framework of Political History*, vol. 4 (reprint, Westport, Conn.: Greenwood Press, 1985); Eugene F. Rice Jr., *The Foundations of Early Modern Europe 1460–1559* (New York: W. W. Norton, 1970), 10–18; J. R. Hale, *War and Society in Renaissance Europe 1450–1620* (Baltimore: Johns Hopkins University Press, 1985).

tween 1537 and 1540, Guicciardini comments on these new developments:

> For in our age methods of warfare have undergone the greatest changes: in that before King Charles of France marched into Italy [1494], the brunt of battle was borne much more by horsemen heavily armed at all points than by foot soldiers; and since the weapons that were used against the towns were very difficult to move and manage, therefore, although armies frequently engaged in battles, there was very little killing. . . . But after King Charles had come to Italy, the terror of unknown nations, the ferocity of infantry organized in waging war in another way, but above all, the fury of the artillery filled all of Italy with so much dread that no hope of defending oneself remained.[2]

The other way of organizing infantry to which Guicciardini refers is most likely the organization of infantry according to Swiss mercenary formations; namely, that large numbers of infantry bearing long pikes were taught to march and maneuver together in a great phalanx.[3] Beginning in the third quarter of the fifteenth century, Swiss mercenaries, so organized, had stunned western European powers by their seeming invincibility; they were able to repel even the most furious cavalry charges and win almost all of their battles. Thereafter, one of the main issues in European warfare for the next fifty odd years was how either to hire enough Swiss mercenaries to fight on your side, or how best to replicate their success with your own infantry.

One of the men most impressed by the Swiss and who did the most to train his troops according to their strategies was Maximilian I of Habsburg.[4] He had already learned respect for Swiss power at the Burgundian court from the councillors who had witnessed the defeat of the troops of Maximilian's father-in-law, Charles the Bold, at the hands of the Swiss in 1476–77.[5] Maximilian in fact began to use Swiss tactics early on, in 1479, in his own battles.[6] Soon thereafter, in the early 1480s, Maximilian began to recruit hired soldiers

---

[2] Francesco Guicciardini, *History of Italy*, trans. and intro. Sidney Alexander (Princeton: Princeton University Press, 1969), 340–41.

[3] Oman, *Art of War*, 63–73.

[4] For a thorough investigation of Maximilian and his armies, see Gerhard Kurzmann, *Kaiser Maximilian I und das Kriegswesen der österreichischen Länder und des Reiches* (Vienna: Österreichische Bundesverlag, 1985).

[5] Peter Krenn, "Heerwesen, Waffe und Turnier unter Kaiser Maximilian I," in *Maximilian I*, (Innsbruck: Tyrolia Verlag, 1969), 86.

[6] Delbrück, *Art of War*, 4.

whom he needed for the ongoing war between the Burgundians and the French, and sometimes, between the Burgundians and himself. He had these mercenary foot soldiers specifically trained to emulate Swiss infantry tactics. Between 1482 and 1486, these soldiers were referred to with increasing frequency as *Landsknechten*.[7] Maximilian's army, including regiments of Landsknechten, was one of the emperor's key resources. Throughout his entire political career, first as prince, then as Roman king (1486) and finally as emperor (1508), Maximilian was almost always at war: with the French (first in the Netherlands, then in Italy), with rebel Burgundian and German estates, with the Hungarians, and with the Venetians. To fund this perpetual warfare and to hire Landsknechten, Maximilian depended greatly on the loans and advances made to him by Upper German merchants, particularly the Fuggers and Hoechstetters of Augsburg.[8]

Important as the Landsknechten were to military efficacy, implementation of artillery was also crucial. As famous as Maximilian is as "Vater der Landsknechte," he is also known for his great interest in the development and use of artillery,[9] thanks in part to *Weißkunig* (ca. 1505–16), Maximilian's heavily constructed autobiography about his youth, education, and battles, where he is shown watching the making of artillery. The *Zeughaus*, or artillery depot, in Innsbruck was built by Maximilian's order (ca. 1500–1505), and he also had inventories of his artillery carefully drawn up (*Zeugbücher* of ca. 1507 and ca. 1512).[10] Maximilian also contributed to the regularization and standardization of artillery manufacture by insisting upon the categorization and organization of artillery according to caliber.

Maximilian seems to have realized the importance of combining these new developments, namely, the emphasized infantry with the new technologies of artillery.[11] The battle of Pavia (1525) proved Maximilian (posthumously) right. By combining the force of the in-

---

[7] Delbrück, *Art of War*, 7.

[8] Hermann Wiesflecker, *Kaiser Maximilian I: Das Reich Österreich und Europa an der Wende zur Neuzeit*, (Vienna: R. Oldenbourg, 1986), vol. 5, chapter 8: "Die neue Wirtschafts- und Finanzpolitik im Dienst der großen Politik und des Krieges," 563–610. For in-depth information about the Landsknechten, see Hans-Michael Möller, *Das Regiment der Landsknechte: Untersuchungen zu Verfassung, Recht und Selbstverständnis in deutschen Söldnerheeren des 16. Jahrhunderts*, Frankfurter historische Abhandlungen, vol.12 (Wiesbaden: F. Steiner Verlag, 1976).

[9] Krenn, "Heerwesen," 88–89; Wiesflecker, *Kaiser Maximilian I*, 5: 557–61.

[10] See catalogue numbers 475–76 in *Maximilian I*, 121–22.

[11] Wiesflecker, *Kaiser Maximilian I*, 5: 547.

fantry armed with both pikes and arquebuses, Charles V's troops were able to lift the French siege of the Italian town of Pavia held by imperial forces and to capture the French king, Francis I, while sustaining dramatically fewer losses despite the numerical superiority of the French.[12]

Some of these important military events provided the subject matter for works by Jörg Breu that will provide the focus for this chapter.[13] Around 1516, Breu painted the frescoes on the Augsburg city hall that depicted Maximilian's ancestors and several battle scenes. Later on, around 1525, Breu commemorated the battle of Pavia in a woodcut. In the analyses of these works, emphasis will not be placed on determining the realities of contemporaneous warfare purportedly reflected therein. Instead, we will want to see how these works respond to certain specific historical conditions and how they construct meaning that is sometimes in accordance with and sometimes in contradiction to those conditions. In short, we will treat Breu's art as part of the cultural discourse surrounding and constructing notions of warfare in the early decades of the sixteenth century. In addition, we will attend to the process in which the articulation of warfare in these works promotes particular political viewpoints.

Warfare and Cultural Production

A number of texts produced roughly within the same period as Breu's drawings, frescoes, and woodcut help us to stake out the parameters of the discourse on warfare as it was articulated in the second and third decades of the sixteenth century.[14] I do not mean to imply that any of these texts directly influenced Breu's art. Instead, I offer these texts as a means to heighten our awareness of the complex interplay between warfare and cultural production. In ana-

---

[12] Oman, *Art of War*, 34–35 and Rice, *Foundations of Early Modern Europe*, 13–14.

[13] Breu's surviving sixteen drawings depicting several of Maximilian's battles and hunting scenes for the emperor's hunting lodge at Lermos (Munich, Staatliche Graphische Sammlung) have not been included in this chapter because of the exentensive and lengthy discussion required to deal concretely with the cycle as a whole.

[14] For a listing of printed books dealing with warfare available in the late-fifteenth and first four decades of the sixteenth centuries, see Maurice Cockle, *A Bibliography of Military Books up to 1642* (1900; reprint, London: Holland Press, 1978), 1–17, 126–33, 197.

lyzing the texts, we will see how little literature is a passive reflection of, or even neutral response to contemporaneous belligerence; instead, we will see how the texts actively construct the concept of warfare to get at other issues of social, national, political, and religious character. These texts actively shape opinions about critical issues. Their use of warfare as part of the rhetorical strategy is particularly effective because warfare, like crime in the late twentieth century, was itself such a high-visibility issue. My readings of Breu's art will also be based on similar assumptions.

The texts we will consider can be divided into two categories: one that constructs warfare as either positive or at least unquestionably necessary, and thus of value; and the other that unequivocally condemns it. Interestingly, the texts also divide into these categories according to geographic origin: the positive texts are Italian, the negative are Northern.[15] On one facet, however, all of the texts agree: namely, the castigation of mercenary forces.

We will begin with the positive. To this category belong *The Courtier*, by Baldassare Castiglione (finished in 1516, published in 1528); *The Prince*, by Niccolò Machiavelli (written 1513, published in 1532); and by the same author, *The Art of War* (published in 1521). All three of these texts express positive sentiments about military activity, although each has its own particular agenda and audience.

In *The Courtier*, Castiglione (1478–1529) has Count Ludovico da Canossa assert that the exercise of arms is the courtier's principal

---

[15] In addition to the Northern texts discussed in detail here, other texts written in the Germanic lands that condemn warfare, especially as it is carried out by mercenaries are: a dialogue between a mercenary and an Einsiedler from 1522 written by Zwingli, a carnival play from the same year written by Niklaus Manuel Deutsch ("Vom Pabst und seiner Priesterschaft"), and Sebastian Franck's *Chronica, Zeytbuch und geschychtbibel*, published in 1531 in Strasbourg. These texts are cited in Christiane Andersson, *Dirnen, Krieger, Narren: Ausgewählte Zeichnungen von Urs Graf* (Basel: G-S Verlag, 1978), 30. Of course, not all Northern texts were critical of war. In his texts "Von der weltlicher Obrigkeit" (1523) and "Ob Kriegsleute auch im seligen Stande sein können" (1526), Luther defended war as long as it was defensive in nature and just. Luther's conception of the two worlds (one having to do with secular things, the other with spiritual) allowed him to sanction war under appropriate conditions. As part of the secular world, war was thus not in contradiction to Christ's teachings pertaining to the spiritual realm; in fact, to follow secular authority, when that authority was truly legitimate, was part of leading a life pleasing to God. See the highly tendentious article by Gustav Kawerau, "Luthers Gedanken über den Krieg," in *Luthers Frühentwicklung (bis 1517/9)* edited by Hans von Schubert (Leipzig: Schriften des Vereins für Reformationsgeschichte, 1916), 37–56, in which the author uses Luther's writings to justify Germany's role in World War I.

task.[16] To this end, he should spend his time participating in activities that strengthen and hone his martial skills, such as wrestling, swimming, and riding (all of which he should perform with the requisite *sprezzatura* [effortless grace]). Count Ludovico maintains that the courtier's main objective in war is glory, and as a swipe at mercenary soldiers, adds: "and whosoever is moved thereto [i.e., to fight in battle] for gain or any other motive . . . deserves to be called not a gentleman but a base merchant."[17] Although somewhat later, Count Ludovico concedes to Pietro Bembo that both letters and arms are equally important, the discussion then moves on to other topics, leaving letters and arms on equal footing as noble accouterments of the ideal courtier.

Castiglione was writing with a definite retrospective accent.[18] His book was meant to re-construct the glories of the court of Urbino under Guidobaldo da Montefeltro, who had died in 1508. But in looking back toward the recent past, Castiglione also managed to blend current with medieval social norms, at least in his construction of a military elite. Although noble birth was not an absolute prerequisite for the courtier (yet remained preferred), nonetheless his arms- and letters-laden courtier, beholden to his lord, was to be a true gentleman and motivated by glory, thus recalling the chivalric knights of the feudal middle ages.

No doubt Castiglione conceived of his audience as one similarly interested in this retrospective courtly and chivalric ideal that he, looking backwards, reconstructed; he thus must have aimed his book at readers from similarly courtly milieux as well as at those of the international social and intellectual elites. The manuscript seems to have been undertaken at the behest of and dedicated to Alfonso Ariosto (1475–1525), a courtier himself with connections to France, although the first printed edition was dedicated to Michel de Silva, bishop of Viseu and a member of the Spanish nobility. Castiglione's text upheld this medieval ideal to similarly oriented readers just at

---

[16] Baldassare Castiglione, *The Book of the Courtier*, trans. Charles Singleton (New York: Doubleday, 1959). The discussion of arms is found on pp. 32–34, 37–39, 69–74.

[17] Castiglione, *Courtier*, 69.

[18] See Peter Burke, *The Fortunes of the Courtier* (University Park, Pa.: Pennsylvania State University Press, 1995), 8–18 for the tradition of values drawn upon by Castiglione. Burke also discusses the reception of Castiglione's book in Italy and abroad, 39–80.

the time at which this ideal was being lethally challenged by mercenaries and gunpowder. The bearing of arms in Castiglione's text
thus functions as one more way of promoting a chivalric ideal and its
attendant conservative social and political notions.

Machiavelli's texts are also addressed to particular elites, and his
ideal is also influenced by past paradigms. But Machiavelli's elites
are those of the Florentine oligarchy, and his ideal is shaped by Roman antiquity. The function of his text is not so much to promote an
ideal even older than Castiglione's as it is to promote a specifically
Florentine militia that will more effectively support the political and
economic agendas of its overlord. But discussing warfare becomes a
way for Machiavelli (1469–1527) to talk about fundamental issues of
nationalism (or, in his case, Florentine localism would be more correct) and the consolidation and preservation of political supremacy.
That Machiavelli was most interested in the essence of power itself,
rather than a particular institutionalization of it, is indicated by the
fact that he worked for the Florentine state under both republics as
well as under the Medicis.

Because of Machiavelli's important role in the Soderini republic
(he was appointed secretary of the republic in 1498 and undertook
several diplomatic missions), he was dismissed from his office when
the republic was toppled and the Medicis returned to power in 1512.
A year later, he was imprisoned, tortured, and then sent into exile.
That same year, he wrote *The Prince* while at his estate in San Cas-
ciano. It is dedicated to the new head of Florence, Lorenzo de' Medici (1492–1519, not to be confused with his grandfather Lorenzo il
Magnifico, who died in 1492) and thus must be seen as part of Machiavelli's efforts to ingratiate himself with the new regime. Machiavelli admits as much in the dedication, stating that his book was
undertaken "since . . . I am desirous of presenting myself to Your
Magnificence with some token of my eagerness to serve you."[19]

In *The Prince*, the ability to wage war is constructed by Machiavelli
as one of the twin girders upon which all states rest (the other being
effective laws), and as the main concern of a prince.[20] Inability to
wage war is a great danger for a prince, since he is thereby made an

---

[19] Niccolò Machiavelli, *The Prince*, trans. and ed. T. Bergin (Arlington Heights:
Harlan Davidson, 1947), xiii.

[20] The discussion of warfare and arms in *The Prince*, which I am paraphrasing
here, is found on pages 33–43 and 75–78.

object of contempt. To remain a successful warrior, he should thus regularly exercise his troops and his own body, whereby hunting is recommended to the prince as an especially useful activity as it kept him in shape and gave him the opportunity to study topography. In addition, the prince is to read the military deeds of the ancients and learn from them.

But there is a particular reason why Machiavelli wishes Lorenzo de' Medici (or anybody else who happens to be in charge, for that matter) to be successful. The book's last chapter is entitled: "Exhortation to Free Italy from the Barbarians." Machiavelli urges the prince to put together an army the right way (i.e., no mercenaries, only local troops, with the prince at its head) and drive all the foreigners out of Italy. The text's penultimate sentence reads: "This barbarian occupation stinks in the nostrils of all of us."[21] With his emphases on excluding foreign mercenary soldiers from the army on the basis that they are evil and unreliable, and on the goal of creating an Italy for Italians only, the issue of warfare in *The Prince* is actually part of the larger issue of nationalism.

In *The Art of War*, which appeared in 1521, shortly before the Medicis were once again swept out of Florence (1523), Machiavelli portrayed in great detail the composition and actions of the ideal army.[22] The book is dedicated to the Florentine nobleman Lorenzo di Filippo Strozzi. Although the text mostly describes the ideal army as one based on the model of the ancient Romans, the underlying assumption of Machiavelli's thought is that the army is an arm of the state. To construct, train, and employ it properly allows the head of state to defend as well as to expand his territory, and to remain uncontested in his exercise of power; power that might otherwise be challenged by an overly ambitious or aggrieved army. To this end, the soldiers should be of good character, of local origin (and both of these characteristics preclude any foreign mercenaries, against which Machiavelli frequently rails), and well trained in another occupation so that when they are no longer needed, they can easily return to a civilian life without becoming a burden on the state. Warfare, in Machiavelli's text, is thus an essential part of the efficacious exercise

---

[21] Machiavelli, *The Prince*, 78.

[22] Machiavelli, *The Art of War* (New York: Da Capo Press, 1965). Most relevant for the philosophical and practical underpinnings of Machiavelli's ideal army are passages in bk. 1, 7–43.

of political power. To follow this line of reasoning, warfare can be justified as a necessity. Although this is only implicit in *The Art of War*, it is explicitly stated in *The Prince*: "[T]hat war is just which is necessary and arms are merciful when there is no hope save in them."[23]

Erasmus of Rotterdam (1466–1536), however, doubted whether any war was just. In his text *The Education of a Christian Prince* (written in 1515–16 and printed in 1516), Erasmus cautions the prince to consider "how disastrous and criminal an affair war is and what a host of evils it carries in its wake even if it is the most justifiable war—if there really is any war which can be called 'just.'"[24] The prince whom Erasmus is addressing is Charles, duke of Burgundy (later to become Emperor Charles V). International nobility and councillors at other courts might be the targeted audience of a slightly later but closely related text, *The Complaint of Peace* (1517), which is less deferential and more strident in tone. Both were written while Erasmus was himself at court as Charles's advisor.

The function of both texts is to dissuade those in power from waging war. Erasmus describes warfare in as varied and negative terms as possible and constructs mutually inflected social, political, economic, and moral arguments against it. In the first place, war is usually commenced for reasons that do not affect the common people. These reasons include greed, stupidity, and nationalism.[25] If, as Erasmus maintains, the prince rules by consent of the people, yet acts against their interests by waging war, his exercise of political power is thus called into question.[26] In addition, the prince is morally compromised by war because he becomes responsible for shedding Christian blood, and because he is forced to deal with "mercenary soldiers, who are absolutely the most abject and execrable type of human being,"[27] indeed "the very scum of the earth."[28] Warfare is also disastrous financially; the prince drains both state and private

---

[23] Machiavelli, *The Prince*, 76.

[24] Desiderius Erasmus, *The Education of a Christian Prince*, trans. and intro. Lester Born (New York: Octagon Books, 1965), 249.

[25] Erasmus, "The Complaint of Peace," in Desiderius Erasmus, *The Praise of Folly and Other Writings*, trans. and ed. Robert Adams (New York: W. W. Norton, 1989), 105 and 109.

[26] Erasmus, *The Education of a Christian Prince*, 252 and "The Complaint of Peace," 107.

[27] Erasmus, *Christian Prince*, 250.

[28] Erasmus, "Complaint of Peace," 112.

coffers by paying for mercenaries and artillery, the latter which Erasmus describes as "machines out of hell."[29]

Erasmus constructs warfare as the total breakdown of society in its moral, social, and economic facets. Even if the prince would fight the most justifiable war and win, the gain can never outweigh the cost:

> [Y]our soldiers are now polluted with the crime of homicide. Add to that the corruption of public morals and social discipline, not to be made whole at any cost. You have exhausted your treasury and plundered your people, burdening the honest tax payer and inciting the underhanded to dishonest means, so that even before the war is over, its consequences are upon you. The arts and crafts languish, business establishments close their doors.[30]

In short, warfare is simply a bad investment and almost any peace is both cheaper and more preferable:

> Hardly any peace is so bad that it isn't preferable to the most justifiable war. Calculate how much a prospective war will cost, both directly and indirectly, and you will see what a poor investment it is.[31]

Although Erasmus is at pains to shape his arguments against war in both moral and practical terms, with a decided emphasis on financial considerations, his main rhetorical weapon remains the teachings of Christ, who is after all, Erasmus reminds his readers, the prince of peace. He repeatedly points to the hypocrisy of Christians waging war against one another and uses other past cultures to highlight this fact.

> Plato called it sedition, not war, when Greeks fight war with Greeks; ... what terms should we apply then when Christians engage in battle with Christians . . .?[32]

Although the Jews waged war against each other in the centuries of the Jewish Bible, they were following God's orders; Christians are to follow the Gospels, which do nothing but teach peace. How can someone who wages war and goes against the fundamental precept of Christ's teachings be called a Christian?[33] Or as Erasmus viscer-

---

[29] Ibid., 102.
[30] Ibid., 112.
[31] Ibid., 106.
[32] Erasmus, *Christian Prince*, 251. He uses this argument also in "Complaint of Peace," 105.
[33] Erasmus, *Christian Prince*, 255.

ally states: "You cannot conceivably address a credible prayer to the father of all men when you have just driven a sword into your brother's bowels."[34]

Erasmus's texts construct warfare as a great evil but also, upon closer reading, as a particular symptom. The main underlying issue for Erasmus is really the lack of true moral leadership on the part of the Christian princes of Europe, whereby morality is defined as living according to the tenets established in the Gospels. For Erasmus, politics and morality are not mutually exclusive concepts but instead must be mutually supportive; only the prince's strict adherence to the highest moral standards justify his exercise of leadership. At present, Erasmus maintains, princes are forgetting the common bond of Christianity that unites them all and are instead blinded by self-interest and greed. War is a symptom of disunity and folly, of a leadership that has forgotten its justification in Christ's teachings and has become too worldly. It would not be impossible to rid the world of war

> if everyone would cease to favor his own cause, if we could set aside all personal feelings and carry out the common aim, if Christ, not the world, was in our plans. Now, while everyone is looking out for his own interests, while popes and bishops are deeply concerned over power and wealth, while princes are driven headlong by ambition or anger, while all follow after them for the sake of their own gain, it is not surprising that we run straight into a whirlwind of affairs under the guidance of Folly.[35]

Erasmus' friend, Thomas More (1478–1535), also criticizes power-hungry princes ever ready to wage war in *Utopia* (written in 1515–16) which Erasmus helped to publish in Louvain in 1516. Like Erasmus, More makes peace the nobler accomplishment of a ruler than war but bemoans the fact that current political thinking is otherwise:

> [T]he most part of all princes have more delight in warlike matters and feats of chivalry . . . than in the good feats of peace, and employ much more study how by right or by wrong to enlarge their dominions than how well and peaceable to rule and govern that they have already.[36]

---

[34] Erasmus, "Complaint of Peace," 97.
[35] Erasmus, *Christian Prince*, 256–57.
[36] Thomas More, *Utopia* (London: J. M. Dent and Sons, 1985), 20.

Unlike Erasmus, however, who praised Francis I of France as especially desirous of peace, More castigates the French drive for Italian
and Netherlandish territory, saying that the king had already more
than enough territory for one man to rule effectively. Besides, waging war has dreadful financial and social consequences: the coffers
are drained, and soldiers returning from war who are maimed or
otherwise untrained turn to thievery to support themselves and thus
become a burden to the common good. About the only thing war is
good for, according to More in his description of the citizens of Utopia, is killing off Swiss mercenary soldiers, thinly disguised in More's
text as the race of Zapoletes:

> They [the Utopians] hire soldiers out of all countries and send them to
> battle, but chiefly the Zapoletes. . . . They be hideous, savage and
> fierce, dwelling in wild woods and high mountains where they were
> bred and brought up. . . . Whosoever lacketh soldiers, there they
> proffer their services for small wages. . . . But they bind themselves for
> no certain time; but upon this condition they enter into bonds, that the
> next day they will take part with the other side for greater wages, and
> the next day after that they will be ready to come back for a little more
> money. . . . The Utopians pass not how many of them they bring to
> destruction, for they believe that they should do a very good deed for
> all mankind if they could rid out of the world all that foul stinking den
> of that most wicked and cursed people.[37]

Mercenary soldiers, specifically the Landsknechten, are the target of
special criticism in Eberlin von Günzburg's 1524 pamphlet *Mich
wundert das kein gelt im land ist*. The pamphlet, written in German and
in the form of a dialogue, must have been intended for a far wider
audience than any of the texts discussed so far, as it was written in
the vernacular. Its purpose, then, was to shape public opinion about
particular issues, including warfare and soldiers. The Landsknechten
get special mention by Günzburg because of their deleterious effect
on the country's morals, and are thus more dangerous to their own
country than any outside foe:

> If the devil doesn't take them and they instead come back home again,
> they spoil all social groups [Stände] with their evil customs: in words,
> dress, deeds, to the detriment of good middle class relationships etc.;
> others are also incited by them to idleness, gambling, guzzling, whor-

---

[37] Ibid., 111–12.

ing etc. and thus they cause more damage to their own fatherland than the enemy [does] through unjustifiable war.[38]

Critique of the Landsknechten is part of Günzburg's criticism of war, which he offers as one of the reasons that money is scarce in Germany. War robs the country not only of money but also of cultivated land and able-bodied men. Political critique is offered here too. In a sentence which echoes both Erasmus and More, Günzburg describes the nobles as more interested in territorial expansion than in beneficial leadership: "If the nobles paid as much attention to making sure that their lands were ruled in the right way as they do to acquiring more land, then we would soon have peace."[39]

But war, like the merchants and clerics who are also thrashed in Günzburg's text, is constructed in such a way as to allow the author to get at the underlying issue: the espousal of Luther's religious and social tenets. Ostensibly, the issue seems to be the lack of currency in the German lands, but each of the phenomena made responsible for the lack points to a corrupt state of affairs that could be corrected if the country would be sustained and guided by true faith, that is, according to Luther, not the pope:

> The French are not as much of a problem for the Emperor as the Pope who is sitting in his capitol and his land—he should defend himself against him, and for that we would gladly give our lives and goods; but we are unwilling to serve in other wars. In short, there is no happiness, no discipline, no fear of God, no loyalty, no faith in our land.[40]

For Günzburg then, like Erasmus, the underlying issue is a moral one, whereby warfare functions as a foil to highlight that issue.

In the texts we have examined, we have seen that warfare, be it

---

[38] Johann Eberlin von Günzburg, "Mich wundert das kein Geld im Land ist," in *Johann Eberlin von Günzburg: Ausgewählte Schriften*, ed. Ludwig Enders, (Halle an der Saale, 1902), 3: 151: "Fueret sie [the *Landsknechten*] aber der tewffel nit hyn so bald und kommen wieder heym, so verderben sie alle stend mit yren bösen siten, in worten, kleidern, wercken, zu grossen schaden burgerlicher beywonung etc. auch andere gereitzt werden durch sie zu mussigkeit, spylen, sauffen, hurrn etc. und also mehr schaden zufuegn yrem eygen vatterlandt durch böse sitten dann vorhynn den veinden durch unbillige krieg."

[39] Ibid, 155: "Wenn die herren sovil acht hetten, das die land wol regirt wurden als sie achten vil landt zu uberkommen, so hette man bald frid."

[40] Ibid., 155: "Sitzt doch der Frantzoß dem keyser nit so gar im landt als der Bapst, welcher dem keyser in seiner hauptstadt und landt sitzt, des sollt er sich weren, und dartzu wolten wir gern leib und gut geben, aber zu andern kriegen seint wir unwillig, kurtz, kein gluck, kein zucht, kein gotsforcht, kein trew, kein glaub ist in unserem land."

judged positively or negatively, acts as a rhetorical construction that
allows the authors to address larger issues. Certainly the success of
that rhetorical strategy depended on the widespread exposure to and
concern about warfare in the second and third decades of the sixteenth century. But the textual discourse of warfare clearly was not
about simply reporting what happened on the battlefield, but was
instead about shaping public opinion through constructing warfare
as a support to a main argument. As a phenomenon, warfare is
hardly a given event; it is competitively interpreted in the varying
texts. Each text struggles to give warfare a meaning, one that is convincing to the reader and tendentious. In this way, warfare, or better
said, its construction and interpretation, becomes a vehicle for shaping political identity. The same holds true in the field of visual discourse, to which we now turn.

In Western culture, the roots of the visual depiction of warfare go
back to some of the earliest known cultures.[41] Examples of these
include the Akkadian victory stele of Naramsin (c.2300–2200 B.C.)
and the Egyptian palette of King Narmor (c. 3200 B.C.). In antiquity, scenes of battle decorated the pediment of preclassical Greek
temples such as at Aegina (c. 490 B.C.), and were found on the
metopes of the Parthenon (447–438 B.C.). Alexander's battle against
the Persian king Darius was depicted in a Hellenistic pebble mosaic
(second to first century B.C.), and the Roman emperor Trajan commemorated his campaign against the Dacians in relief sculpture that
wound up around a giant column (113 A.D.). These are but a few
widely known examples that nonetheless stand in for an extensive
group of images, in practically all possible media, that depict warfare. These examples also indicate how warfare functioned in these
images: almost always as a glorification of a ruler, and almost always
as a means by which national or local identity is established through
confrontation with an other. Many of these works were large-scale
and widely accessible for viewing.

Battles continued to be depicted in the Middle Ages, especially in
the media of smaller-scale luxury objects such as manuscript illumi-
nation and tapestries of the later medieval period.[42] Contemporane-

---

[41] Olle Cederlöf, "The Battle Painting as a Historical Source," *Revue internationale
d'histoire militaire* 1967: 119–44.

[42] J. R. Hale, *Artists and Warfare in the Renaissance* (New Haven: Yale University
Press, 1990), 42–48

ous as well as ancient battles were depicted now for a small, elite
viewing audience that had resources enough to personally commission decorations for their manors, such as tapestries, or who had
received sufficient education to know about ancient history and how
to read the texts in manuscripts and have the leisure time to do so.
Generally, the depictions of warfare during the Middle Ages featured battles which were visually small in scope (having no doubt to
do with the scale of the objects themselves) and which focused on
only a few figures, also in accordance with the small-scale, one-to-
one fighting formations of medieval warfare.[43]

Thus, by the time battles were depicted in the Renaissance, centuries of iconographic tradition were at least potentially available to
artists. This established iconographic tradition is one of the reasons
why it is wrong to treat Renaissance–and Breu's–battle imagery as
transparent, historically accurate eyewitness accounts. The facts of a
particular battle, if available to the artist, may have been less influential on the composition than the artist's training in traditions of representation. The other reason that it is wrong to ask questions demanding historical accuracy from these images lies in their primary
function as political propaganda, where facts become subordinate to
the overall message.

An excellent example of how the basic facts of warfare–such as
who won and who lost–were not as crucial as the claims made in art
about the facts, are the panels painted by Paolo Uccello depicting
the route of San Romano.[44] As part of the Florentine war against
Lucca, the battle occurred on June 1, 1432, and pitted troops fighting for Florence against a mercenary army fighting for Siena and
Milan, allies of Lucca. The panels clearly intimate the victory of the
Florentines; the first panel shows the first commander of the
Florentine troops leading his troops into battle, the second depicts
the enemy Sienese commander, Bernardino dell Ciarda, knocked
down from his horse, and the third shows the second Florentine
commander, Michelotto da Cotignola, attacking the Sienese from
the rear. With all of this action, who could doubt which army would

---

43 Philippe Contamine, *War in the Middle Ages* (London: B. Blackwell, 1984), 303–4.
44 Dating of the three panels (one at the National Gallery in London, one at the
Uffizi in Florence and the third at the Louvre in Paris) range from mid-1430s to
mid-1450s. The information in this discussion of Uccello's panels is based on the
excellent article by Randolph Starn and Loren Partridge, "Representing War in the
Renaissance: The Shield of Paolo Uccello," *Representations* 5 (1984): 33–65.

prove victorious? Yet, as Starn and Partridge point out, who actually won the battle was anything but clear, as both Siena and Florence claimed victory. Uccello's paintings, with their emphatic insistence on recreating the reality of three-dimensional space thus provide assurance that this recreation of the Florentine victory was just as real. The Medicis, in whose palace the paintings initially hung, could thus commemorate a shining moment in Florentine history (whether it was actually true or not didn't much matter, a situation analogous to the deployment of patriot missiles in the Gulf war of 1990—did they work in shielding Israel from Iraqi missiles or didn't they?) thus emphasizing their local patriotism. The paintings, however, also served to justify the involvement of Florence in the war against Lucca, a situation that led to the Medicis' brief exile in 1433. In addition to the political tendentiousness of the panels, Starn and Partridge also point to the panels' inclusion of battle iconography from medieval manuscripts.[45]

The case of Uccello's panels provides a clear warning against expecting transparency from battle images. Yet such images are frequently analyzed according to what they tell us about historical fact.[46] In analyzing Breu's imagery, we will see that neither aesthetic

---

[45] In 1982, Trudl and Rainer Wohlfeil argued that Renaissance military depictions have no iconographic content, especially those in the graphic medium. Iconography, according to their account, is replaced and made obsolete by the desire for knowledge about military facts. Although they are willing to concede that these images still have political content, they maintain that largely no iconographic knowledge is necessary to understand these images as documents of history since the issue for these images was to replicate empirical facts exactly. In other words, the images of *Landsknechten* that they discuss are analyzed in terms of their reality content. Although the tendency to exaggerate is recognized, the images' ability to capture real life is deemed especially important. Rainer und Trudl Wohlfeil, "Landsknecht im Bild: Überlegungen zur 'historischen Bildkunde,'" in *Bauer, Reich und Reformation: Festschrift Günther Franz*, edited by Peter Blickle (Stuttgart: Ulmer Verlag, 1982), 104–19, especially pages 116 and 118–19.

[46] See for example Olle Cederlöf, "The Battle Painting as a Historical Source," 119–44. Cederlöf tries to separate the tendentious from the factual by creating four different categories of battle imagery: glorifying, narrative, analytical, and ornamental. Yet his second and third categories, which are to contain more factually oriented paintings, remain fairly empty. For the Renaissance, he mentions only one painting for both of those categories, namely, Ruprecht Heller's 1529 painting of the battle of Pavia (Stockholm). J. R. Hale's recent book, *Artists and Warfare in the Renaissance*, is a tremendously useful compilation of visual material, but the text often consists of Hale's subjective descriptions of the images and his similarly subjective judgment of the image's aesthetic and/or narrative success. In his discussion of the Uccello paintings (*Artists and Warfare*, 155), Hale is willing to concede that they are not about

judgment nor mere description (based on the assumption of transparency) are effective hermeneutic strategies to get at how these images performed their social and historical work as propaganda. Instead, our line of inquiry will be more along the lines of Keith Moxey's work. Although Moxey has focused on images of Landsknechten per se (rather than battle imagery) produced in Nuremberg in the 1530s,[47] the questions he asks of this material will be similar to ours; namely, how do images construct social identity, how stable is that identity, and how does it function for the images' audiences, including the patron?

As an illustrator of battles, Breu belonged to a large group of international sixteenth-century artists who incorporated military themes in their works. Battle imagery was produced in sixteenth-century Italy by artists such as Michelangelo, Leonardo da Vinci, Giulio Romano, Giovanni Battista Scultori, and Giorgio Vasari. Yet the decisive difference between Italian and Northern battle imagery was the Italians' persistence in representing either antique battles or cloaking contemporaneous ones in antique guise. Northern artists, for the most part, presented modern warfare and in modern dress.

Breu's Northern counterparts include the Germans Albrecht Dürer (especially the artist's treatise on fortification published in 1527), Albrecht Altdorfer, Hans Burgkmair, Hans Schäufelein, Hans Sebald Beham, Erhard Schoen, and Wolf Huber, and the Swiss Urs Graf and Niklas Manuel Deutsch. There are interesting parallels between Deutsch's career and Breu's; both artists were proreformational, and Deutsch, like Breu, was also a writer.[48] Unlike Breu, however, Deutsch did take part in battle, or was at least on the scene, as was his Swiss colleague, Urs Graf.[49]

Several of Breu's Northern colleagues were also involved in pro-

---

actual warfare, but he substitutes the reality of a battle for the reality of a tournament as the decisive influence on the panels.

[47] Keith Moxey, "Mercenary Warriors and the 'Rod of God,'" in *Peasants, Warriors and Wives* (Chicago: University of Chicago Press, 1989), 67–100.

[48] See *Niklaus Manuel Deutsch: Maler, Dichter, Staatsman* (Bern: Kunstmuseum Bern, 1979). Deutsch did not write a chronicle but did author several pro-reformational dialogues and tracts. His art works have been analyzed as stylistically influenced by Augsburg art.

[49] Artists who actually took part in battle or traveled to the scene in order to make sketches for later work are rare in the first third of the sixteenth century. In addition to Graf and Deutsch, the only artist to whom reference is made of attending battle is Jan Cornelisz. Vermeyen, who accompanied Charles V on his Tunis campaign (J. R. Hale, *Artists and Warfare*, 251).

ducing battle imagery made specifically for Habsburg projects. For example, Maximilian's battles appeared in both the woodcut and miniature versions of the *Triumphal Procession*. The woodcut version, containing 147 sheets, was produced between 1512 and 1518.[50] Maximilian himself dictated his ideas for the *Procession* project to his secretary, Marx Treitzsaurwein. It was first printed posthumously, however, in 1526, at the request of Maximilian's grandson, Ferdinand I. In a somewhat contrived manner, scenes from twelve of Maximilian's wars are displayed on carts pushed and pulled by Landsknechten. These woodcuts were designed by Hans Springinklee, a student of Dürer's, but Hans Burgkmair, Albrecht Altdorfer, Leonhard Beck, and Hans Schäufelein also worked on the project, which included several depictions of different groups of infantrymen and knights. Burgkmair, Beck, and Schäufelein were all living and working in Augsburg during their work on the project.

Parallel to the woodcut version, another *Triumphal Procession* was produced between 1512 and 1516 in 109 miniatures painted on parchment by Albrecht Altdorfer and assistants.[51] Here the battles are illustrated mostly from a bird's-eye view on large banners held aloft by Landsknechten.

Another related project, the *Triumphal Arch*, also included battle scenes.[52] Albrecht Dürer, Hans Springinklee, Wolf Traut, and Albrecht Altdorfer worked from 1512 to 1517 on this enormous composite woodcut made up of 192 blocks. Research was done by Maximilian's court historian Johannes Stabius and initial designs were provided by his court artist Jörg Kölderer.

Lastly, Maximilian's battles make up the entire third section of his symbolic autobiography, *Der Weißkunig* (The White/Wise King).[53] The work was begun in the opening years of the 1500s and re-

---

[50] Horst Appuhn, ed., *Der Triumphzug Maximilians I* (Dortmund: Harenburg Kommunikation, 1987).

[51] Franz Winzinger, *Die Miniaturen zum Triumphzug Kaiser Maximilian I* (Graz: Akademische Druck- und Verlagsanstalt, 1973).

[52] *Ehrenpforte des Kaiser Maximilians*, Facsimile ed. (Graz: Akademische Druck- und Verlagsanstalt, 1970). See also *Maximilian I* (Innsbruck: Tyrolia Verlag, 1969), cat. nos. 521–22, pp. 136–38; Eduard Chmelarz, "Die Ehrenpforte des Kaisers Maximilian I," *Jahrbuch der kunsthistorischen Sammlungen der allerhöchsten Kaiserhauses* 4 (1886): 291f.

[53] T. Musper, ed., *Kaiser Maximilians Weißkunig*, 2 vols. (Stuttgart: W. Kohlhammer, 1956); *Maximilian I*, cat. no. 523, pp. 139–40; Hermann Wiesflecker, *Kaiser Maximilian I*, 5: 315–19.

mained unfinished at Maximilian's death in 1519. The text was written by Treitzsaurwein according to Maximilian's initial ideas and constant editing. In 1526 Ferdinand commanded that Treitzsaurwein finish the book, but it was never completed because Maximilian's former secretary died the following year. The book was first printed in its unfinished state in 1775. Most of the 251 woodcut illustrations were done by Hans Burgkmair and Leonhard Beck, both of Augsburg, but Hans Springinklee and Hans Schäufelein also contributed a couple of illustrations each. Although earlier literature tended to view *Weißkunig* as corresponding closely to historical reality, more recent interpretations have focused on the tendentious function of the text as "Gedechtnus," a word that Maximilian himself used to characterize the function of cultural production under his aegis.[54] These images and texts were all to contribute to the commemoration of Maximilian's family and his own deeds, to insure their immortality, and as it turns out, to also insure the interpretation of the family and the deeds as great and glorious.

The *Triumphal Processions*, the *Triumphal Arch* and *Weißkunig* were all projects that involved the depiction of warfare, they were all intimately linked with Maximilian's court, and were all worked on during the second decade of the sixteenth century. All of them included works by Augsburg artists. And all of them were most likely aimed at a socially and economically elite audience; although the projects were carried out in the graphic medium, their size and extent would have made the finished products both enormously costly and, in terms of subject matter, not especially popular.

Thus, when we regard Breu's battle imagery, also produced in connection with the Habsburgs, our working assumption will be that his production is in some ways more typical than unique. Breu was obviously one of several Augsburg artists working at the behest of the Habsburg court, producing images of mostly the same battles illustrated in his colleagues' images.

Nonetheless, Breu's images of warfare merit close scrutiny for sev-

---

[54] Examples of earlier scholarship include two dissertations written at the University of Graz, both analyzing the relationship between the text and history (both even having the same title!): Wolfgang Schweiger, "Der Wert des Weißkunig als Geschichtsquelle," (Ph.D. diss., University of Graz, 1968); Kurt Riedl, "Der Wert des Weißkunigs als Geschichtsquelle," (Ph.D. diss., University of Graz, 1969). In contrast, Jan-Dirk Müller analyzes the text in terms of its construction of history in his book *Gedechtnus: Literatur und Hofgesellschaft um Maximilian I*, 80–91 and 130–48.

eral reasons. First of all, Breu's works in particular offer us examples of war imagery in different media (frescoes and woodcut) and for different audiences. We will thus be in a position to understand how media and audience influence the construction of meaning. Second, in Breu's case we have an artist who is critical of organized authority and yet is producing images meant to uphold it. This situation allows us to examine the possibility of subversive readings. Our examination will not be undertaken in an attempt to resuscitate the notion of artistic intention or to rescue the artist as someone who remained true to his personal convictions no matter what. Instead, we want to look at the possibility of subversive readings in terms of the creative instability of meaning: that even while producing political propaganda there was enough interpretive space within the images for alternative identities and viewpoints.

At odds with these areas of slippage is the works' main task of constructing meaning that is stable and politically tendentious. My thesis is that Breu's art contributed to a discourse of warfare in order to shape political identity. It does this by constructing definitions: of the ruler, as powerful and victorious; of his state, represented by his army, as obedient and self-sacrificing; and of his subjects, the audience, who ideally would be moved by the images to admire and support the ruler. The art works should present these identities and definitions in as convincing a way as possible in order to encourage the audience to align itself accordingly. Thus, the works use a narrative blend of fact and iconographic tradition to create a reality that is visually–and ideologically–convincing. The art works also serve to construct the Habsburg army, including German Landsknechten, as victorious over foreign others, which serves to support Habsburg leadership as well as to encourage national pride. Meaning thus comes about through the interaction of the viewer with the definitions and identities constructed in the art work. The art works' task is to make sure the viewer interacts with and thus interprets the definitions and identities the right, that is, the pro-Habsburg way. This task becomes all the more crucial at times of crisis and challenge to Habsburg hegemony, as we will see. In the sixteenth-century texts discussed earlier in this chapter, we saw how warfare was used to shape opinion about larger issues. In the remainder of this chapter, I will argue that warfare in Breu's work is a potent means by which to address the larger issue of political legitimation and Habsburg authority.

The Augsburg City Hall Frescoes

The frescoes that Breu painted for the exterior of the Augsburg city hall, depicting battle scenes and Maximilian's genealogy, are no longer extant. They were in fact already destroyed in the early seventeenth century when the old city hall was torn down and replaced by a new one, built according to designs of Elias Holl.[55] Although the frescoes are faintly visible in a late-sixteenth-century painting and an early-seventeenth-century etching, identifying the figures, the battles, or even stylistic characteristics of Breu's work is impossible.

Nonetheless, Breu's frescoes–their documentation and their short-lived existence–have much to tell us. They represent a major civic commission given to Breu and indicate how and perhaps even why certain local artists' workshops collaborated with each other. We recall from Breu's description of the project in his chronicle that the frescoes were made by three different artists (Breu, Ulrich Apt, and Ulrich Maurmüller) assisted by apprentices, and that the frescoes cost ninehundred gulden (see chapter 2). The cost of the frescoes, the number of artists involved in their execution, the frescoes' prominent placement on this significant civic structure, and the prestigious patrons all indicate that the city hall frescoes were an extremely important commission. That Breu was involved in this project points to a high regard for his evidently well-known workshop.

The city hall project is also an interesting example of Breu's collaboration with other Augsburg artists.[56] Both Maurmüller and Breu had been Ulrich Apt's pupils; Breu began his apprenticeship in 1493,[57] Maurmüller five years later in 1498.[58] However, in 1502

---

[55] The city hall was torn down 1615–16 and replaced by a new structure designed by the *Stadtmeister* and architect Elias Holl. See *Welt im Umbruch* 1: 121. For Holl's city hall, see Wolfram Baer, Hanno Wlater Kruft and Bernd Roeck, eds., *Elias Holl und das Augsburger Rathaus*, (Regensburg: Friedrich Pustet Verlag, 1985).

[56] None of the extant documents regarding the city hall project specify for what each artist was responsible. This project is the only known example of Breu's collaboration with both Maurmüller and Apt. Examples of Breu's collaboration with other artists, however, are numerous: Maximilian's prayer book (with Lucas Cranach, Albrecht Dürer, Hans Baldung Grien, and Albrecht Altdorfer), the Lermos/Munich hunt and war cycle (with glazier Hans Knoder), and Ferdinand's investiture woodcut (with Heinrich Steiner and Hans Tirol). Breu was also active in large-scale projects in which other artists were involved; for example, work on the Fugger chapel and in St. Moritz (for the latter, see my discussion in chapter 2).

[57] StAA (Stadtarchiv Augsburg), Reichsstadt Schätze 72c, *Einschreibebuch der Maler*, fol. 34r.

[58] Ibid., 72b, fol. 79r. See also Wilhelm, *Augsburger Wandmalerei*, 524–29.

both artists are mentioned in the guild records as independent masters.[59] The cooperation of these two former pupils with their *Lehrmeister* fourteen years after establishing their own independent workshops indicates that the connection between masters and apprentices could remain very strong.

Associations with major workshops were important not only in terms of stylistic influence but also in terms of professional survival; Wilhelm's analysis of the activities of fresco painters between 1500 and 1530 shows that commissions were given to an increasingly smaller number of workshops, and that only the well-established ones survived.[60] To this privileged group belong Apt's, Breu's, and Maurmüller's workshops.[61]

More important for our task here, the Augsburg city hall frescoes are (were) a highly visible example of how the alliance between Maximilian and his city of Augsburg was publicly proclaimed in the face of ongoing antagonism between the emperor and his German estates, and how Habsburg might and glory were celebrated despite Maximilian's stunning military losses on the Italian front. The frescoes are, in short, perfect examples of the forging of intertwined and mutually dependent civic and imperial ideologies. These ideologies of the powerful ruler and the loyal subjects aligned and allied the emperor and his city into a particular political constellation that served to uphold the interests of those in power.

The placement of Maximilian's ancestors and battles on the walls of Augsburg's city hall constructed the emperor as a great military hero of noble lineage. Interestingly, it is exactly the connection be-

---

[59] For Maurmüller, StAA, Archiv des historischen Vereins 54a, *Malerbuch*, fol. 24r; for Breu, StAA, 72c, fol. 38v.

[60] Wilhelm, *Augsburger Wandmalerei*, 72–77. See also his "Werkstattschema" no. 1, 580–81 in which the relationship between the Apt-Breu-Maurmüller workshops is diagramed.

[61] Maurmüller's workshop seems to have received commissions mostly for handiwork such as painting the customs house at Rotes Tor, the city hall clock and keys, and so on (Wilhelm, *Augsburger Wandmalerei*, 526–27). Interestingly, one of Maurmüller's pupils was Bartholome Nußhardt (a.k.a. Nußfelder, Duchheffter; StAA, 54a, fol.168r 1505). Nußhardt appears in Breu's chronicle (25) as "Bartlme Duchheffter, ain maler" and is described here as involved in the provocation of a monk in 1524. Roth (*Reformationsgeschichte*, 1: 227–30) traces Nußhardt's (here Nußfelder) involvement with the Augsburg Anabaptists. Nußhardt is not mentioned in Breu's chronicle again, nor is there concrete documentary evidence that the two artists knew each other, although their acquaintance seems more than likely (common rejection of Catholicism, common acquaintanceship with Maurmüller, small artisanal community).

tween aristocratic ancestry and soldiering that was being loosened at this time. As we have seen, it was no longer mostly knights from the nobility who fought in battle in the sixteenth century. Instead, the role of the mercenary foot soldier was becoming increasingly important. The placement of Breu's frescoes also constructed an identity for the city of Augsburg, namely, as specifically allied with the emperor, and by implication, as especially loyal. By flattering Maximilian, the frescoes also flattered the citizens and government of Augsburg as special imperial allies. The frescoes did nothing short of constructing and sustaining imperial authority, based on lineage and warfare, on the very walls sheltering the city's government, whose task, at least in principle, was to govern the city in accordance with the emperor's wishes. Thus, a civic identity was created for the Augsburgers as dutifully loyal (seen from the emperor's perspective) and as enjoying a special and powerful connection to the emperor (as seen from the perspective of rival cities and/or nobility).

Because the specific content of the frescoes remains unknown (for example, we do not know which ancestors and which battles in particular were included, nor how they were portrayed), questions pertaining to the role of nationalism and to the possibility of subversive readings must be suspended in this case.

The conception of the plans for the city hall frescoes is documented in a letter from the city secretary of Augsburg, Conrad Peutinger, to the Emperor Maximilian and dated June 9, 1516.[62] The letter contains information not only about the city hall frescoes, but also about a suit of armor commissioned from Coloman Helmenschmied, and about woodcuts for *Weißkunig* and *Theuerdank*. This letter highlights both Peutinger's role as middleman between Augsburg artists/craftsmen and the emperor,[63] and Maximilian's patronage of these artisans. Breu's frescoes are here placed within the context of other imperial projects, thus indicating that their conception and content were possibly related to these projects.

Peutinger writes:

---

[62] This letter is published in A. Buff, "Rechnungsauszüge, Urkunden und Urkundenregesten aus dem Augsburger Stadtarchiv," *Jahrbuch des kunsthistorischen Sammlungen des allerhöchsten Kaiserhauses*, 13 (1892): xx–xxi, #8610.

[63] For Peutinger's political and artistic connections to Maximilian, see C. M. Horn, "Doctor Conrad Peutingers Beziehung zu Kaiser Maximilian I," Ph.D. diss. (University of Graz, Austria); and H. Lutz, *Conrad Peutinger*, 1–143.

Furthermore, all gracious Sire, the city council of Augsburg has entrusted me with the task of arranging for the painting of the city hall
there. I would have, amongst other things, Your Imperial Majesty's
house of Roman Emperors and Kings, and also the Kings of Spain
and Sicily painted on it [the building]. I have described this idea on
the sheet designated "C." I most humbly beg of you, your Imperial
Majesty, to let me know as soon as possible whether Your Majesty is in
agreement with this plan or whether Your Majesty would like to suggest another example; and let me know Your Majesty's wish and pleasure herein.[64]

From this passage in Peutinger's letter, we know that the commission
to paint the city hall was, in the direct sense, a civic, not an imperial
commission. We also know that Peutinger was responsible for the
selection of the subject matter and that his initial ideas included the
representation of Habsburg genealogy. The letter also makes clear
that Maximilian is to feel that the project was to be carried out with
the emperor's knowledge and that his consent was sought. Peutinger
indicates that it was actually up to the emperor to decide what
should appear on the city hall—to accept the suggestion of his royal
genealogy, or to suggest an alternative. Thus, Maximilian was encouraged to participate actively in a project that seems, from Peutinger's text, to have been commissioned by the City Council, with
the emperor's participation, however, clearly in mind. In fact, the
report to Maximilian about the project and its presentation as subject to his approval shows that the City Council took deliberate action to draw the emperor's attention to the project. Yet by the time
Peutinger wrote the letter (June 9), work had already begun on the
frescoes; Breu gives the starting date as May 23. Peutinger must
have been confident that Maximilian would agree with the plans.
The primary function of the letter's text, in fact, seems to be to draw
attention to the project and to reassure Maximilian that he would be
involved.

Peutinger's letter also gives rise to a number of questions. From

---

[64] Buff, "Rechnungsauszüge," xx–xxi: "Ferner allergnadigster herre, mir ist von
dem rat zu Augspurg das rathaus daselbs das angeben des gemeels daselbs bevohlen
worden. Nun wird ich under anderem eur kais. maj. geschlecht von Romischen
kaiseren und kunigen auch kunigen von Hispanien und Sicilien daran malen lassen
und des fürnemens, wie ich an dem zedel, hiebei mit C bezaichnet, auf geschriben
hab; dorauf eur kais. maj. in aller undertanigkeit bit, mir hierauf gnadigen bescheid
zu geben und solchs auf das fürderlichst zu tun dan ich bin in derselben arbeit auch
ob eur maj. solchs also gefällig seie oder ain anderen monnung haben wollen, mich
in demselben nach eur maj. beschaid und wollgefallen auch wissen zu halten."

his letter we know only what Peutinger originally and partially envis-
aged. However, his sketch on "sheet C" is not extant; neither is
Maximilian's response. Thus, the letter does not tell us what Peutinger planned in addition to the genealogy; likewise, there is no
textual evidence that Maximilian altered this plan. Peutinger also
does not relate exactly where these figures would appear (this would
have presumably been clear from "sheet C") or which artists would
be responsible for them.

Two of these questions can be answered by assumption. Peutinger
writes about painting the figures of Maximilian's royal ancestors
"on" the city hall ("daran malen lassen"), which indicates that these
were to be exterior frescoes. We can also assume that Maximilian
probably agreed with Peutinger's plan since the emperor was clearly
interested in the use of genealogy as propaganda, to which other
imperial projects attest, as we will discuss further below.

These assumptions are supported by visual documentation provided in later representations of the city hall mentioned earlier. In a
painting by Elias Schemel from ca. 1599 representing the Perlachplatz, part of the city hall is also depicted.[65] On the first segment of
the west facade (facing onto the Perlachplatz), standing figures with
banners are barely visible. Somewhat more can be seen in an etching by Wilhelm Peter Zimmerman.[66] Although dated 1618, three
years after the destruction of the old city hall, the etching depicts an
earlier scene in which the late-Gothic city hall is still standing.[67]
Here further frescoes on the north facade (facing onto the Fischmarkt) are visible: between the windows on all three levels stand
further single figures with banners. The city emblem (the Roman

---

[65] Augsburg, Maximilianmuseum, Städtische Kunstsammlungen, inv. nr.3825;
discussed and reproduced in *Welt im Umbruch*, vol.1, cat. no. 275, 302–3. The catalogue entry cites the *Baumeisterrechnungsbuch*, 1599, fol. 881 (StAA), in which a payment of forty-six gulden to Schemel is noted for a representation of the old city hall.
Elias Schemel was related to Gall Schemel, one of Breu's pupils; cf. *Welt im Umbruch*,
vol. 1, cat. no. 354.

[66] Stadt- und Staatsbibliothek Augsburg, W. P. Zimmerman, *Ernewrtes Geschlechter
Buch*, Augsburg, 1618, illustration to the book's second part.   See also *Welt in
Umbruch*, vol. 1, 365–67, cat. no. 369, and 255, cat. no. 207.

[67] The etching illustrates the Fuggers and other patricians in sleighs on the
Perlachplatz. Exactly when this event took place is not clear, although to judge from
the clothing it must have been in the late sixteenth/early seventeenth century.
Sleighing parties were also popular earlier than this; a woodcut attributed to Breu
the Younger depicts Charles V and Ferdinand in sleighs during the closing phase of
the 1530 Augsburg Reichstag. See W. Hilger, *Ikonographie Kaiser Ferdinand I* (Vienna:
Böhlau Verlag, 1969), 46 and 61, cat. no. 81.

pine cone flanked by two men) stands immediately above the entrance, and above the emblem appears a fresco of a battle scene.

If we combine the information available in Peutinger's letter and these later representations, we can conclude that the single figures probably represent "eur kais. maj. geschlecht von Romischen kaiseren und kunigen (Your Imperial Majesty's house of Roman Emperors and Kings)" and so forth, and that battle scenes were also represented.[68] Again, these latter scenes would have found Maximilian's approval since the Emperor carefully recorded his military confrontations in other projects, as we have discussed earlier.[69]

Further information regarding the city hall project is provided by Wilhelm Rem in his city chronicle. In 1515 he notes that two new rooms were being built in the city hall (one facing the Fischmarkt) and that work was done on the roof and on five red marble columns.[70] A year later, he reports on other renovations and additions: the doors were heightened, the window sills and entrance redone, and "the facade of the city hall, facing the Fish Market, was painted down to the doors, and the doors were also painted; all that cost 900 fl. to paint, and 20 fl. in tips."[71] Thus, we know that at least the frescoes on the north facade visible in Zimmerman's etching were done in 1516. Rem does not mention any other facade.

The city hall frescoes in fact seem to have been part of a large-scale renovation of this important civic structure. Additional projects were carried out in the interior: a wooden ceiling with rosettes and putti, stained glass windows, and panel paintings were made, Netherlandish tapestries were mounted on the walls.[72] It is possible that Breu was also involved in the interior decoration. Campbell Dodgson has attributed a drawing to Breu from ca. 1515 that represents

---

[68] It is unclear how many battle scenes were represented. Only one is visible in Zimmerman's etching, but Julius Baum maintains that further battle scenes were found on the west facade: J. Baum, "Das alte Augsburger Rathaus," *Zeitschrift des historischen Vereins für Schwaben und Neuburg* 33 (1907): 72.

[69] Perhaps these battle scenes were even suggested to Peutinger by Maximilian in the emperor's lost response.

[70] Rem, *Cronica*, 45.

[71] Ibid., 63: "man malet das Ratthaus an der seitten gegen dem Fischmarkt und hinumb bis an thuren, und den thuren malt man auch; das kost als zu malen 900 fl. und 20 fl. zu trinkgelt."

[72] J. Baum, "Das alte Augsburger Rathaus," 66. Baum's information is from another secondary source, A. Buff, *Augsburg in der Renaissancezeit* (Bamberg: n.p., 1893), 21f and 110f. The ceiling is attributed to Adolf Daucher, the designs for stained glass to Hans Burgkmair, the glass work to glaziers Hans Braun and Hans

the calumny of Apelles.[73] Perhaps this drawing was a study by Breu for a fresco planned for the city hall interior. As this scene is an allegory of justice, it would be an appropriate image for the interior, which also functioned as a legal chamber.

Judgment scenes frequently appeared in or on city halls, for example, in Bruges, Brussels, and Louvain.[74] In fact, the very same calumny scene was painted on the northern wall of the *Ratssaal* (Hall of the Council) in Nuremberg during its later renovation in 1520–21.[75] On the same wall in the Nuremberg Ratssaal also appeared Maximilian's triumphal chariot, designed by Dürer and Pirckheimer.[76] If the supposition that Breu's Calumny was for the interior of the Augsburg city hall is correct, then the Nuremberg city hall seems to have shared the combination of justice scenes and adulation of the Habsburgs with the Augsburg counterpart. As the Augsburg project predates the Nuremberg renovation by five years, and as Peutinger was involved in imperial commissions at this time that also involved Nuremberg artists, it is reasonable to suppose that the program for

---

Thoma. Baum's assertion that four panel paintings representing the four seasons were painted by Ulrich Apt in connection with the city hall project has been refuted by Gode Krämer, *Welt im Umbruch*, 1: 117–20, cat. no. 8.

[73] C. Dodgson, "The Calumny of Apelles," *Burlington Magazine* 29 (Aug. 1916), 183–89. Dodgson's attribution and dating is based on stylistic analysis. He briefly traces the development of this image to a basis in Lucian, discusses translations of Lucian in the fifteenth century, and Italian and German representations of this subject, making a case for the image's accessibility to Breu. In fact, Dodgson has shown that Breu's drawing is a copy after an engraving by the Venetian artist Mocetto and uses this to substantiate the hypothesis that Breu was in Venice in 1514/5. Another drawing attributed to Breu (Vienna, Albertina, inv. no. 3460), which portrays the four Habsburg rulers from Albrecht II to Charles V, has also been recognized as a possible study for a fresco because of the viewer's low vantage point (*Welt im Umbruch*, 2: 227–28, cat. no. 607). However, the drawing cannot belong to the 1515–16 project because of the appearance of Charles V as emperor, the status of which he did not attain until 1530.

[74] For Flemish examples of city hall decorations, see the recent articles: Hugo Van der Velden, "Cambyses for Example: The Origins and Function of an *exemplum iustitiae* in Netherlandish Art of the Fifteenth, Sixteenth and Seventeenth Centuries," *Simiolus* 23, no. 1 (1995): 5–39; idem., "Cambyses Reconsidered: Gerard David's *exemplum iustitiae* for the Bruges Town Hall," *Simiolus* 23, no.1 (1995): 40–62; Hans van Miegroet, "Gerard David's *Justice of Cambyses: exemplum iustitiae* or Political Allegory?" *Simiolus* 18, no. 3 (1988) 116–33.

[75] E. Mummenhoff, *Das Rathaus in Nürnberg* (Nuremberg: J. L. Schrag, 1891), 89–96. Mummenhoff attributes the design to Dürer and its execution to Georg Pencz (92–93). See also Matthias Mende, *Das alte Nürnberger Rathaus*, vol.1 (Nuremberg: Stadtgeschichtliche Museen, 1979).

[76] Ibid., 96–97. See also *Gothic and Renaissance Art in Nuremberg 1300–1550*, (Munich: Prestel Verlag, 1986), 36, 130 and 329.

the Nuremberg city hall received decisive impulses from the Augsburg project.

If we compare the exterior frescoes of the Augsburg city hall with
the few examples of known German city hall exteriors, however, it
becomes clear that the Augsburg structure is not typical. Most exterior frescoes, as in Ulm, depict scenes from the Bible and from Roman history and mythology, which exemplify civic virtues. Illusionis-
tic architecture was also used to enhance exteriors, as in Basel.[77]
Frequently represented scenes included the Judgment of Solomon,
David and Goliath, and deeds of selfless bravery performed by
Marcus Curtius, Mucius Scaevola, and Horatius Cochleas.[78] Thus, it
seems that the theme of the Augsburg frescoes is unusual in its focus
on the life and deeds of a contemporaneous individual, the emperor
Maximilian. This preponderance of Habsburg propaganda on the
walls of Augsburg's dominant civic structure can be explained by the
indirect patronage of the emperor himself and by the relationship
between Maximilian and the city of Augsburg.

Maximilian's interest in the representation of his genealogy is evident in a number of imperial projects.[79] Between 1509 and 1512,
Hans Burgkmair executed 92 designs for woodcuts representing the
emperor's genealogy.[80] This project, like the city hall frescoes, was
organized by Peutinger and involved imperial cooperation: Maximilian's historian, Jakob Mennel, supplied the genealogical information. Between 1512 and 1517, Mennel continued to research the
imperial genealogy on commission from Maximilian, and produced
a six-volume study on this subject.[81] Mennel's work informed another genealogical project also entrusted to an Augsburg artist,
Leonhard Beck. *Die heiligen der Sipp- Mag- und Schwägerschaft Kaiser
Maximilians* ("The Sainted Members of the Emperor Maxmilian's
Kin including Female Relatives and In-laws") consisted of 123

---

[77] Both of these fresco projects are somewhat later: Basel ca. 1530, Ulm ca.
1540: Margarete Baur-Heinhold, *Süddeutsche Fassadenmalerei vom Mittelalter bis zur
Gegenwart*, (Munich: J.D.W. Callwey, 1952), 9, 18 and 31.

[78] Ibid., 9–10. Baur-Heinhold refers to a popular source for such scenes (10):
Johannes von Schwartzenberg's *Das büchle Memorial*. The book's introduction specifically mentions the usefulness of depicting these scenes on walls to encourage contemplation. *Das büchle* was published in Augsburg in 1534 by Heinrich Steiner.

[79] See Marie Tanner, *The Last Descendant of Aeneas*.

[80] *Maximilian I*, (Innsbruck: Tyrolia Verlag, 1969), 135–36, cat. no. 520; *Hans
Burgkmair: Das graphische Werk*, (Stuttgart: Staatsgalerie graphische Sammlung, 1973).

[81] See *Maximilian I*, 143, cat. no. 530.

woodcut illustrations and was printed between 1516 and 1518.[82] Maximilian's genealogy also appeared in the large composite woodcut of the emperor's *Triumphal Arch* produced between 1512 and 1516,[83] and a number of his most famous relatives appear in the *Triumphal Procession*, also initiated in 1512.[84] Although no Augsburg artists were involved in the Arch, Hans Burgkmair was mainly responsible for the *Procession*.[85]

In addition to these graphic works, Maximilian's genealogy was represented in other media as well. The emperor's ancestors were celebrated in bronze statues planned for Maximilian's funerary monument in Innsbruck, begun in 1508.[86] Frescoes illustrating the Habsburg family tree were painted in Ambras Castle, and another family tree from ca. 1508 still decorates the walls of another Tyrolian castle, Tratzberg.[87] Maximilian gave Tratzberg to the Tänzl family in exchange for their castle, Berneck, in 1502 but apparently still visited his former property.[88] The frescoes have been attributed to Hans Maler from Schwaz and were probably commissioned by the Tänzl to honor their prestigious guest.[89]

As we have seen, Maximilian was similarly concerned with the representation of his military feats. We have already discussed imperial projects that commemorate his wars earlier in this chapter.

The remarkable frequency with which scenes of genealogy and war appear in commissions for or by Maximilian attests to the emperor's regard for these topics as effective personal propaganda. Maximilian's desire to create memorials to himself, to insure *Gedechtnus*, has itself become legendary in the scholarship on the em-

---

[82] Ibid., 134–35, cat. no. 519.

[83] Ibid., 136–38, cat. no. 521.

[84] Horst Appuhn, ed., *Der Triumphzug Kaiser Maximilians*, 158–60.

[85] Burgkmair was assisted by Hans Springinklee, Hans Schäufelein, Leonhard Beck and Albrecht Altdorfer (Appuhn, *Der Triumphzug Kaiser Maximilians I*, 158–60).

[86] Vinzenz Oberhammer, "Das Grabmal des Kaisers," in *Maximilian I*, 107–12.

[87] Sighard Enzenberg, *Schloß Tratzberg: ein Beitrag zur Kulturgeschichte Tirols*, (Innsbruck: Wagner, 1958), 41–44. The Tratzberg frescoes have been dated on the basis of their stylistic similarity with the documents of consecration of the castle's chapel in 1508. The frescoes are still extant but have been frequently and heavily restored.

[88] Ibid., 26–28.

[89] Ibid., 41 and 44. Cf. another later Habsburg family tree from Jörg Breu the Younger, in: *Welt im Umbruch*, 1: 132–34, cat. no. 23. An *ex libris* (London, British Museum) of the Tänzl has been attributed to Breu the Elder: K. T. Parker, "A Bookplate of the Family of Tänzl von Tratzberg," *Old Master Drawings* 8 (June 1933): 13–4, pl.15.

peror.[90] Prestigious ancestors, among them saints and the most famous and successful rulers of history, as well as victors in battle,
formed an integral part of this *Gedechtnus*, as they imply both a secular and a sacral justification for Maximilian's rule. Maximilian's concern for the execution of projects that convey this message seems to
have reached high points in 1512 and 1516, when many of these
projects were commissioned. A number of texts on warfare discussed
at the beginning of this chapter also date from this same general
period. Maximilian's projects can thus be seen as contributing, as
these texts do, to the discursive formation of warfare, constructing
the positive and elitist notion of battle akin to Castiglione's. The
depiction of military might as the implicit undergirding of political
authority is similar to Machiavelli's ideas. Clearly, Augsburg artists
played an important role in the production of these works.[91] Thus,
the Augsburg frescoes from 1516 must be regarded within the context of this concentrated production of Habsburg *Gedechtnus*.

If we consider again the above list of works, almost all of the
projects shared a common fate: they were either never realized, or
they were completed only after Maximilian's death. Burgkmair's
genealogy and *Weißkunig* were never finished. The hastily and partially completed woodcut *Triumphal Procession* was first published in
1526 by Maximilian's grandson Ferdinand,[92] and the Innsbruck
monument was not completed until 1585.[93] Only the *Sippschaft*, the
Triumphal Arch, and Mennel's genealogy were completed shortly before Maximilian's death.

Although these finished works belonged to the easily reproducible
graphic medium, they could hardly have been intended for popular
consumption. The monumental size and concurrent expense of these
projects allow us to rule out a large audience. The *Sippschaft* must
have been fairly extensive, with its 123 illustrations; the composite
Triumphal Arch was composed of 192 blocks; and Mennel's genealogy
comprised 6 volumes! If we take Ferdinand's instructions for the
printing of the *Triumphal Procession* as representational for these impe-

[90] See especially Jan-Dirk Müller's analysis in his book *Gedechtnus: Literatur und Hofgesellschaft um Maximilian I*.
[91] See: L. Baldass, *Der Künstlerkreis um Maximilian* (Vienna: A. Schroll, 1923); N. Lieb, "Augsburgs Anteil an der Kunst der Maximilianszeit," in *Jakob Fugger, Kaiser Maximilian and Augsburg 1459–1959* (Augsburg: n.p., 1959), 59–76.
[92] Appuhn, *Der Triumphzug Kaiser Maximilians I*, 161.
[93] Oberhammer, "Das Grabmal," 107.

rial projects,[94] it is likely that they were intended largely for members of court. Thus, the audience would have been restricted to a relatively small group.

The Augsburg frescoes, however, must have been one of the first projects to have reached completion. We know from Breu's entry that the frescoes were finished on September 22, 1516. Maximilian must have been present for their completion since we know from Sender's chronicle that the emperor was in Augsburg from September 18 until at least October 11.[95] Maximilian returned to Augsburg for the Imperial Diet in 1518 and stayed in the city from June 24 to September 29.[96] On this occasion, when members of the estates from all over the German territories came to the city, the frescoes' viewership extended even beyond Maximilian and the citizens of Augsburg.

Their extensive audience is another aspect in which the frescoes differ from the other imperial projects briefly discussed. The frescoes were located on the exterior walls of one of the most important buildings in Augsburg. The city hall was not only central to civic life since it housed the city's government, it also stood in the center of town and was surrounded by important public spaces; adjacent to the north side was one of the market places (Fischmarkt), and the Perlachplatz to the west was the gathering place for the citizens on important civic occasions. For example, the citizens were to report to the Perlachplatz in case of fire or siege,[97] and it was here that male citizens swore their oath of loyalty to the annually elected City Council.[98] The Council officials were publicly sworn into office outside the city hall.[99] During the 1524 insurrection, the Perlachplatz consequently served as the arena of confrontation between these officials and the angry citizens.

Because of their location and prominence, Breu's frescoes were

---

[94] *Hans Burgkmair: Das graphische Werk* (Stuttgart: Staatsgalerie graphische Sammlung, 1973) unpaginated; introductory remarks to cat. nr. 204 etc. 200 copies were to be reserved for the court; any leftovers would be in charge of Maximilian's former secretary Marx Treitzsaurwein.

[95] Sender, *Chronik,* 134–35.

[96] Ibid., 135–43.

[97] SSB 2+ Aug. 10, *Außzug der Kriegsordnung. . .* ca. 1524.

[98] Sieh-Burens, *Oligarchie,* 29. For a discussion of the male-dominated political structure of Augsburg's government, see Lyndal Roper, *The Holy Household* (Oxford: Oxford University Press, 1989), 224.

[99] Sieh-Burens, *Oligarchie,* 29 and P. Dirr, "Studien zur Geschichte der Augsburger Zunftverfassung 1368–1548," *Zeitschrift des historischen Vereins für Schwaben und Neuburg* 39 (1913): 186.

accessible to all the citizens of Augsburg, regardless of their social position, and visible to them in a variety of situations: while purchasing items at the market, while swearing the oath of loyalty, while going to the city hall to pay annual taxes.[100] Maximilian's genealogy and military deeds thus formed the backdrop to the citizens' participation in supporting civic institutions of authority. This backdrop at once implied and justified the emperor's ideological omnipresence in civic life. The juxtaposition of imperial and civic authority also represented a political hierarchy, in which the citizens' role was to provide consensus in the form of loyalty, taxes, and civic defense.

Similarly, the members of the City Council, who were responsible for the order and control of civic life, met within these frescoed walls. Their ideal role in the hierarchy was to pass policies favorable to the emperor and to ensure the free imperial city's loyalty to its ultimate leader. In return for this loyalty, the emperor insured protection and bestowed privileges. This exchange of loyalty and protection is made concrete by the pro-Habsburg frescoes on the walls housing the city's legislative body.

Because of Augsburg's importance as a financially dominant city, the frescoes' audience included more than just its citizens. Since Augsburg was one of the most important trading centers in Germany, we can assume that many out-of-town merchants who visited the city also saw the frescoes. In addition, Augsburg was often the host for numerous Imperial Diets, during which the city was filled with national and international dignitaries escorted by their vast entourages. On these occasions, the city hall constituted one of the main areas of focus since the emperor held council here. This multifarious array of people from differing social groups, cities, and countries must be included in the frescoes' audience. Thus Breu's pro-Habsburg propaganda on the walls of the city hall reached a vastly larger audience than any other of Maximilian's projects described earlier.

Almost immediately upon their completion, we can observe a concrete and early example of the important backdrop function of the frescoes. As mentioned earlier, Maximilian was in Augsburg from the second half of September on into October of 1516. The reason for his presence there was to hear accusations brought against Duke Ulrich of Württemberg, one of several German princes who

---

[100] Clasen, *Steuerbücher*, 17.

directly challenged Maximilian's authority.[101] Many princes were summoned to Augsburg and Ulrich's case, clearly meant as an example, was tried. A verdict was both reached and proclaimed at the city hall:

> At this session in the city hall, on October 11, His Imperial Majesty himself, along with many princes and their councillors, declared and announced the just and lawful sentence of Duke Ulrich's banishment; and it was announced around Vespers by his Majesty's herald, accompanied by His Majesty, from the city hall's small bay window, that Duke Ulrich of Württemberg was banned through sentence and law because of his insubordination, wicked deeds, and disobedience.[102]

The trial was held in the city hall and the verdict made public under Breu's frescoes; the "erckerlin" can be clearly recognized in depictions of the city hall as located at the juncture between the north and west facades. The combination of the actual presence of the emperor at the side of his herald, and the freshly finished frescoes glorifying his ancestry and military might must have lent the pronounced judgment special efficacy; Maximilian's illustrious ancestors appeared to ensure that his judgment was wise, and the scenes of successful battles indicated that his punishment for transgression was fearsome.

The glorification of Maximilian on the walls of Augsburg's city hall conveyed a message of solidarity between the emperor and his city. This publicly displayed message was directed at everyone within the city's walls, citizen and visitor alike. The unambiguous advertisement of Augsburg as an imperial city visibly allied with Maximilian was in the self-interest of the project's direct patrons, the City Council. The frescoes were intended to impress visitors with the city's apparently close ties with the emperor, an allegiance that would purportedly make Augsburg a formidable foe (if one were unwise enough to provoke it) and a political force. Analogously, this message was also directed at Augsburg's own citizens. Allegiance to the emperor justified the city's leadership by definition of its status as a

---

[101] Sender, *Chronik*, 134–35 and Wiesflecker, *Kaiser Maximilian I*, 4: 280–81.

[102] Sender, *Chronik*, 135: "auff dise tagsatzung [. . .] hat kai. mt. in aigner person mit besitzung vil fürsten und irer räth auff dem rathaus hie am 11. tag octobris hertzog Ulrich in die ächt mit urtail und recht declariert und erkündt und um vesper zeit durch seiner mt. herold in dem erckerlin auff dem rathaus in beisteeung kai. mt. an des herolds seitten ausgeriefft, daß hertzog Urlich von Wirtenberg von seiner freffenlichait wegen, auch anderer böser händel und unkorsame wegen mit urtail und recht in die acht erkündt sei."

freie Reichsstadt. The illustration of this allegiance on the city hall reminded the citizens of this justification and implied the consequences of questioning its authority. The solidarity between emperor and City Council was intended both to ensure proper government and to discourage local dissent.

The frescoes were also in the interest of their indirect patron, Maximilian. Their glorification of his military deeds and ancestry reached a vast audience, in comparison with other projects that were either never completed or that reached only a circumspect and limited audience. The frescoes also advertised the close allegiance between Maximilian and one of the most economically powerful cities in his empire. Also favorable to Maximilian was the frescoes' indirect reminder to the Augsburg City Council to uphold their part of the bargain: to support the emperor's endeavors by loyally rendering assistance in the form of taxes and soldiers.

The Augsburg City Council could count on an especially large audience for its politicized message broadcast on the walls of its city hall. The last Imperial Diet had been held in 1512 in Trier and Cologne. Maximilian had subsequently attempted to organize another Imperial Diet on several occasions, including in spring 1515, and in January 1516; on both occasions, the Imperial Diet would have been held in Augsburg.[103] Although these efforts were not successful until 1518, it is clear that an Imperial Diet in Augsburg was being planned for the near future. This planning must have initiated the expansion and renovation of the city hall, and the fresco commission. According to Rem, the renovation began in the second half of 1515,[104] in other words, following Maximilian's initial plan for an Imperial Diet in Augsburg. A second phase of renovation, to which Breu's frescoes belong, occurred in 1516, probably also in response to the emperor's repeated attempt to call an Imperial Diet to Augsburg.

In addition to the major event of the planned Imperial Diet, what were the issues that possibly propelled the City Council to commission this overt reminder of imperial excellence and civic consensus? What events could have informed the commission of frescoes illustrating ancestry and battles, scenes that were not commonly found

---

[103] Wiesflecker, *Kaiser Maximilian I,* 4: 280.

[104] There is no date to Rem's entry, but his mention of the city hall work falls between entries dating from November and December 1515 (*Cronica,* 44–45).

on city hall walls? In the second half of 1515 and throughout 1516, Maximilian was involved in activities motivated by dynastic and territorial concerns. Both the Vienna Congress (summer 1515) and the reactivated war against the French in Italy (1516) were important and well-known events that may have influenced the Augsburg City Council's, and more precisely, Peutinger's choice of visual program. The impact these events may have had on the Augsburg program must be seen in combination with the other imperial projects mentioned earlier.

At the Vienna Congress, held between July 10 and 28, 1515, Maximilian was able to ratify crucial documents drawn up in a session of diplomatic negotiations undertaken in the preceding months.[105] Maximilian met with the kings of Poland and Hungary/ Bohemia in Vienna, where they ceremoniously signed and celebrated pacts of peace and mutual support. But Maximilian did more than just contractually secure the empire's eastern border; he incorporated Hungary and Bohemia into the empire by means of marriage and adoption. His grandchildren were promised to the children of the ailing King Wladislaw of Hungary/Bohemia, and Maximilian even adopted Wladislaw's son Ludwig as his own. Dynastic expansion was thus used as a means of territorial expansion, a policy for which the Habsburgs became famous in succeeding generations. The Vienna Congress, with its double wedding, adoption, and securing of the eastern border belongs to Maximilian's most important diplomatic successes. Instrumental in this success was Jakob Fugger of Augsburg, who lent Maximilian jewels and apparel so that the emperor could make a sufficiently splendid appearance in Vienna.

The Vienna Congress was a widely publicized event, described in many broadsheets and pamphlets.[106] Citizens in Augsburg were certainly informed about this event; Fugger's involvement has already been mentioned. In addition, mention of the Vienna Congress appears in both Rem's and Sender's chronicles,[107] and one of the many poems describing the Congress was written by "Erasmus Amman von Augsburg."[108] Maximilian's dynastic and territorial tri-

---

[105] The "Preßburg Verhandlungen" of April and May 1515. My discussion is based on information given by Wiesflecker, *Maximilian I*, 4: 181–201.

[106] Wiesflecker, *Kaiser Maximilian*, 4: 201.

umph in Vienna was thus known to Augsburg and could have influenced Peutinger's decision regarding the city hall frescoes. The illustration of Maximilian's ancestry and battles on the city hall would have reiterated the dynastic and territorial themes of the Vienna Congress.[109] Their depiction in Augsburg would have flattered Maximilian and perhaps served to increase his appreciation of the city. The City Council would thus ensure themselves of the emperor's good grace as well as impress upon visitors from other cities and/or countries its close ties with Maximilian.

Although events at the Vienna Congress might have provided reason to celebrate, and thus to illustrate Maximilian's dynastic relations on the Augsburg city hall, there was no reason for glorification of the emperor's recent military ventures. In fact, Maximilian's wars against Venice and against French invasion of imperial territories in Italy (especially Milan) were grinding to a disastrous end.

While Maximilian was celebrating his triumphs in Vienna, Francis I of France was preparing for an invasion of Italy.[110] By September 1515, Milan and the rest of Lombardy were in the hands of the French. In March 1516, Maximilian led his troops into Lombardy to reconquer his territories from Francis. Initially, the imperial troops were able to push the French out of Brescia and back to Milan. After this initial success, however, followed disaster. On March 26, 1516, Maximilian and his troops reached Milan, at this point a French stronghold. But instead of laying siege to the city and driving the French out of imperial territory, Maximilian's troops revolted; the emperor had once again been unable to pay the Landsknechten, and his Swiss mercenaries refused to fight their countrymen on the French side. Maximilian was forced into a shameful retreat from Italy, during which his uncontrollable troops pillaged and looted. On

---

[107] W. Rem, *Cronica*, 35–36; Sender, *Chronik*, 133–34. Only Sender's chronicle, written for the Fugger, includes mention of Jakob Fugger's loan to Maximilian (134).

[108] Rochus von Liliencron, *Die historischen Volkslieder der deutschen* (Leipzig: F.C.W. Vogel, 1867), 3: 165–70, #291: "Ain hübscher spruch von der kaiserlichen majestat, wie er zu Vienna ist eingeriten mit sambt den kunigen, fürsten und andern herren." The poem closes with: "Eraßm Amann ich mich nenn / zu Augspurg diß gedicht gemacht."

[109] This hypothesis would be substantiated if Hungarian/Bohemian elements were present in the city hall genealogy, but this can no longer be ascertained.

[110] Wiesflecker, *Kaiser Maximilian*, 4: 233–55. Sender does not mention the war against France but Rem does 49–50, in which he criticizes the unsuccessful Maximilian.

May 18, Brescia again fell into the hands of the French. Maximilian's Italian campaign had been a complete failure.

Just three weeks after the fall of Brescia, on June 9, Conrad Peutinger wrote to Maximilian informing him of the city hall project. However, Peutinger was presenting the emperor with a fait accompli as we know from Breu's chronicle that work on the frescoes was begun on May 23, only five days after the fall of Brescia. Since the planning for this large-scale project must have been fairly extensive, its initiation must well predate May 23 and thus well predate the fall of Brescia, the final catastrophe of Maximilian's Italian campaign. It is then probable that the city hall project was commissioned by the City Council during the Italian campaign at a time when Maximilian's defeat was, however, not yet imminent. The city hall frescoes, with their depiction of battle scenes, would then also function as a show of support for the emperor engaged in battle at the time of the commission.

The function of the frescoes was to construct the identity of the emperor on the basis of dynastic exclusivity and military might. Simultaneously, they constructed the identity of the citizens of Augsburg as loyal and favored. But it seems that it was precisely the fragility of these identities that at least in part motivated their larger-than-life articulation on the walls of the Augsburg city hall. The tradition of military glory that the frescoes asserted met an ignominious end just days before the frescoes were begun. In terms of the real relationship between the emperor and Augsburg, Maximilian could never count on the support of his subjects, be they cities or nobility. Maximilian's attempts to structure the relationship between his estates and himself more clearly and more closely were vigorously resisted,[111] and we have already noted the frescoes early function as a backdrop to Maximilian's sentencing of a rebellious duke. With the advent of the Reformation several years later, the relationship between the Catholic Habsburg ruler and his pro-Reformation city became increasingly strained and eventually reached the point of the city's outright disobedience. And in 1524, the populace revolted against the leadership of the City Council in front of the very frescoes that were to have visually justified this leadership. Owing to the rapid political, social and religious changes, the frescoes' message

---

[111] See Hermann Wiesflecker, *Maximilian I: Die Fundamente des habsburgischen Weltreiches* (Vienna: R. Aldenburg Verlag, 1991), 255–79.

had quickly become unconvincing. Their portrayed ideology was outdated almost before they were begun.

The Battle of Pavia

Maximilian's grandson, Charles V, succeeded him as emperor after Maximilian died in 1519. Breu continued to produce pro-Habsburg propaganda during Charles's reign, yet the personal involvement of the emperor in these projects that occurred under Maximilian seems to have been lacking under Charles.[112] Indeed, Charles's patronage of German artists during his reign has never been thoroughly examined,[113] most likely owing to the absence of a documented concern for visual *Gedechtnus* as had existed for his grandfather Maximilian. Art works glorifying Charles and his deeds continued to be produced in the empire,[114] but since the emperor could not speak German and was seldom in these territories, his involvement with their production must have been minimal at the most. The emperor's younger brother Ferdinand, however, seems to have played a more active role in German art patronage; beginning in 1521, Ferdinand was Charles's *Statthalter* (viceroy) in the Austrian and German territories. It was Ferdinand who had Maximilian's *Triumphal Procession* printed in 1526[115] and who engaged Jakob Seisenegger from 1531 as his court painter.[116] Hilger's extensive list of works dealing with Fer-

---

[112] Alfons Lhotsky, ed. *Sonderausstellung Karl V* (Vienna: n.p., 1958), ix.

[113] The exception to this are the works by Titian for Charles, upon which the literature seems to be fixated. But even these analyses are limited as most attempt to "read" Charles's personality and character from the visual information: see G. Poensen, "Bildnisse des Kaisers Karl V," in *Karl V: Der Kaiser und seine Zeit*, edited by Peter Rassow and Fritz Schalk, (Cologne: Bohlau Verlag, 1960) 173–79. In the same collection, see Herbert von Einem, "Karl V und Tizian," 67–93. By contrast, see Hans Ost, *Lambert Sustris: Die Bildnisse Kaiser Karls V in München und Vienna* (Vienna: König Verlag, 1985) for an interesting iconographical examination of the seated portrait of Charles (Munich, Alte Pinakothek).

[114] Especially in the graphic and numismatic media; see Lhotsky, *Sonderausstellung Karl V*. Augsburg artists who were involved, besides Breu, were Loy Hering (cat. no. 52), Veit Kels (no. 57), Daniel Hopfer (no. 137) and his son Hieronymus (no. 142), Christoph Amberger (no. 150) and Breu the Younger (no. 146).

[115] Appuhn, *Der Triumphzug Maximilians I*, 161. Ferdinand's decision to print his grandfather's project may have been in connection with Ferdinand's election as king of Bohemia, as I argue later.

[116] Ferdinand was finally elected German king in 1531. In the same year, he appointed a court painter, which indicates the important official role these artists played at court. For information on Seisenegger, see Kurt Löcher, *Jakob Seisenegger,*

dinand[117] also indicates an active interest in German art patronage on Ferdinand's part.

Charles's lack of patronage of German artists no doubt had something to do with the emperor's relation to his German territories. This relationship was problematic and contested from the very start, beginning with his election in 1519 as King of the Romans (a kind of emperor-elect title held until papal coronation, which in Charles's case, occurred much later, in 1530). Facing stiff competition for the position of Holy Roman Emperor from Francis I of France and Henry VIII of England, Charles assiduously constructed an identity for himself along national and military lines; whereas his propagandists stressed his Germanic ancestry, Charles's military allies flexed their muscles and ousted the ever-troublesome German Duke Ulrich of Württemburg, a strong supporter of Francis I, from the duke's own territories.[118]

In addition to his ideological and physical posturing of power, Charles bribed the electors with huge sums of money to insure his election; the majority of the money came from the Augsburg Fuggers.[119] Evidently, knowledge of the bribery was fairly widespread; the Augsburg merchant Wilhelm Rem mentions it in his chronicle entry from 1519:

> Many goods were given to the electors and others who helped him [Charles] become Roman King [. . .]. It is said that it cost king Charles 1 million in gold to become Roman King. [. . .]. When the electors are supposed to vote, many goods are transferred [to them]. It's a pity: the electors have to swear such an appropriate oath (namely, that when they elect a Roman King, they may not accept any money, gift or promise) but then that's all forgotten.[120]

Hofmaler Kaiser Ferdinands I (Munich: Deutscher Kunstverlag, 1962). For information on Ferdinand's patronage, see Erich Egg, "Der deutsche König und die neue Kunst," *Alte und moderne Kunst* 6 (May 1961): 16–20 and W. Hilger, *Ikonographie Kaiser Ferdinand I.*

[117] See n. 116

[118] Martyn Rady, *Emperor Charles V* (London: Longman, 1988), 16–20.

[119] Ibid., 16; see also *Welt im Umbruch*, 1: 140, no. 30.

[120] W. Rem, *Cronica*, 108–9: "Es ward den kurfürsten und andren, die darzu hulfen, daß er [Charles] römischer kunig ward, gros gutt geschenckt [. . .]. Man sagt, es hab den kunig Karel wol 1 million gold kost, daß er römischer kunig ist worden [. . .]. Als die kurfürsten welen solten, es gieng gros gutt darüber, es ist zu erbarmen, daß die kurfürsten so aine treffentlichen aid miessend schwören, wan sie ainen römischen kunig welen, daß sie kain gelt oder schanckung wellen nemen oder kain verhais; es wirt aber alles vergessen." Rem, who was Protestant, was clearly writing from a confessionally influenced position because his text exonerates Frederick the Wise of Saxony, who was also a contender, from all such dishonest practices.

From Rem's entry, it is clear that such practice–and its implementation by Charles–was recognized and also condemned. The huge sums of money Charles paid indicate that acceptance of his authority and position as future emperor needed a considerable boost in order to convince the electors to vote for him. The payments, and the necessity for them, also seem to have created resentments against Charles, to judge from Rem's albeit proevangelical chronicle entry.

Rem's chronicle further mentions another indication of the unpopularity of Charles and the hesitancy on the part of his German subjects to accept his authority: Charles's written promises to the electors upon which his election was contingent.[121] This was a series of concessions vis-a-vis Charles's exercise of authority in the German territories to which the future emperor had to consent before the electors would agree to vote for him.[122] These concessions betray specific concerns of the German princes having to do with national identity, and with the continued exercise of their own power. Charles had to agree for example to employ only German officials in the German territories, to preserve the rights and privileges of the princes, and to work towards establishing imperial reforms that, for all intents and purposes, would leave ultimate control of the German territories in the hands of the German princes and estates, and not in those of the emperor. Thus, the trajectory was set for continual conflict between Charles and the Germans over the exercise of his imperial authority.

This conflict was exacerbated by several factors, one of course being the Reformation. Confessional differences between the Catholic emperor and Protestant princes provided further rationale for resisting and challenging imperial authority. National identity became another; although he had originally constructed himself as German, the fact that Charles spoke no German and was only infrequently present in his German lands made him resented as an outsider and foreigner. Charles's absence from his German territories for most of

---

[121] It is mentioned in W. Rem, *Cronica*, 109: "Er [Charles] must sich gegen den kurfürsten und gegen dem römischen reich verschreiben, ee er erwelt ward, wie hernach ain copie lautt. (Before [and also in the sense of "in order that"] Charles was elected, he had to give the electors and the empire written promises, as the following copy describes)." Rem clearly recognized that Charles had to make these promises in order to get elected. In Rem's original manuscript, a copy of the document is included (which means that it must have been circulated publicly), but Roth's edition of Rem's chronicle does not include the copy.

[122] Rady, *Emperor Charles V*, 21.

the crucial decade of the 1520s, when the ideological and political battles of the insurgent Reformation were fought, was particularly damaging. As elected Roman King, Charles first visited the German territories in 1520 for his coronation in Aachen. The Diet of Worms immediately followed in 1521 at which Charles was also present. He did not return to Germany until 1530. The unpopular leadership of his brother Ferdinand as viceroy during these eventful years and during Charles's absence failed to fill the power vacuum effectively, a situation of which the princes and estates were only too glad to take advantage.[123]

Thus, the production of Habsburg propaganda assumed a particular urgency in the 1520s. This is perhaps why Charles's victory at the battle of Pavia (February 1525) was aggressively commemorated in almost every available medium, as we will see. It represented, no doubt, a great victory since Charles's forces were able to capture his former election contender and arch military rival, Francis I of France, thus constituting a personal victory as well as establishing imperial control of contested Northern Italian territories (a contest, we remember, that Charles's grandfather, Maximilian, had lost). But the victory at Pavia also created a welcome opportunity to celebrate Habsburg military might and power over a foreign enemy at a time when Habsburg authority continued to be resisted in home territories.

Breu's woodcut depicting the battle of Pavia (made sometime after the February battle in 1525) contributes to the commemoration of this important event and to fashioning pro-Habsburg political identity (plate 1). Military confrontation, here presented with the hallmarks of an eyewitness account (as specific landmarks and terrain are included), nonetheless functions as kind of discourse about nationality, loyalty, and power, creating identities for the viewer that would align him or her with the Habsburg cause. The woodcut constructs Habsburg identity as militarily supreme and victorious over powerful foreign rivals (the French and their attendant Swiss mercenaries) while it also encourages identities of the viewers as celebratory and loyal, in a manner somewhat akin to the Augsburg city hall frescoes. And yet, when we look closer at the woodcut in its specifics, we will also see that a particular German identity is asserted so that the issue of loyalty becomes more complex and multivalent; in view-

---

[123] Ibid., 44–53.

ing the woodcut, the viewer might attach his or her loyalty to the Habsburg cause, or to the specifically German power that made it possible (or to both).

The issue of loyalty in fact seems to be an important part of the woodcut, in terms of both its viewing and its patronage. Directly beneath the inscription in the upper-right-hand corner of the woodcut two coats of arms are suspended, one bearing the initials B. L., the other A. K.[124] These coats of arms most likely refer to the patrons of the work, as coats of arms analogously fulfill this function in the medium of painting. One of the coats of arms clearly identifies one of the patrons as belonging to the Augsburg family of the Langenmantel.[125]

Although some woodcuts contain information about the printer or publisher, it is unusual for a woodcut to make reference to a patron since most woodcuts were not commissioned in the way that, for example, an altarpiece might have been. With the exception of Maximilian's projects, the graphic medium was not the usual medium for the commemoration of donors. Yet in Breu's woodcut, the signs of particular patronage are carefully and strategically displayed. Immediately juxtaposed to the explanatory inscription,[126] they are as important a "text" to be read as the inscription in order to understand the significance of the work. In addition, the combination of both initials and coats of arms is unusual. In most instances, the

---

124 The shield on the left juxtaposed with the initials B. L. corresponds to the one identified as Langenmantel in a 1545 compilation of city council members' coats of arms ("Aines Erbern Rats der Stat Augspurg Eren clainat des 1545 Jars," reproduced in Blendinger and Zorn, *Augsburg*, 172. Roth (annotations to Sender, *Chronik*, 220–21, n. 3) notes that Joachim Hoechstetter was married to Anna Langenmantel von Sparren since 1522. Perhaps Breu's earlier work for the Hoechstetters was influential in his receiving the Pavia commission from a Langenmantel. I have not been able to identify the second shield.

125 For basic information on the woodcut, see Hollstein, *German Engravings, Etchings and Woodcuts*, 4: 174; and Campbell Dodgson, "Beiträge zur Kenntnis des Holzschnittwerks Jörg Breus," *Jahrbuch der Preußischen Kunstsammlungen* 21 (1900): 211–12. I am the first to make the identification of one of the coat of arms to the Langenmantel family.

126 The inscription in German reads: "Ain verzaichnug der belegerten stat Pauia von Francisco dem Künig zu Franckreich, mit erlegung allda seines gantzen höre und aigner person, des Künigs gefencknus von Kayser Karoli kriegsvolck geschehen Freytag morgens den vierundzwaintzigsten Februarij Anno M.D. xxv [a diagrammatic representation of the city of Pavia, besieged by Francis, king of France, showing the defeat there of his entire armies and his own person, with the capture of the king, by the Emperor Charles's troops, on Friday morning the 24th of February 1525]".

coats of arms alone sufficed to identify the source of patronage. Clearly, the donors were at great pains to ensure that their identity should be known.

The donors also seem to have been concerned that the print was literally legible to an audience varied in its educational training. Although the print's fairly large size (a two-block composite measuring 38.1 x 52.5 cm) and the amount of detail and thus of work that went into its manufacture preclude it from the realm of popular consumption, the fact that two different editions were made, one with the inscription in Latin and the other in German, indicates that the donors were concerned with exposure and circulation. And with the insistence on the legibility of their signs of patronage, they were also clearly concerned that those who saw the sheet would register the identity of the patrons.

The woodcut commemorates, in a detailed and specific manner, in a combination of text and image, the defeat of Francis's army and the capture of the French king himself by Charles's imperial troops. The terrain around the city is rendered with attention to particular landmarks, thus creating a sense that the woodcut represents an eyewitness account. In so doing, and in combination with the coats of arms, the woodcut also constructs the donors as loyal to the Habsburgs since they have undertaken to celebrate this glorious Habsburg victory. The crowned emblem with the imperial eagle appears in the upper-left corner of the print, and the action depicted in the woodcut (and reiterated by the inscription) was a moment of ultimate triumph for the Habsburgs: the capture of their arch-enemy, the king of France. Commissioning and acquiring this print displaying this critical moment of triumph was to show solidarity with the imperial cause.

When we look closely at the woodcut, we will note just how glorification of the Habsburgs is accomplished, but we will also note that alternative accents are also set. These alternative accents indicate how art participated in the discourse of warfare in ways similar to those of the texts we analyzed at the beginning of the chapter, and how they tie in with other works by Breu.

Breu's woodcut depicting the battle is impossible to "read" without some knowledge of the historical circumstances.[127] This fact has

---

[127] For a detailed description of the battle of Pavia, see Oman, *Art of War*, 186–207.

interesting implications for both the production and the viewing of the image. Breu must have been given particular details that he was to include (the hypothesis that Breu was not on-site is supported by the fact that certain geographical or topical references are incorrect, as we will see). And although the patrons provided for the brief explanatory text, the inscription does not provide enough information to understand anything other than the result of the confrontation. But since so much detail is included, the result was not the only thing one was to learn from the print. The patrons most likely, then, were aiming for an audience that would have known something about the battle.

Pictured in the upper-left quadrant is the city of Pavia. The viewer is situated so that we are looking at the eastern wall of the city; the Ticino River runs adjacent to the south flank, and the castello, located in Breu's image in the lower right corner of the city, is situated in the north. At the time of the battle, Pavia was held by imperial troops; perhaps the imperial eagle floating in the sky directly above the city was meant to indicate this fact. The ground directly outside the city walls is clearly a place of contest: men with pikes are present, and the bodies of dead and wounded litter the ground.

The city is surrounded by a crescent shape of terrain. This is the French encampment, where Francis's troops, including Swiss mercenaries fighting on his side, have gathered to lay siege to the city. It is possible to identify this crescent as French/Swiss by the presence of Swiss banners (the upright cross) and the kind of covered wagon decorated with fleur-de-lys.

Beyond the French siege encampment is the Mirabello park. This area constitutes the bulk of the image, and it is here where the main confrontation takes place. Imperial troops have been sent to Pavia to lift the siege and rescue their compatriots. They lock the French and their allied troops in the park in engagement, during which the French king is captured and his army defeated. The woodcut illustrates the moment of Francis's capture outside his camp near San Paolo. This capture occurs in the upper-right quadrant of the print, where a building marks the location of San Paolo and an inscription "captio regis F" above a knight on a horse with fleur-de-lys on its caparison marks the capture of the French king.

On the whole, great attention is paid to detail and to topical specificities so that the image gives the impression of being an eyewitness account. This impression is reinforced by the inscription, which refers to the image as a "Verschreibung," something between a sketch and a catalogue. The Ticino stream, for example, is rendered with some topical accuracy, showing how it branches at the city and then flows into the Po River. Landmarks such as the castello, San Paolo, and Mirabello, a hunting lodge shown on the right margin of the image, are also included. The mass of pikemen mixed with a smaller number of cavalry and a few cannon are indicative of actual methods of warfare. The battle of Pavia was historically important because of the successful use of arquebuses to repel cavalry and protect the pikemen.[128] In the woodcut, two infantrymen stand in a clearing in the lower-right quadrant and take aim with their arquebuses at French cavalry (identifiable again by their horses' fleur-de-lys and a banner decorated with the same device) who have turned the other way in retreat. Although these are the only two arquebuses included in the image, they are nonetheless given prominent placement and stand out in the dense mass of soldiers through their spatial and visual isolation.

Despite the inclusion of all these details, there are many inaccuracies.[129] The Ticino River branches out a second time, east of the city, before flowing into the Po. Mirabello, located directly to the east of San Paolo in the woodcut, was actually farther to the north. The Vernacula brook, located to the east of the city and used by the French as their line of contravallation, is completely absent in the woodcut. In addition, the imperial troops are shown (in the foreground) breaking through the wall of the Mirabello park at a point south of Francis's camp at San Paolo, when in reality they breached the wall well north of it. Thus, again we are cautioned against expecting technical veracity from these images, even if inscriptions and details encourage it, and we are reminded that images like Breu's woodcut are very much artistic constructions meant to function in an ideological manner.

One of the image's ideological functions was, of course, to assert imperial—and thus Habsburg—strength and victory. The image accomplishes this in a number of ways: by the inscription; by the imperial double eagle that floats in the sky, triumphant over all; by the

---

[128] Oman, *Art of War*, 33–35.
[129] See the map of Pavia and environs with battle demarcations provided by Oman, *Art of War*, 197.

depiction of Francis's capture; and by the sheer mass of imperial troops that pour in through the breached wall in the foreground in a seemingly endless swell, and who dominate the battlefield. Another indication as to which soldiers are to be viewed as fighting on the "right" side is the banner displaying the Immaculate Conception carried by the imperial troops.[130] No religious devices appear anywhere in the opposing forces; the enemy clearly does not have God on its side, the image intimates.

In addition to asserting Habsburg victory, Breu's woodcut constructs a victorious identity that is particularly national. The imperial troops do not carry banners displaying the Habsburg double eagle. Instead, the banners display the St. Andrew's cross, which identifies the troops specifically as German Landsknechten. Thus the real heroes of the battle, and of the image, are the German troops. Imperial victory is made possible only by the courage and competence of the Germans, and by the German soldiers in particular. No imperial generals are visible. In fact, the presence of commanders and commanders-in-chief is so marginalized that the capture of the French king himself needs a caption to draw our attention to it. Otherwise, as embedded in the middle ground as it is, it would escape notice. Ostensibly, this event would have been the highpoint of the battle. Instead, the focus is more on the soldiers.

Similarly, the enemies of the German soldiers include some men labeled with the French royal fleur-de-lys, but more often their direct combatants are identified as Swiss mercenaries, troops who carry banners with a straight St. George's cross. In this way, the German victory is less a matter of defeating the French than it is one of defeating the Swiss mercenaries. We recall the almost universal condemnation of mercenary troops, particularly of Swiss origin, in the texts on warfare examined in the first part of this chapter. Breu's image contributes to this negative assessment of the Swiss, but in a way that functions to highlight German victory and courage.

Breu's woodcut thus functions to glorify Habsburg authority by

---

[130] Recall Erasmus' indignation in "Complaint of Peace" (104), at the practice of using religious devices in warfare and praying to God for victory in slaughtering other men: "The maddest thing is that over both camps and over both lines of battle the same cross is displayed, on both sides the same prayers for victory are recited. What unnatural procedure is this? Cross fighting with cross, Christ at war with Christ?"

commemorating this turning point in the French-Imperial wars in
Italy. Commissioning and viewing this woodcut thus becomes a way
of expressing loyalty to the Habsburgs. But Breu's image also provides alternative sites for political identity. The battle of Pavia also
becomes a site for the construction of nationalism; it becomes a celebration of specifically German victory rather than of Habsburg authority. Commissioning and viewing the woodcut could thus also be
about national, rather than imperial loyalty. The two of course need
not be mutually exclusive. The brave German troops could be read
as the loyal support and unswerving basis of imperial authority. But
they could also be read as a force that even the emperor had to
reckon with, especially as his international victories depended on
German cooperation and willingness to sacrifice.

Breu's monogrammed woodcut depicting the city of Pavia and the
battle before its defenses belongs to an extensive group of paintings,
drawings, woodcuts, carvings, songs, broadsheets, and poems that
commemorate the battle of Pavia. The sheer quantity of these multi-
media military memorials indicates that this event was of great importance for the Germany of the latter half of the 1520s. We will
examine just why that might be so. First, however, we will briefly
examine the other Pavia memorials in order to understand how this
event has been variously constructed in text and image. This examination will allow us to understand better how Breu's woodcut contributes to the discourse of warfare articulated in the construction of
Pavia.

Several extant texts describe the battle of Pavia. Rochus von Liliencron reproduces a song written by "Hansen von Würzburg"[131] in
which the bravery of the German Landsknechten and their leaders is
praised while the cowardice of the Swiss mercenaries fighting for the
French is castigated.[132] The song also describes the initial situation in

---

[131] Rochus von Liliencron, *Deutsches Leben im Volkslied um 1530* (Berlin: W.
Spemann, 1884), 31–37.
[132] The poem also specifically mentions the use of firearms, and in this regard,
that the fighting was conducted in an honorable and knightly fashion. This assessment is made in the poem, however, in a tongue in cheek manner, as are several
assertions such as paying the Swiss mercenaries back in cash for their previous actions. This ironic distance between the use of firearms and a courtly manner of
waging war indicates that men were aware of how the deployment of firearms was
changing the social dimension of warfare: "Valentin Kop war auch darpei/mit
manchen guten schützen, dar zu mancher frummer lanzknecht/nach eren thet ers
nutzen; das handgeschütz het er bei im/mit sampt zwaien knechten; schiest drein,

which the city of Pavia is held by German troops and is laid siege by
the French king. The Germans were bravely able to hold out until
Ferdinand ordered troops of German Landsknechten to relieve their
beleaguered comrades. As in Breu's woodcut, we notice here the
emphasis on German skill and bravery. Habsburg presence is crucial
but relegated to the background; Ferdinand is mentioned only
briefly as the enabler for more daring-do by the Germans.

Another song, written by "Erasmus" (Amman?)[133] also describes
the battle and the capture of the French king. In addition, one sentence alludes to the continual political intrigues in which the French
were involved against the Habsburgs: "With the year [fifteen-hun-
dred and] twenty-five, the game, which the French had long played,
fell apart."[134] The text of this song has been printed on a broadsheet
that includes a woodcut illustration attributed to Heinrich Vogtherr
d. Ä.[135] Here a group of imperial Landsknechten, clearly labeled as
such by their banner bearing the double-headed Habsburg eagle,
spear their enemies who are floundering in the Vernacula brook
near Pavia. In the background, a fierce fight between knights is depicted. This illustration of the brutalities involved in warfare underlines the author's ambiguous evaluation of the occupation of a soldier, an occupation in which he himself seems to have been involved
according to the text:

> Ten thousand were killed through water [that is, through drowning],
> artillery and weapons; four hundred [of these] were on our side; may
> God let them rest in peace. I wish this for both sides. Whoever wages

---

schiest drein ir frumme lanzknecht!/gar ritterlich wöll wir fechten (Valentin Kop was
also there, accompanied by several good marksmen and pious Landsknechten; he
employed them with honor. He had handguns [arquebuses] and two assistants, to
whom he said "Fire away, fire away you pious Landsknechten! We'll want to fight
like knights!")," Liliencron, *Deutsches Leben im Volkslied*, 35.

[133] Munich, Staats- und Stadtbibliothek, Einbl. I33. Also reproduced in W.
Strauss, *The German Single-leaf Woodcut*, 4: 1410.

[134] "Da man zalt fünff und zwaintzig jar/das spyl hat sich ertrennet/das
Franckenreich hatt trieben lanng."

[135] I believe there was a close connection between Vogtherr and Breu. Vogtherr
was also an author and religiously radical (cf. his *Ain christlich Büchlin* [. . .], Munich,
Staats- und Stadtbibliothek, Res. 4° Hom. 1925). Vogtherr also did a painting of the
Augsburg city hall and Perlachplatz (Maximilian Museum, Augsburg) based on
Breu's drawing of Winter in the Hoechstetter cycle. In addition, the guild book
mentions that it was Vogtherr who took charge of Jörg Breu the Younger's son after
the father died (Augsburg, Stadtarchiv, 54a, fol.192r). In addition, Vogtherr's woodcut of the *Siege of Betulia* (reproduced in W. Strauss, *The German Single-leaf Woodcut*, 4:
1374–75) seems closely related compositionally to Breu's *Battle of Zama*.

war for money and risks his life hoes a hard row [. . .]. It is against
God's law: you should love thy neighbor.[136]

The criticism particularly of mercenary soldiers which is here made
with religious overtones is similar to Erasmus of Rotterdam's condemnation of warfare discussed earlier.

The above two songs would have been available to a fairly large
audience, including those who could not read, as both texts were
clearly meant to be sung or recited; both texts indicate at their beginning to which tune they are meant to be sung. We know at least
Erasmus's song was available in the form of a printed broadsheet.

In contrast to these widely accessible texts, a handwritten poem in
the Austrian National Library must have been of a more private
nature.[137] The poem is dedicated to Ferdinand and Charles (neither
of whom was present at Pavia) and begins with several strophes of
text lauding the Habsburg brothers. In its description of the battle of
Pavia, the text mentions the bravery of the soldiers, the events of the
battle, the capture of the French king, and the cowardice of the
Swiss mercenaries. It especially stresses, however, the central role of
the nobility, both as the motivating factor for the Habsburgs to send
in reinforcements, and as the deciding factor in battle.[138] This focus
on the nobility is much different from the accent on the soldiers set
in Breu's woodcut and in the previous texts, and probably indicates
that the targeted audience of the poem was a small circle of nobility,
most likely members of the Habsburg court.

A fourth text accompanies a composite woodcut, consisting of six
blocks, by Hans Schäufelein.[139] Schäufelein's woodcut does not cor-

---

[136] See my n. 133; "Zehentausent seynndt verseerdt/durch wasser gschoss unnd
waffenn/vierhunndert auch auff unnser seydt/Gott lass zu frydenn schlaffen./Das
wünsch ich in zu bayder seydt[. . .]. Wer kryegt umb gelt/unnd wagt sein leb/der
fiert ein hörtten ordenn./[. . .] es ist wider das Götlich pott/dein nächsten solt du
liebenn."

[137] *Poema Germanicum in laudem Caroli V et Ferdinandi de capto rege Galliae Francisco ad
Ticinam* (Vienna, Österreichische National Bibliothek, Cod. Vindob. 10,017).

[138] The text describes how Charles is informed of the situation in Pavia, and his
reaction is to think about the nobility ("gedacht er an sein adl" [8r]). Ferdinand
shares this concern: "Sein furstlich durchleucht/hielt zeittigen rat den fursten und
herren bedeut/er das frue und spat" ("His Princely Highness [Ferdinand] held council in a timely manner; early and late [i.e., constantly] he though of the princes and
lords" [8v]).

[139] W. Strauss, *The German Single-Leaf Woodcut*, 3: 1042–45, and Lhotsky, *Sonderausstellung Karl V*, 56–57, cat. no. 143.

respond to the details of action and geography given in the text[140] but instead offers a variety of general scenes of warfare: charging knights, casualties, running Landsknechten, firing cannon. The three columns of text contain not only the usual information regarding the battle but also give a brief history of Charles's difficulties with the French from the year of his election to 1525. This history traces the altercation back to confrontations between Maximilian and the French, portraying the latter as a stubbornly evil force and thereby emphasizing the glory of Charles's triumph over such a foe. Again, national identity is asserted through victory over a foreign other, although in this text, national and imperial identities are mutually supportive and intertwined.

In addition to these various texts and woodcut illustrations, several works in other media also depict the battle of Pavia. A drawing attributed to Wolf Huber in Munich,[141] a painting attributed to Jan Vermeyen,[142] and a signed and dated painting from 1529 by Ruprecht Heller[143] all illustrate the 1525 confrontation. The battle also rages on the ornamental crystal top of a seal handle[144] and on the reverse of a commemorative medallion,[145] both from ca. 1530. Like

[140] The details of this text do correspond with those of the three texts discussed above.

[141] Munich, Graphische Sammlung, Hz 34793, reproduced in Peter Halm, "Die Landschaftszeichnungen des Wolfgang Hubers," *Münchner Jahrbuch für bildende Künste* 7, NF (1930): 1f.

[142] See H. Stöcklein, "Die Schlacht von Pavia," in *Beiträge zur Geschichte der deutschen Kunst,* edited by Ernst Buchner and Karl Feuchtmayr 1: 235 (Augsburg: B. Filser Verlag, 1924). Stöcklein also mentions three and illustrates two other undated paintings by unknown artists. One of these is in a London royal collection (237, ill. 146). He attributes this, wrongly, to Breu the Younger. Another is in the Ashmolean at Oxford (239, ill. 147) and a third is in Vienna (236, unillustrated). See also Hale, *Artists and Warfare in the Renaissance,* 189–92, for his discussion of these works (figs. 235–40). In addition to these works, Hale also illustrates a tapestry that illustrates the battle according to a design by Barnaert van Orley (c.1531, Naples, Capodimonte; Hale, *Artists and Warfare in the Renaissance,* 251, fig.324).

[143] Axel Sjöblom, "Ein Gemälde von Ruprecht Heller im Stockholm Nationalmuseum,"in *Beiträge zur Geschichte der deutschen Kunst,* edited by Ernst Buchner and Karl Feuchtmayr (Augsburg: B. Filser Verlag, 1924), 1: 225–29.

[144] The artist is Giovanni dei Bernardi. The seal is in Vienna, Kunsthistorisches Museum, Sammlung für Plastik und Kunstgewerbe, Inv. no. 2244; see Lhotsky, *Sonderausstellung Karl V,* 24–25.

[145] Hilger, *Ikonographie Kaiser Ferdinand I,* 46, cat.nr.208; in Vienna, Kunsthistorisches Museum, Münzkabinett; see also G. Bruck, "Die graphische Vorlage für die Darstellung der Schlacht von Pavia auf der Medaille des Concz Welcz," *Mitteilungen der österreichischen numismatischen Gesellschaft* 12, NF (1961): 3–5.

the woodcut illustrations we considered above, these representations variously depict the ferocious fighting, the bravery of the soldiers and the capture of the French king.

These objects can be divided into two categories: those that depict general, nonspecific battle scenes, and those that illustrate at least to some degree the strategical layout of the actual battle from February 24, 1525, and the specific characteristics of the terrain as described in the various texts. To the former category belong Schäufelein's woodcut, the ornamental crystal seal top, and Wolf Huber's drawing. To the latter category belong the paintings by Heller and Vermeyen, the Viennese medallion, and Breu's woodcut. These latter works illustrate from various perspectives the imperial troops breaking through the wall surrounding the park, the capture of the French king outside San Paolo, the fortifications of the French immediately encircling Pavia, and (except for Heller's painting) the city itself adjacent to the river Ticino.

Breu's woodcut is thus part of a larger arena of cultural production that commemorates the battle of Pavia. Each of these monuments accesses military discourse to articulate other issues, as did the texts by Castiglione, Machiavelli, Erasmus, More, and Günzburg examined at the beginning of this chapter. Regarding the battle of Pavia, the issues here seem to crystallize around the constructions of national and imperial identities through confrontation with a foreign other, and the formulation of relationships between groups within the empire: between German troops and the emperor, and between the nobility and the emperor. Sometimes these relationships are presented as straightforward. German troops are shown "naturally" fighting for the emperor to defeat the French, and in these instances German and imperial identity are mutually supportive. Certainly this is how Breu's woodcut functions at one level. But at another, we can also see how the image appropriates imperial success and redefines it as national victory, thus appealing simultaneously to an audience both of Habsburg loyalists and of German nationalists.

If we return Breu's woodcut to the larger context of the diverse group of texts and art works dealing with the battle of Pavia, all dating approximately from 1525 to 1530, we must ask ourselves why this event provoked such a plethora of commemoration at such a variety of levels at this time. The popular songs and broadsheets ensured the battle's commemoration on a wide and varied level, while Schäufelein's and Breu's woodcuts would have been accessible to a more restricted circle owing to size and intended circulation. The painting and the seal handle indicate that the triumph at Pavia was celebrated at a very high level admitting only a small private audience. Certainly the capture of the French king was a highly important event in that it signified triumph over a longstanding enemy and brought the prospect of peace in Italy and the Netherlandish territories within diplomatic reach. But these hopes soon proved to be in vain. A year later, in 1526, Francis broke the peace treaty negotiated between Charles and France (Peace of Madrid) in the very same year that it was to be ratified, and hostilities resumed in Italy. It seems likely that the concentrated dispersion of messages asserting Habsburg triumph was provoked by the political situation within the empire between 1525 and 1531, a period in which structures of authority were vigorously challenged. Breu's Augsburg was also directly affected by such challenges at a variety of levels.

Exactly contemporaneous to the victory of Charles's troops in Italy were the uprisings of the peasants in southern Germany and Austria. In fact, the manuscript poem describing the battle of Pavia in the Austrian National Library precedes its discussion of the international event with mention of the troubles at home.[146] The text constructs the Peasants' War as an effort by the peasants to drive a wedge between the Habsburgs and the nobility. But, in the text, these social disturbances become a way, as does the battle of Pavia, for the Habsburgs to show their great regard for the Austro/German nobility.

Augsburg, which had already been rocked the year before by the Schilling uprising of 1524, was also affected by the Peasants' War. In the city, security measures were stepped up in an aggressive show of governmental control; soldiers were hired to patrol the streets day and night, only the four main city gates remained open, and at each a city official was posted who inquired of each person their business in the city.[147] Rem reports both events in his chronicle. His version of the battle of Pavia, like the broadsheets previously discussed, is informed by a nationalistic slant in which he asserts that the battle

---

[146] *Poema Germanicum*: "Die pawern mit schallen/wolten den fursten klar ziehen vom adl allen/das war im leid furwar Er stuend dem furstlich bey/mit verstant und that Sein lieb erzaigt er frey/die er zum Adl hat ("with a great noise the peasants wanted to tear the pure prince [Ferdinand] away from the nobility; he was truly sorry about that. He supported them nobly with reason and deed; he freely proved his love for the nobility" 3v–4r).

[147] Sender, *Chronik*, 162–63.

was won owing only to the bravery and untiring determination of the German troops.[148] His reports of the peasant uprising condemn the brutality used to crush them.[149]

Breu discussed neither Pavia or the peasants in his chronicle entry of 1525. He does, however, mention the marriage of Dr. Johann Frosch, formerly the prior of the Augsburg Carmelites.[150] This controversy over the marriage of priests was just one of the issues that was hotly debated in Augsburg between 1524 and 1530 and which caused extensive factionalism and unrest. As we have seen in chapter 2, not only were there conflicts between Catholics and Evangelicals, but the Evangelicals themselves were split into factions regarding the meaning of communion and the mass. In these years, the Lutherans, Zwinglians, and Anabaptists jostled each other physically and ideologically over support, recognition, and ultimately, civic institutionalization.[151]

Outside of Augsburg, the polarization between Catholics and Protestants prior to the 1530 Imperial Diet was becoming politically volatile. Already in 1526, Philip of Hessen had organized the Lutheran princes into an alliance of solidarity and the two diets at Speyer from 1526 and 1529 had failed to accomplish any reconciliation over the Imperial Proclamation of Worms.[152] Added to this internal danger was the advancing threat of the Turks, who had reached Vienna by 1529.

Thus, the situation in the empire during this half a decade seems to have been pervasively precarious. Conflicts based on religious, economic, and social differences were fought out by and affected people from all classes and positions. Mechanisms of control based in religious, economic, and social structures were now being threatened by these conflicts. Images and texts explicating and asserting the glorious victory of Charles's troops at Pavia might have detracted from problems "at home" in the empire by encouraging a feeling of solidarity in the face of a common enemy (the French). The assertion of Habsburg power and control may also have served

---

[148] W. Rem, *Cronica*, 218.

[149] Ibid., 219ff.

[150] Breu, *Chronik*, 33–34; cf. Sender, *Chronik*, 174 and Rem, *Cronica*, 219.

[151] See Broadhead, "International Politics and Civic Society," chapter 5, "Polemics, Pastors and the People" for his discussion of these vying Reformational groups.

[152] Roth, *Reformationsgeschichte*, 1: 274–77.

as a warning to the unruly factions within the empire of the danger in provoking the Habsburgs.[153]

In addition to these widespread threats of disorder and change within the empire to which the images and texts may have been responding, Habsburg power in this period was actively contested. The main conspirator was Duke Wilhelm IV of Bavaria, who, by extensive diplomatic intrigues and political maneuvering, attempted to gain control of the empire.[154] Tensions between the Bavarian dukes and the Habsburgs were already evident at the beginning of the century, which led to Maximilian's involvement in the Bavarian war of succession. Wilhelm could draw on anti-Habsburg sentiment within the empire since the territorial princes felt threatened by the prospect of the consolidation of power in Habsburg hands, which would severely limit their own political and economic options. The economic alliance between the Habsburgs and the most powerful financial houses in the empire (Fugger, Welser, Hoechstetter) was particularly threatening.[155] This prospect of Habsburg hegemony seemed especially likely in 1525, after Charles's victory over France and during which his brother Ferdinand was actively wooing the electoral dukes for their support of his election as German king.[156] A year later, in 1526, Ferdinand was elected king of Bohemia; Wilhelm IV had also been a candidate but had lost this bid for power.

In response to this amassing of Habsburg political power, and to the corresponding anti-Habsburg sentiment, Wilhelm entered into various alliances.[157] In 1526, the Bavarian duke gained the pope's support for his political plans. But the pope was forced into an alliance with Charles after the sack of Rome by Habsburg troops in

---

[153] Charles was not present in the empire between 1521 and 1530, but his brother Ferdinand, who contractually inherited the Reich's territories (1521 and 1522) was left in charge. It does not seem that Charles at this point was very concerned with the situation in the empire, but Ferdinand, in the very midst of things, must have been so.

[154] See the following sources for discussions of Wilhelm's efforts: Götz Freiherr von Pölnitz, "Anton Fugger und die römische Königswahl Ferdinands I," *Zeitschrift für bayerische Landesgeschichte* 16 (1951/2): 317–49; and Alfred Kohler, *Antihabsburgische Politik in der Epoche Karls V: Die reichsständische Opposition gegen die Wahl Ferdinands I zum römischen König und gegen die Anerkennung seines Königtums 1524–1534* (Göttingen: Vandenhoeck und Ruprecht, 1982).

[155] Pölnitz, "Anton Fugger," 318.

[156] Kohler, *Antihabsburgische Politik*, 81–94.

[157] See Pölnitz's analysis in "Anton Fugger," 318–22.

1527. Wilhelm then negotiated with the French, but this constellation was also temporarily extinguished with the peace of Cambrai in 1529 between Francis and Charles. Although an arch-Catholic and active persecutor of Protestants,[158] Wilhelm even joined the Schmalkaldic League in 1531 in order to participate in a structured anti-Habsburg alliance.[159]

Although Wilhelm's efforts to gain political control were eventually frustrated, they continually threatened the Habsburgs' own goal of hegemony within the empire until 1534 when Wilhelm contractually agreed, in the Treaty of Linz, to recognize the election of Ferdinand in 1531 as German king.[160]

Thus, the Habsburgs were faced with a concentrated challenge to their authority and to stability within the empire during the second half of the 1520s. Habsburg rule was actively contested by the Wittelsbach family; the Catholic Church, which Charles as Roman Emperor was duty bound to protect, was being threatened by evangelical reform; the German princes were split along confessional lines and yet to some extent allied against Habsburg hegemony; city governments and territorial princes were threatened by social unrest. In response to these challenges, pro-Habsburg propaganda must have seemed a necessary instrument to assist reasserting control. It seems likely that these challenges prompted Ferdinand's decision to have Maximilian's woodcut *Triumphal Procession* finally printed, and prompted the dispersion of the Pavia images, including the commission given to Breu by Habsburg loyalists. At a time of shifting loyalties, a clear show of alignment with the emperor's party might have been a politically astute strategy, particularly if one was an inhabitant of a city that was defying imperial authority as the Langenmantels of Augsburg were.[161]

In fact, loyalty of the Langenmantel family was actually called into question by the battle of Pavia. A band of renegade German Landsknechten fought against the imperial troops on the side of

---

[158] Cf. Breu's description of Wilhelm's action at Lederer in 1527, *Chronik*, 35–36. Rem also mentions Wilhelm's actions against Protestants which included heavy fines, banishment, and execution: *Cronica*, 198, 201, and 209–10.

[159] Pölnitz, "Anton Fugger," 344.

[160] Kohler, *Antihabsburgische Politik*, 372.

[161] One member of the Langenmantel family, Eitelhans, became a notorious Anabaptist somewhat later in the decade. He was banned from Augsburg in 1527 and then executed in 1528; see *Welt im Umbruch*, vol. 1, #84, 167.

Francis I. They were led by Georg Langenmantel.[162] Hansen von Würzburg's song describing the battle includes the confrontation between the imperial/German captain ("oberster Hauptmann") Jörg (Georg von Frundsberg) and Georg Langenmantel:

> Sir George [Georg von Frundsberg], a noble, dependable knight, stood there with his halberdiers. He spoke: "Foreign guests are coming to call; let us receive them!" Langenmantel positioned his troops against him [Frundsberg] and said: "Sir George, prepare yourself, you must either become my prisoner now or lose your life." Sir George spoke: "So I have to either become your prisoner or lose my life; I have drunk of the cool wine and I will not give up my life to you. I have several fresh Landsknechten who stand here in their breeches. Stick it to them, stick it to them, you pious Landsknechten: these are the real French!"[163]

The text constructs their confrontation in terms of an old-fashioned chivalric standoff between two knights in which such rhetorical posturing and grandiose statements are made as: "prepare yourself, you must either become my prisoner or lose your life." The confrontation also revolves around the fact that German troops are here facing down other Germans, yet the traitor Langenmantel, by dint of his actions, is given an identity that is not German. Herr Jörg prepares the standoff by referring to "foreign guests" and later fires his halberdiers on by saying they are attacking "the real French." Constructing a national identity at the battle of Pavia thus entails defining Germanness by bravery and skill. But when these nouns are no longer mutually interchangeable, then tellingly, it is the first that is changed; Langenmantel is not really "German" because he is a traitor, and that is incompatible with the constructed German identity; therefore, he is even more French than the French.

The fact that Langenmantel's presence is mentioned in Hansen's song indicates that knowledge of his deeds must have been fairly well known. All the more reason for his family then to commission a woodcut celebrating Habsburg triumph as a means of distancing

---

[162] Liliencron, *Die historischen Volkslieder*, 427.

[163] Liliencron, *Deutsches Leben*, 35; "Herr Jörg ein edler ritter fest/stand da mit helleparten Er sprach 'es kummen uns fremde gast/der selben wöll wir warten!' Gegen im zog der Langenmantel da her;/'Herr Jörg versich dich eben, du must hie mein gefangner sein/oder du wilt fristen dein leben.' Her Jörg sprach: 'muß ich dein gefangner sein/oder kost es mich mein leben, So habe ich getruncken des kulen Wein/mein leib wil ich dir nicht aufgeben: ich hab so manichen lanzknecht frisch/stenda in iren halben hosen. Stecht drein, stecht drein ir frummen lanzknecht/das send die rechten Franzosen.'"

themselves from what was perceived as the treachery of their own relative. Not surprisingly, Langenmantel and his men are nowhere to be found in Breu's image. As far as the woodcut is concerned, the event has been entirely eradicated from history. Habsburg glory and German glory are left uncontested, to vie instead with one another.

CHAPTER FOUR

CEREMONY

In the previous chapter, we saw how warfare, both as historical event and as attendant constructed discourse, functioned to bolster Habsburg claims to power during crucial years of contest. In this chapter, we will attend to the ways in which ceremony fulfilled the same function at an equally critical time. During the 1530 Imperial Diet in Augsburg, issues fundamental to the exercise of Habsburg authority and power in the German lands were vigorously debated. Within the highly politicized structure of the Imperial Diet, ceremony became an especially potent and visible means of communicating power structures, both existent and projected.

Ceremony thus constitutes one level of articulation; the commemoration of ceremony in works of art constitutes yet another. A woodcut series by Breu that commemorated a highly visible and politically significant ceremony, the adventus, or triumphal procession of the Emperor Charles V into the city of Augsburg at the start of the 1530 Diet, provides the focus of this chapter. This key ceremony ostensibly celebrates and affirms Habsburg authority, and yet the woodcuts commemorating it allow for alternative readings which, as we will see, make sense in terms of the series' somewhat unlikely patron.

The contemporaneous importance attached to the ceremony of adventus is indicated by the extant related source materials. The ceremony is in fact described in detail in several different printed pamphlets, thus indicating a concern for both exposure and correct interpretation of the ceremony's events and significance. Although these texts are themselves constitutive of opinion about the events, there are enough factual overlaps between them (despite their differing confessional/political positions) that allow us to ascertain in a basic way what happened during the ceremony. To work out the course of events will be our first task. Then we will compare Breu's version of events with the texts in order to get at additional concerns/subject positions made available in the woodcut series.

The 1530 Triumphal Entry of Charles V into Augsburg

The Historical Significance of the 1530 Augsburg Imperial Diet:
Preconditions and Sequence of Events

In order to understand how Breu's woodcut series of Charles's triumphal entry (from here on referred to as adventus) functioned to
shape political identities, we must first examine the political and confessional issues to which the commission, production, and viewing of
this series were responding. This is indeed a necessary and crucial
task since Breu's woodcuts illustrate the commencement of no doubt
the most important political and confessional event in the empire in
1530, the Imperial Diet held that year in Augsburg. During this six-
month meeting, the city of Augsburg provided the forum for the
debate of a variety of critical issues that affected the empire's internal affairs as well as its international relations.

That contemporaneous participants and observers were well aware
of the importance of this six-month-long debate is indicated by the
extensive primary source material produced in response to this event.
The Imperial Diet of 1530 is described in poems, pamphlets, and in
Augsburg city chronicles. These primary materials provide a variety
of accounts of the ceremonial aspects of the Imperial Diet, including
the adventus, as well as offer differentiated versions of issues perceived as especially immediate and important.

These contemporaneous versions of perceived issues offer a necessary corrective to many secondary sources that examine the 1530
Imperial Diet almost exclusively in terms of the confessional debates.[1]
Certainly the production of the *confessio Augustana*, the first officially
drawn up document advancing a relatively unified and defined Lutheran theology, was a major event in the history of religion. But the
confessional debates were carried out simultaneously with those regarding economic, legal, political, and social issues. Of course, many
of these areas of debate intersected, and it is exactly this mutual
penetration of confessional and political spheres that we must bear in
mind in order to grasp the full complexity both of the Diet itself and
of the response to it in Breu's woodcuts.

The preconditions of the 1530 Imperial Diet were of a varied

---

[1] See for example, H. Immenkötter, *Der Reichstag zu Augsburg und die Confutatio*, 2nd
ed. (Münster: Aschendorff, 1979), 11–13.

nature. On the one hand, a triumphal element characterized Charles's presence in the empire for this event. He had been absent from these territories for nine years, he had recently arranged peace settlements with France (Peace of Madrid, 1529) and with Rome, and on February 24, 1530, he had been crowned emperor by Clement VII in Bologna. His return to the empire, his successful diplomatic negotiations, and his coronation and ordination as emperor were all reasons for official celebration.

On the other hand, Charles reentered an empire full of internal conflicts and external threats as discussed in the previous chapter. In the same year that Charles made peace in Italy with France, 1529, the Turks had advanced as far as Vienna and, in fact, even laid siege to the city. The authority of the *Reichsregiment* (imperial cabinet) headed by Ferdinand, the governing institution in Charles's absence, was consistently challenged since 1524–25;[2] we already noted Wilhelm IV's efforts to take advantage of this dissatisfaction with Habsburg policy in order to usurp power within the empire. We also already noted the growing polarization between evangelical and Catholic factions visible in the establishment of the union of Protestant princes. Their refusal to accept the 1529 *Reichstagsabschied* (the official proclamation announcing the end of an Imperial Diet and the measures that had been agreed upon) was a public challenge to higher authority.[3]

For Augsburg, the arrival of the emperor only increased the difficulty of the city's balancing act between Catholic and reformed interests. In contrast to the other Protestant cities—Nuremberg, Strasbourg, and Ulm—Augsburg in fact accepted the 1529 Speyer Proclamation. In contrast to the more conciliatory Proclamation of 1526, the 1529 document forbade any action of the evangelicals and placed the Catholics expressly under imperial protection.[4] This acceptance isolated Augsburg from the other evangelical cities which would have been potential allies in the common resistance to enforced Catholicism. The action also aroused criticism at home since the Lutheran and especially the Zwinglian factions in Augsburg had achieved large followings by 1529; as we have seen in chapter 2, the

---

[2] Kohler, *Antihabsburgische Politik*, 70.

[3] Wolfgang Steglich, "Die Stellung der evangelischen Reichsstände und Reichsstädte zu Karl zwischen Protestation und Konfession 1529/30," *Archiv für Reformationsgeschichte* 62 (1971): 165–66.

[4] Roth, *Reformationsgeschichte*, 1: 281.

city's mayors of the late 1520s themselves were Lutherans and Zwinglians.[5] In his chronicle entry from 1529 describing the City Council's acceptance of the proclamation, Breu sees through the City Council's maneuvering. He interprets the council's decision to accept the proclamation (which Breu condemned in no uncertain terms) as undemocratic and secretive. He then relates how the council attempted to appease the citizens by asserting that the proclamation made no difference and no changes in the city would be made. At the base of these contradictory actions Breu sees the council wavering between popular pressure and the protection of merchant trading interests.[6]

Despite these tensions within the empire, many were optimistic that some sort of compromise between the evangelicals and Catholics, between the emperor, the cities, and the nobility would be reached. The emperor's call to the Imperial Diet, written on January 21, 1530, was conciliatory in tone.[7] An anonymous poem, written at the beginning of the Diet by someone who obviously sympathized with the Reformation, is full of the emperor's praise.[8] "Teutschland sol sich iez freuwen [Germany should now rejoice]," he exclaims, because Charles is in the empire to bring justice and peace. Along with settlement of the confessional debates, the author expects the emperor to initiate a crusade against the Turks, unify the empire under a just regime, and make the roads safe from robbery and murder. Another poem written by an evangelical at the beginning of the Diet gravely petitions Charles, Ferdinand, and all the princes to take responsibility for their subjects and actively protect them from the Turks and from improper faith.[9] Charles is addressed as a rea-

---

[5] Anthony Bimmel and Ulrich Rehlinger were Zwinglian *Bürgermeister*; Georg Vetter and Hieronymus Imhoff were Lutheran. See Sieh-Burens, *Oligarchie*, 136. Breu, however, criticizes the Lutheran *Bürgermeister* Imhoff and Vetter as political/religious opportunists and hypocrites; Breu, *Chronik*, 46.

[6] Breu, *Chronik*, 45.

[7] Roth, *Reformationsgeschichte*, 1: 328–89.

[8] Liliencron, *Die historischen Volkslieder*, 4: 5–6 #421.

[9] Ibid., 1–4, #420: The poem was written by Haug Marschalk. For information on Marschalk, see F. Roth, "Wer war Haug Marschalk genannt Zoller von Augsburg?" *Beiträge zur bayerischen Kirchengeschichte* 6 (1900): 229–34. According to Roth, Marschalk came from a patrician family from Memmingen. He appears between 1508 and 1535 (the same year as his death) in the Augsburg records of employed *raisigen*. These were military men hired by cities in times of war to lead civic contingents as well as in times of peace to be in charge of the *Stadtsöldner*, to act as accompanying guards to civic diplomats during their missions, to patrol the roads leading to and from the city. Roth also relates that Heinrich Steiner and Marschalk worked

sonable ruler who will no doubt recognize the legitimacy of this peti-
tion.

Despite the optimism at its initiation, the 1530 Imperial Diet was
characterized by conflicts at all levels and by a continual staging of
competing power plays. Both the Catholic version of the Diet provided by Sender and the evangelical version in the so-called Langenmantel chronicle offer a similar image of Augsburg between June
and November 1530,[10] an image in which dissension dominates and
in which claims of authority were conspicuously contested.

Already the preparations for the Imperial Diet provided an inaus-
picious start. Charles sent his officials ahead to Augsburg to arrange
quarter for himself and his court. According to the "Langenmantel"
chronicle, these officials behaved with such arrogance and cruel im-
propriety that they created great hostility amongst the populace.[11]
Charles also insisted that the city fire the Landsknechten they had
already hired because the emperor was bringing his own; the City
Council chafed at this demonstration of imperial power.[12] Both
Sender and "Langenmantel" begin their accounts of the 1530 Imperial Diet with descriptions of precautionary security measures undertaken by the City Council in case of disturbances that seemed, given
the volatility of the issues at stake, almost inevitable. Thus, before
the Diet was even begun, both the emperor and the Augsburg City
Council each began flexing their muscles with displays of control
and authority—and already ran into conflict before the emperor
even set foot inside the city.

When Charles did enter the city, the Catholic clergy staged their
own display. After being received at one of the city gates (Rotes Tor)
by the civic greeting committee, Charles was then received by the
Catholic clergy and processed with them to the cathedral where he
was greeted with liturgical chants. Although this was normal proce-

---

together in 1526 on a pamphlet regarding the *Abendmahlstreit.* From Marschalk's
pamphlets (e.g., *Ain Spiegel der Blindn,* Augsburg, Stadt- und Staatsbibliothek, 4° Aug.
881), we know that he was Protestant. I think it is very possible that Breu and
Marschalk were in contact; Breu was also involved in the civic militia in his capacity
as *Unterhauptmann,* he also worked together with Steiner, and Marschalk's critique of
merchants and his admonition to take responsibility for the poor is very similar to
Breu's   chronicle   entries.

[10] *"Langenmantel" Chronik,* Der Chroniken der deutschen Städte vom 14. bis 16.
Jahrhundert, vol. 25 (Leipzig: S. Hirzel Verlag, 1896), 361–409.

[11] *"Langenmantel" Chronicle,* 367; see also Roth's introduction to this chronicle,
361–62, which also stresses Charles's conciliatory attitude.

[12] Ibid., 364–46.

dure for the ceremonial adventus of an emperor,[13] the chants chosen
in 1530 differed from those normally recited, and made specific reference to the threatened position of the Catholic Church. Instead of
the usual celebratory psalms equating the emperor with the messiah
or King David and expressing joy at his advent,[14] the chants that
Sender relates were used stressed the role of the emperor/messiah as
the rescuer from darkness and torment:

> You who are desirable, whom we have been awaiting in the darkness,
> in order that you might lead us forth from this night, from chains in
> prison, our sighs will summon you; with much wailing we have been
> repeatedly seeking you, you who are hope to the hopeless and a great
> comfort in [our] torments. Alleluia![15]

It seems that Charles also viewed his position as emperor of the Holy
Roman Empire in this light.[16] The very next day after his arrival, on
June 16, Charles participated in an elaborate and extremely public
celebration of Corpus Christi, which included high mass and a highly
visible procession through Augsburg.[17] The Protestant princes were
conspicuously missing from this public event, although Charles had
met with them beforehand to express his desire that they should also
participate.[18] Two days afterward, on June 18, Charles sent messen-
gers throughout the city to proclaim that he had forbidden the activity of all preachers other than those whom he had chosen.[19] Similarly, Protestant literature was also censored whereas Catholic litera-

---

[13] I will discuss the ceremony of *adventus* further on in this section. For clerical
receptions of German kings/emperors specifically, see Anna Maria Drabeck, "Reisen
und Reisezeremoniell der römisch-deutschen Könige im Spätmittelalter" (Ph.D.
diss., University of Vienna, 1963), 66–80, and Aulinger, *Das Bild des Reichtages im 16.
Jahrhundert: Beiträge zu einer typologischen Analyse schriftlicher und bildlicher Quellen*
(Göttingen: Vandenhoeck und Ruprecht, 1980), 197–98.

[14] Ludwig Biehl (*Das liturgische Gebet für Kaiser und Reich* (Padeborn: F. Schoningh,
1937) discusses at length the ceremonial chants used at adventus. He also specifically
discusses an "Empfangsordo" from an Augsburg obsequial of 1487, 166–67. The
chants Sender reports as being used, or anything like them in tone, is missing from
this text. Instead, the obsequial's chants stress the power and glory of God and of
him who is anointed and crowned.

[15] Sender, *Chronik*, 276: "Advenisti desiderabilis quem expectabamus in tenebris,
ut educeres hac nocte vinculatos de claustris. Antiphon: te nostra vocabunt suspiria,
te larga requirebant lamenta, tu factus spes desperatis, magna consolatio in tormen-
tis. Alleluja!"

[16] See Peter Rassow, *Die Kaiseridee Karls V dargestellt an der Politik der Jahre 1528–
1540* (Berlin: E. Eberling, 1932), 30.

[17] Sender, *Chronik*, 279–80; *"Langenmantel" Chronicle*, 371–72.

[18] *"Langenmantel" Chronicle*, 370–71.

[19] Ibid., 372 and Roth, *Reformationsgeschichte*, 1: 337–38.

ture was kept in ready supply.[20] These actions of Charles, undertaken even before the Diet was formally opened, were clear, public demonstrations of the emperor's resolve to protect the Catholic Church and to assert his control within the city.

Charles's public displays of authority were also demonstrated in nonreligious areas. As he had been newly crowned and anointed emperor, his presence in the imperial city meant that the city's privileges could be reconfirmed, on condition of his subjects' promise to be loyal and obedient to their emperor.[21] On June 27, the City Council members and the male citizens of Augsburg gathered at the Perlachplatz.[22] Charles stood in the city hall's bay window (and thus surrounded by Breu's frescoes proclaiming Habsburg might and majesty) while the male citizens and council together swore their oath to the emperor "getreu und gehorsam zu sein (to be loyal and obedient)."[23] In return, Charles reconfirmed the city's privileges.

Where the swearing of oaths was not enough for Charles, the emperor put dramatic but veiled threats to effective use. At two key points during the Diet—when the Catholic *Confutatio* was publicly read (August 3), and on the day Charles left Augsburg (November 23)—he had soldiers who had been accused of disobedience publicly executed. The bodies of those executed on the day of Charles's departure[24] were conspicuously left where they had fallen.

Let us look beneath these poses and gestures of power and consider the outcome of the 1530 Imperial Diet. As for the religious debates, no compromise was reached although compromise had seemed a distinct possibility.[25] The evangelicals refused to accept the Diet's Proclamation[26] and this time Augsburg was among them.[27]

---

[20] Roth, *Reformationsgeschichte*, 1: 338.

[21] Drabeck, "Reisen," 45; see also R. Strong, *Art and Power: Renaissance Festivals 1450–1630* (Berkeley and Los Angeles: University of California Press, 1985).

[22] This event is described by *"Langenmantel" Chronicle*, 379–80 and Sender, *Chronik*, 293–94; see also Roth's annotation to Sender, *Chronik*, 293, n. 1.

[23] *"Langenmantel" Chronicle*, 380.

[24] *"Langenmantel" Chronicle*, 385 and 401. Not surprisingly, Sender does not report these executions.

[25] Rassow, *Kaiseridee*, 54–68.

[26] Ibid., 70–71. The 1530 Proclamation gave the Protestants seven months to decide whether or not they would submit to an imperial council, which would be appointed by the emperor. In the meantime, they were not to obstruct the exercise of Catholicism, or to undertake any religious reforms; see F. Roth, *Reformationsgeschichte*, 1: 341–42.

[27] "Langenmantel" reports on the unsuccessful negotiations between Charles and

The Edict of Worms, which had outlawed Luther, his teachings and his followers, was put back into effect,[28] but the emperor lacked troops to enforce it.[29] Charles left Augsburg bitterly disappointed.[30]

Two poems written by evangelicals after the Diet also express grim disappointment. In *"Ain kurzer begriff und inhalt des richtags zu Augspurg"* ("A Short Account and the Contents of the Imperial Diet at Augsburg") the author uses a lengthy description of the Corpus Christi procession in order to condemn Catholicism, which he makes responsible for the unresolved conclusion of the Diet.[31] He describes Charles as a ruler who could have accomplished much if his advisers had not been so corrupt.[32] In another poem, the author proclaims: "Es ist der reichstag für und nichts beschlossen!"[33] This second author's main concern is that the conflict might now come to war. In order to persuade Charles, who is presented as an honest and pious man,[34] not to wage war against his subjects, the author reminds him of his duty to those subjects whom he has sworn to protect in his oath as emperor. These subjects include not only powerful princes but also "die ganz gemein" who is being led astray by the Pope.[35] The author even asserts that the empire's support of Charles and of his claim to imperial authority depend on his refraining from violence.[36] This kind of statement is a dramatic example of how Habsburg authority failed to be considered as absolute and unconditional by German subjects, and thus required the constant rearticulation and reaffirmation.

Despite the inconclusiveness of the religious debate, the 1530 Im-

---

the City Council regarding the latter's refusal to accept the Proclamation, 394–400. In his efforts to align the council, Charles appeals to the special relationship between the city and the Habsburgs in the past, especially between Augsburg and Maximilian (394–95). Charles also promises the council protection if they have been pressured into their decision by the *Gemein* and warns them of the danger of knuckling under to the mob (395). "Langenmantel" also reports that Charles was especially bitter that Augsburg had refused to cooperate (400).

[28] Rassow, "Die Reichstage zu Augsburg in der Reformationszeit," in *Die geschichtliche Einheit des Abendlandes*, edited by P. Rassow (Cologne: Bohlau, 1960), 285.

[29] Rassow, *Kaiseridee*, 71–72.

[30] *"Langenmantel" Chronicle*, 400; Rassow, *Kaiseridee*, 29.

[31] Liliencron, *Die Historischen Volkslieder*, 4: 10–15

[32] Ibid., 15.

[33] Liliencron, *Deutsches Leben*, 1–6 #1: "The Diet is over and nothing has been decided!"

[34] Ibid., 3.

[35] Ibid., 4.

[36] Ibid., 4.

perial Diet was successful in other areas. That the confessional debate was not even of absolute primary importance for Charles is
indicated by the quarrel regarding the agenda that ensued immediately after the Diet was officially opened. According to "Langenmantel," the argument between Charles, Ferdinand and the Catholic princes on the one hand, and the evangelical princes and cities
on the other, lasted from Monday, June 20, to Friday, June 24, and
focused on the issue whether to consider the confessional question or
the Turkish campaign first.[37]

Although the evangelical factions succeeded in bringing their concerns to the forefront (the *Confessio* was read on June 25), other issues
were also considered during the 1530 Imperial Diet. Debates were
held concerning monopolies, coinage regulations, penal law and
criminal procedure, organization and function of the empire's government and supreme court, the relationship between Germany and
Rome, civil order and regulation,[38] and the agreement of the princes
and cities of the empire to maintain peace with one another (*ewige
Landfriede*).[39] Ultimately, these debates centered around the institutionalization of centralized power within the empire. The more firmly the Habsburgs could institutionalize exercise of their power, the
more stable the empire would become, and the easier it would be for
the Habsburgs to maintain their claims of imperial authority. From
the German estates' position, of course, the entrenchment of Habsburg power meant a highly significant limit to their own.

These efforts to exert control extended from the major empire-
wide issues mentioned earlier, down to minute details of quotidian
life. In the civic order drawn up at the 1530 Imperial Diet, detailed
regulations were imposed on everything from drinking and swearing,
to dressing and selling.[40] The Diet Proclamation from 1530 also

---

[37] *"Langenmantel" Chronicle*, 373. Sender does not report this.

[38] "Römischer kayserlicher Majestät Ordung und Reformation guter Policey im
heiligen römischen Reich, zu Augspurg Anno 1530 auffgericht" printed in *Neue und
vollständige Sammlung der Teutsche Reichsabschiede*, Frankfurt am Main, 1747), vol.1, part
2, 332–44. This is a fascinating document that reveals much about quotidian life in
ca. 1530 by its attempts to regulate that life. Detailed regulations are given regarding
the swearing of oaths, blasphemy, drinking, clothing (according to status and rank,
beginning with the peasants and ending with the aristocracy), usurious contracts, the
selling of ginger, use of correct weights and measurements, bearing of arms and
accepted behavior for social fringe groups like beggars, gypsies, fools, pipers, street
singers, and apprentices.

[39] Immenkötter, *Reichstag*, 11–13.

[40] See my n. 38 this chapter.

gave instructions that anything new to be printed must first receive official permission, and the document must include the name and location of the printer.[41] In addition, the proclamation also forbade the destruction of religious art objects.[42] The attempts to regulate specifically these phenomena indicate that they were of such importance that they were the source of controversy and debate, and thus, of potential instability.

One aspect of the 1530 Imperial Diet was especially successful, seen from the Habsburg perspective. Throughout the summer and fall of 1530, Charles carried on negotiations with the electors regarding Ferdinand's election as German king.[43] Election to this office would guarantee Ferdinand's—and thus Habsburg—succession to the imperial throne after Charles. Ferdinand's main rival, we remember, was Wilhelm IV of Bavaria. Already in 1529, Wilhelm had procured Albrecht of Brandenburg's assurance that the cardinal of Mainz would vote for the duke of Bavaria.[44] During the Diet's negotiations, however, Albrecht was one of the first to promise his vote to the Habsburgs.[45]

Charles was able to make rapid progress with his negotiations. After contact between the emperor and the electors over this issue was initiated in July, intensive negotiations followed in August. By the end of the month or the beginning of September, most of the electors had been won.[46] After a loan from the Fuggers and subsequent negotiations,[47] all the electors signed a contract with Charles and Ferdinand on November 13, 1530, that guaranteed pro-Habsburg votes.[48] Six days later, Charles issued the Diet Proclamation.

Ferdinand was indeed made king soon after the end of the 1530 Diet in November. He was elected in Cologne and already crowned in Aachen in January 1531. Charles rewarded the Fuggers for their

---

[41] *Teutsche Reichsabschiede*, vol.1, part 2, 314, §58.

[42] Ibid., 312, §42.

[43] Kohler, *Antihabsburgische Politik*, 115-7.

[44] Pölnitz, "Anton Fugger," 322; Albrecht sold his vote at an enormously high price that included guarantees of privileges, properties, donations, a lump sum of 100,000 fl., and an annual pension for the rest of his life of 5,000 fl.

[45] Ibid., 332.

[46] Ibid., 334; Kohler, *Antihabsburgische Politik*, 117-24.

[47] Kohler, *Antihabsburgische Politik*, 124. The contract which documents the loan is dated October 15, 1530. Pölnitz, "Anton Fugger," 340–41 estimated that it cost the Habsburgs 1,200,000 fl. to have Ferdinand elected.

[48] Pölnitz, "Anton Fugger," 342.

indispensable help in this highly important matter, without which the Habsburgs would not have secured the needed votes. Not only were the Fuggers accorded social privileges such as elevation to the nobility, but they were also accorded tremendous economic and political privileges. Their properties, their capital, and their persons were all expressly placed under imperial protection. They were free to live and trade anywhere in the empire, and they were free from civilian duties, from taxation, and from the jurisdiction of the Augsburg civil court. These privileges were granted for all eternity.[49] The strong wording of the 1530 Diet Proclamation regarding the outlawing of monopolies,[50] and Ferdinand's electoral promise from January 7, 1531, to end the arbitrary and destructive reign of the trading companies,[51] were in reality nothing but verbal gesturing. The Habsburgs, who now controlled the highest offices of power within the empire, had made the Fuggers untouchable.

The 1530 Imperial Diet was an extremely complicated event during which a number of important issues were debated. The critical debate on the confessional issue remained unsolved, and the events of the Diet in fact served only to increase the polarization of Catholic and evangelical factions. Although Charles was unsuccessful in gaining control of the confessional situation in the empire, as he had wished, he did succeed in attaining an important objective: the election of Ferdinand as king. Now that Ferdinand was king, his authority, which had consistently been challenged when he was *Statthalter* (viceroy), would be contractually and ideologically strengthened, thus bolstering the claims and exercise of Habsburg hegemony.

Critical as these debates were, the public displays of conflicting power struggles must also be counted as important events during the 1530 Diet. We have recognized these displays in numerous incidents: in processions, liturgical chants, the swearing of oaths, executions, and public proclamations. The chronicles indicate that these displays were viewed by sensitized and engaged audiences who were ready to interpret these events, however, in accordance with their own political and confessional positions.

In these claims and counterclaims of power and control, the role of ceremony becomes especially important, where ritual becomes a

---

[49] Ibid., 342.
[50] *Teutsche Reichsabschiede*, 327, §135–37.
[51] Pölnitz, "Anton Fugger," 343.

subtle yet efficacious instrument with which to convey information about what is and about what should be. The ceremony of adventus, with all its implications of classical ruler ideology, was ideally suited for the display of power and thus could form a potent reaffirmation of power in the face of challenge and contest.

We must view Breu's woodcuts within this context of conspicuously conflicting power plays and within the context of both confessional and political debate. We must also consider the ceremony of adventus both theoretically and practically in order to understand the meanings and resonances of this ceremony, and how it was staged and constructed.

The Tradition of Adventus

The ceremony of adventus as used by Charles and his Habsburg predecessors was based on an ancient and elite tradition that began with the celebration of the gods' epiphany and was adopted in turn by Hellenistic rulers and Roman emperors. Christ's entry into Jerusalem, as described in the Gospel of John, adopted these same ceremonial elements of acclamation and celebration, and provided the model for the adventus ceremonies of Christian emperors and medieval kings.[52] Already associated with these early precedents was the production of commemorative art, especially coins often showing an emperor on horseback, addressing his subjects and preceded by a personification and triumphal arches.[53] In some instances, images of the emperor could even take his place and were themselves the acclaimed object of adventus.[54]

The tradition of adventus thus drew on and displayed the powerful ideological concept of the ruler's interdependent divine and imperial nature. The ceremony indeed was a celebration of this dual nature and of its appearance to and presence within a city.[55] The enactment of adventus activated other connotations as well. The ceremony was also associated with triumph and accession,[56] elements that we noted as fundamental to Charles's adventus.

But the ceremony not only provided a forum for the emperor to

---

[52] Ernst Kantorowicz, "The King's Advent," *Art Bulletin* 26 (1944): 230.

[53] Ibid., 213, and 218–19.

[54] Sabine MacCormack, *Art and Ceremony in Late Antiquity* (Berkeley and Los Angeles: University of California Press, 1981), 67–68.

[55] Ibid., 23, and 56.

[56] Ibid., 34.

publicly display his right to and exercise of power, it also provided a forum for his subjects to demonstrate their acceptance of that right and exercise; adventus was a display both of power and of consensus,[57] which demonstrated at least formally the theoretical and practical interdependence between the emperor and the people. This interdependence was certainly a major factor at the 1530 Diet, especially for the imperial city of Augsburg. Here we witnessed another ceremonial event solemnly proclaiming this interdependence; the male citizens' oath of loyalty and obedience for the exchange of imperial privileges. We should also recall here the post-Diet poem that rhetorically reminded Charles that his position as emperor was dependent, at least in theory, on his subjects' consensus. And yet, because of confessional differences between the Catholic emperor and many of the Augsburg citizens who were evangelical, that consensus was not a matter of certainty.

Related to its celebration of the simultaneously divine and imperial nature of the ruler is the function of the adventus ceremony to render hierarchy visual and public.[58] Here the relationships between the emperor, members of court, territorial princes, ecclesiastics, and his "simple" subjects from civic and rural communities were put on display, each group accorded a specific physical position in the ceremony that corresponded to its access to and possession or lack of power.[59] This visual enactment of hierarchical relationships was of great importance for Charles's 1530 adventus because of the challenges to that hierarchy that we discussed earlier.

In the late Middle Ages and early Renaissance, adventus consisted of a composite of various ceremonies.[60] It was initiated by the ruler's

---

[57] Ibid., 18.

[58] Ibid., 82. For examples of this phenomenon in eighteenth-century France, see Norbert Elias, *Die höfische Gesellschaft* (Frankfurt am Main: Suhrkamp Verlag, 1983), especially chapter 5: "Etikette und Zeremoniell."

[59] For this aspect in somewhat later ceremonies of adventus, see Karl Möseneder, "Das Fest als Darstellung der Harmonie im Staat am Beispiel der Entrée Solennelle Ludwigs XIV 1660 in Paris," and Hubert Ekalt, "Zur Funktion des Zeremoniells im Absolutismus." Both these articles appear in *Europäische Hofkultur im 16. und 17. Jahrhundert*, edited by A. Buck (Hamburg: Haus Wedell, 1981), 2: 130–34, and 411–19, respectively.

[60] My discussion is here based on Drabeck, *Reisen und Reisezeremoniell* and R. Aulinger, *Das Bild des Reichstages*. Winfried Dotzauer's article "Die Ankunft des Herrschers: Der fürstliche Einzug in die Stadt," *Archiv für Kulturgeschichte* 55 (1973): 245–88 draws heavily on Drabeck. See also J. Jacquot, *Fêtes et cérémonies au temps du Charles Quint* (Paris: Editions du Centre National de la Recherche Scientifique, 1960).

approach to the city where he was officially greeted, followed by his
procession through the city to the main church or cathedral. Usually, the ruler was greeted first by ecclesiastics bearing relics, which
the ruler was to venerate, and then by the civic representatives.[61] We
know that Maximilian's first act of his 1493 adventus to Basel was to
dismount from his horse and kiss a golden cross offered to him by an
ecclesiastic that contained relics of the True Cross.[62] The ecclesiastical greeting, veneration of relics, and liturgical reception in the cathedral appear to have been the main events.[63]

During its course through the city, the procession might pass by
floats and tableaux, or witness plays or pass through triumphal
arches. This was indeed the case in Charles's 1515 adventus to
Bruges, where various tableaux and floats made reference to specific
political and civic concerns such as the fear of the Turks and the
disastrous consequences of Bruges's silted harbor.[64] The triumphal
arch constructed for Charles's 1541 Nuremberg adventus is illustrated in a woodcut attributed to Peter Flötner[65] and described in a
poem by Hans Sachs.[66] Faux castles were stormed, bombarded,
burned, and exploded at Charles's Munich adventus on June 10,

---

[61] Drabeck, *Reisen*, 34–36.

[62] Ibid., 22–23.

[63] Ibid., 50.

[64] See G. R. Kernodle, "Renaissance Artists in the Service of the People: Political Tableaux and Street Theaters in France, Flanders and England," *Art Bulletin* 25
(1943): 59–64; and Remy de Puys, *La tryumphante et solemnelle entrée . . . de très houle, très
puissant et très excellent prince monsieur Charles prince des Hespaignes* (facsmile ed., Bruges:
n.p., 1950). This is a nineteenth-century reprint of a 1515 Paris edition, printed by
Gilles de Gourmont, of the manuscript description (ÖNB Cod. Vindob. 2591) of
Remy de Puys. However, de Gourmont's edition is illustrated by woodcuts that illustrate only the floats and tableaux and do not correspond to the manuscript illumina-
tions. Three plays were held during Charles's 1530 Munich adventus. After the emperor entered the city gates, he passed three tableaux depicting the stories of Hester,
Thamaris, and Cambysis, all stories that refer to justice and wise leadership. These
plays are mentioned in pamphlet 1178 (see my n. 67) fol.Aii.v and in another pamphlet *Ain kurze anzaygung und beschreybung römischer keyserlicher Maiestat einreyten erstlich von
Innspruck gen Schwatz, volgend zu Munchen und zu letst gen Augspurg.* This latter pamphlet
appears as "Beilage VI," 60–84, in Ernst Salomon Cyprian, *Historia der Augspurgischen
Confession* (Gotha, 1730) where it is attributed to Sturm (in my text referred to as
"Sturm"). In her article "Augsburg und die Reichstage," 3: 13, n. 67, Aulinger cites
Cyprian's information but wrongly asserts that these plays took place in Augsburg.
The text states unambiguously that these plays were held in Munich. I was unable to
find any reference in the primary source material to plays or tableaux held in
Augsburg.

[65] Strauss, *Woodcut*, 3: 787.

[66] Sachs, *Kayserlicher mayestat Caroli V einreyten zu Nürnberg in des hayligen reichs stat den
xvi Tag Februarii deß 1541 jars*, cited in Dotzauer, "Die Ankunft des Herrschers," 272.

1530.[67] Perhaps this violent display of military might organized and sponsored by Wilhelm IV, and the complete lack of the emperor's presence in the woodcut illustrating this display,[68] may indeed indicate the political tension between the emperor and the Bavarian duke.[69]

With this background of the ideology and practice of adventus in mind, let us now turn to Charles's 1530 arrival at Augsburg. By using contemporaneous reports of this event found in pamphlets and Sender's chronicle,[70] we can get a basic idea of the events of June 15, 1530. It is important to first establish these basic facts since they comprise a baseline against which we will measure Breu's rendition of the same ceremony.

---

[67] This is described in the pamphlet: *Keiserlicher Maiestat einreitung zu Munchen den x. tag Junii im M.CCCCC. und XXX jar*, Augsburg, Stadt- und Staatsbibliothek, 4° 1178.

[68] This military show is illustrated in a three-part woodcut printed by Niclas Meldeman and attributed to Hans Sebald Beham; Strauss, *Woodcut*, 2: 272ff.

[69] The pamphlet text does not give any indication of perceived hostility, but rather highly praises the expense of what is seen as a show of honor: "ynn summa/es ist ein solcher pracht gewesen/ das ich nicht gleub das keiserlicher maiestat yn gantzen reich der gleichen ehre geschehen werde den kein unkost daran gespart worden [war]." We do not know who the author of this pamphlet is. The text accompanying Meldeman's three-part woodcut, however, stresses the fact that the woodcut was made in honor of the dukes of Bavaria. Its function is supposedly the dissemination of the dukes' respectful reception of the emperor, which technically is not illustrated: "Zu eren den hochgebornen Fürsten und Herrn/herrn Wilhelm und Ludwig gebrüdern [. . .] meinen gnedigen herrn ist diese aigentlich verzeichnus gestelt. Die schonhait und kostlichkeit/dadurch KM [Kaiserlich Majestät] unser allergnedigster Herr zu irer KM in das heilig reych un hoch genanter MGH [meines gnädigen Herrns] stat München ankunfft von iren FG [fürstlichen Gnaden] mit sonderlicher eererpietung entpfangen[.] Durch mich Niklauß Meldeman bürgern zu Nurnberg als hochgedachten MGH zu unterthenigstem Dienst und darmit solch auch an andere orth und zu andern zeyten außgebrait und kunt gemacht würd/ytzo in der druck verfertigt und außgangen."

[70] The pamphlets used are (1).*Von keyserliche Maiestat einreytten/ auff den Reychstag gen Augspurg*, Augsburg, Stadt- und Staatsbibliothek, 4° Aug. 1179; (2).*Keiserlicher Maiestat einreitung zu Munchen den x. tag Junii*, Augsburg, Stadt- und Staatsbibliothek, 4° 1178; (3).Caspar Sturm, *Wiewol hievor in dreyen underschidlichen büchlein beschrieben und im Truck außgangen wie die Rö. Kai. Maie. von Inßbruck auß zu Schwatz München und volgend auff angesetzten Reychstag Anno etc. 1530 zu Augspurg eingeritten*, Augsburg, Stadt- und Staatsbibliothek, 4° 1201; (4)."Sturm," *Ain kurze anzaygung und beschreybung* . . . in Cyprian, *Historia*, 60–84. The appropriate pages in the "Langenmantel" and in Sender's chronicles are found on 368–70 and 262–79, respectively. In her reconstruction of the adventus, Aulinger (*Das Bild des Reichstages*, 332–35) relies mostly on Sender's chronicle. Although she briefly discusses Breu's woodcuts (335–39), she fails to analyze the differences between Breu's description and the written reports. Her findings reappear in condensed form a year later in "Augsburg und die Reichstage," 3: 12–15. I will be taking issue more specifically with Aulinger's conclusion in the course of the discussion.

The Augsburg Adventus of 1530

Charles and his entourage approached Augsburg on June 15, 1530. The emperor was met at the bridge on the river Lech outside the city by a greeting committee consisting of electors, nobility, diplomats, and ecclesiastics who had already arrived in Augsburg. To the embarrassment of the princes, Charles and Ferdinand dismounted, although this was against protocol. The princes hurriedly followed the Habsburg example and were greeted by Charles and Ferdinand with friendly handshakes. Albrecht of Brandenburg then held a long speech to welcome Charles, who expressed his thanks for the welcome through Count-Palatine Friedrich.[71]

Sender's report of this first stage of adventus is the most detailed, yet he omits two significant details. Pamphletist 1178 reports that the cardinals of Salzburg and Trient did not dismount from their horses during the greeting ceremony and in fact the papal legate, Cardinal Campeggio, was even physically absent from it.[72] This refusal of the ecclesiastics to participate as and with the others illustrates the tensions already inherent in this Imperial Diet and the efficacious use of ceremony to give expression to this tension. Sender's omission of these facts also indicates the tendentious nature of the textual sources; the Benedictine monk seems to have withheld any details that might have reflected negatively upon the Catholic clergy and its participation in the ceremony.

After the exchange of speeches, Charles was helped back onto his horse by six princes, including the duke of Saxony and the count of Hessen (both Protestant), and the procession moved on toward the city gate. Here began the second stage of adventus, where the emperor and his entourage were greeted by the citizens of Augsburg. The imperial procession had already been met outside the gates by Landsknechten, and by representatives from the various guilds, including the Fuggers and other merchants. The two present and two former mayors of Augsburg and four other members of the City Council officially welcomed Charles at Rotes Tor in the name of the city.[73] All artillery was then fired.[74]

It is at this point that the pamphletists describe the order of the

---

[71] Sender, *Chronik*, 262; pamphlet 1179, Aii r; pamphlet 1178, Aiii r.

[72] Pamphlet 1178, Aiii r–v. This pamphlet is especially anti-Catholic.

[73] The greeting committee consisted of the two present *Bürgermeister*, Georg Vetter and Hieronymus Imhoff (both Lutheran), the two former *Bürgermeister*, Ulrich

imperial procession.[75] Sender's description does not appear until the third stage of adventus but does not differ substantially from the pamphletists' reports,[76] except for the appearance of Charles, which we will discuss later. The reports are not completely identical with one another in terms of the exact order of each and every group participating in the procession, but the details agree with one another to a sufficient extent to generally reconstruct the procession as it moved through the city.

The procession began with a show of force. First came the thousand Landsknechten whom Charles had hired to maintain order. Then came the courtly and military entourages of the various princes, electors, aristocrats, and ecclesiastics. Interspersed with these were members of the Spanish court. A number of aristocratic page boys followed riding Ferdinand's and Charles's best horses. Next came the members of court, the imperial advisers, and foreign diplomats, interspersed with trumpeters and drummers. The princes' heralds and court chamberlains followed.[77]

The next part of the procession contained the tip of the imperial hierarchy. It was proceeded by the elector of Saxony as the supreme marshall of the empire carrying the drawn imperial sword. He was accompanied by Margrave Joachim of Brandenburg and Count-Palatine Ottheinrich. This group was followed by archbishops Albrecht of Brandenburg and Mainz, and Hermann of Cologne.[78] The order of this particular constellation was established in the Golden Bull which stipulated that the archbishops of Trier, Cologne, and Mainz (in their capacities as ecclesiastics and electors) should proceed first, followed by the elector of Saxony as supreme marshall.[79] The order

---

Rehlinger and Anthony Bimmel (both Zwinglian), and the following members of the city council: Conrad Rehlinger, Simprecht Hoser, Stephan Eysselin and Conrad Peutinger; see Roth, annotation to Sender, *Chronik*, 18, n. 1.

[74] Sender, *Chronik*, 273; 1179, Aii r-v; 1178, Aiii v.

[75] 1179, Aii v- Aiiii r; 1178, Aiii v.

[76] Sender, *Chronik*, 274–76.

[77] Sender reports that the princes process in groups of three or four, that there are four heralds and two *Hofmeister* belonging to the emperor and Ferdinand (275). Pamphlet 1179 has Ferdinand in among the princes, whereas Sender and 1178 do not; "Sturm," 68. Pamphlet 1178 reports that members of the Bohemian nobility processed with the German princes so this is perhaps from where the confusion stems.

[78] Sender, *Chronik*, 275; 1178, Aiiii v; "Sturm," 68; and 1179 Aiii r, have all ecclesiastics following Charles.

[79] Aulinger, *Das Bild*, 195–96.

here has been reversed. Instead, the elector of Saxony processed in front of the archbishops, who have, in effect, been moved further back in the procession but therefore also closer to the emperor, thus increasing their projected rank and status. This small but significant change in protocol is entirely in keeping with Charles's perception of his function as protector of Christianity as embodied by the Catholic Church,[80] which he was to defend at the 1530 Imperial Diet.

Following Mainz and Cologne came Charles. The emperor is described as riding a white stallion and dressed in a golden robe.[81] Pamphlet 1178 states that Charles wore a small Spanish hat. The pamphlets describe Charles at this point as riding under a baldachin of red, green, and white velvet, the city colors of Augsburg.[82] The baldachin was supported by six poles, three on one side bearing the imperial eagle, three on the other bearing the city emblem.[83] The structural unity of and interdependence between imperial city and empire, between Augsburg and Habsburg, is here graphically illustrated by this baldachin. Six members of the City Council carried the baldachin over Charles[84] as he rode from the city gate at Rotes Tor[85] through the city to St. Leonard's Church on the Perlachplatz.

Sender, pamphlet 1178, and "Sturm"[86] report that Ferdinand and Campeggio followed directly behind Charles.[87] This placement of Ferdinand directly adjacent to Charles represented another breach of protocol. As king of Bohemia, Ferdinand instead should have followed somewhere in the procession after Charles.[88] Yet the emperor expressly desired this change of protocol to be implemented.[89] Charles's specific placement of Ferdinand close to his own person surely signified the emperor's desire to present his brother as his protegé, as a viceroy who acted on imperial authority. This physical and political proximity of Ferdinand to Charles must also have indicated Charles's support of Ferdinand's bid for the Roman kingship,

[80] Rassow, *Kaiseridee*, 30.
[81] 1179, Aiii r; 1178, Aiiii v.
[82] 1179, Aiii r; 1178, Aiii v.
[83] Sender, *Chronik*, 273.
[84] According to Sender (*Chronik*, 273) these six were Hans Rehlinger, Wilhelm Rehlinger, Franz Hoffmair, Laux Schellenberger, Ulrich Sultzer and Mang Seitz.
[85] *"Langenmantel" Chronicle*, 370.
[86] Sender, *Chronik*, 275; 1178, Aiiii v; "Sturm," 68.
[87] Only 1179 has Ferdinand in among the princes who processed in front of the duke of Saxony.
[88] Aulinger, *Das Bild*, 196.
[89] Ibid., 331–32.

support which would be activated during the negotiations regarding the election during the Diet.

The direct proximity of Cardinal Campeggio represented the same breach of protocol. Here again Charles was most likely expressing his protection of and cooperation with the Catholic Church, as did the movement of the archbishops' position noted earlier. "Sturm" reports, however, that the position of Ferdinand and Campeggio was not uncontested. Before the city was reached, "Sturm" relates that Campeggio even tried to ride directly next to Charles, but he was prevented from doing so. "The electors and princes in no way wanted to permit or allow anything but that His Imperial Majesty should ride alone; neither the said Cardinal nor his Royal Majesty nor any other prince [should accompany the emperor]."[90] "Sturm's" report illustrated how the symbolically significant proximity to Charles was jealously guarded by the German princes and electors who here seem united in their rejection of a combined display of Habsburg and papal claims.

The third stage of adventus was initiated at St. Leonard's, where Charles received the welcome of the ecclesiastics. Here Charles passed from under the civic baldachin to the ecclesiastical one made of white damask and carried by six cathedral chapter members (*Domherren*).[91] It is under the ecclesiastical baldachin where Sender describes Charles, but as bare-headed and shorn.[92] In this third stage, the religious ceremonies of adventus were enacted. In our general discussion of adventus, we saw that usually the main and immediate activities performed were religious ceremonies. That these should be confined here during the 1530 Augsburg adventus to this single and relatively late stage of adventus indicates that Catholic ceremony was feared to be too provocative to be practiced to the full extent within the city confines.

The procession, now including the ecclesiastics, moved from the Perlachplatz to the cathedral. Sender remarks that every common

---

[90] "Sturm," 69: "Also haben churfürsten und fürsten kainswegs gestatten noch zugeben wollen weder mit gedachten Cardinal [Campeggio] noch mit ku. maiae. [Ferdinand] oder nemandts andern fürsten sonder wollen kai. maiae. [Charles] soll allain frey reyten." In his account of the Munich adventus, "Sturm" reports that Charles rode together with Ferdinand at his right and Campeggio at his left.

[91] *"Langenmantel" Chronicle,"* 370, and 1178, Bi v, report that Charles's horse shied at this point and did not want to go under the ecclesiastic baldachin.

[92] Sender, *Chronik*, 274–75.

citizen was barred from the cathedral on this occasion,[93] no doubt also in an effort to minimize confrontations based on widespread anti-Catholic sentiment on the part of the populace. Sender reports that the service was both triumphal and orderly.[94] However, pamphletist 1178 reports that Cardinals Campeggio and Lang of Salzburg had a fight at the high altar as to which one of them was to bestow the benediction upon Charles.[95] After the service, the princes and electoral dukes accompanied Charles to his quarters, where there was a brief discussion before everyone retired for the night.[96]

Viewed superficially, Charles's 1530 adventus celebrated the rites of acclamation, triumph, power, and consensus generally associated with the ceremony of adventus as we have seen. The imperial procession must have been truly spectacular, with the sheer number and splendor of its dazzling princes, mighty soldiers, and foreign diplomats. Sender remarks: "As long as the city of Augsburg has stood, never has there been seen so many foreigners from so many nations as at this Diet held at Augsburg."[97] "Sturm" asserts that the splendor of the participants clothing was overwhelming and indescribable.[98]

Although Charles's Augsburg adventus must have been colorful and impressive, his reception by the city of Augsburg pales in comparison with the show put on by Wilhelm IV of Bavaria in Munich. In addition to the large-scale and spectacular destruction of faux buildings already mentioned, the city also staged a joust between fishermen on the Isar River, and three different tableaux, followed the next day by a hunt.[99] No such events were organized by the city of Augsburg, thus indicating that the element of consensus was in this case presented as conspicuously guarded.[100]

In comparison to other ceremonies of adventus, we were also able to note several shifts of accent, signaled by changes in protocol and in reaction to specific concerns. We saw Charles moving his protegés

---

[93] Ibid., 276.

[94] Ibid., 276–77.

[95] 1178, Bi v.

[96] Sender, *Chronik*, 263–64; 1179, Aiii r; 1178, Bi v.

[97] Sender, *Chronik*, 263–64: "Allenweil Augspurg gestanden ist, ist nie sovil fremdsvolck aus so vil nationen gesechen worden [. . .] als auff disen reichstag gen Augspurg."

[98] "Sturm," 69–70.

[99] Ibid., 63–65 and Cyprian, *Historia*, 60–80.

[100] After all, Duke Wilhelm IV, who staged this apparently brilliant show of acclamation and celebratory consensus was at the same time plotting to undermine Habsburg authority by becoming king himself.

Ferdinand, Campeggio, and the archbishops closer to his person in order to signal his support and protection of them. Religious ceremonies were de-emphasized in response to the incendiary potential for religious conflict in the city. The liturgical ordo chanted by the ecclesiastics was changed in order to include references of the church's beleaguered position and the expectation of imperial rescue.

Once aware of these changes, we realize that Charles's 1530 adventus was far from a straightforward display of imperial power and splendor and of civic consensus and acclamation. Instead, it seems that considerable diplomatic maneuvering took place in a delicate balancing act between the assertion of authority and the willingness to compromise. That this maneuvering at times degenerated into some hard jostling is indicated by one pamphletist's assessment of Charles's adventus procession: "In these entry and departure processions, all kinds of confusions and quarrels took place among the German princes regarding who should go before or after."[101]

Breu's Woodcut Series

Just as Charles's adventus manipulated ceremony to make hierarchy and power visible, so also did Breu's woodcuts manipulate Charles's adventus to comment on that power. If we compare the woodcuts with the actual ceremony and with other triumphal processions, we can begin to recognize how the woodcuts performed their function of propaganda. But propaganda for whom? We will see that on one level, the series commemorates Charles's adventus as a splendid ceremony, as a manifestation of Charles's military might and magnificent court. In this way, the series clearly functions as an articulation of Habsburg propaganda. But on another level, we again note that alternative sites for identity are created, sites around which particularly a German aristocratic and even an anti-Habsburg identity could coalesce. The woodcuts thus are not a straightforward glorification of Habsburg authority, but instead seem both to assert and to contest that authority. The meanings created by the woodcuts are ambiguous, even contradictory, multivalent to an extreme. But it is their multivalence that makes the woodcuts so deeply political.

We do not know Breu's reaction to Charles's 1530 adventus; the

---

[101] 1178, Bi v: "Ynn diesen ein und auszug haben sich allerley Irrungen und Zank unter den deudschen Fürsten zugetragen des vor und nach zugs halben."

artist's chronicle lacks entries for that year. This is a possible indication that Breu may have been extremely busy during the Imperial
Diet. We know that he was working on the woodcut series sometime
after the adventus procession, and that he may also have been working on *Battle of Zama* for Wilhelm IV at this time.[102] If Breu were still
active in 1530 as an *Unterhauptmann*, however, then he would have
indeed been very busy, as "Langenmantel" repeatedly refers to the
active role of the civic militia as a peace-keeping force within the
city.[103] We also do not know the exact date or circumstances of
commission which might have provided us with information about
Breu's source. We do not know whether the artist was sent out to
observe the procession (something he would probably have done as a
citizen of Augsburg anyway) in order to be able then to portray it, or
if the idea for the commission came after June 15. We must assume
that Breu either saw the procession himself or read any number of
the pamphlets if his memory needed refreshing. Contrary to
Maximilian's *Triumphal Procession*, which illustrated an event that
never actually happened,[104] Breu's woodcuts do specifically refer to
certain groups and individuals who really did participate in this particular procession on June 15, 1530.

The question of Breu's source of visual information remains unsolved. Aulinger postulates that Breu was probably working in con-
juncture with the imperial herald, Caspar Sturm.[105] Sturm was the
author of various pamphlets describing the Diet's ceremonials,[106]
and Aulinger sees enough similarities between these pamphlets and
Breu's woodcuts to warrant a conclusion of cooperation. Aulinger's
analysis is not decisive, however. On the one hand, some of Breu's
woodcuts are closer to Sender's account; for example, the procession

---

[102] The painting is placed at c. 1530 by Goldberg, *Die Alexanderschlacht und die
Historienbilder*, 25.

[103] "*Langenmantel*" *Chronicle*, 366 and 379, where members act as heralds. It is
possible then that Breu might have known Caspar Sturm through their shared quasi-
military position (Aulinger hypothesizes this as well, "Augsburg und die Reichstage,"
14), but Breu's woodcuts are not based on Sturm's reports (see following discussion).

[104] Appuhn, *Triumphzug*, 157.

[105] Aulinger, "Augsburg und die Reichstage," 14.

[106] Ibid., n. 323 and n. 328. For information on Sturm, see D. Kolde, "Der
Reichsherold Caspar Sturm und seine literarische Tätigkeit," *Archiv für Reformationsgeschichte* 4 (1907): 117–61; and K. Schottenloher, "Kaiserliche Herolde des 16. Jahrhunderts," *Historisches Jahrbuch* 49 (1929): 460–71. See also Sturm's portrait sketched
in 1520 by Dürer at Aachen in the artist's sketchbook from his Netherlandish journey (Musée Condé, L.340).

of the princes in groups of four and the illustration of Charles's and Ferdinand's chamberlains agree closely with the Benedictine monk's description. On the other hand, as we shall see, Breu's version differs importantly from any of the printed sources. Although Aulinger regards these differences as examples of artistic licence,[107] I will argue that they instead account for the series' articulation of ideology. Breu's deviations from the procession as we know it to have existed are too consistent in character to be explained away either by artistic license or by lack of information. We can assume that these deviations from the texts and from the ceremony were probably made at the behest of the unnamed patron. Aulinger assumes that if Charles did not commission the woodcuts, then the patron must have been a member of his court and therefore a Catholic.[108] The woodcut series does contain clues that can be interpreted to indicate the possibility of certain patrons, as the following analysis will show.

The composite reconstruction of Breu's series illustrated in Strauss is, in terms of the arrangement of the sheets, incorrect,[109] as are some of the labels accorded to various sheets.[110] Breu's procession can be divided into two parts. One part contains four sheets depicting knights bearing various arms: "Trumpeter and Six Crossbowmen" (plate 3), "Captain and Six Crossbowmen" (plate 4), "Ten Hungarian Lancers" (plate 10), and "Two Groups of Lancers" (plate 11). These groups of sheets clearly display another hand than Breu's especially evident in the faces of the lancers and crossbowmen following the captain. Only the group of crossbowmen and trumpeter seem to be by Breu. This fact and the presence of the trumpeter blowing his horn, perhaps signaling the beginning of the procession, may indicate that this sheet opened the series.[111] From the written sources we know that soldiers were found both at the beginning and at the end of the 1530 procession. Ferdinand's soldiers, for example, came toward the end of the procession. Thus, we can hypothesize that the two groups of crossbowmen formed the beginning of the woodcut procession,

---

[107] Aulinger, *Das Bild*, 334–35.

[108] Aulinger, *Das Bild*, 194.

[109] For example, we know that the duke of Saxony followed the princes, but Strauss has him preceding them.

[110] For example, Strauss's "Court Chamberlain and Page" are really the emperor's and the king's court chamberlains. Aulinger (*Das Bild*, 338, n. 40) identifies Strauss's "Nine Knights" as *Reichsfürsten*; both authors are incorrect (see my discussion). Strauss even mistakes Ferdinand for Charles and vice-versa.

[111] Maximilian's *Triumphal Procession* opens with Preco blowing his trumpet.

while the two groups of lancers formed the close. The "Hungarian Lancers" must have belonged to Ferdinand's entourage and thus must have appeared later in the procession. Placing two groups of soldiers at the end of the woodcut series also avoids an unceremonious termination of the procession, which would otherwise come to an abrupt halt with the depiction of the emperor as it appears in Strauss. Neither Maximilian's *Triumphal Procession* nor textual or pictorial reports of Charles's processions in 1515 in Bruges[112] or 1530 in Bologna[113] terminate with the depiction of Charles; instead, he is followed by several different groups who then comprise the end of the procession.

The second part of Breu's woodcut series is comprised of the remaining six sheets. In contrast to the preceding four sheets which depict anonymous soldiers, these six sheets depict participants in the procession, all of them aristocratic and most of them at least potentially identifiable.

On the basis of the pamphlets and chronicles, I would argue that the first sheet in this part of the series is the one depicting what Strauss has labeled "Nine Knights on Horseback" (plate 4). Aulinger identifies these men as "Reichsfürsten."[114] Both of these identifications are incorrect. The nine men are all dressed similarly; they wear small brimmed black hats (some with plumes, some without) and white capes over black tunics. The farthest man in the front row rides a mule. The overgarment of the man next to him bears a cloverleaf cross. In the same row, the man in the foreground turns and looks back to the second row. The turning of his torso reveals a sword cross emblem on the breast of his tunic. The two crosses identify these men as knights belonging to the Spanish orders of Santiago (the sword cross) and of Calatrava (the cloverleaf cross).[115] Although

[112] Vienna, Österreichische Nationalbibliothek, Cod. Vindob. 2591, based on Remy de Puys report. See the facsimile Sydney Angelo, ed. *La Tryumphante Entree de Charles Prince des Espagnes en Bruges 1515* (Amsterdam: Theatrum Orbis Terrarum, 1973).
[113] Lhotsky, *Sonderausstellung Karl V*, 57–58, no. 144; 38 etchings done by Nicolas Hogenberg. Reproduced in *La Coronacion Imperial de Carlos V* (1530; reprint, Madrid: Joyas Bibliograficas, 1958).
[114] Strauss, 1: 336; Aulinger, *Das Bild*, 338, n. 40.
[115] Fifteenth-century depictions of the knights of these orders substantiate this identification. The portrait of the Master of Santiago Frey Don Alvaro de Luna (1445–53) depicts him as wearing a white mantel bearing the sword-cross emblem. A miniature in the Alba Bible depicts the Master of Calatrava Frey Don Luis de Guzman (1414–43) wearing a white mantel bearing the clover-leaf cross. Below him

none of the chronicles or pamphlets mention specifically knights of Spanish orders participating in the procession, Sender does note that many members of the Spanish court, including knights, processed wearing golden and black tunics.[116]

The next group to follow would be the aristocratic page boys on stallions (plate 5). The woodcut depicts three of them, seen from the back, side, and front, each one dressed in splendid costumes trimmed with a plethora of plumes. The central figure is dressed in what appears to be a Turkish costume, perhaps to indicate the origin of his mount; Sender reports that the handsome horses came from Turkey, England, and Poland.[117] Certainly the fantastic costumes also lend an exotic, cosmopolitan air to Charles's court. The awkwardness in the details of the pages' faces indicates that this sheet was probably drawn by an assistant in the Breu workshop.

Next comes Charles's and Ferdinand's chamberlains Count Adrian von Rois and Wilhelm Freiherr von Roggendorf-Mollenburg (plate 6).[118] The emperor's chamberlain, von Rois, mounted on his armored steed and viewed in strict profile, looks very much like

---

stand knights of the order dressed in black tunics upon which are also emblazoned the clover-leaf cross. These illustrations are found in Desmond Seward, *The Monks of War* (St. Albans: Paladin, 1974), figs. 12 and 15 respectively. These orders included knights and clerics; the man in the woodcut riding the mule is probably a cleric belonging to one of the two orders. Their exotic headgear indicates that these men are clearly not members of the German/Austrian aristocracy. At first I thought they may have been knights of the Order of St. John because Charles gave them the island of Malta in early 1530, which might have explained their inclusion in the 1530 procession. But the insignia of the Order of St. John is the eight-point cross, which Breu's figures definitely do not wear. I was also tempted to identify them as knights belonging to the Order of the Holy Sepulcher. As the later discussion will show, we can identify one of the princes depicted on another sheet as Count-Palatine Ottheinrich. In 1521, Ottheinrich made a pilgrimage to Jerusalem where he and several of his noblemen were dubbed knights of the Holy Sepulcher (A. v. Reitzenstein, *Ottheinrich von der Pfalz* [Bremen: Angelsachsen-Verlag, 1939], 48). This was obviously an important event in Ottheinrich's life as he commemorated this event twenty years after its occurrence in a tapestry from 1541 (now in the Bayerisches Nationalmuseum, Munich; reproduced in Reitzenstein, *Ottheinrich*, 55). We also know that several of the noblemen who accompanied Ottheinrich to Jerusalem and who were made knights there also participated in the 1530 procession (Reitzenstein, *Ottheinrich*, 143). Tempting as this identification is, it is, however, not plausible as these knights clearly wore on their robes the Jerusalem cross, which is in no way similar in appearance to the cloverleaf- or sword-cross depicted in Breu's woodcut (see V. Cramer, *Der Ritterorden vom Hl. Grabe von den Kreuzzügen bis zur Gegenwart*, (Cologne: J. P. Bachem, 1952).

[116] Sender, *Chronik*, 274.
[117] Ibid., 275.
[118] Identified by Sender, *Chronik*, 275 and "Sturm," 68.

Burgkmair's woodcut of Maximilian on horseback (1508). But here in Breu's version, twenty-two years after Burgkmair's, it is not the emperor seated in powerful majesty on his striding horse but his court chamberlain. And this latter figure seems to have been made faintly ridiculous, almost overcome by the mass of feathers exuberantly sprouting from his helmet. Even the horse looks strangely coquettish, with its open mouth, heavy-lidded eye, and the two long curly plumes that softly frame its armored face. The horse also wears decorative coverings that depict at its withers a scene of calamity, and at its chest a depiction of vanity(?).[119] Next to van Rois is Ferdinand's chamberlain, Wilhelm Roggendorf, who was a member of the Order of Calatrava since 1523.[120] The greater sophistication in the execution of the faces in this sheet and the following three indicates that these were done by Breu. This would seem logical as these sheets depict the most important people in the procession in terms of social rank. The commission may indeed have stipulated that Breu must himself be responsible for these important figures rather that his workshop assistants.

Four princes surrounded by five Landsknechten follow (plate 7). Aulinger has identified them as Philip of Hessen, George of Saxony, and Ludwig and Wilhelm of Bavaria.[121] The identification of Wilhelm of Bavaria is plausible if one compares the first prince on the left with Wertinger's portrait of Wilhelm now in the Alte Pinakothek in Munich.[122] The square-trimmed beard, long straight nose and pronounced eyebrows are shared by both figures. The other identifications suggested by Aulinger, however, are surely incorrect. The third prince from the left is certainly not Wilhelm's brother Ludwig,

---

[119] Neither Aulinger nor Rolf Biedermann in his catalogue entry in *Welt im Umbruch*, 1: 171–72, no. 91 deal with this decoration and its possible significance. Biedermann's order of procession is also incorrect. I cannot identify the scene at the horse's withers: at the top, a fortress or city stands in flames, below it are five nude figures, two on the right appear to be fleeing, one at the center lies on his back dead or injured(?). The scene at the horse's chest could be identified as either vanity or an allegory of prudence: a nude figure looks at a round object (a mirror?) held by another figure. On top of the chamberlain's helmet appears a nude torso holding a round dish-like object; I do not know to what this refers.

[120] Hermann Kellenbenz, *Die Fuggersche Maestrazgopacht (1524–42): Zur Geschichte der spanischen Ritterorden im 16. Jahrhundert* (Tübingen: Mohr Verlag, 1967), 65.

[121] Aulinger, *Das Bild*, 338.

[122] The portrait is from 1526. See Goldberg and Salm, *Alte Pinakothek Katalog II Altdeutsche Malerei*, 197, cat. no. 17, reproduced on 284.

who was thirty-five in 1530 and who wore a beard.[123] Similar objections must be raised against Aulinger's identification of the first prince as Philip of Hessen. Breu's figure is bearded but Philip apparently was not.[124] The second prince cannot be George of Saxony, who was quite old already in 1530. Cranach's portrait of George from 1537[125] shows the Saxon prince as bearded, elderly, and balding, whereas Breu's figure appears to have a thick head of hair, is clean-shaven and seems powerfully built.

In light of the physiognomic discrepancies between Breu's figures and Aulinger's candidates as we know them from contemporaneous portraiture, we need to reidentify the former. We have already identified the first prince as Duke Wilhelm IV. We can also include the duke's brother Ludwig in the group, but he is not the third prince, as Aulinger suggests, but the fourth from the left, who is bearded and looks middle-aged. Hans Wertinger's portrait of the duke (1516, Bayerisches Nationalmuseum in Munich), with his bushy beard, thick moustaches, and rather blank stare, suggests a similarity to Breu's figure. We can identify the powerfully built prince next to Wilhelm as Count-Palatine Ottheinrich. We know from Barthel Beham's portrait of 1535 that Ottheinrich was a large, hefty man.[126] The strikingly large head of Breu's figure seems very similar to Ottheinrich's characteristically massive head as portrayed by Beham. Breu's prince is, however, unbearded, whereas some likenesses of the Count-Palatine around 1530 show him sporting a beard.[127] However, two medallions from ca. 1520 portray Ottheinrich as beardless, and here too, the characteristically large head seems similar to that of Breu's figure.[128] The third prince can be identified as Ott-

---

[123] Painting by Hans Wertinger of Ludwig X of Bavaria, 1516, Munich, Bayerisches Nationalmuseum.

[24] See the painting of Philip by Hans Krell, reproduced in H. Nihi, *Karl V*, Reinbeck, 112 and the engraving of ca. 1630 by Johann Dürr, reproduced in *Welt im Umbruch*, 1: 179–80.

[125] This portrait appears on a wing of Cranach's triptych in the chapel of St. George in the Meißen cathedral; reproduced in *Das Jahrhundert der Reformation in Sachsen*, ed. H. Junghans (Berlin: Evangelische Verlagsanstalt, 1989), fig.2.

[126] In the Alte Pinakothek, Munich, inv. no. 5316; reproduced in Reitzenstein, *Ottheinrich*.

[127] Medallion of Ottheinrich and his brother Philip by Matthes Gebel, 1528, and a portrait tapestry of 1533, both illustrated in Reitzenstein, *Ottheinrich*, 35 and 120 respectively.

[128] One by Hans Schwarz, another by Hans Daucher, both illustrated in Reitzenstein, *Ottheinrich*, frontispiece and 77 respectively.

heinrich's brother Count-Palatine Philip. The slim face and straight, bluntly cut hair of Breu's figure seem identical to Philip's likeness as it appears in Daucher's medallion of 1522[129] and Baldung Grien's early portrait of him in 1517.[130]

The identification of Breu's princes, from left to right as Wilhelm IV, Ottheinrich, Philip, and Ludwig X is not only physiognomically plausible, it also makes sense ideologically and historically. Aulinger's constellation did not make sense confessionally, genealogically, or functionally. The four princes as we have identified them were related to one another. The brothers Ottheinrich and Philip were first cousins to the brothers Ludwig and Wilhelm. A few months prior to the Augsburg adventus, in October 1529, Ottheinrich married Ludwig and Wilhelm's sister, Susanna, thus also making him their brother-in-law.[131] In addition, pamphlet 1179 and Sender[132] both mention that the retinues of Ludwig and Wilhelm were followed by those of Ottheinrich and Philip. This indicates that the close ancestral relation between these two pair of brothers determined the order of procession of their retinues, and, one would conclude, of their own persons as well.

After the four princes comes Elector John the Steadfast (plate 8). He is portrayed here in his function as supreme marshal of the empire, a position that allowed him to carry the drawn sword of the empire before the emperor. Sender and "Sturm"[133] report that he was flanked by Elector Joachim of Brandenburg and by Ottheinrich, who processed in the stead of another cousin, Elector Ludwig. In Breu's rendition, however, Joachim has been eliminated and Ottheinrich moved up with his brother and cousins. In the woodcut, John processes accompanied only by four Landsknechten and an imperial herald.

The next sheet in Breu's series depicts, from left to right, Ferdinand, Charles, possibly Count-Palatine Friedrich, and Cardinal Campeggio (plate 9). I have based my identification of the third man

---

[129] Reitzenstein, *Ottheinrich*, 77.

[130] *Alte Pinakothek*, 42, illustrated, 263. The striking similarities between Breu's figures of the Palatine brothers and other art works of earlier date raise the possibility that the artist might have had access to at least the medallions and used these as the basis for the portraits.

[131] H. and M. Rall, *Die Wittelsbacher in Lebensbilder* (Regensburg: Friedrich Pustet Verlag, 1986), 237.

[132] 1179, Aii v; Sender, *Chronik*, 275.

[133] Sender, *Chronik*, 275; "Sturm," 68.

as Friedrich on a medallion, possibly by Daucher, from ca. 1515, which portrays the Count-Palatine.[134] The slightly wavy hair and prominent nose are the same on the medallion and in the woodcut. Even the hat with the lozenge-shaped decoration on the underside of the brim is similar. He bears somewhat of a resemblance to Breu's Count-Palatine Philip as portrayed on the princes' sheet. And indeed, Friedrich was Philip and Ottheinrich's uncle. The two brothers ruled the palatinate Neuburg under Friedrich's regency from 1505 to 1523.[135] Campeggio is identifiable by his cardinal's hat.

Breu's depiction of Charles agrees with the written sources insofar as he wears a light colored brocaded tunic, a small black hat, and is mounted on a white horse. Ferdinand's dress at the Augsburg adventus is not recorded in the sources, but "Sturm" describes him as he appeared at the Munich adventus just five days earlier as dressed more expensively and ostentatiously than his brother the emperor.[136] Sender describes Ferdinand's appearance on November 23, 1530 as he left Augsburg wearing "a black velvet tunic and a small gold chain around his neck,"[137] a description that exactly fits Breu's depiction.

In the woodcut, the four men ride abreast of one another. Closest to the viewer is Ferdinand, seen in strict profile. He seems oblivious to all that happens around him; his face is composed, his eyes directed straight ahead. He sits straight on his horse and grasps his baton. Next to him rides his brother, Charles V. The emperor is speaking to Friedrich, the man on his left. Charles's mouth is open and he gestures with his left hand, his index finger outstretched, clearly making a point. Friedrich is turned toward Charles, listening. He stretches his hand out with the palm towards Charles as if to underline his reception of the emperor's words. Campeggio observes the discussion; he is turned toward the two men but is not included in their conversation.

This configuration of these four men riding together is found nowhere in the texts. Charles, we remember, was described as riding alone beneath first a civic and then an ecclesiastical baldachin. As for the other men, Pamphlet 1179 has Ferdinand riding in front of

---

[134] Reproduced in Reitzenstein, *Ottheinrich*, 35.
[135] Rall, *Die Wittelsbacher*, 237.
[136] "Sturm," 64.
[137] Sender, *Chronik*, 327: "ain schwarz samatin rock und ain klaines guldin kethelin am hals."

Charles with the princes, and pamphlet 1178, Sender, and "Sturm" have Ferdinand and Campeggio riding directly behind Charles. Count-Palatine Friedrich is mentioned only at the initial stage of adventus at the Lech bridge. Here he acts as Charles's interpreter and thanks the greeting committee for their welcome:

> After this speech, the emperor, king and Count-Palatine Friedrich withdrew and discussed how and in what form he would thank the princes. Thereafter, Friedrich very politely thanked the princes in the name of the emperor with a nice short speech.[138]

However, according to the texts, this conversation did not take place on horseback during the procession, and not in the presence of Campeggio, who, according to pamphlet 1179, was absent at that moment. We should recall at this point "Sturm's" report of the bickering that went on during the adventus between the princes, who wanted Charles to ride alone, and Campeggio and Ferdinand, who wanted to ride next to him. The discrepancies in the textual sources mentioned above as to where exactly Ferdinand, Charles, and Campeggio were placed in the procession, and in what combination, underlines both how important and contested spatial proximity to the emperor was, and how the sources are anything but reliable on all counts and instead seem to follow their own agendas in constructing the procession.

As mentioned earlier, Breu's woodcut procession would then draw to a close with the two groups of lancers (plates 10–11).

Here we must ask ourselves: out of the many groups that processed into Augsburg on June 15, 1530, why were specific groups chosen for representation? And how did their presence function? Let us briefly review the procession from the beginning. The crossbowmen and lancers must have been meant to indicate Charles's military might and thus his power within the empire. The lancers at the end of the procession must have functioned similarly to articulate his brother Ferdinand's power. Also connected with Charles were the Spanish knights of the Orders of Santiago and Calatrava. As king of Spain, Charles was head of both orders. It is interesting to note,

---

[138] Sender, *Chronik*, 263: "Nach dieser oration [the welcome speech held by the Archbishop of Mainz] ist der kaiser und kinig mit Pfalzgraff Friedrichen auff ain ort tretten und [hat] sich beratschlagt, wie und was gestalt er den fürsten dank sagen well. Darnach hat Pfalzgraff Friderich in namen des kaisers den fürsten mit ainer kurtzen zierlichen red danck gesagt gantz hofflich." This is also described in 1178, Aiii r; not mentioned in "Sturm" or 1179.

however, that certain key elements of modern militia are either absent from or de-emphasized in the procession as depicted by Breu. The Landsknechten, who comprise the nonaristocratic infantry, are literally marginalized in the woodcuts, functioning more as framing devices than as significant members of a fighting force. Firearms are nowhere represented. Maximilian's *Triumphal Procession* included depictions of both these military resources that, as we discussed in chapter 3, were fundamentally changing the theories and practices of warfare. In Breu's woodcuts, Charles's and Ferdinand's armies are made up of either aristocratic knights or men of high military rank, all on horseback, and all armed with conventional weapons. Thus, the plebeian and unchivalrous elements (infantry and firearms) of warfare are erased or marginalized. Their displacement is a way of articulating claims to the nobility and to the traditional values and techniques of the Habsburg army.

The page boys and the court chamberlains certainly added a ceremonious touch with their splendid costumes and fine horses. They become signifiers of the wealth and magnificence of Charles's court.

Here we have reached the sheet with the four princes. This sheet and the one depicting Charles and others are key to the hypothetical identification of the series' patron(s). If we compare these four princes with any of the other eight sheets (excluding for a moment the one depicting John of Saxony), we immediately notice a formal difference. All the other groups portrayed, whether soldiers or aristocrats, are characterized by movement and interaction. In each one of these groups, some men turn toward each other and converse, some look back, some bend forward. This various multidirectional movement creates an atmosphere of spontaneity, thus enlivening the woodcut figures and making their procession seem more lifelike. In contrast to these informal groups, however, the princes process in frozen seriousness. They do not interact with one another but stare determinedly ahead, motionless, emotionless. As we have already noted, each of their faces is detailed, characteristic, and distinct. By these formal means, of creating careful likenesses, and of creating an atmosphere of solemnity and majesty specifically around these figures, Breu has highlighted the presence of these four princes.

The importance of the Wittelsbach princes is again emphasized by the presence of Count-Palatine Friedrich at the side of the emperor. We have already seen how the proximity to Charles was jealously guarded and vehemently contested. We have also seen from the texts that Friedrich did not ride alongside Charles, and yet Breu has depicted him as doing so. In light of these two sheets—one depicting the solemn portraits of the two pairs of brothers, and the other depicting Friedrich as Charles's left-hand man—we can hypothesize that Breu's series was commissioned by one of these Wittelsbach princes to celebrate the family's participation in the procession here portrayed as especially glorious. The lack of civic and ecclesiastical baldachins also acts to remove the event from its specific locality (in the city of Augsburg), thus opening the image up to the possibility of an interpretation fixed more on Wittelsbach and Habsburg than on its Augsburg context.

Two different but not necessarily mutually exclusive political identities are fashioned by Breu's adventus woodcuts. Glorification of the Wittelsbachs has been subtly blended with pro-Habsburg propaganda in the woodcut series. Charles's breach of protocol and adjacent placement of Ferdinand and Campeggio is here faithfully recorded, with the slight alteration of the insertion of Count-Palatine Friedrich as an integral component of this highest constellation of power. And the Wittelsbach princes prominently take their place among the other loyal Habsburg subjects as embodied by the knights, Landsknechten and chamberlains. By their prominence and key positions in the procession, the Wittelsbach princes are depicted as important members of the imperial hierarchy but also as faithful and loyal subjects of Charles. The prints can thus be read as a celebration both of Charles's power and of Wittelsbach loyalty.

In fact, the Wittelsbach princes had recently served Charles well. Friedrich and Philip (along with the chamberlain Wilhelm von Roggendorf) had been active in repelling the Turkish attack of Vienna in 1529.[139] And Philip had been the only German prince at Charles's imperial coronation in Bologna, where he had carried the sword of the empire before Charles.[140]

Nevertheless, the projection of the Wittelsbach princes as devoted subjects of Habsburg is at first extremely surprising in light of the fact that Wilhelm was at this very time actively contesting Ferdinand's efforts to be elected Roman king. This seemingly fundamental contradiction between political image and political reality, however, probably provided the motivation for the commission. Breu's

---

[139] Reitzenstein, *Ottheinrich*, 114.
[140] Ibid., 115.

woodcut provides a smoke screen of loyalty with which to obscure Wilhelm's intrigues, in a manner similar to Schäufelein's woodcut of Charles's 1530 Munich adventus. The image projected an uncomplicated, harmonious relationship between the emperor and his subjects, although we know that in reality this was not the case. Nevertheless, this projection and the image's positive presentation of the Habsburg court would have been pleasing to those princes and factions supporting the Habsburgs as well as members of court. Presumably, this would have been the audience for Breu's woodcut series and may have even included Ferdinand and Charles as well as Wittelsbach family members.

That the Wittelsbachs commissioned Breu to produce this image seems logical. We know that Breu was already working for Wilhelm IV at this time, which makes the duke an obvious choice for the patron. We also know that in the 1530s, Wilhelm sent some of his artists to his cousin Ottheinrich, who was building his residence in Neuburg.[141] This circulation indicates that certain artists were patronized simultaneously by different members of the Wittelsbach family. Breu the Younger in fact did work for Ottheinrich in 1536–37 (just at the time of Breu the Elder's death)[142] so that an active, ongoing patronage relationship between the Wittelsbach and the Breu families seems very likely.

As much as the woodcut series seems to assert Habsburg authority, it also seems in other ways to contest it. If we ask ourselves now not what has been represented but how it has been done so, and not who has been included but who has been left out, we become aware of a subtle anti-Habsburg slant. This would have served an audience of insiders who might have been privy to Wittelsbach plans to contest Habsburg hegemony in the German territories, thus even serving to justify those plans.[143]

Let us again review the procession with the question of how groups have been represented in mind. The representation of Charles's and Ferdinand's military might—the four groups of soldiers—is actually very limited. If we compare Breu's adventus to Maximilian's *Triumphal Procession*, we notice that to Breu's four sheets of soldiers

---

[141] Hans Rott, *Ottheinrich und die Kunst*, Mitteilungen zur Geschichte des Heidelberger Schloßes (Heidelberg: C. Winter Verlag, 1905), 19.

[142] Ibid., 15–16, 184–85, and 189–90.

[143] Ottheinrich later became a Protestant, but not until the early 1540s (Reitzenstein, *Ottheinrich*, 154).

are twenty-five of Maximilian's, including the scores of tournament knights. The pamphlets and chronicles that recorded the 1530 Augsburg adventus agree on the large number of knights and soldiers who took part in the procession. This military presence, however, is represented only minimally in Breu's version.

Charles's Spanish knights also belonged to the emperor's entourage. Yet in order to pay back his still outstanding election debt to the Fuggers, Charles was forced to lease out the administration of these orders' extensive and profitable landholdings to Augsburg merchants.[144] Previously leased to the Fuggers, the administration was leased to Bartholomäus Welser's company from 1533 to 1538; the negotiations for this new contract were worked out during the Augsburg Diet in October 1530.[245]

The court chamberlains and the pages have been represented in almost overwhelming pomp, especially in comparison with the simple appearance of the emperor. We can perhaps perceive a critical note in the seemingly ridiculous overabundance of plumage and finery, and the possible negative commentary on the tack of von Rois's horse.

We have already discussed the representation of Breu's hypothetical patrons, the Wittelsbach princes. Here we can perceive no negative commentary from their solemn and stately procession, which again speaks for their identity as patrons. Instead, they in fact seem to have been depicted with singular seriousness and formality.

Skipping the image of John of Saxony again for a moment, let us move on the image of Charles and the others. Breu has hardly created a very flattering image of the newly crowned and anointed emperor. Breu's woodcut is like a botched press photograph. It is as if Charles has forgotten, as Ferdinand has not, to look at the camera and has been caught with his mouth open and his finger wagging instead of solemnly posing in stately grandeur. Breu seems to have been aware that his presentation of Charles was radically understated. As a hint to the viewer, the artist has placed a bareheaded Landsknecht (all others wear headgear) directly in front of Charles to identify him as the emperor. This act of reverence, however, is mini-

---

[144] Kellenbenz, *Maestrazgopacht*, 6.
[145] Ibid, 9–11.

mal. None of the other Landsknechten are taking any notice of Charles.

Especially in comparison to other triumphal imagery do we notice Breu's minimalist approach. Maximilian is seated in glory and splendor in Dürer's triumphal chariot, wearing the imperial crown, holding his scepter, crowned and surrounded by the personification of virtues.[146] This was undoubtedly Schäufelein's model when he created a composite woodcut of Charles's triumphal chariot in 1537.[147] Here Charles is seated in strict profile under an imperial baldachin, crowned by the figure of victory, holding the imperial insignia, surrounded by famous Habsburg relatives. The Latin inscription praises the emperor's deeds and asserts that he was unanimously elected by the German princes, an election wholeheartedly approved of by the German people.[148] Hogenberg's depiction of Charles's procession from the Bologna Cathedral as newly anointed emperor shows him riding beside the pope under an imperial baldachin, wearing the imperial crown and an elaborate cloak.[149] Breu's depiction of Charles displays none of this grandiose splendor, although the actual Augsburg adventus ceremony provided such scenes, such as Charles's procession under the red-green-white civic baldachin or under the white damask baldachin of the ecclesiastics. Even if one were to take into account the emperor's preference for simple fashion, as remarked on at the Munich adventus, compositional devices would have been available to the artist to highlight Charles's importance. For example, Breu could have depicted Charles as riding alone in severe and simple solemnity, in a pose of suitable majesty. But the artist has not taken advantage of such devices in his construction of the emperor's image. In fact, Breu's depiction of Charles has such a low profile that Strauss mistook Ferdinand for Charles and identified him as the emperor.

In terms of formal grandeur, the high point of Breu's procession is not the emperor, but the Protestant Elector John of Saxony. The only man to process alone without equals, he sits in calm dignity on his powerful horse, the sword of the empire resting over his shoulder. His face is seen in strict profile and framed by the broad brim of his

---

[146] Appuhn, *Triumphzug*, pl.122a–g.
[147] Strauss, *Woodcut*, 1031–41.
[148] Lhotsky, *Sonderausstellung Karl V*, 66–7, no. 152.
[149] Ibid., 57–8, no. 144.

plumed hat. He is accompanied by an imperial herald, who according to the texts, actually accompanied the person of the emperor. By moving the official, whose place was with the emperor, next to John, the position and importance of the Protestant elector is therefore increased and emphasized. The Landsknecht behind the elector's horse looks up at John with an expression of reverence, while another Landsknecht at John's side raises his hand in acclamation. Through manipulation of formal devices, Breu has invested the figure of John with greater majesty than the figures of either Charles or Ferdinand.

Associated with his emphasis on John is Breu's complete neglect of the ecclesiastic participants, other than Cardinal Campeggio. We know from the texts that archbishops preceded and followed Charles. But they are nowhere to be found in Breu's version. The only ecclesiastic depicted is Campeggio, of whom neither Charles, nor Friedrich nor Ferdinand take any notice.

Breu has also eliminated the presence of Joachim of Brandenburg, who according to the texts, rode next to John. The lack of another figure of similar rank formally allows the viewer to concentrate on John's majestic and noble appearance. The herald who accompanies him is visually almost obliterated by John's imposing frame. We can surmise that this elimination was motivated not only by formal but also by political considerations. Joachim, brother of Albrecht of Brandenburg, was strongly anti-Lutheran and entered into formal alliances with other Catholic princes, including the dukes of Bavaria, in their active attempts to quash the Reformation.[150] Clearly the presence of Joachim on this sheet would not necessarily have met with Wittelsbach disapproval.

So why then the emphasis on the Protestant elector John of Saxony and the erasing of the Catholic Joachim of Brandenburg? It might perhaps be tempting to read this as the result of the artist inserting his own evangelical sympathies into the picture. This certainly remains a possibility, but perhaps there might be another explanation as well, one that not necessarily completely supplants the first. Perhaps the primary intent of the print series was to build German aristocratic identity in opposition to the Habsburg threat to that group's ultimate authority and control of the German territories. The dividing line between "us" and "them" would therefore be drawn

---

[150] Junghans, *Reformation in Sachsen*, 53.

between the German princes on the one hand, and the Habsburg family on the other. In other words, the dividing line would not be drawn between confessional categories, between pro-Reformational and Catholic, but between national and foreign or international. In fact, the removal of the objectionable figure of Joachim (seen from an Evangelical perspective) and the heroizing of the figure of John might even have been a kind of conciliatory and inclusive gesture on the part of the Wittelsbachs to signal their willingness to overlook confessional difference in order to encourage aristocratic German community.

Fear of Habsburg intervention in and restriction of their ability to exercise power was in fact a powerful force unifying German princes no matter what their confession. That confessional identity was at times even regarded as secondary, and national identity as primary, is demonstrated by the fact that Wilhelm at one point even became a member of the Schmalkaldic League of Protestant princes in order to join in their opposition to Charles V. The duke became a member in 1531, just one year after the Augsburg Diet. Seen in this light, Breu's woodcuts perhaps might even have functioned as a cautious kind of advertising for Wilhelm's bid for power and perhaps even to make his membership in the Schmalkaldic League more credible. The Wittelsbachs are portrayed as powerful within the imperial hierarchy, but could even be read as a rival to Habsburg control by those so inclined. But Wittelsbach power would be inclusive, tolerant, and based on national versus confessional identity, seeming to ensure a place for all German princes. In this way, circulated to the right people, Breu's woodcut series could have been a powerful yet subtle tool for building crucial alliances needed by the Wittelsbachs in their bid for power.

Breu's woodcut adventus is an extremely complex series of images. To understand the significance of what was represented, how it was done so, and what was not represented, we had to sift through various layers. At the base was the antique and medieval tradition of adventus. Superimposed on this ceremonial tradition was the 1530 Augsburg adventus as described by the pamphlets and chronicles. At this level, changes of protocol indicated concerns arising from the specific historic situation of this particular adventus. Charles expressed his support for the contested Catholic Church and for Ferdinand by allowing Campeggio, the archbishops of Mainz and Cologne, and his brother, to process in his direct proximity. The reception which the city of Augsburg prepared for Charles's adventus seems to have gone smoothly, although it was decidedly low key compared to Charles's welcome in the Catholic city of Munich. Religious displays were kept at a minimum to prevent provocation of the evangelical factions visiting and resident in Augsburg.

Breu's woodcut series presents a second level of superimposition. This level is particularly complicated because of the conflicting signals available about the Wittelsbachs and the Habsburgs, as well as about the relationship between them. Contrary to the actual procession, the four Wittelsbach princes ride forward together in the woodcut as a solid unit characterized by a special solemnity. Another Wittelsbach prince occupies the most sanctified space of the whole procession: at the side of the emperor. This position of honor underlines Wittelsbach access to power. Yet his addition does not necessarily threaten Habsburg authority and its dynastic claims. The very person Wilhelm was attempting to oust, Ferdinand, is accorded a prominent place in the woodcut: at Charles's right hand and closest to the viewer. Wittelsbach princes are portrayed as participants in a procession comprised only of loyal elements. This projection of loyalty is similar to Wilhelm and Ludwig's dramatically staged welcome of Charles to Munich. The woodcuts as well as the fireworks must have been intended to detract attention from the Wittelsbach challenge of Habsburg hegemony by covering political intrigue with a spectacular show of consensus.

Breu's woodcuts depicting the 1530 Augsburg adventus of Charles V thus functioned in a stunning variety of ways. By accessing the discourse of the adventus ceremony, the series fashions a number of political subject positions for the viewers, which most likely included the Wittelsbachs (as patrons) and other German aristocrats who might have been recipients of the woodcuts. The Wittelsbach princes could have sent the series to virtually anyone they were trying to impress, the point being that the series allowed for different elements to be stressed. On one level, the woodcuts "document" Wittelsbach participation in the ceremony. This participation can be read both as Habsburg-loyal (and thus would be useful if the prints were given to those who expected the Wittelsbachs to support the Habsburgs, i.e., members of the court) as well as Habsburg-challenging (and thus useful for those viewers who were informed about Wilhelm's plans). The prints could also assure Protestant princes that the powerful Wittelsbachs were tolerant of confessional differences (when in fact

Wilhelm had several pro-Reformational citizens of his territories executed during the second half of the 1520s), or at least that these differences were not seen by them as a hindrance to German aristocratic community. The prints could thus function as an aid to the formation of alliances between the Wittelsbachs and other princes, as well as a reassurance that the Wittelsbachs were loyal subjects of the emperor whose splendid ceremony they helped to commemorate.

In the indeterminacy of its meaning, in its offering a spectrum of political subject positions oscillating between national and Habsburg, and in its negation of certain unpleasant facts about the patrons (here, Wittelsbach subversion), Breu's depiction of the 1530 adventus functions similarly to his depiction of the battle of Pavia discussed in chapter 3. In so doing, it also challenges our notions of how political art operates. Instead of works that are immediately knowable, the meaning of which is fixed, stable, and one-dimensional, Breu's art negotiates between competing and contradictory political interests to produce meanings and identities that are themselves complex, ambiguous, and multivalent.

CHAPTER FIVE

HISTORY

Thus far, we have been considering how certain works by Breu engaged particular discourses of warfare and ceremony in order to legitimate and substantiate a projected Habsburg hegemony. The works discussed were executed in different media (frescoes, and single and serial woodcuts) and aimed at a variety of audiences, ranging from general and widespread (for example, whoever happened to walk past the Augsburg city hall) to more exclusive and limited (for example, whoever could read the Latin inscription on the battle of Pavia woodcut). In fashioning imperial and proimperial identities, the works responded to particular historical circumstances and contexts, often asserting Habsburg control and dominance in the face of serious threats to that dominance. And yet, we have also seen that works ostensibly functioning as pro-Habsburg propaganda simultaneously offered alternative subject positions, allowing, for example, the embrace of specifically local and German (versus international and imperial) identities.

In this final chapter, I would like to turn to two further works by Breu that both clarify and complicate this book's main thesis. The works in question are two paintings completed by Breu in 1528 and ca. 1530 for Duke Wilhelm IV (Wittelsbach) of Bavaria. Analysis of these works allows us to add the medium of panel painting to our discussion as well as to add an audience somewhat more definitely circumscribed by courtly rituals and protocol. More significantly, these paintings are important examples of the kind of profoundly political and subtly ambiguous art we have been discussing so far. Like the other works analyzed here, these paintings also access a particular discourse, in this case history, in order to fashion political positions in the face of specific historical conditions. I will argue that these paintings were meant to challenge and undermine Habsburg authority by constructing narratives, based on Roman history, that sanction revolution and that offer alternative leadership. To consider these paintings, then, is to attend to the complicity between the production of history, art, and theories of state under the aegis of humanism in Early Modern Germany. The paintings also provide instructive examples of how complicated the relationships between art, history, power, and meaning can be.

Breu's work for Wilhelm also further complicates the artist/patron relationship. We have already noted Breu's general ambiguity about the Habsburgs and his distrust of and even disdain for institutions of authority throughout his city chronicle. Yet as his work evidences, Breu was nonetheless willing to work for the emperors and their supporters. But Breu was also willing to work for their challengers, in this case Wilhelm. This seems doubly surprising, as the artist makes several negative references to Wilhelm in his chronicle.

In three separate entries, Breu describes the Bavarian duke as arrogant, vengeful, and a persecutor of the common man. He relates how Wilhelm commanded his mounted troops to ride through the farmers' grainfields when the duke failed to find the evangelical preacher he had sought to capture in their village:

> As they [the duke and his men] were unable to accomplish anything, they rode with horse and wagon through the grain[fields] of the poor farmers. That was his [i.e., Wilhelm's] command, despite the fact that he had neither the power nor the right to forbid or to instigate anything; instead, he was like a brutal madman, he persecuted the people within and without his territory.[1]

The artist also describes how the duke condemned the daughter of an unskilled laborer to death because she was suspected of belonging to the Anabaptists. In Breu's narrative, the young woman's brave words, her unshakable faith in the face of death, and the great grief expressed by the crowd as it witnessed her execution, function to highlight Breu's reference to Wilhelm as "der löblich fürst (the praiseworthy prince)" as ironic, and to engage the reader's sympathies entirely with the woman as the victim of the duke's persecution.[2] Later, Wilhelm is mentioned as head of the Swabian League, and the goal of his current campaign, according to Breu, was "den armen leuten das ir abzuschlaifen und sie zu verderben (to make off with the possession of the poor and to ruin them)."[3] These references

---

[1] Breu, *Chronik*, 35–6: "da sie nichts konnten ausrichten, da zogen sie den armen paurn durch das traidt, wa es am höchsten, mit roß und wägen hindurch. das was sein bevelch, darzu er weder fueg noch recht etwas zu pieten oder zu schaffen hett, sunder war als ein wietrich, durchechtet das volck ausser und innerhalb seinem landt."

[2] Breu, *Chronik*, 42.

[3] Breu, *Chronik*, 46.

to Wilhelm are made in the years 1527, 1528, and 1529, respectively, in other words, at exactly the time when Breu was working for the duke.

The two panels that Breu painted for Wilhelm depict (1) the suicide of Lucretia and the oath of her kinsmen (plate 12), and (2) the victory of Publius Cornelius Scipio over Hannibal at the battle of Zama (plate 13); both are currently in the Alte Pinakothek in Munich.[4] The paintings are fairly large in scale: *Lucretia* measures 103.5 cm x 148.5 cm, *Battle of Zama* 162 cm x 120.8 cm. (both have been trimmed to dimensions somewhat smaller than their original format seems to have been intended).[5] Breu signed and dated the Lucretia panel; above the cornice, in the right half of the painting, appears the date 1528 and Breu's monogram. Directly below the date is a tablet bearing the inscription "HOC OPVS FeCIT IEGRIVS PREW DE AVG" ("this work was made by Jörg Breu of Augsburg"). *Battle of Zama* is also signed twice; on a signpost that has fallen over and which is rendered in carefully perspectival view, the artist has written his name, "IORG PREW," and on a stone directly beneath the signpost appears his monogram. No date is found on the painting, but art historians have estimated that it was produced around 1530.[6]

Unfortunately, no contracts or records of payments for the paintings are known to exist. The provenance of the paintings is relatively straightforward, however. Both panels display Wilhelm's coat of

---

[4] Inventory Number 7969 and 8 respectively; Gisela Goldberg and Christian zu Salm, *Altdeutsche Malerei*, 202–11, especially 207–9; and Gisela Goldberg, *Die Alexanderschlacht*, especially 18–25.

[5] G. Goldberg, *Die Alexanderschlacht*, 20 and 25; see also Gisela Goldberg, "Die ursprüngliche Inschrifttafel der *Alexanderschlacht* Albrecht Altdorfers," *Münchner Jahrbuch der bildenden Kunst* 19, 3. Folge (1968): 121–26.

[6] See previous note 4. Volkmar Greiselmayer has suggested that the painting is to be dated in or after 1535 because of similarities he sees between Breu's depiction of the town of Naragarra in the Munich painting, and the view of Tunis appearing in Erhard Schön's 1535 woodcut of the conquest of Tunis by Charles V. I, however, am not struck by any particularly emphatic similarity: Breu's fortress appears on a large hill, not found in Schön; Breu's city gates are round whereas Schön's are square; Breu's city is accessible through many gates whereas Schön's appears to have only one. To my knowledge, Greiselmayer's suggestion has not been taken up by any other art historians. See Volkmar Greiselmayer, "Die Historienbilder Herzog Wilhelms IV von Bayern und seiner Gemahlin Jacobäa: Versuch einer Interpretation," 6 vols. (Habilitationsschrift, Universität Erlangen, 1991) 1: 174.

arms, thus indicating ducal patronage, and both are mentioned in an inventory taken in 1598 of the ducal art collection.[7]

On the basis of the dimensions, the inclusion of Wilhelm's coat of arms, and the inventory, we know that Breu's paintings were actually part of a large cycle of sixteen history paintings executed by different artists between 1528 and 1540. In addition to Breu, Hans Burgkmair (Augsburg, 1473–1531), Barthel Beham (Nuremberg, 1502–40), Albrecht Altdorfer (Regensburg, ca. 1480–1538), Abraham Schöpfer (Munich, fl. 1533), Hans Schöpfer (Munich, ca. 1505–ca. 1566), Ludwig Refinger (Munich, ca. 1510–ca. 1549) and Melchior Feselen (Ingolstadt, ca. 1495–1538) contributed paintings. The cycle depicts scenes from the lives of eight virtuous women from the Jewish Bible, Roman history, and legends of the saints (in paintings executed in horizontal format) and eight virtuous men from Greek and Roman history (in vertical format).[8]

In its recourse to certain iconographic and literary traditions, as well as in the sheer monumentality of its scale, Wilhelm's history

---

[7] In the Lucretia panel, Wilhelm's coat of arms is suspended from the left arch separating the fore- from the middle ground; his wife Jacobäa's hangs from the right arch. In the battle panel, Wilhelm's coat of arms appears in the bottom right foreground on a tablet set into the ground. The 1598 inventory of the ducal art collection was undertaken by Johann Fickler (referred to as the "Ficklersches Inventar"): Staatsbibliothek Munich, Cod. germ. 2133.

[8] In chronological order, the paintings belonging to the cycle are: 1528: Hans Burgkmair, *Esther and Ahasver* (dated and signed, no coat of arms), Munich, Alte Pinakothek, Inv. Nr. 689; Jörg Breu, *Lucretia* (dated and signed, coats of arms of Wilhelm and Jacobäa), Munich, Inv. Nr. 1969; 1529: Melchior Feselen, *Cloelia* (dated and signed, coats of arms of Wilhelm and Jacobäa), Munich, Inv. Nr. 13; Albrecht Altdorfer, *Alexander and Darius* (dated and signed, no coats of arms), Munich, Inv. Nr. 688; Hans Burgkmair, *Victory of Hannibal at Cannae* (dated and signed, no coats of arms), Munich, Inv. Nr. 5328; 1530: Barthel Beham, *Empress Helena and the Finding of the True Cross* (dated and signed, coats of arms of Wilhelm and Jacobäa), Munich, Inv. Nr. 684; ca. 1530: Jörg Breu, *Battle of Zama* (signed, undated, Wilhelm's coat of arms), Munich, Inv. Nr. 8; 1533: Abraham Schöpfer, *Mucius Scaevola* (signed and dated, no coat of arms), Stockholm, National Museum, Inv. Nr. 295; Melchior Feselen, *Caesar Lays Siege to Alesia* (signed and dated; coats of arms of Wilhelm and Jacobäa), Munich, Inv. Nr. 686; 1535: Hans Schöpfer, *Virginia* (signed and dated, coats of arms of Wilhelm and Jacobäa), Munich, Inv. Nr. 13099; 1537: Hans Schöpfer, *Susanna and the Elders*, (unsigned, dated, coats of arms of Wilhelm and Jacobäa), Munich, Inv. Nr. 7775; Ludwig Refinger, *Horatius Cocles* (signed [signature may be later addition] and dated, coats of arms of Wilhelm and Jacobäa), Stockholm, National Museum, Inv. Nr. NM 294; 1540: Ludwig Refinger, *Marcus Curtius* (unsigned, dated, coats of arms of Wilhelm and Jacobäa), Munich, Inv. Nr. 687; ca. 1540: Ludwig Refinger, *Titus Manlius Torquatus* (unsigned, undated, coats of arms of Wilhelm and Jacobäa), Stockholm, National Museum, Inv. Nr. NM 296; lost: *Queen of Sheba*; *Judith*. There is, however, no complete consensus about the exact composi-

cycle constitutes one of the major monuments of humanist culture in Early Modern Europe. Its inclusion of famous men from classical antiquity places the cycle within the *uomini famosi* tradition, which has its Early Modern beginnings in Petrarch's (1304–1374) text *De viris illustribus*.[9] Characteristic of humanist intellectual enterprises especially south of the Alps, Petrarch's text revisits the sources of classical antiquity in order to present ancient heroes as examples for modern scrutiny. In his preface, Petrarch plainly states: "For, unless I am mistaken, this is the profitable goal for the historian: to point up to the readers those things that are to be followed and those to be avoided, with plenty of distinguished examples provided on either side."[10] Such an endeavor, whereby ancient events, conditions and personages are intellectually and textually constructed as relevant for contemporary times as examples of actions and behavior either to emulate or eschew, points to the cyclical and exemplary view of history undergirding the production of humanist culture.[11] This assumption about history will also be of fundamental importance for deciphering the political message of Wilhelm's history cycle.

South of the Alps, Petrarch's textual catalogue of famous men was translated into the fresco medium. Throughout the second half of the fourteenth century, the walls of the Carrara palace in Padua were decorated with frescoes depicting men and scenes from their lives as described by Petrarch.[12] Fresco cycles by Giotto for King

---

tion of the cycle. Eschenburg ("Altdorfers *Alexanderschlacht*," 58) doubts that the 1540 depiction of Marcus Curtius by Ludwig Refinger belonged to the original conception of the cycle. The Munich catalogue of 1963 includes two further paintings which have been suggested to belong to the cycle (Jörg Breu the Younger, *Queen Artemesia Conquers Rhodes*; and an anonymous Netherlandish/Northwest German painting depicting Judith and Holofernes) but which the authors assess as dubious: Goldberg and Salm, *Altdeutsche Malerei*, 204, 210 and 214–15.

[9] On Petrarch and humanism, see Nicholas Mann, *Petrarch* (Oxford: Oxford University Press, 1984). See also Charles Nauert, Jr., "The Birth of Humanist Culture" in *Humanism and the Culture of Renaissance Europe* (Cambridge: Cambridge University Press, 1995), 8–51.

[10] Benjamin Kohl, "Petrarch's Prefaces to *De viris illustribus*," *History and Theory* 13 (1974): 132–44.

[11] Ernst Breisach, *Historiography: Ancient, Medieval and Modern*, 2nd ed. (Chicago: University of Chicago Press, 1994), 153–62.

[12] Annegrit Schmitt, "Der Einfluß des Humanismus auf die Bildprogramme fürstliche Residenzen" in *Höfischer Humanismus*, ed. August Buck, Deutsche Forschungsgemeinschaft, Mitteilung XVI der Kommission für Humanismusforschung (Weinheim: VCH Verlagsgesellschaft mbH, 1989), 215–57; here 219–27. See also Theodor Mommsen, "Petrarch and the Decoration of the *Sala Virorum Illustrium* in Padua," *Art Bulletin* 34 (1952): 95–116.

Robert of Anjou in Naples (ca. 1330) and by Andrea Castagno for the Carducci family in Legnaia (ca. 1450), among others, were similarly influenced by this return to classical antiquity as a source for moral and political models characteristic of humanist cultural production.[13] Such cycles participated in a project of representing famous men and thus, of imparting prestige to those who owned the walls graced by such depictions by indicating the patrons' learning, economic welfare, and social status, and by implying the patrons' similarity to their chosen heroes.

Women were sometimes included within these fresco cycles, as we know from the literary references to Giotto's cycle in Naples and from the still extant frescoes by Castagno in Legnaia. Depictions of famous women, however, do not seem to be rooted as much in the *uomini famosi* tradition (for obvious reasons) as in the medieval tradition of the Nine Worthies, which celebrated three pagan, three Jewish and three Christian women along with their nine male counterparts.[14] In 1519, Hans Burgkmair produced a woodcut series illustrating the Nine Worthies.[15] In addition, catalogues of women such as Boccaccio's *De clara mulieris* (1371) and Christine de Pisan's *Le Livre de la cité des dames* (1405) described historic and legendary women and their lives and deeds.[16]

In illustrating the deeds of eight famous men and eight famous women, Wilhelm's cycle thus clearly partakes of both humanist and medieval traditions. Yet not one of these texts or pictorial cycles provides the exact model for the duke's paintings. Only six of the famous men of Petrarch's text appear in the paintings (Alexander, Hannibal, Scipio, Caesar, Horatius Cocles, and Titus Manlius Torquatus), only five of the nine female worthies (Lucretia, Esther, Helena, Virginia, and Judith) and only two of the nine male worthies (Alexander and Caesar).[17] In addition, Wilhelm's cycle differs from

---

13 Christiane Joost-Gaugier, "Giotto's Hero Cycle in Naples: A Prototype of *donne illustri* and a Possible Literary Connection," *Zeitschrift für Kunstgeschichte* 43 (1980): 311–18; C. Joost-Gaugier, "A Rediscovered Series of *uomini famose* from Quattrocento Venice," *The Art Bulletin* 58 (1976): 184–95; and her "Castagno's Humanistic Program at Legnaia and its Possible Inventor," *Zeitschrift für Kunstgeschichte* 45 (1982): 274–82.

14 B. Eschenburg, "Altdorfers *Alexanderschlacht*," 56.

15 Burgkmair's woodcut series illustrating the nine worthies was made between 1516 and 1519; see Strauss, 2: 440–45.

16 Glenda McLeod, *Virtue and Venom: Catalogs of Women from Antiquity to the Renaissance* (Ann Arbor: University of Michigan Press, 1991).

17 Eschenburg has pointed this out, "Altdorfers *Alexanderschlacht*," 56.

previous illustrations of these figures, which usually feature the individual standing in an undifferentiated space, in the narrative detail and breadth in which each of the figures is embedded. The fact that there is no complete agreement between textual and visual sources, on the one hand, and the duke's paintings, on the other, indicates that although Wilhelm's cycle was inspired in a general way by the *uomini famosi* and the Nine Worthies traditions, its composition responded to particular issues or interests of a more local and specific character and thus needs to be read within the defined context of Wilhelm's court and his politics. The cycle is also singular in that, to my knowledge, no other art work of similar humanist character and of comparable breadth existed in Germany before or during Wilhelm's lifetime.

The importance of the Munich history cycle thus makes the paucity of literature on it all the more surprising. Several interrelated factors may aid in explaining this fact. As a whole, the sixteenth-century Catholic dukes of Bavaria have not received widespread attention (Wilhelm IV, reigned 1508–50; Albrecht V, 1550–79; Wilhelm V, 1579–97, died 1626). In traditional historiography conceptualizing the sixteenth century primarily as a titanic struggle resulting in the birth and consolidation of Protestantism, Wilhelm and his successors were simply on the wrong side of the confessional divide.[18] Seen in relation to the European-wide stage upon which the drama of Protestantism was acted out, the unswervingly Catholic Wittelsbach dukes remained minor actors on a provincial scale.

In addition, Wilhelm in particular seems to have failed to capture a sustained degree of historical interest. In terms of art patronage, he is overshadowed by his son and successor, Duke Albrecht V, who exhibited a taste for more classical and Italianate art.[19] Thus, Albrecht's patronage and artistic preference coincided with an aes-

---

[18] Thomas A. Brady, "Some Peculiarities of German Histories in the Early Modern Era," in *Germania Illustrata: Essays on Early Modern Germany Presented to Gerald Strauss*, ed. Andrew Fix and Susan Karant-Nunn, Sixteenth Century Essays and Studies, Volume 18 (Kirksville: Sixteenth Century Journal Publishers, 1992), 197–216, here 199–200.

[19] Otto Hartig's article "Die Kunsttätigkeit in München unter Wilhelm IV und Albrecht V 1520–1579" (*Münchner Jahrbuch der bildenden Kunst* 1933, NF, 147–225), for example, is mostly concerned with Albrecht's patronage. His discussion of Wilhelm encompasses twenty-two pages; Albrecht, in contrast, is discussed in the remaining fifty-five pages. This discrepancy is of course also due to the apparent increase in art patronage during Albrecht's reign, thus making him understandably the preferred object of art historical research.

thetic paradigm accepted by later art historians that privileged an Italian High Renaissance style (based on the reiteration of classicism) over a German late-medieval one. Furthermore, the prominence that Wilhelm's great-grandson, Kurfürst (Electoral Duke) Maximilian I (1597–1651) achieved in German politics and the international movement of the Counter Reformation at the turn of the century and beyond also served to detract attention from his less glamorous relative.[20] If historians of Bavaria sought a figure who epitomized the Duchy's transcendence from a backwater province to a player on the worldstage, it was Elector Maximilian I who fit the bill, not Duke Wilhelm IV.

Indeed, Wilhelm's reign seems to have been rather unremarkable. His contributions to history seem to have remained solidly on the local level: keeping any form of confessional alternatives to Catholicism from taking root inside his territory, and regaining power from the begrudging hands of his estates.[21] Perhaps his unsuccessful challenge to Habsburg hegemony was even viewed by subsequent historians with embarrassment, smacking as it might of conspiracy and disloyalty, and proving another reason for consideration of his reign in anything other than a purely perfunctory mode. To date, no systematic or critical appraisal of his reign has been produced.[22]

As Wilhelm paled in comparison to such contemporaneous princely patrons as Alfonso d'Este, Federigo Gonzaga, and Cosimo I de' Medici, in terms of both the amount of the work commissioned and its dominant aesthetic, so has his history cycle languished in art historical literature. Attempts to treat the cycle as a whole are, perhaps understandably, rare.[23] The extended period of construction

[20] See, for example Hubert Glaser, ed., *Um Glauben und Reich: Kurfürst Maximilian I; Beiträge zur Bayerischen Geschichte und Kunst 1573–1657*, Wittelsbach und Bayern, vol. 2, 2 vols., (Munich: Hirmer Verlag and Piper Verlag, 1980).
[21] Gerald Strauss, "The Religious Policies of Dukes Wilhelm and Ludwig of Bavaria in the First Decade of the Protestant Era," *Church History* 28 (1959): 350–73.
[22] The best source of information on Wilhelm are the following entries found in vol. 2 of Andreas Kraus, ed., *Handbuch der bayerischen Geschichte* 2nd ed., (Munich: C. H. Beck'sche Verlagsbuchhandlung, 1988): Heinrich Lutz and Walter Ziegler, "Das konfessionelle Zeitalter: Die Herzöge Wilhelm IV und Albrecht V," 324–92; Dieter Albrecht, "Staat und Gesellschaft 1500–1745," 625–63; and idem, "Die kirchlich-religiöse Entwicklung 1500–1574," 702–35.
[23] Greiselmayer, Eschenburg, and Goldberg are the exceptions, although Eschenburg and Goldberg's work intimates a hermeneutic privileging of Altdorfer's work already in their titles respectively: "Altdorfers *Alexanderschlacht* und ihr Verhältnis zum Historienzyklus Wilhelms IV" and *Die Alexanderschlacht und die Historienbilder Herzog Wilhelms IV.*

(thirteen years) and the number of artists involved (eight) makes such an undertaking extremely complex, although the uncanonical status of most of the artists, and indeed of the patron, has no doubt also discouraged sustained analysis. Most attention has been focused on Albrecht Altdorfer's contribution to the cycle, the *Victory of Alexander over Darius at the Battle of Issus* from 1529, a work that is often even included in art history survey textbooks in the unfailingly thin sections on sixteenth-century German art.[24] Altdorfer's construction of landscape on a cosmic scale and his spiritual and aesthetic affinities with Romanticism and Modern art (in particular, German Expressionism) have been especially singled out for praise.[25] In most instances, Altdorfer's painting is considered in splendid isolation from its fifteen other companion pieces, based on the assumption that it either metonymically stands in for the entire cycle, or that its perceived aesthetic predominance merits exclusive focus.

In all accounts, however, scant attention is paid to Breu's two paintings. Almost without exception, they are perfunctorily described in terms of their subject matter, if mentioned at all.[26] Yet it seems clear that Breu's paintings belong to a crucial moment in the cycle's production, namely the first phase of work; within the first three years, that is between 1528 and 1530, almost an entire half of the cycle (seven paintings) was produced. In contrast, the next seven paintings were produced over a period of ten years, with several years' interruption in between (the remaining two paintings belonging to the cycle according to the 1598 inventory are now lost and their dates are unknown, thus making it impossible to assign them a place within the production phases of the cycle). The paintings produced within this first phase, in roughly chronological order, are as

---

[24] Horst de la Croix et al., *Gardner's Art Through the Ages*, 9th ed. (Chicago: Harcourt Brace Jovanovich, 1991), 722–23; "This sudden opening up of space, with its subordination of the human figure to the cosmic landscape, bespeaks a new view of nature–a view that will see human beings as insignificant notes in an infinite universe. . . . In this first vision of the immense space and power of the cosmos, Altdorfer seems to suggest a theme that all subsequent philosophers, scientists and churchmen, as well as artists, will confront–the insignificance of human life." (722); Frederick Hartt, *Art: A History of Painting, Sculpture, Architecture*, 4th ed., vol. 2 (New York: Harry N. Abrams, Inc, 1993), 743, 745–46.

[25] For bibliography, see Eschenburg, "Altdorfers *Alexanderschlacht*," 36 n. 1; and Goldberg and Salm, *Altdeutsche Malerei*, 206; and recently, Christopher Wood, *Albrecht Altdorfer and the Origins of Landscape* (Chicago: University of Chicago Press, 1993), esp. 19–23 and 201–2.

[26] The exception to this is Greiselmayer; his arguments will be discussed below.

follows: (1) Jörg Breu, *Lucretia*, 1528; (2) Hans Burgkmair, *Esther and Ahasver*, 1528; (3) Albrecht Altdorfer, *Victory of Alexander over Darius at the Battle of Issus*, 1529; (4) Hans Burgkmair, *Victory of Hannibal over the Romans at Cannae*, 1529; (5) Melchior Feselen, *Cloelia*, 1529; (6) Barthel Beham, *Empress Helena and the Finding of the True Cross*, 1530; (7) Jörg Breu, *Victory of Scipio over Hannibal at the Battle of Zama*, ca. 1530.

The inclusion of Breu's paintings within this first phase of production is significant on a number of counts. First, it demonstrates that Breu's work is most likely informed by the original conception of the cycle and thus by the context of events and situations around 1528–1530. Second, it indicates that Breu's participation was sought right from the first, and that he must have been considered artistically on a par with his colleagues Burgkmair, Altdorfer, and Beham. Thus, Breu joins artists who worked for a wide range of important clients and whose reputations in modern times have fared much better than his own. In contrast, the cycle's paintings done after this first phase were executed by artists of much more local repute. Third, and from a methodological standpoint, the interpretation offered here for Breu's two paintings must work when the panels are seen not only within the context of the political situation at the end of the 1520s but also within the context of the other paintings from this first phase of production.

I argue that the primary political context for Breu's paintings, and for the others belonging to this first phase, is Wilhelm's negotiations to wrest power from the Habsburgs and to consolidate it in his own hands.[27] As discussed in the previous chapters, the period between 1526 and 1531 constitutes the main thrust of Wilhelm's challenge. During this time, he entered into various alliances and negotiations to check the expansion of Habsburg control and to place himself in the foreground as a viable alternative leader. Already at the Nuremberg Diet of 1524, discussion occurred about who would be the next

---

[27] Eschenburg also makes this point ("Altdorfer's *Alexanderschlacht*," 53–54) but makes her argument in a general way for the cycle as a whole. She discusses Breu's *Battle of Zama* only briefly (66–67) and concludes by comparing it with Altdorfer's, whereby Breu's work is deemed less clear in its message than the Regensburg artist's. She does not discuss his *Lucretia* at all. Greiselmayer also points to the relevancy of Wilhelm's political ambitions, particularly within the context of Breu's depiction of Lucretia (*Die Historienbilder*, 1: 242–54). He notes a general parallel between the story of Lucretia, a narrative describing a change of power structure, and Wilhelm's desire for the same. As evidence, he points to the tondi relief sculptures on the pilasters as indicative of struggles for power, and to the parallel importance, suggested by the

Roman king. This position was absolutely crucial since it meant that whoever was Roman king was also the de facto successor to the imperial throne. The logical choice, from the Habsburg point of view, was Charles's brother, Archduke Ferdinand. Despite Wittelsbach challenge, Ferdinand had been elected Bohemian king in 1526, and his continuing bid for the Roman kingship made the German estates decidedly nervous. Ferdinand's status as Bohemian king, which represented a strengthening of the empire's eastern borders under the Habsburg aegis, as well as Charles's impressive victory over the French at the battle of Pavia in 1525, all signaled the increasing consolidation of power in the hands of the Habsburg dynasty. If Ferdinand also became Roman king, then the continuation of control would be dynastically ensured.

Wilhelm opposed Ferdinand's candidacy by stepping forward as a candidate himself. Because of the nature of the Roman kingship, Wilhelm was, in essence, also proclaiming himself a contestant for the position of next Holy Roman Emperor. In 1526, the duke gained a promise of support for this enterprise from the Pope.[28] However, after Rome was sacked by imperial troops beginning in May 1527, Clement VII was forced into negotiating with Charles V and thus could not politically afford at that moment to support Wilhelm's anti-Habsburg plans. So the duke turned to Francis I of France instead, but this ally also fell by the wayside through the 1529 Peace of Cambrai, which united Charles with Francis. Turning to sources closer to home, Wilhelm next struck up negotiations with the Elector and Cardinal Albrecht of Mainz. The elector agreed to support Wilhelm's candidacy in return for a variety of financial, political, and cultural concessions, yet Albrecht did not remain true to his word; during the negotiations at the 1530 Augsburg Imperial Diet, the elector of Mainz agreed instead to back Ferdinand, who was duly crowned in Aachen early in 1531. In response, Wilhelm again approached Francis I, as well as Henry VIII of England,

---

composition, of Lucretia's suicide and her kinsmen's oath—in other words, that the political consequences of the rape and suicide are literally foregrounded. I agree with Greiselmayer on both these points, but my argument will involve a much closer reading of the painting. Curiously, Greiselmayer drops the issue of Wilhelm's ambitions when he discusses Breu's *Battle of Zama* (167–79) and interprets the painting instead primarily within the context of the westward advance of the Turks. I will argue that Wilhelm's ambitions also remain central for the interpretation of this painting.

[28] Götz Freiherr von Pölnitz, "Anton Fugger," 319.

Friedrich I of Denmark, Johann Zapolya of Hungary, and even joined the Schmalkaldic League of Protestant princes (Pact of Saalfeld), all in 1531, in what would seem a desperate attempt at creating a vast, last-minute alliance against Habsburg.

But 1531 also marked the beginning of delicate negotiations between Bavaria and Habsburg over a possible rapprochement.[29] Thus, Wilhelm was engaged in a diplomatic war on two fronts, participating in parallel yet diametrically opposed negotiations. By the time the next paintings in his history cycle were executed, in 1533 and 1535, the Bavarian opposition to Ferdinand's kingship had faltered and then formally ceased: in the Contract of Linz (September 11, 1534), the Bavarian dukes Wilhelm and his coregent and brother Ludwig contractually recognized Ferdinand as Roman king.[30]

This period of intense diplomatic negotiation during which Wilhelm contested Habsburg authority by making his own bid for power coincides with the first phase of his history cycle's production and in fact informs its function: to signal a legitimate and desirable change of leadership, and to suggest that the new leader, replacing Habsburg, should be Duke Wilhelm IV of Bavaria. An important part of my argument, however, will be that the cycle in general, and Breu's two paintings in particular, perform this function with a degree of ambiguity that is entirely suitable for highly political paintings. Their political nature in fact consists of the paintings' multivalence, their refusal to offer narratives that can be read simply, clearly, and unequivocally. Instead, the very number of competing and shifting subject positions they construct allows a variety of observers to invest the paintings with a variety of meanings. What the paintings thus signify exactly and precisely in terms of Wilhelm's political stance is not entirely clear. Instead of reading this as the paintings' failure to signify adequately, my argument is to read this as the paintings' success in providing a truly political statement: one that is ambiguous and cannot be pinned down. The paintings thus fulfill the dream of every politician: to be able to speak out of both sides of one's mouth at once. Up till now, those few scholars who have attempted to read Wilhelm's cycle in terms of its political message have sought for an underlying hermeneutic or contextual struc-

---

[29] Kohler, *Antihabsburgische Politik*, 211.
[30] Kohler, *Antihabsburgische Politik*, 372.

ture according to which the paintings in the cycle would all neatly line up and thereby reveal their meaning. Foregrounding the paintings' multivalence and their shifting positions therefore represents a radically new way of understanding this major monument to humanism north of the Alps.

That Wilhelm's political ambitions were couched in the language of Roman antiquity in Breu's paintings is a tribute to the politically tendentious production of history that characterized so much of humanist ideas and the writing it inspired in the fifteenth and sixteenth century both north and south of the Alps. In Italy, histories written by Lionardo Bruni (1370–1444), Poggio Bracciolini (1380–1459), and Niccolò Machiavelli (1469–1527) all connected ancient history with contemporaneous events and situations, usually in the service of creating a specifically Florentine identity sanctioned by its connection to antiquity. History thus becomes a powerful political tool with which to argue for certain forms of government, foreign relations, warfare, local versus enemy identity; in short history becomes the ideological basis for the production of theories of state.

Machiavelli in particular is very explicit about the relation between past and present and the importance of this relation for affairs of state. Although Machiavelli was not so much a humanist as a well-educated civil servant, Machiavelli's texts respond to those of humanist predecessors. In his *Florentine Histories* (1520–25), for example, he specifically praises the histories of Bruni and Bracciolini as worthy of imitation but also points out how his work will extend theirs; he will provide a more thorough account of internal politics in Florence than they, who, according to Machiavelli, had focused more on external relations and foreign affairs.[31] Indeed, Machiavel-

---

[31] Niccolò Machiavelli, *Florentine Histories*, trans. Laura Banfield and Harvey Mansfield Jr. (Princeton: Princeton University Press, 1988), 6: "My intent, when I at first decided to write down the things done at home and abroad by the Florentine people, was to begin my narration with the year of the Christian religion 1434, at which time the Medici family . . . gained more authority than anyone else in Florence; for I thought that Messer Leonardo d'Arezzo [Bruni] and Messer Poggio [Bracciolini], two very excellent historians, had told everything in detail that had happened from that time backwards. But when I read their writings diligently so as to see with what orders and modes they proceeded in writing, so that by imitating them our history might be better approved by readers, I found that in the descriptions of the wars waged by the Florentines with foreign princes and peoples they had been very diligent, but as regards civil discords and internal enmities, and the effects arising from them, they were altogether silent about the one and so brief about the other as to be of no use to readers or pleasure to anyone."

li's critical interest in ancient sources stems directly from the rediscovery, editing, and translating of ancient texts undertaken by humanists.

It is in fact in Machiavelli's response to the first ten books of
Livy's *Ab urbe condita* (Livy: 64 B.C.–12 A.D.; text begun ca. 29 B.C.
and worked on until his death) where he constructs a relationship
between past and present that is, at least ideally, dynamic and inter-
active, as well as politically potent. *The Discourses on Livy* are comprised of Machiavelli's annotations made while reading Livy and
were written, with several interruptions, mostly between 1515 and
1517. They were published posthumously in 1531.

In the introduction to Book 1, Machiavelli contrasts the realm of
art, in which antiquity is honored and imitated, with the realm of
affairs of state, in which it is not:

> When we consider . . . how much honor is attributed to antiquity, and
> how many times . . . a fragment of an ancient statue has been bought
> at a great price so that the buyer may have it near him to decorate his
> house or to have it imitated by those who take pleasure in that art; and
> when we see, on the other hand, the powerful examples which history
> shows us that have been accomplished by ancient kingdoms and re-
> publics, by kings, captains, citizens and legislators who have exhausted
> themselves for their fatherland, examples that have been more often
> admired than imitated (or so much ignored that not the slightest trace
> of this ancient ability remains), I cannot but be at the same time both
> amazed and sorry.[32]

Machiavelli here advocates the idea that events from antiquity
should ideally provide models, not just for art, but also for government and politics. In fact, he goes on to argue, ancient wisdom provides the very foundations of civil law and medicine in their modern-
day practices; by dint of negative argument, Machiavelli also intimates that knowledge of antiquity should also provide the foundations of statecraft: "Nevertheless, in instituting republics, maintaining
states, governing kingdoms, organizing the army and administering a
war, dispensing justice to subjects, and increasing an empire one
cannot find a prince or a republic that has recourse to the examples
of the ancients."[33]

The reason for this neglect of ancient examples, according to Ma-

---

[32] Niccolò Machiavelli, "The Discourses," in *The Portable Machiavelli*, ed. and
trans. Peter Bondanella and Mark Musa (New York: Viking Penguin, 1979), 170.

[33] Machiavelli, "The Discourses," 170.

chiavelli, lies not in the fact that historical information is unknown, but rather in the fact that it is not used properly, that is, that it is not imitated:

> This, in my opinion, arises . . . from not possessing a proper knowledge of histories, for in reading them we do not draw out of them that sense or taste that flavor which they have in themselves. Hence it happens that an infinite number of people read them and take pleasure in hearing about the variety of incidents which are contained in them without thinking to imitate them, for they consider imitation not only difficult but impossible.[34]

Thus it is not enough to read history, one must instead read it properly. Enjoyment and entertainment are not sufficient values to be extracted from the text, rather text should be the basis for action just as the past must be the basis for the present. The raison d'etre of Machiavelli's text is to redress the current situation in which history is read for the wrong reasons:

> "I wish to write what I, according to my knowledge of ancient and modern aVairs, judge necessary for a better understanding of them [i.e. Livy's books], so that those who read these statements of mine may more easily draw from them that practical knowledge one should seek from an acquaintance with history books."[35]

The basis for the potent link between past and present, and the justification for taking history so seriously, is explained later on in Machiavelli's text. Past and present are inextricably linked because human nature does not essentially change. Constantly repeating patterns of behavior and of situations can thus be charted across history. The cast of characters changes but in essence, the script does not:

> Anyone who studies present and ancient affairs will easily see how in all cities and all peoples there still exist, and have always existed, the same desires and passions. Thus it is an easy matter for him who carefully examines past events to foresee future events in a republic and to apply the remedies employed by the ancients, or, if old remedies cannot be found, to devise new ones based upon the similarity of the events. But since these matters are neglected or not understood by those who read, or, if understood, remain unknown to those who govern, the result is that the same problems always exist in every era.[36]

---

[34] Machiavelli, "The Discourses," 170–71.
[35] Machiavelli, "The Discourses," 171.
[36] Machiavelli, "The Discourses," 252.

Because of this link, history becomes an especially useful tool in pre-
dicting events in the future and influencing conditions in the present.
Yet it is precisely because those who govern remain unaware of the
uses of history that problems continue to recur, no matter what the
geographic and chronological specifics. Therefore, according to Machiavelli, history should be of particular concern for those involved
in affairs of state.

If history then has the power to reveal the past and to explain the
present and even shape the future, and since the main area of focus
would appear to be affairs of state, then there is politically much at
stake in the production of history. What gets to be defined as the
stuff of history, what gets to be chosen as examples to follow and
examples to scorn has enormous political consequences since in
choosing and evaluating such elements from the past, one is also
ultimately making statements about the present. Looking back at ancient history is therefore not about returning to a textual given and
passively accepting a totality of neutral facts. Instead, it is about actively shaping the past in order to justify or condemn the present
and to give shape to the future.

North of the Alps, history and politics, past and present were also
connected in humanist and humanist-inspired texts. There, too, as in
Italy, that connection is articulated in a self-conscious manner revealing an awareness of the political implications of writing and
reading history. These implications range from the formation of national identity to the ability to anticipate situations in affairs of state,
functions with which Italian writers also credited the production of
history, as we have seen. Such are also the uses of history as articulated by northern humanist authors in their texts.[37]

In his forward to *Epitome rerum germanicarum*, printed in 1505, Jakob
Wimpfeling (1450–1528) specifically states that he wrote the book so
that Germans would be able to visualize and to become familiar
with their past, which, according to Wimpfeling, included military
and intellectual triumphs resulting from the great strength of German character.[38] For Wimpfeling, reading history was the way for

---

[37] For a discussion of the humanist theories of history, see Rüdiger Landfester,
*Historia Magistra Vitae: Untersuchungen zur humanistischen Geschichtstheorie des 14. bis 16.
Jahrhunderts* (Geneva: Librairie Droz S.A., 1972).

[38] Jakob Wimpfeling, *Epitome rerum germanicarum*, 1505, cited in Joseph Knepper,
Jakob Wimpfeling 1450–1528: Sein Leben und seine Werk, (1902; reprint, Nieuwkoop: B.
de Graaf, 1965), 155.

present Germans to become acquainted with their past. What constitutes that past has been carefully selected by the historian, however.
The focus here is on German greatness, from military deeds to
moral character. The function of history in Wimpfeling's text is to
construct a great and inspiring German past as the basis for a national identity that current Germans would be proud to assume.

Wimpfeling's younger colleague and court historiographer to Wilhelm IV from 1517, Johannes Aventinus (1477–1534), also remarked
on the uses of history in his texts. However, Aventinus did not stress
the construction of national identity (to which his texts nonetheless
greatly contributed) so much as the knowledge history offers of the
way things are in the world and the way they are yet to be. In other
words, knowledge of the past helps to explain the present and predict the future. Aventinus also refers to the difficulties involved in
writing history.

From 1517 to 1521, Aventinus was involved in writing a history of
Bavaria that Wilhelm IV had commissioned from him.[39] In 1522, an
excerpt from the *Annales Boiarum* was translated from Latin into German and published in Nuremberg.[40] Aventinus uses the introductory
texts to the excerpt to reflect on his work and assert its importance.
In dedicating the work to his princely patrons, the Wittelsbach
brothers Wilhelm IV, Ludwig X, and Ernst, Aventinus draws attention to his labor and sacrifices expended and made in writing the
history: "According to your Princely Graces' command and instructions, I have now finished the chronicle in Latin, which I have written with great effort and hard work, and not without physical and
emotional exertion. I now publish this excerpt in German for your
Princely Graces' honor, benefit and gracious pleasure, and also for
the praise and use of the entire region."[41] The purpose of the history

---

[39] For information on Aventinus's life and work, see Gerald Strauss, *Historian in
an Age of Crisis: The Life and Work of Johannes Aventinus 1477–1534* (Cambridge Mass:
Harvard University Press, 1963). Aventinus's role as humanist at the Munich court
and his possible influence on Wilhelm's history cycle will be discussed further below.

[40] Johannes Aventinus, *Bayrischer Chronicon im Latein nun verfertigt und in siben puecher
getailt ein kurzer auszug* (Nuremberg: Frd. Peypus, 1522) reproduced in: *Johannes
Turmair's genannt Aventinus sämtliche Werke*, ed. K. Akademie der Wissenschaften (Munich: Christian Kaiser, 1881), 1: 108–70.

[41] Aventinus, *sämtliche Werke*, 1: 109: "Auß E.F.G. befelch und darlegen hab ich
die chronica mit grosser müe und schwerer arbeit nit on leibs und gemüts kreften
verschwentung im latein nun verfertigt und disen außzug E.F.G. zu er, wolfart, gne-
digem gefallen auch gemainer landschaft zu lob und nutz in teutsch durch den druck
auß lassen geen . . ."

is entirely political: the text is made in the first place to honor and please the princes, although Aventinus concedes that it would also serve the princes' subjects as well. In the introduction to the excerpt itself, Aventinus again stresses the work involved in writing history and then describes its use for prognostication:

> And so, after I have rested somewhat after bearing such an excessive burden, it is my intention to take up this burden yet again and to translate in German, as swiftly as possible, the entire history [i.e., the *Annales Boiarum*], which is quite useful and entertaining, and in many ways more reliable than predicting future things, good and evil, through the constellations or through astrology; so one who pays attention to such things and who wants to be able to count on one thing after another can see, understand, and examine [these things] in the reflection of the world's course.[42]

To write history, then, is so difficult that it is a burden, yet its usefulness outweighs its laboriousness. Here the activity and position of the court historian is skillfully defended: the writing of history, because of the difficulties involved and the skills needed, is not for everyone. But for the prince to gather the fruits of the historian's labor is a worthwhile enterprise because it will allow him to predict what might happen in the future, an extremely valuable political asset.

Aventinus spent the rest of his life translating his *Annales Boiarum* into German, a process he began in 1526. His introduction to this work sets similar accents:

> Introductory dedication to my gracious lords the princes, in which it is briefly explained: the use of history; the effort, work, and even dangers undertaken by the historian; and what kinds of art and diligence are necessary in order to write chronicles. . . . [43] The texts chronicling the history of the world from its beginning on are not begun for the entertainment of everyone. Instead, they are intended to provide a counterfeit of truth, to bring truth to the light of day, to show, as if in a mirror, the world's course, and to explain how and why a state and its people may remain unified and at peace and how and why they may

---

[42] Ibid., 110: "Und so ich nach solcher überschwenklichen pürde etwa ein wenig gerastet und verblasen, hab ich vor, disen Last wider auf mich zuladen und auf das furderlichist die ganzen historien zu verteutschen, welche gar nutzlich und kurzweilig ist, als in der vil gwißlicher dann ab dem gestirn oder sternsehen kunftige ding, gut und pöß, gleichwie in der weltlauf spiegel ein ietlicher, der solchs in acht haben und eins auf das ander rechnen wil, sehen, versten und abnemen mage. . ."

[43] Aventinus, *sämtliche Werke*, 4 pt. 1: 5: "Vorred zu meinen genedigen herren den fürsten, darin kurz angezaigt der nutz der historien, müe und arbait auch ferlikait des schreibers, was kunst auch und fleiss not sei, chronica zue beschreiben."

together become prosperous and blessed. On the other hand, one also
sees in the old, well-written histories what the sources are from which
spring jealousy, hate, war and wrath, insurrection, ruin and exploita-
tion of both land and people; one also sees that these things cannot be
avoided unless one gets at the source from which such evil is nourished
and does away with it.[44]

Like Machiavelli, Aventinus insists that history is not for entertainment but is instead about understanding the course of world events.
History's function is to reveal the true causes underlying situations of
peace and prosperity as well as of war and dissention. With such
knowledge, one is then empowered to change destructive situations
and avert disaster.

In all of the humanist texts touched on so far, we note a consistently articulated position about the uses of history. Its entertainment
value is acknowledged but downplayed whereas its political value is
foregrounded. The construction of national/local identity and the
ability to understand and thus to influence situations and even to
predict events in the future are highlighted as resources particularly
important for affairs of state and for those who govern. Interesting
especially in light of this chapter's concern with the relationship between history and art are the rhetorical parallels drawn by the northern humanists between history as textual narrative and history as
visual narrative. This topos in historical writing goes back to the
ancient historians Polybius and Livy and is taken up in humanist
historiography.[45] Wimpfeling writes his text so that people can visualize, or literally make a picture of the great German past. Aventinus
refers to his writing of history as art ("Kunst") and states that historical chronicles were made in order to provide a visual counterfeit of
truth—"das man die warheit abmale."

The political tendentiousness of producing history in the Renaissance was not without its critics. In fact, firm evidence of this practice

---

[44] Ibid., 10: "Es seind die chronica von anfang der welt her nit darumb angefangen, das sie iederman gefallen sollen, sunder erdacht worden, das man die
warheit abmale und an das leicht, an den tag brechte und als in aim spiegel der welt
lauf anzaigte, den rechten grund herfür legte, wie und warumb land und leut...in
guetem wesen, frid und ainigkait bleiben, erhalten reich und selig mit einander
werden mügen. Herentgegen auch siecht man in den alten rechtgeschribnen
geschichten, aus was ursachen aller neid und has, krieg und unwillen, aufruer,
verderben und ausreutung beder, land und leut, erwachsen und wie solchs nit
vermiden kan pleiben, man tue dan die ursach, den rechten grunt als den prun ab,
daraus solch pös übel entspringt."
[45] Landfester, *Historia Magistra Vitae*, 140–41.

is provided precisely through its critique. In his bitterly satirical work *Über die Fragwürdigkeit, ja Nichtigkeit der Wissenschaften, Künste und Gewerbe* (On the dubiousness, even triviality, of the sciences, arts and crafts), written in 1526, Agrippa von Nettesheim castigates the abuses he insists are all too often involved in the production of history.[46]

He begins his text with the usual definition of history as a narrative of events, deeds, and ideas meant to inspire people either to imitate or to reject them. Therefore, history is an important didactic tool that brings the past alive before the eyes of the beholder, and here Agrippa too employs a parallel between history and art: "In the writing of history, great ideas, actions and their results, and the deeds of kings and great men are placed chronologically and geographically in sequence, before the eyes of the viewer, as in a living picture."[47]

But already in his first sentence, "The writing of history is a representation of events involving praise or critique thereof (Die Geschichtsschreibung ist die mit Lob oder Kritik verbundene Darstellung von Ereignissen),"[48] Agrippa asserts that history is not a neutral depiction of events but one that entails a critical positioning, either positive or negative, of the narrator vis-à-vis his material. Agrippa goes on to analyze the motivations underlying the adoption of certain positions by historians. These motivations determine not only what critical stance the historian will take but also determine the relationship between the historian and the truth.

The desire to entertain, a motive de-emphasized by Aventinus and Machiavelli, is twice mentioned by Agrippa as a reason that historians take liberties with the truth:

> In order to offer their readers something entertaining, some authors add invented things to those that are true, or they leave out what is true. ... [49] Numerous historians do not write primarily in order to

---

[46] Agrippa von Nettesheim, *Über die Fragwürdigkeit ja Nichtigkeit der Wissenschaften, Künste und Gewerbe* (1526), transl. Gerhard Güpner, conclusion by Siegfried Wollgast (Berlin: Akademie Verlag, 1993).

[47] Ibid., Kapitel 5: Geschichtsschreibung, 32–36; here 32: "[Die Geschichtsschreibung] stellt große Ideen, Handlungen und deren Ergebnisse, Taten von Königen und großen Männer zeitlich und räumlich geordnet dem Betrachter als lebendiges Bild vor Augen."

[48] Ibid., 32.

[49] Ibid., 33: "Manche Autoren fügen auch, um ihren Lesern Unterhaltsames zu bieten, zum Wahren noch Erfundenes hinzu oder lassen Wahres weg..."

report the truth; instead, they write primarily in order to entertain the reader. That is why they do not write according to how everything really happened but rather they write according to how well things fit together as a narrative.[50]

Narrative structure and narrative delight take precedence over telling the truth for these historians, according to Agrippa.

Other disreputable historians position themselves according to the wishes of their patrons and write only what they think will please them. In order to flatter their patrons, they tamper with the truth:

> One must accuse further historians of even worse crimes committed against the truth. Motivated by toadyism or by the demands of their patrons, they consciously provide false representations. This is also true of those people, who, in writing history, allow themselves to be led by party interests; they include in their texts only that which is in line with their own wishes, while they misinterpret, down-play or even totally leave out anything else and therefore produce biased, butchered, even corrupted history. . . . In this they count on the fact that their lies will not be short of assistants and interested parties, and that the important men, in whose interests all this transpires, will feel flattered. Princes engage such historians, as Plutarch says, just for the purpose of minimizing the achievements of others and of inflating their own historical consequence through the invention of little tales.[51]

Agrippa reserves special scorn for particularly obsequious historians (to whom he refers as "Speichellecker," literally "saliva lickers") who invent genealogies for their princes linking their houses with those of antiquity. Where no appropriate ancestors can be found, these histo-

---

50 Ibid., 35: "Zahlreiche Historiker schreiben nicht in erster Linie um Wahres zu berichten sondern um dem Leser Vergnügen zu bereiten...deshalb schreiben sie auch nicht so wie sich alles tatsächlich ereignet hat, sondern so, wie es sich erzählerisch gut gestalten läßt. . ."

51 Ibid., 34: "Weiteren Historiern muß man noch schlimmere Vergehen gegen die Wahrheit vorwerfen: sie geben [. . .] aus Liebedienerei oder auf Verlangen ihrer Gönner bewußt falsche Darstellungen. Das trifft natürlich ebenfalls auf die Leute zu, die sich bei ihrer Geschichtsschreibung von Parteiinteressen leiten lassen und nur das anführen, was ihren eigenen Wünschen entspricht, während sie alles andere umdeuten, abschwächen, oder ganz weglassen und damit einseitige, verstümmelte, ja korrupte Geschichtsschreibung betreiben. [. . .] Dabei bauen sie darauf, daß es ihnen nicht an Helfern und Interessenten für ihre verlogenen Geschichten fehlt und daß die Herren, um derentwillen all das geschieht, sich geschmeichelt fühlen. [. . .] Fürsten halten sich solche Geschichtsschreiber, wie Plutarch sagt, eigens zu dem Zweck, mit Hilfe von deren Talenten die Leistungen anderer zu schmälern und die eigenen durch erfundene Histörchen zu historischer Größe aufzubauen."

rians do not shy away from either inventing some or resorting to mythical figures.[52]

In relation to the *uomini famosi* tradition, Agrippa is also skeptical. He finds the adulation of many of these famous men from Greek and Roman history suspect and even misguided. In a passage naming many of the figures appearing in Wilhelm's history cycle, Agrippa blasts the historical commemoration of great generals of antiquity whom he refers to as "megalomaniacal bandits and world-famous plunderers":

> Historians report on many things but one cannot accept everything they say [as true]; some also sanction things that one in no way can approve of. Very many of them represent the most awful things as examples worthy of imitation. They loudly sing the praises of Hercules, ... Darius, Alexander, Pyrrhus, Hannibal, Scipio, Pompey and Caesar, while in reality they have glorified megalomaniacal bandits and world-famous plunderers. Although the above-named have all been supremely successful in their command of power, they nonetheless and indubitably acted in a reprehensible and even criminal fashion.[53]

Agrippa's critique comes no doubt in response to the writing of politically tendentious histories, the production of which abounded in early sixteenth-century Germany. Most of these actively construct a German national identity through the twin strategies of asserting both an affinity with and a fundamental difference to the ancient Romans. These arguments about German national identity are often tied together with justifications for the passing of the Roman Empire into the hands of the Germans during the Middle Ages.

Jakob Wimpfeling discusses the western borders of empire in his work *Germania* (1501) in order to assert their German character and thus the legitimacy of German rule in these areas.[54] The German character of the Rhineland was already designated as such by the

---

[52] Ibid., 35.

[53] Ibid., 36 "Die Geschichtsschreiber berichten vieles, doch nicht alles kann man hinnehmen; manche billigen auch Dinge, die man keines falls gutheißen kann; sehr viele stellen jedoch auch die allerärgsten Dinge als nachahmenswerte Beispiele dar: In den höchsten Tönen preisen sie Herakles, [. . .] Dareios, Alexander, Pyrrhos, Hannibal, Scipio, Pompeius und Cäsar. Und dabei haben sie eigentlich doch nur größenwahnsinnige Banditen und weltweit bekannt gewordenen Freibeuter verherrlicht. Mögen die Genannten auch höchst erfolgreiche Machthaber gewesen sein, so haben sie doch ganz gewiß verwerflich, ja verbrecherisch gehandelt."

[54] Theobald Bieder, *Geschichte der Germanenforschung*, Part I: 1500–1806 (Leipzig: Theodor Weicher, 1921), 7–8.

ancient Romans, who referred to the inhabitants of that territory as "Germani," a term that Wimpfeling defines as meaning "brothers." Thus, German character is defined by the similarities between the Germans and the Romans.[55] Three other humanists, Conrad Celtis, Conrad Peutinger, and Heinrich Bebel, also promulgated this Roman definition of "Germani" as based on affinity.[56]

Another important political issue discussed by Wimpfeling in 1501 was whether the French had any relevant claim to the imperial crown. In order to refute any French claims to either the Rhineland territory or the imperial crown, Wimpfeling set about to prove that the Franks and Charlemagne were really German, thus negating any French connections to either that the French might have otherwise used to bolster their claims.[57] Wimpfeling emphasizes the historical continuity between the ancient Roman Empire and the German Holy Roman Empire of Charlemagne a few years later in his 1505 *Rerum germanicarum epitome.* Here he asserts that the Roman emperors Diocletian, Decius, Probus, Jovianus, and Valentinianus were all actually German, and thus it is only right that the Holy Roman Empire is now again in German hands.[58]

Other humanist authors promoted the idea of continuity between the ancient Romans and contemporaneous Germans, a tactic that supports the argument by affinity. Andreas Althamer, for example, maintained in 1529 that most of the German nobility stemmed from (and thus were related to) Roman noble families.[59] In addition to Wimpfeling, the humanists Heinrich Bebel (1472–1518),[60] Matthias Philesius,[61] Hieronymus Gebwiler (1473–1545),[62] Conrad Peutinger (1465–1547) and Cuspinian[63] all either implied or insisted on the

---

[55] Frank Borchardt, *German Antiquity in Renaissance Myth* (Baltimore: Johns Hopkins University Press, 1971), 99.

[56] Bieder, *Geschichte*, 16 and Borchardt, *German Antiquity*, 114.

[57] Borchardt, *German Antiquity*, 99.

[58] Bieder, *Geschichte*, 9–10.

[59] Andreas Althamer, *Scholia in C. Tacitum Rom. historicum de situ, moribus populisque Germaniae*, (Nuremberg: 1529); cited in Borchardt, *German Antiquity*, 161.

[60] Borchardt, *German Antiquity*, 113.

[61] Philesius published a translation of Caesar in 1507 that included a listing of emperors from Caesar to Maximilian; Borchardt, *German Antiquity*, 115.

[62] Hieronymus Gebwiler, *Libertas Germaniae* (1519), cited in Borchardt, *German Antiquity*, 155.

[63] Paul Joachimson, *Geschichtsauffassung und Geschichtsschreibung in Deutschland unter dem Einfluss des Humanismus*, (1910; republished Aalen: Scientia Verlag, 1968), 205–9. Both authors were engaged in writing compendia on emperors (Kaiserbuch) ranging from ancient Rome to their present times.

continuity between the Roman and the German empires, whereby the transference of power from one to the other was completely legitimate.

An alternative strategy for constructing German national identity in humanist texts to the argument by affinity was the argument by difference, although many authors combined both strategies in a single text, as we will see. German identity in these texts is constructed in opposition to, or at least in competition with, ancient Roman identity. The rediscovery of Tacitus's (c.55–c.117) work *Germania* (98 A.D.) provided an important impetus for this strategy as the ancient author himself favorably contrasts the purity of German society to his own.[64]

Tacitus's text was rediscovered by Poggio Bracciolini in a monastery in Hersfeld in 1425. He brought the manuscript back to Italy where it was copied numerous times by other humanists. The first editions were printed in Venice (1470) and Nuremberg (1473). It was not, however, until the 1496 edition, printed in Leipzig and edited by Enea Silvio Piccolomini that the text received widespread attention from German humanists.[65] Piccolomini used the *Germania* to refute German complaints about paying tribute money to the church in Rome by contrasting the primitive state of Germany in antiquity, as discussed by Tacitus, and its modern and highly cultured state. The credit for this change, Piccolomini argued, was the highly beneficial influence of the Catholic Church, and thus Germany should continue to make its payments. Any current difficulties in Germany were not caused by these payments, Piccolomini insisted, but by the cities' and princes' lack of obedience to the emperor and to the church.

But Piccolomini's argument had an entirely different effect than the papal legate had intended. Instead of accepting it as a justifica-

---

[64] Tacitus, *The Agricola and the Germania*, transl. H. Mattingly and S. Handford (New York: Penguin Books, 1970). For the German reception of Tacitus, see the following: Hans Tiedemann, *Tacitus und das Nationalbewußtsein der deutschen Humanisten* (Berlin: Emil Eberling, 1913); Hans Kloft, "Die Idee einer deutschen Nation zu Beginn der frühen Neuzeit: Überlegungen zur *Germania* des Tacitus und zum *Arminius* Ulrichs von Hutten," in *Arminius und die Varusschlacht: Geschichte, Mythos, Literatur*, ed. Rainer Wiegels and Winfried Woesler (Munich: Ferdinand Schöningh, 1995), 199–209 and Ludwig Krapf, *Germanenmythos und Reichsideologie: Frühhumanistische Rezeptionsweisen der taciteischen Germania* (Tübingen: Niemeyer, 1979).

[65] I am here following Tiedemann (5–7) and Kloft's (200–206) argument about Piccolomini and the German reception of Tacitus.

tion for Germany's dependence on Rome, German humanists got hold of Tacitus and used his text as a basis for constructing a positive and entirely independent German identity.

Wimpfeling asserted that what might be loosely regarded as a German state ("das Germanentum") had existed since Homer's time and was thus extremely ancient.[66] German society was therefore older than the ancient Romans, proven by the "fact" that the German city of Trier was supposedly much older than the city of Rome.[67] Indeed, another German humanist, Michael Coccinius, claimed in 1506 that the Germans had already established a great empire that existed parallel to the Roman one, and were thus already in possession of one empire when the Roman one was transferred to them in the Middle Ages.[68] These ancient Germans were famous for their valor in war; they alone, according to Wimpfeling, were powerful and belligerent enough to offer Alexander the Great serious resistance.[69]

The antiquity of German society, and the prowess of the Germans in war, are often repeated topoi in German humanist historiography. Conrad Peutinger followed Tacitus's lead in maintaining in 1506 that the Germans all stemmed from Tuisco, a son of Noah.[70] In the hands of Hieronymus Gebwiler, the ancient Greek hero Herakles becomes a German.[71] In his *Oratio ad regem Maximilianum de laudibus atque amplitudine Germaniae* (1501), Heinrich Bebel claims that the Germans' courage and ferocity in war were world-famous since antiquity.[72] Aventinus, writing for Duke Wilhelm and his brothers, makes a similar claim and includes a few Bavarian twists: the Franks descended from a royal Bavarian family, and Charlemagne himself was a Bavarian. The "facts" that Bologna was once the capital of Bavaria, and that Alexander the Great conquered the entire world,

---

[66] Wimpfeling, *Rerum germanicarum epitome* (1505); cited in Bieder, *Geschichte*, 9.

[67] Ibid., cited in Borchardt, *German Antiquity*, 100.

[68] Michael Coccinius, *De imperii a Graecis ad Germanos translatione* (Strasbourg, 1506); cited in Borchardt, *German Antiquity*, 115.

[69] Ibid., cited in Bieder, *Geschichte*, 10.

[70] Conrad Peutinger, *Sermones convivales in quibus multa de mirandis Germaniae antiquitatibus referuntur* (1505), cited in Borchardt, *German Antiquity*, 114. Bieder dates the *Sermones* to 1506, *Geschichte*, 7).

[71] Hieronymus Gebwiler, *Libertas Germaniae* (1519); cited in Borchardt, *German Antiquity*, 155.

[72] Cited in Bieder, *Geschichte*, 17. Borchardt dates the *Oratio* to 1504, *German Antiquity*, 109).

except Bavaria, are presented as evidence of the military skill and
bravery of the Bavarians in particular.[73]

The humanists' interest in constructing the Germans as a people
at least as ancient and powerful as the Romans is perhaps most
cogently articulated in their treatment of Arminius, tribal leader of
the Germanic Cherusci. Although Conrad Peutinger and Willibald
Pirckheimer (1470–1530) both mention his name in early texts, the
discovery in 1515 of another work by Tacitus, this time the *Annals*,
stimulated further and more detailed interest in this historical figure.[74] In 9 A.D., Arminius had defeated Augustus's commander,
Publius Quinctilius Varus, in the Teutoburg forest (just south of
present-day Osnabrück and Bielefeld) and slaughtered the Roman
troops. Tacitus's text narrates the continued resistance against
Tiberius's commander, Germanicus, offered by Arminius, and the
battles that he won.[75] Tacitus also briefly reports that once Germany
had been cleared of Romans, Arminius himself tried to become king,
but the Cherusci wanted to remain free and Arminius was murdered
by his own relatives. In summing up Arminius' career, Tacitus has
this to say:

> He was unmistakably the liberator of Germany. Challenger of Rome—
> not in its infancy, like kings and commanders before him, but at the
> height of its power—he had fought undecided battles and never lost a
> war. He had ruled for twelve of this thirty-seven years. To this day the
> tribes sing of him. Yet Greek historians ignore him, reserving their
> admiration for Greece. We Romans, too, underestimate him, since in
> our devotion to antiquity we neglect modern history.[76]

The "liberator of Germany" was enthusiastically embraced by some
German humanists. Wilhelm's court historiographer Johannes Aventinus not only includes Arminius (whom he calls "Herzog Erman")
in his *Bayerische Chronik* but also quotes the above cited passage from

---

[73] Aventinus, cited in Borchardt, *German Antiquity*, 167–72. See also references to
Aventinus in Hedwig Riess, *Motive des patriotischen Stolzes bei den deutschen Humanisten*
(Berlin: Emil Eberling, 1934), 8 and her footnote 54.
[74] Hans Gert Roloff, "Der Arminius des Ulrich von Hutten" in *Arminius und die
Varusschlacht: Geschichte, Mythos, Literatur*, ed. Rainer Wiegels and Winfried Woesler
(Munich: Ferdinand Schöningh, 1995), 211–38; here 213.
[75] Tacitus, *The Annals of Imperial Rome*, revised ed., transl. Michael Grant (New
York: Penguin Books, 1971), 64–71, 81–86, 119.
[76] Tacitus, *Annals*,119.

Tacitus almost verbatim.[77] It was in Ulrich von Hutten's dialogue between Arminius and the great generals of classical antiquity, however, where the Cheruscer is celebrated most fervently as a national hero. The work, *Arminius: Dialogus Huttenicus quo homo patriae amantissimus patriae laudem celebravit*, was published posthumously in 1529, although it is not known exactly when Hutten actually wrote the dialogue. A likely post quem date is the year 1515, during which Hutten was in Italy and read the newly discovered annals of Tacitus that provided him with information for his work.[78] Hutten's dialogue was later reprinted in 1538 and 1557 under the supervision of Philip Melanchthon who issued the text together with Tacitus's *Germania* and Melanchthon's own commentary on the latter.[79] *Arminius* was not translated into German until 1815.[80]

In the dialogue, Arminius pleads his own case before Minos, judge of the underworld, that he, Arminius, should be proclaimed the greatest military leader in history. Arminius argues that Minos's previous judgment, which ranked Alexander the Great, Scipio Africanus, and Hannibal as the greatest leaders (in that order), was unfair because Minos had never even taken Arminius into account in the first place. This oversight, it is discovered, was the fault of biased histories that ignored the accomplishments of this great German (a situation to which even Tacitus had referred in the *Annals* as we have seen). Hutten, then, like Tacitus as well as Agrippa von Nettesheim and other humanists, was well aware of the partisan nature of his-

---

[77] Johannes Aventinus, *Sämmtliche Werke*, vol. 4 pt. 2, 604–6. His quotation of Tacitus (606) is as follows: "Herzog Erman (wie dan Tacitus der Römer von ihm sagt) ist on allen zweifel [...] ain erlediger Germanien und teutscher nation, der nit im anfang, da es noch clain und schwach war, das römisch volk reich und kaisertumb wie ander künig, fürsten und herren, sunder do es am allermächtigisten und glücksäligisten gewesen ist, angegriffen und zeckt hat. Wie wol er in dem schlachten, ernach mit den Römern gehabt, ie ob ie under gelegen, ist er doch nie mit streit überwunden und des kriegs müed worden, hat zwelf jar gestracks aneinander mit grossen eren und macht den krieg wider die Römer gefüert und wolgestreckt bis an sein end. [...] Es singen und sagen noch von im die Teutschen [...] (den kriechischen historien, die allain ir sach gros achten, ist er unbekant, den römischen chroniken nit so gar wol vermärt) [...]."

[78] The 1529 edition was printed in Hagenau; Roloff, "Der Arminius," 212. Lucian also was influential on Hutten's dialogue.

[79] Jacques Ride, "Arminius in der Sicht der deutschen Reformatoren," in *Arminius und die Varusschlacht: Geschichte, Mythos, Literatur*, ed. Rainer Wiegels and Winfroed Woesler (Munich: Ferdinand Schöningh Verlag, 1995, 239–48; here 244.

[80] Roloff, "Der Arminius," 212. Roloff reproduces the entire dialogue 222–38 in Latin and German.

toriography. The particularly anti-German stance of some Italian
historians was excoriated, for example, in 1518 in Franciscus Ire-
nicus's (1495–c.1559) *Germaniae exegeseos libri XII*.[81]

In order to combat the biased accounts of other historians, Arminius calls on Tacitus as his witness, who delivers the pronouncement from the *Annals* as cited above. Minos is impressed by Arminius and his star witness. However, he cannot reverse any judgment once it has been made. Thus, as a way of honoring Arminius,
Minos pronounces him equal to the two Brutuses who likewise freed
Rome from dictators: Lucius Junius Brutus, who expelled the Etruscan king Tarquinius Superbus after the rape of Lucretia in 509 B.C.
and Marcus Junius Brutus who murdered Julius Caesar in 44 B.C.
Minos addresses Arminius with the words: "But because you were
the liberator of Germany and because you made war for the cause
of freedom–and, in everyone's opinion, you turned out to be the
victor–it pleases me to place you among both the Brutuses and to
accord you first place among the liberators of the fatherland."[82]
Arminius's placement as first among these two famous Romans
means that Germany is a nation that has ancient heroes who are
equal to if not superior to those of ancient Rome. And because
Minos agrees in the course of the dialogue that Arminius's military
deeds even outstrip those of Alexander the Great, Germany's greatness in this instance even surpasses that of ancient Greece.

Hutten's *Arminius* is not only an important humanist text that constructs a German national identity on the basis of a glorious past
equal to if not superior to that of ancient Rome; it also has, I believe,
important resonances for the political positions embraced by
Wilhelm IV and intimated by his paintings. I am not suggesting that
Hutten's dialogue necessarily provides the originary text for the
duke's history cycle, although most of the main male characters
present in the text (Alexander, Hannibal, and Scipio) are also present
in the paintings executed in the first phase of production which represent the deeds of famous men. Even Junius Lucius Brutus, mentioned by Minos in the text, is accorded prominence in Breu's paint-

---

[81] Bieder, *Geschichte*, 21.
[82] Ulrich von Hutten, *Arminius*, reproduced in Roloff, "Der *Arminius*," 235: "Weil
du aber der Befreier Deutschlands warst und den Krieg für die Freiheit unternom-
men hast und nach Meinung aller als Sieger hervorgegangen bist, [. . .] gefällt es
mir, dich den beiden Brutus zuzugesellen und dir unter den Vaterlandsbefreiern die
erste Stelle einzuräumen."

ing representing the death of Lucretia. None of the women from the
painting cycle are mentioned in the dialogue, however, and the other
male figures from the text (Arminius, Minos, Tacitus, and Marcus
Junius Brutus) are found nowhere in the paintings. Furthermore,
there is no concrete evidence that Wilhelm knew the dialogue; it was
not published until 1529, a year after the history cycle was begun,
although it might have been possible that the duke, who had received
a humanist education in his youth, saw it earlier in manuscript
form.[83] However, no distinct ties between Ulrich von Hutten and the
Wittelsbach court in Munich are traceable, although it can be shown
that Wilhelm's court historiographer Aventinus shared some of the
same acquaintances of Hutten, including Hutten's brother-in-law,
Sebastian von Rotenhan, with whom he corresponded in 1530 and
1531.[84]

What I am suggesting is that *Arminius* provides useful evidence
that within humanist circles, most of which were albeit completely
loyal to the emperor, the legitimacy of the exercise of power was
debated.[85] Wilhelm might not have been familiar with this particular
text, but he may indeed have been familiar with some of the reasoning and the issues presented there. Most importantly, Hutten's text
articulates important justifications for certain political ideas that I
believe are suggested in the duke's paintings.

After Minos's pronouncement proclaiming Arminius as the fore-
most liberator of the fatherland, Alexander, Scipio, and Hannibal
are allowed to raise objections. Those that the generals do raise are
ones that would also pertain to Wilhelm's goal of ousting the Habsburgs from power and taking over control of the empire himself. In

---

[83] Claudia Willibald discusses Wilhelm's humanist education in her article "Das
chronicon Bavarorum des Veit von Ebersberg," *Zeitschrift für bayerische Landesgeschichte*
30 (1987): 493–541. For humanism in Bavaria, see Heinrich Lutz and Alois Schmidt,
"Von Humanismus zur Gegenreformation," in *Handbook der bayerischen Geschichte*, 2nd
ed., ed. Andreas Kraus, (Munich: C. H. Beck Verlagsbuchhandlung, 1988), 2: 861–
75.

[84] Gerald Strauss, *Historian in an Age of Crisis*, 257 and his footnotes 11 and 12 on
292. Indeed, the community of German humanists, although geographically dispersed between places like Augsburg, Vienna, Strasbourg, Tübingen, and Ingolstadt,
seems to have been nonetheless a fairly close-knit group of scholars who corresponded and visited with one another. The interwoven network of humanists
emerges very clearly in Joachimson's work *Geschichtsauffassung und Geschichtsschreibung in
Deutschland unter dem Einfluss des Humanismus*.

[85] Hutten also was at least initially completely loyal to Maximilian and his successor Charles. The enemy of the Germans which he is addressing in his dialogue is
the Church of Rome, not the Holy Roman Emperor (Riess, 40–41).

the dialogue, Alexander the Great reminds Arminius that the Cheruscer had sworn an oath of loyalty to the Romans and that therefore Arminius's war against his former allies was not appropriate: "That is just what is generally said: it was not for you to turn against those whose yoke you once bore. . . . You gave your word."[86] Scipio joins in and levels the charge of betrayal ("Treulosigkeit") at Arminius.[87] Finally Hannibal accuses Arminius of attempting to substitute his own rule over his people for that of the Romans: "although you brag about how you lifted the foreign yoke from your people, you burdened them with your own."[88]

Each of these charges could also be leveled at Wilhelm if he were to achieve his political goals. The issues of loyalty and betrayal were indeed relevant since Wilhelm, as a member of the German nobility and also as a relative of the Habsburgs, was expected to support the emperor who also happened to be his second cousin.[89] Any attempt by Wilhelm to unseat the Habsburgs would thus be viewed as both a political and a familial betrayal. The duke's further desire, to himself take over the reins of power, is also exactly equivalent to Hannibal's accusation of Arminius.

The defenses that Arminius offers in the face of these charges provide viable justification for his—and for Wilhelm's intended—actions. Arminius admits swearing an oath of loyalty to the Romans but says that he did not swear an oath to suffer indignities. The inhumane, violent, and unjust actions of the Romans rendered their authority over the Cherusci null and void and thus, Arminius argues, he was no longer bound to keep his oath.[90] Rome had lost its legitimacy as a power; it was no longer a "rechtmäßige Obrigkeit (legal authority)" but a tyranny and thus resistance was justifiable. Similarly, Arminius answers the charges of betrayal by saying that all tyrant slayers were disloyal. As examples of these, he names the two Brutuses, who because of their actions, had earned the greatest re-

---

86 Hutten, *Arminius*, 235.

87 Hutten, *Arminius*, 237: "Das ist es gerade, was man allgemein sagt: dir habe es nicht zugestanden, von denen abzufallen, deren Joch du einmal empfangen hattest [. . .] du hattest dein Wort gegeben."

88 Hutten, *Arminius*, 237: "[. . .]obwohl du dich rühmst, das fremde Joch von Deinem Volke genommen zu haben, hast du ihnen das deinige auferlegt [. . .]."

89 Wilhelm's mother Kunigunde was the emperor Maximilian's sister, thus making Maximilian Wilhelm's uncle. The current emperor, Charles V, was Maximilian's grandson and thus Wilhelm's second cousin.

90 Hutten, *Arminius*, 235.

spect and eternal fame. As they had done, Arminius acted the way he did because he was influenced by a just cause, namely, to resist injustice.[91] Finally, he denies ever pursuing the idea of becoming king but does say that it would have only been fair, for all he had done for his people, if they would have made him king. Instead, he had simply wanted to retain power in order to protect the common good and the newly won freedom.[92]

The text of *Arminius* thus basically provides a sanctification of revolution based on the construction of the current regime as unjust and therefore unworthy of obedience and support. In the case of *Arminius*, the unjust regime was also odious because it was foreign. Wilhelm could make similar claims about Charles V, who remained mostly absent from his German territories and did not even literally speak their language.[93] Charles's focus was more international, and although he worried about the French in Italy during the 1520s, confessional and political troubles were left to brew in Germany. Charles's inability to stop the Reformation (or in other words, the spread of heresy, as many Catholics perceived it) and the sack of Rome in 1527 at the hands of the imperial troops represented serious incursions on the part of the Holy Roman Emperor whose very authority was based as much on his function as protector of the church as it was on his function as ruler of secular affairs.[94]

In making his bid for power, Wilhelm could thus draw on a number of situations and perceptions that questioned the legitimacy of Habsburg right to rule. Indeed, the state and leadership thereof was a matter of current debate, not only in city halls but also between the covers of books, and I will argue, within the frames of Wilhelm's history paintings.

How was the German state conceptualized at this time? The definition of the German nation was of great importance to the humanist project of cultural production. In 1486, the modifier "deutscher Nation" had been officially appended to the phrase "heilige rö-

---

[91] Hutten, *Arminius*, 237.

[92] Hutten, *Arminius*, 237.

[93] Heinrich Lutz, "Die deutsche Nation zu Beginn der Neuzeit: Fragen nach dem Gelingen und Scheitern deutscher Einheit im 16. Jahrhundert," *Historische Zeitschrift* 234 (1982), 529–59, here 532; see also Bernd Moeller, *Deutschland im Zeitalter der Reformation*, Deutsche Geschichte, ed. Joachim Leuschner, vol. 4 (Göttingen: Vandenhoeck und Ruprecht, 1977), 68.

[94] Borchardt, *German Antiquity*, 250, discusses the medieval conception of empire that continued to influence Renaissance ideas.

mische Reich," but what that meant exactly was open to discussion.[95] We have already seen how German national identity was
constructed in some humanist texts. Still others grappled with other
elementary constituents of definition, such as the meaning of the
word "Germania," the description of the nation's borders and territories, and the characterization of its indigenous inhabitants.[96] This
project of producing an all-encompassing *Germania Illustrata* was particularly embraced by Conrad Celtis and Johannes Aventinus but
was never fully realized.[97]

Many humanist texts also commented on political components of
the German nation as state. In addition to the emperor, who held
the position of head of state, three basic groups wielded varying degrees of political power in the nation: the electors, the princes, and
the cities. Representatives of these three groups were to meet with
the emperor during the Imperial Diets, which ideally were to be
called into session annually in order to carry out the nation's business. The institution of the Imperial Diet, along with that of the
Kammergericht, which took the highest instance of judicial decision
away from the emperor, were created in order to check the emper-
or's power by increasing the role of his estates in decision and policy
making.[98] These institutional efforts were the results of the basic conflict in the nation between the emperor's desire to consolidate power
in his hands, and the estates' desire to retain as much power as
possible in theirs.[99]

Humanists positioned themselves vis-à-vis this conflict in a consistently proimperial manner.[100] Nonetheless, many of their texts articulate concern about the tensions among political and social groups in
the empire. Jakob Wimpfeling discusses relationships between what
he defines as the state's main classes (*Stände*), namely, the clergy, the
princes, and the laity/non-aristocracy (*geistlichen, fürstlichen und bürgerlichen*) in *Germania* (1501). Here he expresses concern that the empire
will be harmed by the tension between the three groups, and he

---

[95] Moeller, *Deutschland im Zeitalter der Reformation*, 11.
[96] Discussed in Hans Tiedemann, *Tacitus und das Nationalbewußtsein der deutschen Humanisten*.
[97] Joachimson, *Geschichtsauffassung und Geschichtsschreibung*, chapter 6 "Germania Illustrata," 155–87.
[98] Moeller, *Deutschland im Zeitalter der Reformation*, 14–16.
[99] Lutz, "Die deutsche Nation," 532.
[100] Tiedemann, *Tacitus*, 138.

singles out the particularly difficult relationship between the princes and the burghers.[101] This relationship is also the subject of Ulrich von Hutten's poem *Beklagung der freistädte deutscher nation oder Vermahnung an die freien und Reichsstädt deutscher nation.*[102] In the text, Hutten promotes an alliance between the cities and the lower aristocracy (*die Adel*) against the princes who, according to Hutten, betray the nation and the emperor, oppress the other classes, and suppress the word of God by their persecution of Luther.[103] The princes' refusal to surrender any of their own power for the sake of the empire, and their lack of support of the emperor, is further castigated by Piccolomini,[104] Wimpfeling, Bebel,[105] and Aventinus.[106] Agrippa von Nettesheim spares no hyperbolic device in order to portray the royal courts as places of moral corruption where virtue is banished and vice reigns supreme. He compares the court to a comet portending evil, an infectious epidemic and a rabid dog:

> The court is essentially just a gathering of mythic giants; or, more precisely stated, an association of ill-reputed aristocratic windbags, a stage for the most nauseating of subjects, a school of the most atrocious morals, an asylum for the most loathsome criminals. Here is the home

---

[101] Wimpfeling, cited in Knepper, *Jakob Wimpfeling*, 140–41.

[102] Reproduced in *Hutten, Müntzer, Luther*, 4th ed., introduction by Siegfried Streller (Berlin: Aufbau Verlag, 1982), 1: 6–14.

[103] Hutten, *Beklagung*: "Ihr frummen Städt, nun habt in acht/Des gmeinen deutschen Adels Macht/Zieht den zu euch, vertraut ihm wohl;/ich sterb, wo's euch gereuen soll!/Ihr seht, daß euch und ihn zugleich/Beschweret der Tyrannen Reich/ Die ietzt all ander Ständ verdrückt/[. . .] Ich mein die frommen Fürsten nit [. . .] Allein die Bösen rühre ich/Durch die itzt ganze Land beschwert.," (6); "Doch will ich sagen mein Verstand/Verraten ist ganz deutsche Land/Das Reich die Fürsten hant verkauft.," (8); "Der [the emperor] zeucht nun von uns uber Meer./Sie [the princes] wolln nit, daß er wiederkehr,/Denn allen Gwalt des Kaisers hie/Von ihm gegeben bhalten sie. [. . .]. Drüm haben s'noch eins gfangen an,/Verbieten Doktor Luthers Lehr/Als ob sie ergens sträflich wär./Dann Wahrheit mögen s'leider nit/Ist wider ihren Brauch und Sitt/Dann sollt Gotts Wort in Wesen stahn/Ihn' wurd ihr Gut und Macht zergahn [. . .] Drüm förchten wir die Türken nit,/Dann sie uns wohnen täglich mit [. . .]. Gott nie verwegner Menschen schuf/Dann seind in diesem Regement [. . .]. Drüm widerz'streben ist uns not/Entgegen aller Oberkeit./ Drüm, fromme Städt, euch macht bereit/Und nehmt des Adels Freundschaft an,/So mag man diesen widerstahn/Und helfen deutscher Nation/Vermeiden Schaden Spott und Hohn." 12–13.

[104] Piccolomini, cited in Kloft, "Die Idee einer deutschen Nation," 203–5.

[105] Paul Ulrich, *Studien zur Geschichte des deutschen Nationalbewußtseins im Zeitalter des Humanismus und der Reformation* (Berlin: Verlag Dr. Emil Ebering, 1936), 32; and Tiedemann, *Tacitus*, 143–47.

[106] Aventinus, "Ursachen des Türkenkrieges" in Aventinus, *Sämmtliche Schriften*, 1: 172–242; here 177–82.

of arrogance, pride, conceit, rapaciousness, lewdness, extravagance, envy, wrath, gluttony, violence, impiety, evil, betrayal, cunning, malice, cruelty, and whatever other depravities and corrupted morals one can possibly think of. . . . Here all crimes rage like storms, and that is why all virtues are horribly ship-wrecked here. No greater punishment can be inflicted upon a city than that it becomes the residence of a potentate; where the court is held or wherever it is moved, it brings the most terrible misery, like a comet portending evil and like an infectious epidemic. If the court moves away, it leaves behind it irreparable damage, like a rabid dog does through his poison. [107]

In their commentaries on particular political and social groups, these humanist texts consistently criticize the behavior of the princes, indicating that their political function of leadership was being called into question. This was certainly the case outside of Germany as well, where texts like Erasmus's *On the Education of a Christian Prince* and Machiavelli's *The Prince* were produced and which sought to define appropriate leadership albeit within vastly different parameters. The humanist texts discussed above also articulate an awareness of tension and competition between political and social groups within the empire. Wilhelm's history cycle, in its implied critique of the Habsburgs, is a physical manifestation of that tension and competition. The cycle's glorification of Wilhelm can be seen to legitimate the claims to power made by a prince whose own class was much maligned by some humanists.

Wilhelm's cycle of history paintings, and Breu's two contributions to it in particular, can be seen to respond to some of the main political and intellectual trends affecting the German territories as established so far in this chapter: the politically tendentious production of

---

[107] Agrippa von Nettesheim, *Über die Fragwürdigkeit*, 161–62: "Der Hof is im Grunde nur eine Versammlung von Giganten, genauer gesagt, eine Vereinigung übelbeleumdeter adliger Windbeutel, eine Bühne übelster Subjekte, eine Schule der verruchtesten Sitten, ein Asyl für abscheulichste Verbrecher. Hier ist die Heimstatt [. . .] für Hochmut, Stolz, Einbildung, Raffgier, Unzucht, Luxus, Neid, Zorn, Völlerei, Gewalt, Gottlosigkeit, Bosheit, Verrat, List, Tücke, Grausamkeit und was sonst noch an Lastern und verderbten Sitten denkbar ist. [. . .] Hier toben alle Verbrechen wie Stürme, und deshalb leiden hier auch alle Tugenden entsetzlich Schiffbruch. [. . .] Kein größeres Verhängnis kann ein Stadt treffen, als daß sie zur Residenz eines Potentaten wird, denn wo Hof gehalten wird oder wohin er verlegt wird, dahin bringt er wie ein unheilverkündender Komet und wie eine ansteckende Seuche größtes Unglück; zieht der Hof aber weg, dann hinterläßt er wie ein tollwütiger Hund durch sein Gift unheilbare Schäden." Agrippa is writing here about the royal court of kings (Kapitel 68 "Die königliche Haus- oder Hofhaltung," 161–63) but the same could be said no doubt for any royal court.

history under the influence of German humanism; and the debates about appropriate leadership. Wilhelm IV was directly involved in both of those trends. He actively promoted the production of historiography at his court in his patronage of the humanist historian Aventinus, and he actively contested the leadership of the Habsburgs. He also commissioned the cycle of paintings that constitutes a politically tendentious version of ancient history precisely because, in its recourse to and retelling of history, it contributes to the debate about appropriate leadership by promoting Wilhelm IV as the new and legitimate ruler. And yet it does so in a sufficiently subtle way as to match the duke's own delicate political negotiations.

In its emphasis on the political, and in its use of antique sources (in the case of both of Breu's paintings, the source is Livy), Wilhelm's history cycle displays fundamental affinities with the humanist production of history. As we have seen in these texts, antiquity is held up as a model to be honored and especially to be emulated, particularly within the realm of politics and statecraft. Ancient history was meant to educate and used to prognosticate. Although some humanists argued about the appropriate degree, ancient history also had entertainment value as well. Furthermore, humanist historiography was crucial to the construction of a national identity. In some cases, this national identity was defined in part by military prowess and by affinity or competition with the ancient Romans. I believe that Wilhelm's history cycle as a whole, and Breu's paintings in particular, partake of these same functions and strategies. In Breu's art, history, like warfare and ceremony, is a cultural discourse, used to shape identity and to articulate relationships of power and thus to fashion political identity.

With such a close connection between the history cycle and the production of humanist history texts in terms of function, it is tempting to search for a humanist author who might have worked out the cycle's program. One humanist immediately and logically comes to mind: Wilhelm's court historiographer Johannes Aventinus. Barbara Eschenburg in fact argues for the plausibility of his influence on the initial program and on Altdorfer's painting in particular.[108] Following Gisela Goldberg's lead, Eschenburg points to relevant passages from Aventinus's work in which the humanist argues for the rel-

---

[108] Eschenburg, "Altdorfers *Alexanderschlacht*," 44-54.

evancy of the ancient past to the present, and in which he also criticizes Western military policies, making these shortcomings responsible for the victories of the Turks.

There are problems with the Aventinus theory, however. In a text
drafted probably in 1526 and reworked in 1529, Aventinus is openly
critical about the princes' lack of support of the emperor.[109] His anticlerical tendencies are also clearly visible here, something Wilhelm
would have found profoundly disturbing in the very years the duke
fought to keep his territories loyally Catholic. In addition, the humanist was briefly imprisoned in October 1528 for his connections
to evangelical reformers and for sympathy with their cause, in the
same year in which the first paintings of the history cycle were completed.[110] Even if we were to assume that Wilhelm was simply willing
to overlook confessional differences when it came to cultural production, or that Aventinus's plan for the cycle significantly predated his
ideological disagreements with his patron, there is simply not enough
evidence in Aventinus's writings to link him definitively to the cycle.
He does not, for example, describe the battle of Zama between Scipio and Hannibal, and he has very little to say about the story of
Lucretia. In fact, he recommends that the reader should instead consult Livy for the details:

> [Tarquinius Superbus] was at last expelled and, along with all his rela-
> tives and supporters, driven out of Rome because of adultery, in that
> his son abused the chaste woman Lucretia. Thus, the monarchy's
> name and power was forever done away with in Rome, and freedom
> and the administration by the common man, as in Switzerland, was
> instituted. The Roman empire blossomed under this state of freedom,
> as Titus Livy describes in such full detail that it is not necessary to
> write much more about it here. Whoever would like to know about it
> should read the German translation of Livy, which would be much
> more useful than cramming himself full of food and drink and wasting
> time with other foolish activities that are useful neither to God nor the
> world.[111]

---

[109] Aventinus, "Ursachen des Türkenkrieges," in Aventinus, *Sämmtliche Schriften*, 1:
172–242. Eschenburg also calls attention to this passage in her article, "Altdorfers
Alexanderschlacht," 48–49.

[110] G. Strauss, *Historian an in Age of Crisis*, 168–9.

[111] Aventinus, 4, pt. 1: 287: "[Tarquinius Superbus] ward zulest von eines
ebruchs wegen, damit sein sun die frummen frauen Lucretiam schmäht, verjagt und
aus der stat Rom mit allen den seinen [. . .] vertriben. Und wart der küniglich nam
und g'walt zue Rom zue ewigen zeiten abgetan, der frei stand und verwaltung des

In addition, the idea that the program for the cycle was firmly set in the mid- to late 1520s by Aventinus and then simply carried out over a thirteen-year period does not take into consideration the fundamental political changes during that time, and the shifts in the cycle's accents. Instead, I believe that the cycle evolved over this extended period, responding to the changing political climate in a flexible way.

Furthermore, the search for an originary text seems unnecessarily limiting and methodologically dubious. Even if a text were found that exactly described what was depicted in the paintings, the correlation between text and image does not necessarily generate significant meaning. Instead, our task is to attend to ways in which history and antiquity were produced in art in order to generate political meanings by establishing relationships of power and providing identity.

In Breu's paintings, events from ancient history are carefully staged in architectural and landscape settings. Breu's *Lucretia* narrates Livy's story of the rape and suicide of Lucretia in 509 B.C. (*Ab Urbe Condita*, bk.1, sec. 57–60) from left to right and from foreground to background (plate 12). The continuous narrative is set inside a splendid building that overlooks a kind of composite view of the city of Rome. Through the double arches of the structure, one can see the Pantheon and Trajan's column. At the panel's left margin, between the square piers, we can see Lucretia asleep in her bed, presumably before the king's son Sextus Tarquinius rapes her. Lucretia's suicide, witnessed by her male kin, occurs in the left foreground. This group of witnesses include Lucretia's husband Tarquinius Collatinus and his friend Lucius Junius Brutus, Lucretia's father Spurius Lucretius, and his friend Publius Valerius. Although her family, and even she herself, exonerate her of all guilt, she kills herself so that no abuse of chastity will go unpunished in the future through her example. With the words "not in time to come shall ever unchaste woman live through the example of Lucretia," she plunges a knife into her breast

---

g'main mans, wie in der schweiz, angenummen. Und hat under diesem freien stant das römisch reich hoch aufgenummen, wie Titus Livius nach der leng beschreibt, ist nit not hie vil krumps davon weiter zue machen; wer's gern wissen well, der les den teutschen Titum Livium, ist im vil nutzer dan das er dieweil fress und sauf und mit anderem narrenwerk die zeit unnützlikch verzer, das weder got noch der welt nuz ist."

and dies.[112] In the right foreground, the men swear an oath on the knife extracted from Lucretia's body to avenge the matron's violation by expelling from Rome the king Tarquinius Superbus, and his family, thus ending the institution of monarchy. This oath was initiated by Lucius Junius Brutus, the nephew of the Roman king. In the middle ground, Lucretia's body is carried out into the public domain of the marketplace; further back, Brutus can be seen addressing a crowd of citizens and exhorting them to take up arms against the king.

The painting thus literally sets the stage for the overthrow of the Roman monarchy. It does not tell the end of the story—in which the king and his family are driven into exile and Brutus and Lucretia's husband Collatinus are made the consuls of Rome—but the educated viewer was provided with enough visual clues about which story was being told and would be able to furnish the tale's conclusion for her- or himself.

Breu constructs antiquity in his painting through fanciful details of architecture and costume. The men in the foreground wear sandals, cuirasses, and togas that are meant to signify Roman antiquity. Besides the representation of actual Roman structures, the foreground architecture is decorated with a pastiche of antique elements: rondels on the piers depict scenes of pagan sacrifice and battles between nude men; the exuberantly composite capitals include bucrania and shell motifs; and above the cornice at the upper left, a statue of Mercury may be seen.

And yet, distinct elements of contemporaneity are also found in the painting. Lucretia's dress, with its tassels and puckered sleeves, her jewelry, and coiffure are decidedly "modern" and not antique. In addition, the man standing to her left (our right) in the left foreground bears a striking resemblance to Duke Wilhelm IV. The duke's coat of arms, and that of his wife's, are in fact suspended from the arches in much the same way as coats of arms were affixed to family property. The placement of the Bavarian coat of arms in such a manner, built into the scene and comprising part of the architectural decoration, not only indicates Wilhelm and Jacobäa's patronage of the painting in a naturalistic, nonintrusive way, but also

---

112 Livy, *The History of Rome*, trans. B. O. Foster (Cambridge, Mass. and London: Harvard University Press and William Heinemann, 1919), vol. 1, bk. I, sec. 58, p. 203.

suggests their involvement in the narrative itself. The significance of
these contemporaneous elements will be discussed below.

Thus, the world of antiquity is evoked through narrative content
and surface detail, albeit, in good humanist style, with clues that this
event from ancient history has modern relevance. By virtue of the
narrative content of Livy's history and of the narrative accents of
Breu's painting, relationships of power are established and political
identities are offered in this construction of ancient history. Clearly,
according to both Livy and Breu, Lucretia is meant to be a sympathetic figure in her courage and her innocence. In comparison to
other depictions of Lucretia in Northern Renaissance art which are
highly erotic in tone, Breu's figure retains the composure and de-
meanor of the Roman matron of Livy's story. Paintings by Lucas
Cranach (1529, University of Houston; and 1530, Munich, Alte
Pinakothek) and Albrecht Dürer (1518, Munich, Alte Pinakothek)
and prints by Hans Baldung Grien (1522, woodcut) and the Beham
brothers (Barthel's engraving from c. 1524, Hans Sebald's woodcut
of 1530 and engraving of c. 1541–5) for example, focus on the lone
figure of Lucretia, sometimes nude, sometimes in a state of undress,
thrusting a phallic sword into her breast and swooning with an expression mixing pleasure and pain. Other images, such as prints by
Heinrich Aldegrever (engraving, 1539) and Georg Pencz (engraving,
c. 1546) focus on the rape scene during which Lucretia and Tarquinius wrestle together naked in bed. In Breu's painting, however,
Lucretia remains composed and calm. Although her dress is opened
at the throat and chest to reveal her breasts, this part of her body is
not emphasized or made voluptuous as in other images such as the
ones mentioned above. Breu's Lucretia addresses the viewer directly
with a look of gentle sadness, pleading that the viewer empathize
with her situation.

If Lucretia is sympathetic and courageous, then so are the men
who swear to avenge her violation. Breu depicts them gesturing vigorously within their noble hall. The popular support that Brutus's
exhortation enjoys, indicated by Breu by the crowd assembled before
him in the background, also adds to the legitimacy of their deeds
and the story's conclusion: the overthrow of the monarchy. The
glory of the Roman republic that Brutus instituted is also vindicated
by subsequent writers of Roman history, as the informed viewer
would know. Thus, the viewer is encouraged to adopt a subject position sympathetic to Lucretia, her kinsmen, and her supporters, be-

cause they are themselves represented as worthy of sympathy and because they are the ones who, according to the judgment of history, will wield power correctly. In opposition to the corrupt rule of Tarquinius Superbus, Brutus and Collatinus will take charge of the republic and Rome will be governed fairly. These subject positions are also politically tendentious as they serve to align the viewer with particular political positions.

Breu's production of Livy's history is intensely theatrical. The elaborate architecture provides a stagelike setting for the actors, who pose, gesticulate, and cast significant glances in a studied and self-conscious way. Indeed, the arcade separating fore- from middle ground presage the proscenium arches promulgated by Sebastian Serlio for theatrical productions. And yet, significant members of the cast are missing from this play: the antagonists. The proud king and his lecherous son are completely absent. Even the rape scene is omitted. Indeed, the entire painting seems full of their absence, a presence implied but not reified, a blank that can be filled in with a number of different options. The absence of the enemy is part of the painting's politicized content, as I will argue below.

Breu's second painting for the history cycle, depicting the battle at Zama between Scipio and Hannibal,[113] reifies the enemy in an epic version of Rome versus Carthage (plate 13). If *Lucretia* represents a call to arms, then the *Battle of Zama* represents the force of arms in action.

According to Livy, the battle at Zama was the decisive confrontation in the Second Punic War between the Roman general Scipio and the Carthaginian Hannibal (in 202 B.C.) which resulted in the decisive victory of the Romans and the final downfall of Hannibal.[114] Although Hannibal had led many successful battles on the Italian peninsula, Scipio succeeded in driving him all the way back to North Africa and defeating him at Zama, southwest of Carthage. Thus, Scipio not only rid Italy of Hannibal, he also soundly defeated him

---

[113] The tablet with inscription at the top margin of the painting is a later addition from the seventeenth century, although it does correctly identify the scene below ("P. Cor Scip: Afr. De Hannibale et Car: Victoria" = the victory of Publius Cornelius Africans over Hannibal and the Carthaginians); Goldberg, *Die Alexanderschlacht*, 25.

[114] Livy, *The War with Hannibal*, trans. Aubrey de Selincourt, introduction Betty Radice (London: Penguin, 1965), 653–64. This edition basically reproduces Books 29–30 of Livy's *History of Rome*.

in his own home territory and thoroughly subdued the Carthaginians.

Breu represents the battle, as he did the story of Lucretia, by simultaneously evoking antiquity and the present. Scipio's army is identified by banners bearing the letters SPQR (senatus populusque Romanus [the senate and the Roman people]). The walled town and fortress flanked by tents and soldiers in the right background are labeled "NADAGRA," a reference to Scipio's camp at Naragarra.[115] The elephants that Hannibal had strategically placed in the front lines of his army are included in Breu's rendition, although they are found in the middle- and background of the battlefield. The painting's foreground space is reserved for the struggle between the Roman and Carthaginian cavalry, the decisive confrontation that afforded Scipio final victory, according to Livy. Scipio himself is included in the depiction, in the lower-right corner. Although we see him only from behind, the inscription on his horse's caparison ("Cipio Affricani") identifies his figure.

Yet the sixteenth-century present intrudes on this event from ancient Roman history. Breu has rendered Scipio's Roman army as "modern" European cavalry while Hannibal's soldiers wear the pointed turbans of "modern" Turks. The confrontation between the Muslim Turks and Catholic Europe, a political and religious issue since the medieval crusades, had newly acquired an even greater urgency; in 1529, Turks got as far west as Vienna and laid siege to the city. Altdorfer's painting for the duke's cycle dated 1529 and depicting Alexander the Great's victory in 333 B.C. over the Persian general Darius similarly equates the victorious Western army with a modern European one and the defeated Eastern army with the Turks. In this way, the West's ancient enemies (Persians and Carthaginians) are equated in both Altdorfer's and Breu's paintings with the West's modern enemies, the Turks.

One important subject position offered by the painting seems relatively clear: no one in ca. 1530 wanted to sympathize with the Turks. Contemporary broadsheets in fact depicted the Turks as horrible savages who raped Christian women and murdered their children.[116] Instead, an appropriate subject position suggested by the

---

[115] Livy, *The War with Hannibal,* 654.
[116] Keith Moxey, *Peasants, Warriors and Wives: Popular Imagery in the Reformation* (Chicago: University of Chicago Press, 1989), 76–78.

painting is to identify with the victorious ancient Roman/modern European army. Such a position would be in keeping with humanist texts' construction of German identity by affinity with the ancient Romans. Yet the relationship of power between the two forces of East and West, although clearly established in historical hindsight for the third-century B.C. conflict, is not so certain in either the painting or the painting's context. Just who will emerge victorious from the seething melee of men and animals is not immediately evident on the painting's surface, just as the eventual Turkish retreat from Vienna in no way signaled the West's final and conclusive victory over the East. Thus the painting becomes a kind of articulation of a historically informed wish-fulfillment: although yet in the thick of the battle, the Europeans will emerge triumphant over the Turks just as Scipio defeated Hannibal in the fierce battle at Zama.

Other modern-day intrusions include Duke Wilhelm's coat of arms, and the initials H W ("Herzog Wilhelm"[117]) located on a small tablet at the bottom right of the painting; next to the tablet lies a fallen signpost upon which the artist has signed his name. A white stallion ridden by a helmeted knight leaps over the tablet and sign. Directly behind him rides a knight who appears to bear the likeness of the Habsburg Emperor Maximilian I (d. 1519). The significance of his inclusion will be discussed later.

In the versions of ancient history narrated in Breu's paintings, relationships of power are constructed in which certain groups, designated in history texts and the paintings as either morally virtuous (Lucretia and her supporters) or militarily superior (Scipio's Roman army), are represented as overcoming an enemy designated as foreign, other, and ultimately vanquished (the Tarquinian kings, who were Etruscan, and Hannibal's Carthaginian army). With this power structure in place, the viewer is encouraged to adopt subject positions in line with the virtuous and victorious groups, in other words, with the Romans. This sympathetic attitude toward the Romans, their function as historical exempla, and their relationship to the Germans are all in keeping with the humanist production of history as we have seen.

Upon closer inspection, however, Breu's paintings offer further

---

[117] Gisela Goldberg has suggested this interpretation of the initials, *Die Alexanderschlacht*, 25.

definitions of just who the virtuous and victorious might be. Here the
paintings can be seen to participate in the debate about legitimate
leadership and theories of state. They serve Wilhelm's interests by
drawing attention to different forms and components of a state that
accommodate Wilhelm's desire to take over leadership of Germany.
The definition of who is virtuous and victorious in the paintings, I
argue, has several layers. On the first layer, lying on the surface of
the narrative, it is the Romans, as we have seen. On another layer,
however, it is Duke Wilhelm of Bavaria.

According to Livy, the story of Lucretia is ultimately the story of
corrupt government. In the pages preceding the story of Lucretia,
Livy describes the reign of Tarquinius Superbus (543–510 B.C.) in
strongly negative tones.[118] Livy criticizes the king for making the
plebeians labor too intensely and for neglecting to consult with the
senate. Thus, affairs of state were conducted entirely on the basis of
the king's desires and needs, instead of on the basis of his people's:

> For this king was the first to break with the custom handed down by
> his predecessors, of consulting the senate on all occasions, and gov-
> erned the nation without other advice than that of his own household.
> War, peace, treaties and alliances were entered upon or broken off by
> the monarch himself, with whatever states he wished, and without the
> decree of people or senate. The Latin race he strove particularly to
> make his friends, that his strength abroad might contribute to his secu-
> rity at home.[119]

To make matters worse, Livy reveals that Tarquinius Superbus had
no right to rule to begin with; in order to ascend the throne, he had
the former king murdered, who was also his father-in-law. The only
words of praise Livy has for the king is to concede that "he was not a
bad general in war."[120]

The government of Tarquinius Superbus therefore lacked legitimacy, not only in terms of the rights of hereditary ascension, but
also in terms of the sovereign's lack of the appropriate relationship
with his subjects. Like von Hutten's later argument in *Arminius*,
Livy's narrative demonstrates that a government lacking legitimacy
will ultimately fail to command its subjects' loyalty. The action of the
king's son, the rape of Lucretia, was merely the straw that broke the

---

[118] Livy, *The History of Rome*, bk. 1, sec. 49–56, pp. 171–95.
[119] Livy, *The History of Rome*, 173.
[120] Livy, *The History of Rome*, 183.

camel's back, a catalyst that allowed the Romans to mobilize themselves against a government and a leader who ruled without consideration of their needs. What followed the fall of the monarchy in Rome was a republic in which Brutus and another man held the offices of consul.

In Wilhelm's own day, six forms of government were recognized and discussed: monarchy/principality, aristocracy, democracy, tyranny, oligarchy, and anarchy.[121] The first three were seen as related to the second three, and the relative merits of each of the first three was open to debate. According to these categories, the Roman Republic as established by Lucius Junius Brutus and Lucretia's husband corresponded, not to a democracy, but to an aristocracy, where only a few men controlled and exercised power. Machiavelli recognized the limited nature of the Roman republic instituted at the overthrow of the monarchy:

> And when it happened that her [Rome's] kings lost their power for the reasons and in the ways described earlier, nonetheless those who drove them out, having immediately established two consuls in place of the king, drove out only the title of king and not royal power; so that, as there were in that republic the consuls and the senate, it came to be formed by only two of the three above-mentioned elements, that is, the principality and the aristocrats.[122]

When analyzed in this way, the historical narrative of Lucretia becomes an appropriate vehicle for articulating Wilhelm's goals to challenge the Habsburg monarchy. As discussed earlier, Habsburg rule could be construed as both foreign and corrupt, with the perennially absent emperor refusing to consult with the German princes on important issues in a manner similar to the description of Tarquinius Superbus's reign.

Furthermore, there is contemporaneous precedence for the interpretation of the Lucretia narrative on an entirely political level having to do with the legitimacy of state and leadership. Interesting in terms of the theatricality displayed in Breu's paintings, these precedents come from the realm of theater. In 1527, one year before

---

[121] See Agrippa von Nettesheim, *Über die Fragwürdigkeit*, chapter 55 "Politik," 114–18; and Machiavelli, *The Discourses*, 176–79. Machiavelli uses the term "principality" for "monarchy," but as far as their definitions go, the two terms mean the same thing.

[122] Machiavelli, *The Discourses*, 180–81.

Breu completed his depiction of Lucretia, two dramas were written about her. One, written by the Swiss theologian Heinrich Bullinger, parallels the overthrow of the Roman monarchy with the overthrow of aristocratic rule and the consolidation of power in the hands of the guilds in Zurich.[123] Although this interpretation of Lucretia would not have been appropriate for Wilhelm's situation, Bullinger's drama nonetheless attests to the willingness to reinterpret ancient history in a modern, political, and tendentious sense.

The other drama was written by Hans Sachs. Although the opening commentary to the play refers to a "Spiegel der zuchtigen Weyber [mirror of chaste women]," the closing commentary makes clear that the drama is less about women and much more about the state and leadership:

> Now honorable sirs, see how, because of this dastardly deed, the Roman people and senate expelled King Tarquinius and his eldest son Tarquin, who was defeated at Gabia, as the historians report. So the Roman government, which was established by Romulus and which lasted for 244 years, suddenly came to an end, just as today unjust power cannot be sustained. Where such power is tyrannical, there it provokes discord and insurrection and in the end falls into ruin. However, where there is a praiseworthy government—one that is just, merciful, mild, gentle, true to its constituents, benevolent, cautious, wise and always truthful—the territory and the people remain obedient and at peace. The territory grows increasingly honorable and prosperous because God protects it and gives it strength, might and vigor: so says Hans Sachs from Nuremberg.[124]

---

[123] Discussed in Derek von Abbe, *Drama in Renaissance Germany and Switzerland* (Melbourne: Melbourne University Press, 1961), 42–43.

[124] Hans Sachs, "Tragedia von der Lucretia, auß der beschreybung Livii, hat 1 actus und 10 person" in *Hans Sachs*, ed. Adalbert von Keller, vol. 140 (Tübingen, 1979), 3–14, here 13–14. "Nun secht an, ihr ersamen herr!/Durch dise lesterliche that/Das römisch volck und der senat/Vertrieben konig Tarquinium/Mit seinem eltesten Sohn Sextum/Der zu Gabia ward erschlagen/Als die historien thut sagen./Also das königlich regiment/Zu Rohm nam also geling end/Das von Romulo gstanden war/Zwey hundert vier und vierzig jar./Also noch heut zu disem tag/Unrechter gwalt nicht bleiben mag./Wo er tyrannisieret nur/Richt er an zwitracht und auffrur/Und geht zu drümmern an dem end./Aber ein loblich regiment,/Gerecht, barmherzig, milt, sanftmütig,/Ihrn unterthan trew, lind und gütig,/Fürsichtig, weiss, warhaft allzeit,/Da bleibt in frid land und leut/Und bleibt gehorsam iederman [. . .]./Das Land nimbt zu an ehr und gut,/Wann Gott hat sie in seiner hut/Und verleicht ihn kraft, macht und sterck./So spricht Hans Sachs von Nurembergk."

In Sachs's text, an unjust government that does not take care of its constituents is bound to fall, whereas a just government is rewarded by unity, prosperity, loyalty, and God's grace. This is the lesson meant to be learned from the dramatization of Livy's story, a lesson to be applied to Sachs's own time ("Even just as it is today [Also noch heut zu disem tag]. . ."). Sachs does not specify which form that government should take; its legitimacy is based solely on its moral virtue. Agrippa von Nettesheim comes to a similar conclusion; the form of government is not the critical issue, the suitability and talents of the leader(s) is: "However, in the end, the integrity and the capacity of the administrators weigh more heavily for the ideal administration of a state than some philosophy, ingenious system or theoretical knowledge. One person, a few people, or an entire population can all exercise leadership in an ideal fashion–if they are morally upright and capable."[125]

The story of Lucretia, and contemporaneous receptions of it, indicate that it was ideally suited for debating the legitimacy of government and leadership. As such, it was also ideally suited for Wilhelm's purposes to cast aspersions, by implication, on the Habsburg right to rule. Furthermore, the story and the painting of Lucretia also provide Wilhelm with an appropriate opportunity to advance his own political leadership, which would supplant that of the Habsburgs, as legitimate and just. This is accomplished by emphasizing historical and visual parallels between Wilhelm and Brutus.

The historical Brutus, the man who galvanized resentment against the king and his family and who eventually took over control, was the king's own nephew. Tarquinius Superbus's sister was Brutus's mother. Similarly, Wilhelm was Maximilian of Habsburg's nephew; Maximilian's sister, Kunigunde, was Wilhelm's mother. In order to underscore the parallels between the historical situation in the ancient Roman monarchy and in the modern Holy Roman Empire, Breu portrays the figure of Brutus in the left foreground as Wilhelm IV. This figure, to Lucretia's left (our right) can be identified as Brutus because he is the same figure in the right foreground who

---

[125] Agrippa von Nettesheim, *Über die Fragwürdigkeit*, 118: "Letztlich hat aber für die ideale Regierung eines Staates die Rechtschaffenheit und Befähigung der Regenten größeres Gewicht als irgendeine Philosophie, ein kunstreiches System oder theoretisches Wissen. Vorbildlich die Herrschaft führen können einer, einige wenige oder das gesamte Volk–wenn sie rechtschaffen und fähig dazu sind."

initiates the oath sworn on Lucretia's dagger. And that initiator, according to Livy, was Brutus. Comparison with Hans Wertinger's portrait of Wilhelm IV from 1526 (Alte Pinakothek, Munich) reveals significant similarities between the duke and the figure in Breu's painting. The long nose, ear-length hair, moustache, and square-trimmed beard are shared by Breu's figure and Wertinger's portrait. A further portrait of Wilhelm in the cycle, who appears as a by-stander in Hans Schöpfer's panel from 1535 depicting the story of Virginia, substantiates the claim that the duke wished to be seen within the context of ancient history. The argument here is that accessing this context also meant accessing specific notions about virtue that could be applied to the duke himself.

In addition, the figure of Brutus/Wilhelm in Breu's painting stands adjacent to Wilhelm's coat of arms suspended from the arch. The placement of the coat of arms within the architectural setting serves to imply that the space contained within the architecture also belongs to the duke and thus may make reference to the Wittelsbach court in Munich. In a similar way, Hans Schöpfer included the towers of the Frauenkirche in Munich in his city scape of Rome, as Gisela Goldberg has pointed out.[126] The appearance of Wilhelm's coat of arms in Breu's painting also legitimizes the duke's claims to authority by placing his house historically in Roman antiquity.

In the painting, Brutus is equated with Wilhelm. This equation would presumably include both the ultimate victory as well the moral virtue of both men. Knowledge of Livy's account of Lucretia and resentment against Habsburg hegemony could stimulate an informed viewer to thus equate Tarquinius Superbus, the king of Rome who ruled unwisely, with Charles V of Habsburg, the Holy Roman emperor, at whose command Rome had recently been sacked. Wilhelm's direct gaze out at the viewer in the guise of Brutus, the man who would overthrow the king and take control, could be read as a signal of Wilhelm's own challenge of authority and of his own readiness and suitability for leadership. That Wilhelm's plan would not necessarily include the institution of a republic in the strict sense does not detract from the applicability of Lucretia's story to the duke's desires. As we have seen in contemporaneous reception of Livy's text, it was the legitimacy, not the form of government, that

---

[126] G. Goldberg, *Die Alexanderschlacht*, 55.

was at stake. Furthermore, Brutus's consulship was recognized by Machiavelli as rule of the aristocracy, with monarchical elements still present, not a democracy. This form of rule would probably indeed have been in line with Wilhelm's goals.

If Breu's painting of Lucretia argues for the legitimacy of Wilhelm's political leadership, the artist's rendition of the battle of Zama argues for the duke's military leadership. We recall from chapter 3 that the ability to wage war successfully was an important component of political leadership, and from this chapter, that military prowess was constructed by some humanists to be an essential component of specifically German identity.

Military leadership was an issue of particular relevance after the 1529 Turkish siege of Vienna as this event pointed out the inability of the Western powers and their military to effectively keep the Turks away from Western territories. We have already noted that the Carthaginian soldiers are dressed as Turks in Breu's painting, and Eschenburg has already made the connection between the work (and Altdorfer's) and the perceived need of a crusade against the Turks.[127]

Current dissatisfaction with military organization, in some cases directly related to the West's impotence in dealing with the Turks, was articulated in some sources. Eschenburg quotes from Aventinus's ca. 1529 text in which the humanist compares the Roman, Turkish, and German military and finds the first two similar to each other, with Germany the odd man out.[128] The similarity between the ways in which the Turkish and Roman armies are organized, financed, and then put into action explains the Turks' success over the Germans, according to Aventinus. However, Eschenburg does not make the connection between Aventinus's praise of the Turks' practice of pursuing their foes even into enemy territory, and the history of the Second Punic War. Scipio not only drove Hannibal from the Italian peninsula, he also pursued him into Hannibal's own North African territory and defeated him there at Zama. The battle

---

[127] Eschenburg, "Altdorfers *Alexanderschlacht*," 43 and 66.

[128] Aventinus, "Anzaigung wie und in was wege das alt römisch regiment sein kriegsregiment mit den gestiften kriegsleuten hab gestelt und angericht und wie man noch auf heutigen tag, wil man anderst dem Türken ain pleiblichen widerstand tun, sölch aufrichten möcht" in *Sämmtliche Werke*, 1: 243-53. Quoted in Eschenburg, "Altdorfers *Alexanderschlacht*," 44.

of Zama, then, is an example of a particularly effective military strategy that deals decisively with the enemy, in contrast to the current
lack of decisive military action against the Turks.

In his pamphlet, Aventinus argues for reorganizing the military
according to the ancient Roman model. In *The Art of War*, Machiavelli does the same. In particular, Machiavelli uses the Roman military to argue conservatively for an army that is made up only of
local citizens and for the continued employment of cavalry.[129] In
making these arguments, Machiavelli is reacting to the increasing
employment of infantry troops made up of foreign mercenaries,
whereby the cavalry played an increasingly insignificant role. These
two issues are also relevant to the battle at Zama. Livy describes how
Hannibal's army was impacted negatively by the fact that it mixed
Carthaginians with many other nationalities. Hannibal's harangue of
his army seems to have been a complicated procedure because it
involved interpreters, and he was still in the act when the Romans
already came upon him. And when they attacked, the Roman war-
cry was more effective because all the soldiers spoke the same language: "There were . . . factors which seem trivial to recall, but
proved of great importance at the time of action. The Roman war-
cry was louder and more terrifying because it was in unison, whereas
the cries from the Carthaginian side were discordant, coming as they
did from a mixed assortment of peoples with a variety of mother-
tongues."[130] Livy further credits the attack of the cavalry with the
final defeat of Hannibal's polyglot army.[131]

The battle of Zama as historical event thus could be seen as an
example of an efficacious military strategy and organization put into
action as a critical commentary on the lack of either in the current
military. In addition, the battle of Zama as painted narrative indicates that this successful strategy and organization is needed in dealing with contemporary foes (the Turks), and that there is someone
who could provide this military leadership. In the historical event,
that leader is of course Scipio Africanus. In the painting, however,
Scipio's leadership is visually minimalized. We have already noticed
his figure in the bottom right-hand corner of the panel. However, we

---

[129] Machiavelli, *The Art of War*, Book 1 (7–43) contains his argument that soldiers
should be local citizens, whereas Book 2 (44–82) explains the role of the cavalry.

[130] Livy, *The War with Hannibal*, 661–62.

[131] Ibid., 663.

see him only from the back, and without the label on his horse's saddle-blanket, it would be impossible to identify him at all.

Instead of focusing on Scipio, our eyes are drawn instead to the leaping white stallion and his rider in the right foreground. They are given visual prominence by size, color and placement. The stallion and the rider are larger than any of the other figures; they also stand out from the dense, interlocking pattern of soldiers by virtue of the stallion's brilliant white color and the fact that the one corner of unencumbered space in the entire painting, besides the sky, is found beneath and between the stallion's hooves. It is also in this strangely vacant place that Breu has chosen to insert Wilhelm's coat of arms and the artist's own signature. While Scipio stands with his back to the viewer and turns away from the battle in action, the rider on the white stallion charges energetically into the fray, the cavalry following him behind and off to his right side.

Who is this brave knight, who, in the confused and swirling mass of soldiers, provides the only moment of vigorous forward thrust, leading the calvary into its ultimately victorious attack? Livy's text provides no answer. The painting, however, might provide its own clue. I believe that the juxtaposition of Wilhelm's coat of arms, the initials H W (for "Herzog Wilhelm"), and the knight on the white stallion are significant, and that upon closer inspection we are meant to identity the knight with Wilhelm. Commemorative equestrian portraits of generals, princes, and emperors often include the personage's coat of arms or clarifying inscription situated below the horse's hooves. Examples of this can be seen in the Italian quattrocento frescoes in the Cathedral of Florence by Paolo Uccello (equestrian portrait of Sir John Hawkwood, 1436) and Andrea Castagno (portrait of Niccoló da Tolentino, 1456).

Both of Breu's paintings can thus be seen to promote Wilhelm IV as a great leader. In *Lucretia*, it is his political leadership that is represented as legitimate and forceful; in the *Battle of Zama*, it is his military leadership that is represented as vigorous and effective. And yet the paintings also offer alternative interpretations that compete with the interpretation I have been laying out above which focuses on Wilhelm's leadership. In fact, one could even speak of issues of dissimulation, in both the historical and the visual narratives.

Livy's story of Lucretia includes the transformation of Brutus from a man people believed to be somewhat lacking in wits, to the founder of the Roman Republic. Brutus in fact had acted as if he were unintelligent in order to save himself from his uncle's treachery. Livy describes Brutus as:

> a young man of a very different mind from that which he pretended to bear. Having heard that the leading men of the state, and among them his own brother, had been put to death by his uncle, he determined to leave nothing in his disposition which the king might justly fear . . . , resolving to find safety in contempt, where justice afforded no protection. He therefore deliberately assumed the appearance of stupidity . . . ; he even accepted the surname Brutus [meaning dullard], that behind the screen afforded by this title, the great soul which was to free the Roman people might bide its time unseen.[132]

Dissimulation even plays a small but crucial role in the battle of Zama. Preceding the battle, Scipio and Hannibal meet for a lengthy discussion (Livy's own narrative construction). Although Hannibal sues for peace, Scipio rejects the offer. The two commanders then part and each returns to his soldiers in order to verbally prepare them for battle. In his carefully arranged harangue meant to inspire his troops with courage and confidence, Scipio included information that he supposedly gleaned from his discussion with Hannibal. Livy states, however, that Scipio used his meeting with Hannibal in his speech to convey what he wished, and what would benefit his troops, rather than what actually transpired between the two commanders: "Furthermore, he [Scipio] made good use of his conference with Hannibal, which, as it had taken place without witnesses, he was free to misrepresent in any way he pleased."[133] Dissimulation then was a necessary strategy of physical and political survival and one which, through Livy's narrative, clearly enjoyed historical sanction. Both Brutus and Scipio know how to use dissimulation to their advantage and are ultimately successful in their endeavors.

It would also have been at times in Wilhelm's best interests to dissimulate. Although the duke could count on resentment of the Habsburgs in his challenge of their authority, the success of that challenge was far from certain. Indeed, Wilhelm ultimately failed in his endeavor. We see him maintaining a careful facade of loyalty, for example, in the great celebration he staged for Charles's adventus at Munich in 1530, immediately preceding the emperor's visit to

---

132 Livy, *The History of Rome*, bk. 1, 195.
133 Livy, *The War with Hannibal*, 659.

Augsburg, and which was discussed in chapter 4. At no time was Wilhelm's challenge officially and openly issued, and as we have seen, the duke was quite prepared to carry on simultaneous negotiations with and against the Habsburgs.

Wilhelm's paintings are just as careful, and in the alternative interpretations they offer, they also can be seen to dissimulate. In each painting, visual elements are provided–and in the case of *Lucretia*, also negated–which point to very different meanings. Thus, a variety of political subject positions are offered to the viewer, encouraging rather than foreclosing on multivalence.

In *Lucretia*, we have already noted the absence of the antagonists: the Roman king and his son. This perhaps was a precautionary strategy undertaken so that the equation of the ancient and the Habsburg monarchy remained at the level of implication. In this way, the painting avoids becoming an outright statement of clear political antagonism, a statement that could be held against Wilhelm if his bid for power failed, as it in fact did.

In addition, the inclusion of the figures of Adam and Eve above the cornice in the right half of the painting provides a ready-made moralizing interpretation of the scene below. The content of the painting becomes an indictment of the sin of lust, as exemplified by Eve tempting Adam with the apple, and as transferred onto the narrative of Lucretia, the unwitting temptress and object of Sextus Tarquinius's lust. The fall of the monarchy is equated with the fall of man from grace. Thus, the content of the painting is shifted from politically charged and highly specific to morally charged and historically generalized.

In the *Battle of Zama*, the presence of the Emperor Maximilian behind the knight we have identified as Wilhelm might also function as a kind of hermeneutic decoy, this time meant to signify Habsburg loyalty. To include Maximilian in the number of Scipio's victorious troops was certainly a way of honoring an emperor who had taken such a vital interest in warfare, as we have seen in chapter 3. Even if the knight was identified by some as Wilhelm, Maximilian's direct proximity to his nephew might have been interpreted as Wilhelm literally receiving backing from his famous (albeit deceased) uncle. In many ways pertinent to the history cycle, Wilhelm followed Maximilian's lead: many of the artists he commissioned to produce its paintings, especially from the first phase of production, were those who had previously worked for Maximilian (Altdorfer, Breu, Burgkmair).[134] In addition, he seems to have taken the idea of employing a court historiographer from his uncle.[135]

Furthermore, when both of the paintings are viewed within the context of the entire cycle, they could be interpreted as simply a manifestation of Wilhelm's humanist education and a signal of his knowledge of and appreciation for classical antiquity, without necessarily any political component involved. These famous men and women from past history could be viewed simply as moral exempla, as providing a generalized theme of virtue cumulatively articulated in a broad expanse of rich oil paintings, which in sum also point to the duke's financial resources and the splendor of his court.

Thus, a number of different interpretations of Breu's paintings are all possible and in fact seem to be encouraged by elements within the art works. If we now take into consideration possible original locations of the paintings, it becomes clear why the insistence on multivalence was such a good idea.

It is not known for certain where the paintings originally hung or even where they were displayed during the thirteen years of the cycle's continuing production. Otto Hartig suggests that the paintings hung in the duke's garden *Lusthaus* ("pleasure house") on the basis of some letters of Italian diplomats who visited the Munich court in 1530 and of a text written in 1565 by Samuel Quicchelberg.[136] Gisela Goldberg, I believe quite rightly, treats Hartig's theory with skepticism.[137] The paintings mentioned by the sixteenth-century sources do not necessarily correspond to those of the history cycle. The one Italian, Cesare Gracio, who is most specific in his reference to the paintings, describes them as depicting landscapes and scenes of hunting, dancing, and battling.[138] Yet the history cycle as it existed in 1530 did not include pure landscapes or scenes of hunting or dancing. On the basis of earlier examples of *uomini famosi* cycles, Goldberg argues for a much more official and representative location than a garden pleasure house for the duke's history cycle, such as an audience hall. Structures that might come into question could be the palacelike building also located in the garden that the diplo-

---

[134] Eschenburg notes this as well, "Altdorfers *Alexanderschlacht*," 57.

[135] Joachimson, *Geschichtsauffassung und Geschichtsschreibung*, 199.

[136] Hartig, "Die Kunsttätigkeit," 151–58.

[137] Goldberg, *Die Alexanderschlacht*, 59–61.

[138] The letter is reproduced in Hartig, "Die Kunsttätigkeit," 153–55 and Goldberg, *Die Alexanderschlacht*, 60.

mats also mention, as Goldberg suggests, or even perhaps the newly constructed portion of the ducal residence.[139]

Even if we cannot pin down the exact location of the room in which the paintings actually hung, the scale, size, and character of the history cycle, even as it existed in 1530, was sufficiently grandiose to merit display in an important and semipublic space, such as an audience hall, somewhere within the residential complex. Such a cycle was not meant for private, intimate delectation, but for open display and serious contemplation. Clearly, a cycle such as Wilhelm's, meant to signify its patron's wealth and learning by its broad historical and physical sweep, called for an audience. Who constituted such an audience?

In order to answer that question, we have to speculate on who would have had access to the semipublic spaces of the residence, such as an audience hall. This would include members of Wilhelm's court, in other words, certain members of the German nobility. Such an audience might indeed have been sympathetic to Wilhelm's political goal to provide German leadership in place of Habsburg hegemonic control, given the political tensions within the empire. The members of the nobility might indeed have viewed the paintings and understood their careful promulgation of Wilhelm's projected claims to power.

Access to such spaces in Wilhelm's residence was not confined to members of court alone, however. As we know from Charles's visit to Munich in 1530, diplomats, foreign dignitaries, members of the Roman curia, and even the Habsburg emperor himself visited Wilhelm's court and could have seen the paintings. This group of people represents an audience of powerful men much more diverse in their political allegiances. One such potential political allegiance would have been to the Habsburgs. Therefore, to make a clear statement challenging the Habsburgs in a medium potentially accessible to powerful Habsburg supporters (or even to members of the Habsburg family themselves) would have been unwise. Instead, it behooved Wilhelm to articulate his aims in a circumspect and ambiguous way. When viewing the paintings, unsuspecting Habsburg supporters could interpret them simply as illustrations of ancient history appropriate by precedence and tradition to the halls of a prince. In

---

[139] Otto Meitinger, "Baugeschichte der Neuveste," *Oberbayerisches Archiv für vaterländische Geschichte* 92 (1970): 31ff.

other words, a political interpretation was not necessary in order to
invest meaning in or extract it from the cycle. If Wilhelm practiced
delicate political and diplomatic negotiations surrounded by his
paintings, for example, within the confines of an audience hall, then
the paintings themselves had to be diplomatic. To signify several
things at once, to offer those in the know appropriate political positions while simultaneously offering those who should not know still
others, is an example of profoundly political and diplomatic activity.

The interpretation of Breu's two paintings as signifying, in a politically cautious manner, Wilhelm's bid for leadership is not inconsistent with the other five paintings produced within the first phase
of production (1528–ca.1530). All of the other paintings can be interpreted as responding to contemporary issues that Wilhelm might
have used to justify his intended actions. Hans Burgkmair's *Victory of
Hannibal over the Romans at Cannae* (1529) and Melchior Feselen's
Cloelia (also 1529) provide narratives, based on Livy, that feature
Rome in trouble at the hands of foreign enemies. In Burgkmair's
painting, Hannibal, who has yet to be defeated by Scipio at Zama, is
depicted defeating the Roman army near the Italian city of Cannae.
The story of Cloelia takes place during the siege of Rome at the
hands of the Etruscan king Porsenna (508 B.C.). Cloelia is a Roman
woman who had been sent as a hostage to Porsenna but manages to
escape with several other women. Feselen's painting depicts the siege
camp of Porsenna, and the escape of the Roman women. Porsenna
demands that the women be sent back to him, although the king
subsequently allows Cloelia to return to Rome as a reward for her
bravery. Cloelia's audience with Porsenna upon her return to the
Etruscan king's camp appears in the middle foreground of Feselen's
painting, in which Porsenna is depicted in strict profile, mounted on
his horse, holding his baton of command. In other words, Porsenna
looks very much like equestrian portraits of rulers, including, for example, Burgkmair's woodcut of the Emperor Maximilian on horseback from 1508. Both of these paintings representing foreign enemies threatening Rome might be making reference to the sack of
Rome by Charles's imperial troops in 1527, an action that, as discussed previously, could be seen as seriously undermining the legitimacy of Habsburg right to rule as Holy Roman Emperor. Especially
the equestrian portrait in Feselen's painting could be read as an indictment of the emperor, in which the Etruscan king Porsenna
stands in for Charles.

Altdorfer's *Battle of Issus* can be seen to respond to the same issues as Breu's *Battle of Zama*, namely, to the threat of the East (in the sixteenth century, the Turks) to the West, and the need for capable and effective military leadership to vanquish that threat.

Burgkmair's *Esther and Ahasver* (1528) and Beham's *Empress Helena and the True Cross* (1530) both make references to religious issues. Queen Esther personally intervenes to save her people, with whom God had made his covenant, from slaughter at the hands of the Persians. The Empress Helena rescues Christ's cross, sign of the new covenant, from oblivion and destruction. Both women make clear and active demonstrations of their faith, the consequences of which serve to preserve and protect the faith of others. In a similar manner, Wilhelm could be seen as the defender of his faith by his active persecution of the Anabaptists and Lutherans in his territories, and his staunch loyalty to Rome. This constituted a very different position, it might be argued, from the one adopted by Charles, whose troops in 1527 terrorized the pope and almost destroyed Rome.

These other paintings in the cycle produced during the first phase of production thus do not contradict the reading of Breu's panels and in fact serve to bolster and further the claims made there. Therefore, the interpretation I have offered for Breu's paintings seems consistent with their larger, immediate, artistic context: the first portion of the entire history cycle.

Breu's contributions to Wilhelm's history cycle provide instructive examples of how complex the relationship among art, history, power, and meaning can be. A Zwinglian artist, known for his production of pro-Habsburg art (in itself an interesting situation, as we have seen), paints two panels for the main Habsburg rival, Wilhelm IV of Bavaria, a man the artist singled out for criticism on several occasions in his chronicle. The panels participate in a humanist discourse of history, fashioning German identity and commenting on the nature of the state through the retelling of ancient history. In doing so, the panels provide a number of equally suitable yet competing subject positions: as educated viewers who enjoy understanding the historical references for their own sake, as visitors to the court who are impressed by the scale of Wilhelm's art patronage, as viewers who incline toward a national, pro-Wittelsbach position, and those who incline toward an imperial, pro-Habsurg one. The paintings are vigorously multivalent and thus, I have argued, perfectly suited for their intensely political function.

CONCLUSION

In reflecting upon his experiences in Rome, where between 1786 and 1788 he had seen and studied the art of classical antiquity, Goethe remarked: "The most decisive effect of all works of art is that they carry us back to the conditions of the period and of the individuals who created them."[1] In considering the trajectories traced by the preceding chapters, examining the art of Jörg Breu the Elder has afforded us insight into a highly volatile and extremely dynamic period in the history of Early Modern Germany. In the process, we have become familiar not only with political conditions but also with a politically astute and successful artist whose reception in our own day has languished unnecessarily. We have seen how Breu constructed visual narratives of warfare, ceremony, and history in response to various historical and political circumstances. The function of these narratives was to shape political identity. Commissioning, viewing, purchasing, or displaying these works have here been interpreted as politically meaningful acts in which the patron/audience responds to political issues articulated in the work of art. By doing so, the patron/audience is thus aligned with a variety of ideological assumptions supporting the particular issues. Through this alignment, political community is created and potentially mobilized, focused either on consensus or critique of existing or projected structures of power.

Yet Breu's art has also demonstrated that this relationship between art and politics is decidedly complicated. Analyzing Breu's art in its historical context and with regard to its potential audiences revealed that the political identity fashioned therein was not monolithic but in fact multifarious. Issues of civic identity intersected and also competed with issues of imperial identity (as in the frescoes for the Augsburg city hall); national identity undergirded and also outstripped imperial identity (as in the battle of Pavia woodcut); and local aristocratic identity presented itself as simultaneously supportive and subversive with regard to imperial identity (the adventus se-

---

[1] Goethe, *Italian Journey*, trans. W. H. Auden (London: Penguin Books, 1962), 489.

ries and Breu's history paintings for Wilhelm IV of Bavaria). Even the artist's own identity, as fashioned in his city chronicle, was socially and politically complicated and contradictory.

The complexity that emerges from this study has two important consequences. First, it emphasizes the importance of conceptualizing identity as multivalent and flexible. As the consideration of the Reformation's institutionalization in Augsburg has shown, what it meant to be evangelical (as a follower of Luther, Zwingli, Karlstadt, or Müntzer) was still very much in the process of being worked out in the 1520s and 1530s. As the analysis clearly demonstrates, these boundaries of confessional identity were still decidedly permeable and elastic; individuals constructed their confessional identities according to a surprisingly wide spectrum of social and political postitions. The same can be said for political identity, oscillating between imperial, national, and civic/local poles. The relationship between these poles was always different according to time and place.

Second, recognizing the complexity of mutually inflected social, confessional, and political relationships and identities leads the historian also to understand the vital role played by art and other forms of cultural production in at least attempting to confine if not to control such complexity. When identities are constantly in a state of flux, when sources and structures of power are consistently contested, then the need to reiterate or redefine those identities, to assert or reconfigure those structures becomes particularly urgent. Art is one of the most important vehicles by which people have sought to fix identity and justify power. This being said, however, the indeterminacy of meaning in a work of art always leaves things open to other interpretations. In the case of Breu's art, this indeterminacy has been recognized as an advantage, allowing for his works' distinct flexibility in fashioning and accomodating a variety of political identities. This flexibility is also an advantage to the historian, who is thus called upon to understand a range of historical and hermeneutic possibilities; questions dealing in an informed manner with issues of historical causality and relativity, and with the meaning of art, never have just one answer.

Attending to Breu's work reveals that the creation of political identity is a crucial function of art, and that this creation is a complex and historically revealing process. This insight is as relevant to Early Modern Germany as it is to our intensely visual postmodern culture. We need to understand how political identities are shaped today in contemporary art and especially in the widely accessible visual media of television, film, and increasingly, the internet. How are these identities manipulated? Whose interests do they serve? To what social, economic, and political conditions are they responding? What are the larger consequences of embracing or rejecting such identities? Issues vital to historical inquiry of Early Modern Germany regarding the nature of the relationship between art and politics, between image and power structures, still urgently need thoughtful and critical attention if we are to be responsible citizens of our global village. To have learned this lesson for the past will hopefully encourage us to learn it also for the present.

BIBLIOGRAPHY

I. *Primary Sources*

Angelo, Sydney, ed. *La Tryumphante Entree da Charles Prince des Espagnes an Bruges 1515.* Amsterdam: Theatrum Orbis Terrarum, 1973.

Anschlag, undated (ca. 1524). "Außzug der Kriegsordnung." Augsburg, Staats- und Stadtbibliothek, 2° Aug 10, nr. 25.

Anschlag, Sept. 11 1537. Augsburg, Staats- und Stadtbibliothek, 2° Aug 10, nr. 81.

Anschlag, Sept. 18 1542, "Ordnung und befelch ains ersamen Rats wie sich gemeine Burgerschafft mit harnisch und woehr versehen soll." Augsburg, Staats- und Stadtbibliothek, 2° Aug 10, nr. 83.

Appuhn, Horst, ed. *Der Triumphzug Kaiser Maximilians I* (1516–1518). Dortmund: Harenberg Kommunikation, 1979.

—. *Der Theuerdank.* Dortmund: Harenberg Kommunikation, 1979.

Aventinus. *Johannes Turmair's genannt Aventinus sämtliche Werke.* 5 vols. Edited by the königliche Akademie der Wissenschaften. Munich: Christian Kaiser, 1881.

Brant, Sebastian. *Das Narrenschiff.* Basel, 1494. Reprint, Leipzig: Verlag Philipp Reclam jun., 1986.

Breu, Jörg. *Die Chronik des Malers Georg Preu des Älteren.* Die Chroniken der deutschen Städte vom 14. bis ins 16. Jahrhundert, ed. Friedrich Roth, vol. 29. Leipzig: S. Hirzel Verlag, 1906.

—. List of names, signed by Breu as "maller und underhauptmann" dated 1520. Augsburg, Stadtarchiv, Nachtrag I, 1519–1525.

—. Untitled, undated letter to guild wardens, loose paper inserted in *Satzungsbuch des Malerhandwercks* 1437–1547. Augsburg, Stadtarchiv, Reichsstadt, Schätze, 72a.

Castiglione, Baldesar. *The Book of the Courtier.* Translated by Charles Singleton. New York: Doubleday, 1959.

La Coronacion imperial de Carlos V. 1530. Reprint, Madrid: Joyas Bibliograficas, 1958.

Dürer, Albrecht. *Schriften und Briefen.* Edited by Ernst Ullmann. West Berlin: Verlag das europäische Buch, 1984.

Eberlin von Günzburg, Johann. "Mich wundert das kein gelt im land ist." In *Johann Eberlin von Günzburg: Ausgewählte Schriften,* edited by Ludwig Enders, 3: 147–81. Halle an der Saale: Max Niemeyer, 1902.

Ehrenpforte des Kaisers Maximilian I. Facsimile edition, Graz: Akademischer Druck- und Verlagsanstalt, 1970.

Einschreibebuch der Maler, Bildhauer, Goldschläger und Glaser, 1480–1542. Augsburg, Stadtarchiv, Reichsstadt, Schätze, 72c.

Einschreibebuch der Maler, Bildhauer, Goldschläger und Glaser, 1480–1548. Augsburg, Stadtarchiv, Reichsstadt, Schätze, 72b.

Einschreibebuch der Maler, Bildhauer, Goldschläger und Glaser, 1480–1624. Augsburg, Stadtarchiv, Archiv des historischen Vereins, 54a.

Erasmus, Desiderius. "The Complaint of Peace." In *Desiderius Erasmus: The Praise of Folly and Other Writings,* edited by Robert Adams, 88–116. New York: W. W. Norton, 1989.

—. *The Education of a Christian Prince.* Translated by Lester Born. New York: Octagon Books, 1965.

Gerichtsbücher. Augsburg, Stadtarchiv, 1502, 1510, 1513, 1520.

Geschichtsbeschreybung unsers aller gnedigsten Herren des Ro. Kayser Carls des fünfften Beleh-

nung umb das hochloblich Erzhertzogthumb osterlich. Augsburg, Staats- und Stadtbibliothek, 4° Aug 1200.

Guicciardini, Francesco. *History of Italy.* Translated by Sidney Alexander. New York: Macmillan, 1969.

Hutten, Müntzer, Luther. 4th edition. Edited by Siegfried Streller. Berlin: Aufbau Verlag, 1982.

Hutten, Ulrich von. *Arminius.* 1529. Reprinted in Hans Gert Roloff, "Der *Arminius* des Ulrich von Hutten." In *Arminius und die Varusschlacht: Geschichte, Mythos, Literatur,* edited by Rainer Wiegels and Winfried Woesler, 222–38. Munich: Ferdinand Schöningh Verlag, 1995.

——. *Beklagung der freistädte deutscher Nation oder Vermahnung an die freien und Reichsstädte deutscher Nation.* Reprinted in *Hutten, Müntzer, Luther.* 4th ed. Edited by Siegfried Streller, 6–14. Berlin: Aufbau Verlag, 1982.

Jäger, Clemens. *Die Weberchronik von Clemens Jäger.* 1929. Die Chroniken der deutschen Städte vom 14. bis ins 16. Jahrhundert, ed. Friedrich Roth, vol. 34. Göttingen: Vandenhoeck und Ruprecht, 1966.

Kopialbuch. Dillingen an der Donau, Fugger Archiv, 6.I.3.

Keiserlicher Maiestat einraitung zu Munchen den x. Tag Junii im M.CCCCC. und XXX jar, 1530. Augsburg, Staats- und Stadtbibliothek, 4° 1178.

Die Langenmantel Chronik. Die Chroniken der deutschen Städte vom 14. bis ins 16. Jahrhundert, vol. 25. Leipzig, S. Hirzel Verlag, 1896.

Livy. *The History of Rome.* Vol. 1. Translated by B. O. Foster. Cambridge, Mass.: Harvard University Press, 1919.

——. *The War with Hannibal.* Translated by Aubrey de Selincourt. London: Penguin Books, 1965.

Machiavelli, Niccolò. *The Art of War.* Revised edition of the Ellis Farneworth translation. New York: DaCapo Press, 1965.

——. "The Discourses." In *The Portable Machiavelli,* edited and translated by Peter Bondanella and Mark Musa, 167–418. New York: Viking Penguin, 1979.

——. *Florentine Histories.* Translated by Laura Banfield and Harvey Mansfield Jr. Princeton: Princeton University Press, 1988.

——. *The Prince.* Translated and edited by Thomas G. Bergin. Arlington Heights: Harlan Davidson, 1947.

More, Sir Thomas. *Utopia.* 1515–16. London: J. M. Dent and Sons, 1985.

Musper, T. H., ed. *Kaiser Maximilians Weißkunig.* 2 vols. Stuttgart: W. Kohlhammer, 1956.

Nettesheim, Agrippa von. *Über die Fragwürdigkeit ja Nichtigkeit der Wissenschaften, Künste und Gewerbe.* 1526. Translated by Gerhard Güpner. Berlin: Akademie Verlag, 1993.

Neue und vollständigere Sammlung der Teutsche Reichsabschiede. Frankfurt am Main, 1747.

Poema Germanicum in laudem Caroli V. et Ferdinandi de capto regis Galliae Francisco da Tacinam. Vienna, Österreichische Nationalbibliothek, cod. Vindob. 10,017.

de Puys, Remy. *La tryumphante et solemnelle entrée . . . de très houle, très puissant et très excellent prince monsieur Charles prince des hespaignes,* Facsimile edition. Bruges: n.p., 1950.

Ratdolt, Erhard. *Die autographische Aufzeichnungen Erhard Ratdolts 1462–1523.* Vienna, Österreichische Nationalbibliothek 15473. Edited by Robert Diehl and H. Reichner. Vienna: n.p., 1932.

Ratsbücher. Augsburg, Stadtarchiv, 1520.

Rem, Lukas. *Tagebuch des Lukas Rem aus den Jahren 1494–1541: Ein Beitrag zur Handelsgeschichte der Stadt Augsburg.* Edited by B. Greif. Augsburg: n.p., 1861.

Rem, Wilhelm. *Cronica newer geschichten von Wilhelm Räm.* Die Chroniken der deutschen Städte vom 14. bis ins 16. Jahrhundert, ed. Friedrich Roth, vol. 25. Leipzig: S. Hirzel Verlag, 1896.

Sachs, Hans, *Tragedia von der Lucretia, auß der beschreybung Livii, hat 1 actus und 10 person,* reprinted in *Hans Sachs.* Edited by Adalbert von Keller, 12: 3–14. Tübingen: H. Laupp, 1979.

Satzungsbuch des Malerhandwercks, 1473–1547, Augsburg, Stadtarchiv, Reichsstadt, Schätze, 72a.

Sender, Clemens. *Die Chronik von Clemens Sender von den ältesten Zeiten der Stadt bis zum 1536.* Die Chroniken der deutschen Städte vom 14. bis ins 16. Jahrhundert, ed. Friedrich Roth, vol. 23. Leipzig: S. Hirzel Verlag, 1894.

Steuerbücher. Augsburg, Stadtarchiv, 1502–1537.

"Sturm, Caspar." "Ain kurze anzaygung und beschreybung römischer kayserlicher Maiestat einreyten erstlich von Innspruck gen Schwatz, volgend zu Munchen und zu letst gen Augspurg." In *Historia der Augspurgischen Confession,* by Ernst Cyprian, 60–84. Gotha, 1730.

Sturm, Caspar, *Wiewol hievor in dreyen underschidlichen büchlein beschrieben und im Truck außgangen wie die Rö. Kai. Maie. Von Inßbruck auß zu Schwatz, München [und] zu Augspurg eingeritten.* ... Augsburg, Staats- und Stadtbibliothek, 4° 1201.

Tacitus, Cornelius. *The Agricola and the Germania.* Translated by H. Mattingly and S. Handford. New York: Penguin Books, 1970.

—. *The Annals of Imperial Rome.* Rev. ed. Translated by Michael Grant. New York: Penguin Books, 1971.

Tetleben, Valentin von. *Protokoll des Augsburger Reichstages 1530.* Edited by Herbert Grundmann. Göttingen: Vandenhoeck und Ruprecht, 1958.

Urgichten. Augsburg, Stadtarchiv: Sigmund Guttermann (29.1.1534; 3.2.1534; 5.2.1534; 7.2.1534), Elisabeth Guttermann (3.2.1534; 5.2.1534), Barbara Hirsthin (6.2.1534), Ursula Weißkopfin (2.8.1534), Katharina Schwegglin (11.2.1534), Magdalena Boglerin (1.2.1534).

Vasari, Giorgio. *Lives of the Artists.* Vol. 1. 1550. Reprint, London: Penguin Books, 1965.

Von kayserlich Maiestat einreytten auff den Reychstag gen Augsburg. Augsburg, Staats- und Stadtbibliothek, 4° Aug 1179.

Wahrhafftig anzaygung wie Kaiser Carl der fünfte ettlichen Fürsten auf dem Reychstag zu Augsburg im MCCCCCXXX jar gehalten Regalia und Lehen under dem fan gelihen. Augsburg, Staats- und Stadtbibliothek, 4° Aug 1199.

Zechpflegerrechnungen, St. Moritz. Augsburg, Stadtarchiv, Reichsstadt, Schätze, 11, I.

Zimmerman, Wilhelm Peter. *Ernewrtes Geschlechter Buch.* (Augsburg, 1618). Augsburg, Staats- und Stadtbibliothek, 2° Aug 125.

Zwingli, Ulrich. *Herr Ulrich Zwingli Leerbiechlein wie man die knaben christlich unterwysen und erziehen soll.* (Augsburg, 1524). Ausgsburg, Staats- und Stadtbibliothek, 4° Th H 2995.

II. *Secondary Sources*

Abbe, Derek von. *Drama in Renaissance Germany and Switzerland.* Melbourne: Melbourne University Press, 1961.

Albrecht, Dieter. "Die kirchlich-religiöse Entwicklung 1500–1575." In *Handbuch der bayerischen Geschichte,* 2nd ed. Edited by Andreas Kraus, 2: 702–35. Munich: Beck'sche Verlagsbuchhandlung, 1988.

—. "Staat und Gesellschaft 1500–1745." In *Handbuch der bayerischen Geschichte,* 2nd ed. Edited by Andreas Kraus, 2: 625–63. Munich: Beck'sche Verlagsbuchhandlung, 1988.

Andersson, Christiane. *Dirnen, Krieger, Narren: Ausgewählte Zeichnungen von Urs Graf.* Basel: GS-Verlag, 1978.

Andersson, Christiane, and Charles Talbot. *From a Mighty Fortress: Prints, Drawings and Books in the Age of Luther 1483–1546.* Detroit: Detroit Institute of Art, 1983.

Aulinger, Rosemarie. "Augsburg und die Reichstage." In *Welt im Umbruch: Augsburg zwischen Renaissance und Barock*. 3: 9–24. Augsburg: Augsburger Druck- und Verlagshaus, 1981.

—. *Das Bild des Reichstages im 16. Jahrhundert: Beiträge zu einer typologischen Analyse schriftlicher und bildlicher Quellen*. Göttingen: Vandenhoeck und Ruprecht, 1980.

Augsburger Buchholzschnitt der Frühdruckzeit: Aus der Sammlung Kurt Bösch. Augsburg: H. Mühlberger, 1986.

Baldass, Ludwig von. *Der Künstlerkreis Kaiser Maximilians*. Vienna: A. Schroll, 1923.

Bauer, Clemens. "Conrad Peutingers Gutachten zur Monopolfrage." *Archiv für Reformationsgeschichte* 45 (1945): 1–43 and 145–96.

Baur-Heinhold, Margarete. *Süddeutsche Fassadenmalerei vom Mittelalter bis zur Gegenwart*. Munich: J.D.W. Callwey, 1952.

Baum, Julius. "Das alte Augsburger Rathaus." *Zeitschrift des historischen Vereins für Schwaben und Neuburg* 33 (1907): 63–73.

—. *Altschwäbische Kunst*. Augsburg: B. Filser Verlag, 1923.

Baer, Wolfram, Hanno-Walter Kraft, and Bernd Roeck, eds. *Elias Holl und das Augsburger Rathaus*. Regensburg: Friedrich Pustet Verlag, 1985.

Beenken, Hermann. "Beiträge zu Jörg Breu und Hans Dürer." *Jahrbuch der preußischen Kunstsammlungen* 56 (1935): 61–3.

Bieder, Theobald. *Geschichte der Germanenforschung, Part I: 1500–1806*. Leipzig: Theodor Weicher Verlag, 1921.

Biehl, Ludwig. *Das liturgische Gebet für Kaiser und Reich: Ein Beitrag zur Geschichte des Verhältnisses von Kirche und Staat*. Padeborn: F. Schöningh, 1937.

Blendinger, Friedrich, and Wolfgang Zorn, eds. *Augsburg: Geschichte in Bilddokumente*. Munich: C. H. Beck'sche Verlagsbuchhandlung, 1976.

Blickle, Peter. *Communal Reformation: The Quest for Salvation in Sixteenth Century Germany*. Translated by Thomas Dunlap. New Jersey: Humanities Press, 1992.

—. *The Revolution of 1525: The German Peasants' War from a New Perspective*. Translated by Thomas A. Brady Jr. and H. C. Erik Midelfort. Baltimore: John Hopkins University Press, 1981.

Bodmer, Jean Pierre. *Chroniken und Chronisten im Spätmittelalter*. Bern: Francke Verlag, 1976.

Borchardt, Frank. *German Antiquity in Renaissance Myth*. Baltimore: John Hopkins University Press, 1971.

Brady, Thomas A. Jr. "The Social Place of a German Renaissance Artist: Hans Baldung Grien (1484/5–1545) at Strasbourg." *Central European History* 8 (1975): 295–315.

—. "Some Peculiarities of German Histories in the Early Modern Period." In *Germania Illustrata: Essays on Early Modern Germany Presented to Gerald Strauss*, edited by Andrew Fix and Susan Karant-Nunn, 197–216. Kirksville: Sixteenth Century Journal Publishers, 1992.

Breisach, Ernst. *Historiography: Ancient, Medieval and Modern*. Chicago: University of Chicago Press, 1994.

Broadhead, Philip. "International Politics and Civic Society in Augsburg During the Era of the Early Reformation 1518-1537." Ph.D. diss., University of Kent, 1981.

Bruck, G. "Die graphische Vorlage für die Darstellung der Schlacht von Pavia auf der Medaille des Concz Welcz." *Mitteilungen der österreichischen numismatischen Gesellschaft*, NF 12 (1961): 3–5.

Buchner, Ernst. "Bemerkungen zum 'Historien- und Schlachtbild' der deutschen Renaissance." In *Beiträge zur Geschichte der deutschen Kunst*. Edited by Ernst Buchner and Karl Feuchtmayr, 1: 240–59. B. Filser Verlag: Augsburg, 1924.

—. "Der ältere Breu als Maler." In *Beiträge zur Geschichte der deutschen Kunst*. Edited by Ernst Buchner and Karl Feuchtmayr, 2: 273ff. Augsburg: B. Filser Verlag, 1928.

Buchner, Rudolf. *Maximilian I*. Göttingen: Musterschmidt Verlag, 1970.)

Buff, A. *Augsburg in der Renaissancezeit.* Bamberg: n.p., 1893.

——. "Rechnungsauszüge, Urkunden und Urkundenregesten aus dem Augsburger Stadtarchiv." *Jahrbuch des kunsthistorischen Sammlungen des allerhöchsten Kaiserhauses* 13 (1892): xx–xxi, #8610.

Burke, Peter. *The Fortunes of the Courtier.* University Park: Penn State University Press, 1995.

Bushart, Bruno. *Die Fuggerkapelle bei St. Anna in Augsburg.* Munich: Deutscher Kunstverlag, 1994.

Cederlöf, Olle. "The Battle Painting as a Historical Source." *Revue internationale d'histoire militaire* 1967: 119–44.

Chmelarz, Eduard. "Die Ehrenpforte des Kaisers Maximilian I." *Jahrbuch der kunsthistorischen Sammlungen des allerhöchsten Kaiserhauses* 4 (1886): 289–319.

Christensen, Carl. *Art and the Reformation in Germany.* Athens: Ohio University Press, 1979.

——. *Princes and Propaganda: Electoral Saxon Art of the Reformation.* Kirksville: Sixteenth Century Journal Publishers, 1992.

Clasen, Claus-Peter. *Anabaptism: A Social History.* Ithaca: Cornell University Press, 1972.

——. *Die Augsburger Steuerbücher um 1600.* Augsburg: H. Mühlberger, 1976.

——. *Die Augsburger Weber.* Augsburg: H. Mühlberger, 1981.

Cockle, Maurice. *A Bibliography of Military Books up to 1642.* 1900. Reprint, London: Holland Press, 1978.

Contamine, Philippe. *War in the Middle Ages.* London: B. Blackwell, 1984.

Cramer, V. *Der Ritterorden vom Hl. Grabe von den Kreuzzügen bis zur Gegenwart.* Cologne: J. P. Bachem, 1952.

Cuneo, Pia. "Art and Power in Augsburg: The Art Production of Jörg Breu the Elder." Ph.D. diss., Northwestern University, 1991.

——. "Propriety, Property and Politics: Jörg Breu the Elder and Issues of Iconoclasm in Reformation Augsburg." *German History* 14 (1996): 1–20.

Cyprian, Ernst Salomon. *Historia der Augspurgischen Confession.* Gotha, 1730.

Czok, Karl. "Bürgerkämpfe und Chronistik im deutschen Spätmittelalter: Ein Beitrag zur Herausbildung bürgerlicher Geschichtsschreibung." *Zeitschrift für Geschichtswissenschaft* 10 (1962): 637–43.

Davis, Natalie Zemon. *Fiction in the Archives.* Stanford, Calif.: Stanford University Press, 1987.

Delbrück, Hans. *History of the Art of War within the Framework of Political History.* 1900. Vol. 4. Reprint, Westport, Conn.: Greenwood Press, 1985.

Dirr, P. "Studien zur Geschichte der Augsburger Zunftverfassung 1368–1548." *Zeitschrift des historischen Vereins für Schwaben und Neuburg* 39 (1913): 144-243.

Dodgson, Campbell. *Catalogue of Early German and Flemish Woodcuts Preserved in the Department of Prints and Drawings in the British Museum.* 2: 108–19 and 423–32. 1911. Reprint, Liechtenstein: Quarto Press in association with the British Museum Production, 1980.

——. "Beiträge zur Kenntnis des Holzschnittwerks Jörg Breus." *Jahrbuch der preußischen Kunstsammlungen* 21 (1900): 192–214.

——. "The Calumny of Apelles." *Burlington Magazine* 29 (1916): 183–89.

——. "Ein Miniaturwerk Jörg Breus d. J." *Münchner Jahrbuch der bildenden Kunst,* NF 11 (1934): 198–200.

Dörnhöffer, Friedrich. "Ein Cyclus von Federzeichnungen mit Darstellungen von Kriegen und Jagden Maximilians I." *Jahrbuch der kunsthistorischen Sammlungen des allerhöchsten Kaiserhauses* 18 (1897): 1–55.

Dotzauer, Winfried. "Die Ankunft des Herrschers: der fürstliche Einzug in die Stadt." *Archiv für Kulturgeschichte* 55 (1973): 245–88.

Drabeck, Anna Maria. "Reisen und Reisezeremoniell der römisch-deutschen Könige im Spätmittelalter." Ph.D. diss., University of Vienna, 1963.

Dresler, Adolf. *Augsburg und die Frühgeschichte der Presse*. Munich: Pohl Verlag, 1952.

Dworschak, Fritz. "Der Meister der Historia (Niclas Preu)." In *Kunst der Donauschule 1490–1540: Malerei, Graphik, Plastik, Architektur*. Linz: Landesverlag, 1965, 96–103.

Ecker, Gisela. *Einblattdrücke von den Anfängen bis 1555: Untersuchungen zu einer Publikationsform literarischer Texte*. 2 vols. Göppingen: Kümmerle Verlag, 1981.

Edelman, Murray. *From Art to Politics: How Artistic Creations Shape Political Conceptions*. Chicago: University of Chicago Press, 1995.

Egg, Erich. "Der deutsche König und die neue Kunst." *Alte und moderne Kunst* 6 (1961): 16–20.

Einem, Herbert von. "Karl V und Tizian." In *Karl V: Der Kaiser und seine Zeit*, edited by Peter Rassow and Fritz Schalk, 67–93. Cologne: Böhlau, 1960.

Ekalt, Hubert. "Zur Funktion des Zeremoniells im Absolutismus." In *Europäische Hofkultur im 16. und 17. Jahrhundert*. Vol. 2. Edited by August Buck, 411–19. Hamburg: Haus Wedell, 1981.

Elias, Norbert. *Die höfische Gesellschaft*. Frankfurt am Main: Suhrkamp Verlag, 1983.

Elsas, M. J. *Umriss einer Geschichte der Preise und Löhne in Deutschland vom ausgehenden Mittelalter bis zum Beginn des neunzehnten Jahrhunderts*. Vol. 1. Leiden: A. W. Sijthoff, 1936.

Enzenberg, Sighard, Graf von. *Schloß Tratzberg; ein Beitrag zur Kulturgeschichte Tirols*. Innsbruck: Wagner, 1958.

Eschenburg, Barbara. "Altdorfers *Alexanderschlacht* und ihr Verhältnis zum Historienzyklus Wilhelms IV." *Zeitschrift des deutschen Vereins für Kunstwissenschaft* 33 (1979): 36–67.

Essenwein, A. "Hans Tirols Darstellung der Belehnung Ferdinands I." *Mitteilungen aus dem Germanischen Nationalmuseum* 2 (1887–89): 1–22.

—. *Hans Tirols Holzschnitt darstellend die Belehnung König Ferdinands mit den österreichischen Erblanden durch Kaiser Karl V auf dem Reichstag zu Augsburg am 5. September 1530*. Frankfurt am Main: Heinrich Keller, 1887.

Fichtner, Paula Sutter. *Ferdinand I of Austria: The Politics of Dynasticism in the Age of the Reformation*. New York: Columbia University Press, 1982.

Freiheit und Ordnung: Reformation in Augsburg. Augsburg: Selbstverlag der Evang.-Luth. Gesamtkirchengemeinde Augsburg, 1987.

Freud, Sigmund. *Leonardo da Vinci and a Memory of his Childhood*. Edited by Peter Gay. New York: Norton, 1989.

Frenzel, G. "Entwurf und Ausführung in der Nürnberger Glasmalerei der Dürerzeit." *Zeitschrift für Kunstwissenschaft* 15 (1961): 31–59.

Gamber, Ortwin. "Ersteller, Erzeuger und Liefernormen des Augsburger Harnisches." In *Welt im Umbruch: Augsburg zwischen Renaissance und Barock*. 3: 171–75. Augsburg: Augsburger Druck- und Verlagshaus, 1981.

Giehlow, Karl. "Beiträge zur Entstehungsgeschichte des Gebetbuches Kaiser Maximilians I." *Jahrbuch der kunsthistorischen Sammlungen des allerhöchsten Kaiserhauses* 20 (1899): 30–112.

Glaser, Hubert, ed. *Um Glauben und Reich: Kurfürst Maximilian I; Beträge zur bayerischen Geschichte und Kunst 1573–1657*. 2 vols. Munich: Hirmer und Piper Verlag, 1980.

Goethe, J. W. von. *Italian Journey*. Translated by W. H. Auden. London: Penguin Books, 1962.

Goldberg, Gisela. *Die Alexanderschlacht und die Historienbilder des bayerischen Herzogs Wilhelm IV und seiner Gemahlin Jacobäa für die Münchner Residenz*. Munich: Hirmer Verlag, 1983.

—. "Die ursprüngliche Inschrifttafel der *Alexanderschlacht* Albrecht Altdorfers." *Münchner Jahrbuch der bildenden Kunst* 19, Folge 3 (1968): 121–26.

Goldberg, Gisela, and Christian zu Salm. *Altdeutsche Malerei: Alte Pinakothek München, Katalog II*. Munich: F. Bruckmann Verlag, 1963.

Gothic and Renaissance Art in Nuremberg 1300–1550. Munich: Prestel Verlag, 1986.

Gottlieb, Gunther, and Wolfram Baer, eds. *Geschichte der Stadt Augsburg: 2000 Jahre von der Römerzeit bis zur Gegenwart*. 2nd ed. Stuttgart: Konrad Theiss Verlag, 1985.

Greiselmayer, Volkmar. "Die Historienbilder Herzog Wilhelms IV von Bayern und seiner Gemahlin Jacobäa: Versuch einer Interpretation." 6 vols. Habilitationsschrift, University of Erlangen, 1991.

Gross, Hanns. "The Holy Roman Empire in Modern Times: Constitutional Reality and Legal Theory." In *The Old Reich: Essays on German Political Institutions 1495–1806*, edited by James A. Vann and Steven Rowan, 3–29. Brussels: Les Editions de la Librairie Encyclopedique, 1974.

Grüber, Pia Maria, ed. *Kurzweil viel ohn' Maß und Ziel: Augsburger Patrizier und ihre Feste zwischen Mittelalter und Neuzeit*. Munich: Hirmer Verlag, 1994.

Hale, John Rigby. *Artists and Warfare in the Renaissance*. New Haven: Yale University Press, 1990.

——. *War and Society in Renaissance Europe 1450–1620*. Baltimore: John Hopkins University Press, 1985.

Halm, Peter. "Die Landschaftszeichnungen des Wolfgang Hubers." *Münchner Jahrbuch der bildenden Kunst* NF, 7 (1930): 1–110.

Hans Burgkmair: Das graphische Werk. Stuttgart: Staatsgalerie graphische Sammlung, 1973.

Hartig, Otto. "Die Kunsttätigkeit in München unter Wilhelm IV und Albrecht V 1520–1579." *Münchner Jahrbuch der bildenden Kunst* NF, 10 (1933): 147–225.

Hartung, Fritz. "Die Wahlkapitulationen der deutschen Kaiser und Könige." *Historische Zeitschrift* 3. Folge, 11 (1911): 306–44.

Hartung, J. "Die Augsburger Vermögenssteuer und die Entwicklung der Besitzverhältnisse im 16. Jahrhundert." *Jahrbuch für Gesetzgebung Verwaltung und Volkswirtschaft im deutschen Reich* 19 (1895): 867–83.

Hilger, Wolfgang. *Ikonographie Kaiser Ferdinands I. (1503–1564)*. Vienna: Böhlau, 1969.

Hofmann, Werner, Eckhard Schaar, and Gisela Hopp, eds. *Köpfe der Lutherzeit*. Munich: Prestel Verlag, 1983.

Hofmann, Werner and Peter-Klaus Schuster, eds. *Luther und die Folgen für die Kunst*. Munich: Prestel Verlag, 1983.

Holborn, Hajo. *A History of Modern Germany: The Reformation*. Princeton: Princeton University Press, 1982.

Hollstein, F.W.H. *German Engravings, Etchings and Woodcuts ca. 1400–1700*. 4: 157–84. Amsterdam: M. Hertzberger Verlag, 1954.

Horn, Christine. "Conrad Peutingers Beziehung zu Kaiser Maximilian I." Ph.D. diss., University of Graz, 1977.

d'Hulst, Roger Adolf. *Flämische Bildteppiche des XIV. bis XVIII. Jahrhunderts*. Brussels: Kunstverlag l'arcade, 1961.

Huth, Hans. *Künstler und Werkstatt der Spätgotik*. 4th edition. Darmstadt: Wissenschaftliche Buchgesellschaft, 1981.

Immenkötter, H. *Der Reichstag zu Augsburg und die Confutatio*. Münster: Aschendorff, 1979.

Jacquot, Jean. *Fêtes et cérémonies au temps du Charles Quint*. Paris: Editions du Centre National de la Recherche Scientifique, 1960.

Joachimson, Paul. *Geschichtsauffassung und Geschichtsschreibung in Deutschland unter dem Einfluss des Humanismus*. Leipzig, 1910. Reprint, Aalen: Scientia Verlag, 1968.

——. "Zur städtischen und klösterlichen Geschichtsschreibung Augsburgs im 15. Jahrhundert." *Alemania* 22 (1894): 1–32 and 123–59.

Joost-Gaugier, Christiane. "Castagno's Humanistic Program at Legnaia and Its Possible Inventor." *Zeitschrift für Kunstgeschichte* 45 (1982): 274–82.

——. "Giotto's Hero Cycle in Naples: A Prototype of *donne illustri* and a Possible Literary Connection." *Zeitschrift für Kunstgeschichte* 43 (1980): 311–18.

—. "A Rediscovered Series of *uomini famose* from Quattrocento Venice." *Art Bulletin* 58 (1976): 184–95.

Junghans, Helmar, ed. *Das Jahrhundert der Reformation in Sachsen.* Berlin: Evangelische Verlagsanstalt, 1989.

Kantorowicz, Ernst. "The King's Advent." *Art Bulletin* 26 (1944): 207–31.

Kauffmann, Thomas DaKosta. *Court, Cloister, and City: The Art and Culture of Central Europe 1450–1800.* Chicago: University of Chicago Press, 1993.

Kawerau, Gustav. "Luthers Gedanken über den Krieg." In *Luthers Frühentwicklung (bis 1517/9).* Edited by Hans von Schubert, 37–56. Leipzig: Verein für Reformationsgeschichte, 1916.

Kellenbenz, Hermann. "Augsburger Wirtschaft 1530 bis 1620." In *Welt im Umbruch: Augsburg zwischen Renaissance und Barock.* 1: 50–71. Augsburg: Augsburger Druck- und Verlagshaus, 1980.

—. *Die Fuggersche Maestrazgopacht (1525–1542): Zur Geschichte der spanischen Ritterorden im 16. Jahrhundert.* Tübingen: Mohr Verlag, 1967.

—. "Wirtschaftsleben der Blütezeit." In *Geschichte der Stadt Augsburg.* 2nd ed. Edited by Gunther Gottlieb and Wolfram Baer, 258–301. Stuttgart: Konrad Theiss Verlag, 1985.

Kern, E. "Studien zur Geschichte des Augsburger Kaufmannshauses der Hoechstetter." *Archiv für Kulturgeschichte* 26 (1936): 162–98.

Kernodle, G. R. "Renaissance Artists in the Service of the People: Political Tableaux and Street Theaters in France, Flanders and England." *Art Bulletin* 25 (1943): 59–64.

Kloft, Hans. "Die Idee einer deutschen Nation zu Beginn der frühen Neuzeit: Überlegungen zur *Germania* des Tacitus und zum *Arminius* Ulrichs von Hutten." In *Arminius und die Varusschlacht: Geschichte, Mythos, Literatur,* edited by Rainer Wiegels and Winfried Woesler, 197–210. Munich: Ferdinand Schöningh Verlag, 1995.

Knepper, Joseph. *Jakob Wimpfeling 1450–1528: Sein Leben und seine Werke.* 1902. Reprint Nieuwkoop: B. De Graaf, 1965.

Kohl, Benjamin. "Petrarch's Prefaces to *De viris illustribus.*" *History and Theory* 13 (1974): 132–44.

Kohler, Alfred. *Antihabsburgische Politik in der Epoche Karls V: Die reichsständische Opposition gegen die Wahl Ferdinands I zum römischen König und gegen die Anerkennung seines Königtums (1524–1534).* Göttingen: Vandenhoeck und Ruprecht, 1982.

Kolde, D. "Der Reichsherold Caspar Sturm und seine literarische Tätigkeit." *Archiv für Reformationsgeschichte* 4 (1907): 117–61.

Krämer, Gode. "Jörg Breu als Maler und Protestant." In *Welt im Umbruch: Augsburg zwischen Renaissance und Barock.* 3: 115–33. Augsburg: Augsburger Druck- und Verlagshaus, 1981.

Kramer-Schlette, Carla. *Vier Augsburger Chronisten der Reformationszeit; die Behandlung und Deutung der Zeitgeschichte bei Clemens Sender, Wilhelm Rem, Georg Preu und Paul Hektor Mair.* Lübeck: Matthiesen Verlag, 1970.

Krapf, Ludwig. *Germanenmythos und Reichsideologie: Frühhumanistische Rezeptionsweisen der taciteischen Germania.* Tübingen: Niemeyer, 1979.

Kraus, Andreas, ed., *Handbuch der bayerischen Geschichte.* 2nd ed. Vol. 2. Munich: C. H. Beck'sche Verlagsbuchhandlung, 1988.

Kraus, J. *Das Militärwesen der Reichsstadt Augsburg.* Augsburg: H. Mühlberger, 1980.

Krenn, Peter. "Heerwesen, Waffe und Turnier unter Kaiser Maximilian I." In *Ausstellung Maximilian I,* exhibition catalogue, 86–92. Innsbruck: Kulturreferat Tirol, 1969.

Kroher, E. "Breu d. Ä, Jörg." *Kindlers Malerei Lexikon.* 2: 528–34. Cologne: Lingen Verlag, 1979.

Kunst der Reformationszeit. Berlin: Elefanten Press, 1983.

Kurzmann, Gerhard. *Kaiser Maximilian I und das Kriegswesen der österreichischen Länder und des Reiches.* Vienna: Österreichische Bundesverlag, 1985.

Landfester, Rüdiger. *Historia Magistra Vitae: Untersuchungen zur humanistischen Geschichtstheorie des 14. bis 16. Jahrhunderts.* Geneve: Librairie Droz, 1972.

Lhotsky, Alphons, ed. *Sonderausstellung Karl V*, exhibition catalogue. Vienna: n.p., 1958.

Lieb, Norbert. "Augsburgs Anteil an der Kunst der Maximilianszeit." In *Jakob Fugger, Kaiser Maxmilian und Augsburg 1459–1959*, edited by Götz Freiherr von Pölnitz, 59–76. Augsburg: n.p., 1959.

——. *Die Fugger und die Kunst.* Munich: Schnell & Steiner, 1952.

Liliencron, Rochus, Freiherr von. *Die historischen Volkslieder der Deutschen.* Vol. 3. Leipzig: F.C.W. Vogel, 1867.

——. *Deutsches Leben im Volkslied um 1530.* Berlin: W. Spemann, 1884.

Löcher, Kurt. *Jakob Seisenegger: Hofmaler Kaiser Ferdinands I.* Kunstwissenschaftliche Studien, vol. 31. Munich: Deutscher Kunstverlag, 1962.

Lutz, Heinrich. *Conrad Peutinger: Eine politische Biographie.* Augsburg: Verlag die Brigg, 1958.

Lutz, Heinrich, "Die deutsche Nation zu Beginn der Neuzeit: Fragen nach dem Gelingen und Scheitern deutscher Einheit im 16. Jahrhundert," *Historische Zeitschrift,* 234, 1982, 529–59.

Lutz, Heinrich, and Alois Schmidt. "Von Humanismus zur Gegenreformation." In *Handbuch der bayerischen Geschichte.* 2nd ed. Edited by Andreas Kraus, 2: 861–75. Munich: C.H. Beck'sche Verlagsbuchhandlung, 1988.

Lutz, Heinrich, and Walter Ziegler. "Das konfessionelle Zeitalter: Die Herzöge Wilhelm IV und Albrecht V." In *Handbuch der bayerischen Geschichte.* 2nd ed. Edited by Andreas Kraus, 2: 324–92. Munich: C. H. Beck'sche Verlagsbuchhandlung, 1988.

Lutz, R. *Wer war der gemeine Mann? Der dritte Stand in der Krise des Spätmittelalters.* Munich: Oldenbourg, 1979.

MacCormack, Sabine. *Art and Ceremony in Late Antiquity.* Berkeley and Los Angeles: University of California Press, 1981.

Martin Luther und die Reformation in Deutschland. Frankfurt am Main: Insel Verlag, 1983.

Maximilian I. Innsbruck: Tyrolia Verlag, 1969.

Mann, Nicholas. *Petrarch.* Oxford: Oxford University Press, 1984.

Mayer, E. W. "Forschungen zur Politik Karls V während des Augsburger Reichstags von 1530." *Archiv für Reformationsgeschichte* 13 (1916): 40–73 and 124–46.

Mayr, Anton. *Die großen Augsburger Vermögen in der Zeit um 1618 bis 1717.* Augsburg: Selbstverlag der Stadt Augsburg, 1931.

Mayr, Michael. *Das Jagdbuch Kaiser Maximilians I.* Innsbruck: Verlag der Wagner'schen Universitäts-Buchhandlung, 1901.

McLeod, Glenda. *Virtue and Venom: Catalogs of Women from Antiquity to the Renaissance.* Ann Arbor: University of Michigan Press, 1991.

Meitinger, Otto. "Baugeschichte der Neuveste." *Oberbayerisches Archiv für vaterländische Geschichte 92* (1970): 31ff..

Mencke, J. B. "Geschichtsschreibung und Politik in den deutschen Städten des Spätmittelalters." *Jahrbuch des kölnischen Geschichtsvereins 33* (1958): 1–84 and 34/5 (1960): 85–194.

Mende, Matthias. *Das alte Nürnberger Rathaus: Baugeschichte und Ausstattung des Grossen Saales und der Ratsstube.* Exhibition catalogue, vol. 1. Nuremberg: Stadtgeschichtliche Museen, 1979.

Menz, Cäsar. *Das Frühwerk Jörg Breus des Älteren.* Augsburg: Kommissionsverlag Bucher Seitz, 1982.

Michalski, Serge. *The Reformation and the Visual Arts: The Protestant Image Question in Western and Eastern Europe.* London: Routledge, 1993.

Moeller, Bernd. *Deutschland im Zeitalter der Reformation.* Göttingen: Vandenhoeck und Ruprecht, 1977.

Möller, Hans-Michael. *Das Regiment der Landsknechte: Untersuchungen zu Verfassung, Recht und Selbstverständnis in deutschen Söldnerheeren des 16. Jahrhunderts.* Wiesbaden: F. Steiner Verlag, 1976.

Mommsen, Theodor. "Petrarch and the Decoration of the *Sala Virorum Illustrium* in Padua." *Art Bulletin* 34 (1952): 95–116.

Morrall, Andrew. "Saturn's Children: A Glass Panel by Jörg Breu the Elder in the Burrell Collection." *Burlington Magazine* 135 (1993): 212–4.

Möseneder, Karl. "Das Fest als Darstellung der Harmonie im Staat am Beispiel der Entrée Solennelle Ludwigs XIV 1660 in Paris." In *Europäische Hofkultur im 16. und 17. Jahrhundert,* edited by August Buck, 2: 130–34. Hamburg: Haus Wedell, 1981.

Moxey, Keith. *Peasants, Warriors and Wives: Popular Imagery in the Reformation.* Chicago: Chicago University Press, 1989.

Müller, Jan-Dirk. *Gedechtnus: Literatur und Hofgesellschaft um Maximilian I.* Munich: W. Fink Verlag, 1982.

Mummenhoff, E. *Das Rathaus in Nürnberg.* Nuremberg: J. L. Schrag, 1891.

Nauert, Charles Jr. "The Birth of Humanist Culture." In *Humanism and the Culture of Renaissance Europe,* 8–51. Cambridge: Cambridge University Press, 1995.

Niederwolfsgruber, F. *Kaiser Maximilians I Jagd- und Fischereibücher: Jagd und Fischerei in den Alpenländern im 16. Jahrhundert.* Munich: Bayerischer Landwirtschaftsverlag, 1965.

Niklaus Manuel Deutsch: Maler, Dichter, Staatsmann. Bern: Kunstmuseum Bern, 1979.

Oberhammer, Vinzenz. "Das Grabmal des Kaisers," in *Maximilian I.* Innsbruck: Tyrolia Verlag, 1969, 107–12.

Oman, Charles. *A History of the Art of War in the Sixteenth Century.* New York: E. P. Dutton, 1937.

Ost, Hans, *Lambert Sustris: Die Bildnisse Kaiser Karls V in München und Wien.* Vienna: W. König Verlag, 1985.

Overfield, James. "Germany." In *The Renaissance in National Context,* edited by Roy Porter and Mikuláš Teich, 92–122. Cambridge: Cambridge University Press, 1992.

Parker, K. T. "A Bookplate of the Family of Tänzl von Tratzberg." *Old Master Drawings* 8 (1933): 13–14, pl. 15.

Peters, Ursula. *Literatur in der Stadt: Studien zu den sozialen Voraussetzungen und kulturellen Organisationsformen städtischer Literatur im 13. und 14. Jahrhundert.* Tübingen: Mohr Verlag, 1983.

Pfeiffer, Rudolf. "Conrad Peutinger und die humanistische Welt." In *Augusta 955–1955: Forschungen und Studien zur Kultur- und Wirtschaftsgeschichte Augsburgs,* edited by Hermann Rinn, 219–28. Munich: n.p, 1955.

Piper, Ernst. *Der Stadtplan als Grundriß der Gesellschaft: Topographie und Sozialstruktur in Augsburg und Florenz um 1500.* Frankfurt am Main: Campus Verlag, 1982.

Poensen, G. "Bildnisse des Kaisers Karl V." In *Karl V: Der Kaiser und seine Zeit,* edited by Peter Rassow and Fritz Schalk, 173–79. Cologne: Bohlau Verlag, 1960.

Pölnitz, Götz, Freiherr von. "Anton Fugger und die römische Königswahl Ferdinands I." *Zeitschrift für bayerische Landesgeschichte* 16 (1951/2): 317–49.

—. "Augsburger Kaufleute und Bankherren der Renaissance." In *Augusta 955–1955: Forschungen und Studien zur Kultur- und Wirtschaftsgeschichte Augsburgs,* edited by Hermann Rinn, 187–218. Munich: n.p., 1955.

—. *Jakob Fugger: Kaiser, Kirche und Kapital in der oberdeutschen Renaissance.* 2 vols. Tübingen: Mohr Verlag, 1949.

Porter, Roy, and Mikuláš Teich, eds. *The Renaissance in National Context.* Cambridge: Cambridge University Press, 1992.

Rady, Martyn C. *Emperor Charles V.* London: Longman, 1988.

Rajkay, Barbara. "Die Bevölkerungsentwicklung von 1500–1648." In *Geschichte der Stadt Augsburg: 2000 Jahre von der Römerzeit bis zur Gegenwart,* edited by Gunther Gottlieb and Wolfram Baer, 252–58. Stuttgart: Konrad Theiss Verlag, 1985.

Rall, H., and M. Rall. *Die Wittelsbacher in Lebensbilder*. Regensburg: Friedrich Pustet Verlag, 1986.

Rasmussen, Jörg. "Bildersturm und Restauratio." In *Welt im Umbruch: Augsburg zwischen Renaissance und Barock*. 3: 95–114. Augsburg: Augsburger Druck- und Verlagshaus, 1980.

Rassow, Peter. *Die Kaiseridee Karls V dargestellt an der Politik der Jahre 1528–1540* Berlin: E. Ebering, 1932.

—. "Die Reichstage zu Augsburg in der Reformationszeit." In *Die geschichtliche Einheit des Abendlandes; Reden und Aufsätze*, 278–93. Cologne: Böhlau, 1960.

Reitzenstein, Alexander, Freiherr von. *Ottheinrich von der Pfalz*. Bremen: Angelsachsen-Verlag, 1939.

—. "Die Plattner von Augsburg." In *Augusta 955–1955: Forschungen und Studien zur Kultur- und Wirtschaftsgeschichte Augsburgs*, edited by Hermann Rinn, 265–72. Munich: n.p., 1955.

Rice, Eugene F. Jr. *The Foundations of Early Modern Europe 1460–1559*. New York: W. W. Norton, 1970.

Ride, Jacques. "Arminius in der Sicht der deutschen Reformatoren." In *Arminius und die Varusschlacht: Geschichte, Mythos, Literatur*, edited by Rainer Wiegels and Winfried Woesler, 239–48. Munich: Ferdinand Schöningh Verlag, 1995.

Riedl, Kurt. "Der Wert des Weißkunigs als Geschichtsquelle." Ph.D. diss., University of Graz, 1969.

Riedmüller, Ludwig. "Ein vergessenes Freskobild des älteren Jörg Breu." *Archiv für die Geschichte des Hochstifts Augsburg* 5 (1916–19): 629–31.

Riehl, W. "Augsburger Studien 1857: der Stadtplan als Grundriss der Gesellschaft." In *Kulturstudien aus drei Jahrhunderten*, 5th ed. Stuttgart: Cotta Verlag, 1896.

Riess, Hedwig. *Motive des patriotischen Stolzes bei den deutschen Humanisten*. Berlin: E. Ebering, 1934.

Rinn, Hermann, ed. *Augusta 955–1955*. Munich: n.p., 1955.

Roloff, Hans Gert. "Der Arminius des Ulrich von Hutten." In *Arminius und die Varusschlacht: Geschichte, Mythos, Literatur*, edited by Rainer Wiegels and Winfried Woesler, 211–38. Munich: Ferdinand Schöningh Verlag, 1995.

Roper, Lyndal. "Mothers of Debauchery: Procuresses in Reformation Augsburg." *German History* 6 (1988): 1–19.

—. "Discipline and Respectibility: Prostitution and the Reformation in Augsburg." *History Workshop* 19 (1985): 3–10.

—. *The Holy Household*. Oxford: Oxford University Press, 1989.

—. "Work, Marriage and Sexuality: Women in Reformation Augsburg." Ph.D. diss., University of London, 1985.

Roth, Friedrich. *Augsburgs Reformationsgeschichte*. 2 vols. Munich: Theodor Ackermann, 1901 and 1904.

—. "Einleitung" to Jörg Breu. *Die Chronik des Malers Georg Preu des Älteren*. Die Chroniken der deutschen Städte vom 14. Bis ins 16. Jahrhundert, ed. Friedrich Roth, vol. 29. Leipzig: S. Hirzel Verlag, 1906.

—. "Wer war Haug Marschalk genannt Zoller von Augsburg?" *Beiträge zur bayerischen Kirchengeschichte* 6 (1900): 229–34.

Rott, Hans. *Ottheinrich und die Kunst*. Heidelberg: C. Winter Verlag, 1905.

Röttinger, Heinrich. "Breu-Studien." *Jahrbuch der kunsthistorischen Sammlungen des allerhöchsten Kaiserhauses* 28 (1909): 31–44.

—. "Zum Holzschnittwerk Jörg Breu des Älteren." *Repertorium für Kunstwissenschaft* 31 (1908): 48–62.

Rowlands, John. *German Drawings from a Private Collection*. London: British Museum Publications, 1984.

Schade, Gunter, and Klaus-Peter Arnold, eds. *Kunst der Reformationszeit*. West Berlin: Elefanten Press, 1983.

Schmelzing, Wilhelm H. von. "Geschichtliche Beiträge zu Kunstwerken des deutschen Museums in Berlin." *Jahrbuch der preußischen Kunstsammlungen* 57 (1936): 10–14.

Schmid, Klaus-Peter. *Luthers Acta Augustana 1518.* Augsburg: FDL-Verlag, 1982.

Schmid, W. "Notizen zu deutschen Malern." *Repertorium für Kunstwissenschaft* 14 (1896): 285–86.

Schmidt, Heinrich. *Die deutschen Städtechroniken als Spiegel des bürgerlichen Selbstverständnisses im Spätmittelalter.* Göttingen: Vandenhoeck und Ruprecht, 1958.

Schmitt, Annegrit. "Der Einfluß des Humanismus auf die Bildprogramme fürstlicher Residenzen." In *Höfischer Humanismus,* edited by August Buck. (Deutsche Forschungsgemeinschaft, Mitteilung XVI der Kommission für Humanismusforschung.) Weinheim: VCH Verlagsgesellschaft mbH, 1989.

Schottenloher, K. "Kaiserliche Herolde des 16. Jahrhunderts." *Historisches Jahrbuch* 49 (1929): 460–71.

Schuster, Peter-Klaus. "Bilderkult und Bildersturm: Reformatorische Ablehnung der Bilder." In *Luther und die Folgen für die Kunst,* edited by Werner Hofmann. Munich: Prestel Verlag, 1983.

Schwab, E. "Einiges über das Wesen der Städtechronik." *Archiv für Kulturgeschichte* 18 (1928): 258–86.

Schweiger, Wolfgang. "Der Wert des Weißkunigs als Geschichtsquelle." Ph.D. diss., University of Graz, 1968.

Scribner, Robert W. *For the Sake of Simple Folk: Popular Propaganda for the German Reformation.* Cambridge: Cambridge Univerisity Press, 1981.

—. *The German Reformation.* Atlantic Highlands: Humanities Press International, 1986.

—. "Germany." In *The Reformation in National Context,* edited by Bob Scribner, Roy Porter, and Mikulá Teich, 92–122. Cambridge: Cambridge University Press, 1992.

Seward, Desmond. *The Monks of War.* St. Albans: Paladin, 1974.

Sieh-Burens, Katarina. "Die Augsburger Stadtverfassung um 1500." *Zeitschrift des historischen Vereins für Schwaben und Neuburg* 77 (1983): 125–49.

—. *Oligarchie, Konfession und Politik im 16. Jahrhundert: Zur sozialen Verflechtung der Augsburger Bürgermeister und Stadtpfleger 1518–1618.* Munich: E. Vogel Verlag, 1986.

Silver, Larry, "Forest Primeval: Albrecht Altdorfer and the German Wilderness Landscape." *Simiolus* 13 (1983): 4–43.

—. "Die guten alten istory: Emperor Maximilian I, *Teuerdank,* and the Heldenbuch Tradition." *Jahrbuch des Zentralinstituts für Kunstgeschichte* 2 (1986): 71–106.

—. "Paper Pageants: The Triumphs of Emperor Maximilian I." In *Triumphal Celebrations and the Rituals of Statecraft,* edited by Barbara Wisch and Susan Scott Munshower, 292–331. Papers in Art History from the Pennsylvania State University, vol. 6 pt. 1. University Park: Penn State University Press, 1990.

—. "Prints for a Prince: Maximilian, Nuremberg and the Woodcut." In *New Perspectives on the Art of Renaissance Nuremberg,* edited by Jeffrey Chipps Smith, 6–21. Austin: The Archer M. Huntington Art Gallery, College of Fine Arts, University of Texas, 1985.

—. "Shining Armor: Maximilian I as Holy Roman Emperor." *Museum Studies: The Art Institute of Chicago* 12 (1985): 8–29.

Simon, M. "Johannes Frosch." In *Lebensbilder aus dem bayerischen Schwaben,* edited by Götz Freiherr von Pölnitz, 2: 181ff. Munich: M. Hueber, 1953.

Sjöblom, Axel. "Ein Gemälde von Ruprecht Heller im Stockholm Nationalmuseum." In *Beiträge zur Geschichte der deutschen Kunst,* edited by Ernst Buchner and Karl Feuchtmayr, 1: 225–29. Augsburg: B. Filser Verlag, 1924.

Stälin, C. F. "Aufenthaltsorte Kaiser Maximilians I seit seiner Alleinherrschaft 1493 bis zu seinem Tod 1519." *Forschungen zur deutschen Geschichte* 1, Göttingen (1862): 349–83.

Starn, Randolph, and Loren Partridge. "Representing War in the Renaissance: The Shield of Paolo Uccello." *Representations* 5 (1984): 33–65.

Steglich, Wolfgang. "Die Stellung der evangelischen Reichsstände und Reichsstädte zu Karl zwischen Protestation und Konfession 1529/30." *Archiv für Reformationsgeschichte* 62 (1971): 165ff.

Stelzer, Winfried. *Die Belagerung von Kufstein.* Vienna: Österreichischer Bundesverlag, 1969.

Stiassny, R. "Jörg Breu und Hans Knoder." *Zeitschrift für bildenden Kunst* 9, NF (1897): 296–98.

—. "Ein monumentaler Holzschnitt." *Kunstchronik* 2, NF (1890–1): 34–5.

Stöcklein, H. "Die Schlacht von Pavia." In *Beiträge zur Geschichte der deutschen Kunst,* edited by Ernst Buchner and Karl Feuchtmayr, 1: 230–39. Augsburg: B. Filser Verlag, 1924.

Strauss, Gerald. *Historian in an Age of Crisis: The Life and Work of Johannes Aventinus 1477–1534.* Cambridge Mass., Harvard University Press, 1963.

—. "The Religious Policies of Dukes Wilhelm and Ludwig of Bavaria in the First Decade of the Protestant Era." *Church History* 28 (1959): 350–73.

Strauss, Walter, ed. *The Book of Hours of the Emperor Maximilian the First.* New York: Abaris Books, 1974.

—, ed. *The German Single-leaf Woodcut 1500–1550.* Vol. 1. New York: Hacker Books, 1974.

Strong, Roy. *Art and Power: Renaissance Festivals 1450–1630.* Berkeley and Los Angeles: University of California Press, 1985.

Tanner, Marie. *The Last Descendant of Aeneas: The Hapsburgs and the Mythic Image of the Emperor.* New Haven: Yale University Press, 1993.

Thieme-Becker: Allgemeine Lexikon der bildenden Künstler. Vol. 4. Edited by H. Vollmer. Leipzig: E. A. Seemann Verlag, 1910.

Tiedemann, Hans. *Tacitus und das Nationalbewußtsein der deutschen Humanisten.* Berlin: E. Ebering Verlag, 1913.

Thiem, Günther, and Christian Beutler. *Hans Holbein der Ältere: Die spätgotische Altar- und Glasmalerei.* Augsburg: H. Rosler, 1960.

Trevor-Roper, Hugh. *Princes and Artists: Patronage and Ideology at Four Habsburg Courts 1517–1633.* New York: Harper and Row, 1976.

Ullmann, Ernst, ed. *Kunst und Reformation.* Leipzig: VEB E. A. Seemann Verlag, 1983.

Ulrich, Paul. *Studien zur Geschichte des deutschen Nationalbewußtseins im Zeitalter des Humanismus und der Reformation.* Berlin: E. Ebering Verlag, 1936.

Van der Velden, Hugo. "Cambyses for Example: The Origins and Function of an *exemplum iustitiae* in Netherlandish Art of the Fifteenth, Sixteenth and Seventeenth Centuries." *Simiolus* 23 (1995): 5–39.

—. "Cambyses Reconsidered: Gerard David's *Justice of Cambyses*: Exemplum iustitae for the Bruges Town Hall." *Simiolus* 23 (1995): 40–62.

Van Miegroet, Hans. "Gerard David's *Justice of Cambyses*: Exemplum iustitae or Political Allegory?" *Simiolus* 18 (1988): 116–33.

450 Jahre Staats- und Stadtbibliothek Augsburg: Kostbare Handschriften und alte Drucke. Augsburg: Paul Kieser, 1987.

Vogt, Wilhelm. "Johann Schilling der Barfüßermönch und der Aufstand in Augsburg im Jahre 1524." *Zeitschrift des historischen Vereins für Schwaben und Neuburg* 6 (1879): 1–32.

Warnke, Martin. *Cranachs Luther: Entwürfe für ein Image.* Frankfurt am Main: Fischer Taschenbuch Verlag GmbH, 1984.

Weber, Dieter. *Geschichtsschreibung in Augsburg: Hektor Mülich und die reichsstädtische Chronistik des Spätmittelalters.* Augsburg: Verlag H. Mühlberger, 1983.

Wegener, Wolfgang. "Die Scheibenrisse für die Familie Hoechstetter von Jörg Breu dem Älteren und deren Nachfolge," *Zeitschrift für Kunstgeschichte* 22 (1959): 17–34.

Wehmer, Carl. "Ne Italo cedere videamur: Augsburger Buckdrucker und Schreiber um 1500." In *Augusta 955–1955: Forschungen und Studien zur Kultur- und Wirtschaftsgeschichte Augsburgs*, edited by Hermann Rinn, 145–72. Munich: n.p., 1955.

Weissmann, Ronald. "Reconstructing Renaissance Sociology: The Chicago School and the Study of Renaissance Society." In *Persons in Groups: Social Behavior as Identity Formation in Medieval and Renaissance Europe*, edited by Richard Trexler, 39–46. Binghamton: Medieval and Renaissance Texts and Studies, 1985.

Wentzel, H. "Glasmaler und Maler im Mittelalter." *Zeitschrift für Kunstwissenschaft* 3 (1949): 53–62.

Wheatcroft, Andrew. *The Habsburgs: Embodying Empire*. London: Penguin Books, 1996.

Wiesflecker, Hermann. *Kaiser Maximilian I; das Reich, Österreich und Europa an der Wende zur Neuzeit*. 5 vols. Vienna: R. Oldenbourg Verlag, 1971–86.

——. *Maximilian I: Die Fundamente des hapsburgischen Weltreiches*. Vienna: R. Oldenbourg Verlag, 1991.

Wilhelm, Johannes. *Augsburger Wandmalerei: Künstler, Handwerker und Zunft 1368–1530*. Augsburg: H. Mühlberger Verlag, 1983.

Willibald, Claudia. "Das chronicon Bavarorum des Veit von Ebersberg." *Zeitschrift für bayerische Landesgeschichte* 30 (1987): 493–541.

Winzinger, Franz. *Die Miniaturen zum Triumphzug Kaiser Maximilians I*. Graz: Akademische Druck- und Verlagsanstalt, 1973.

Wohlfeil, Rainer, and Trudl Wohlfeil. "Landsknecht im Bild: Überlegungen zur historischen Bildkunde." In *Bauer, Reich und Reformation: Festschrift für Günther Franz zum 80. Geburtstag am 23. Mai, 1982*, edited by Peter Blickle and Wilhelm Abel, 104–19. Stuttgart: Ulmer Verlag, 1982.

Wolff, Janet. *The Social Production of Art*. London: Macmillan, 1981.

Wood, Christopher. *Albrecht Altdorfer and the Origins of Landscape*. Chicago: University of Chicago Press, 1993.

Zapalac, Kristin. *In His Image and Likeness: Political Iconography and Religious Change in Regensburg 1500–1600*. Ithaca: Cornell University Press, 1990.

Zimmermann, H. "Urkunden und Regesten aus dem K. und K. Haus-, Hof-, und Staatsarchiv in Wien." *Jahrbuch der kunsthistorischen Sammlungen des allerhöchsten Kaiserhauses* 1 pt.2, (1883): LXVI, #400.

Zorn, Wolfgang. *Augsburg: Geschichte einer deutschen Stadt*. 2nd ed. Augsburg: H. Mühlberger Verlag, 1972.

——. "Michael Keller." In *Lebensbilder aus dem bayerischen Schwaben*, 7: 161–72. Munich: M. Hueber, 1959.

INDICES

PEOPLE

PLACES

Aachen 122, 148, 160n.106, 188
Alesia 181n.8
Augsburg 1-3, 6, 10n.12, 13, 15-29, 31-
39, 40n.73, 42n.81, 44, 47-50, 54,
56-57, 62-72, 74-76, 79-81, 84, 100,
103-104, 108-118, 123, 129n.135,
133-134, 136, 139-146, 149, 151-
158, 160, 166-168, 170, 172-173,
175-176, 180-181, 206n.84, 229,
235; Cathedral 20, 41n.79, 143,
157-158; Church of the Holy
Cross 42n.79, 68, 78; City Hall 2,
13, 22, 26, 47, 56-59, 67-68, 85,
102-103, 105-109, 112, 114-115,
117-118, 122, 129n.135, 145, 178,
234; Fischmarkt 106-107, 112;
Franciscan Church 21-22, 43, 53;
Fugger Chapel, St. Anna 64, 69,
102n.56; Horbruck 28n.41; In der
Grottenau (krottenau) 68, 74, 78;
Perlachplatz 106, 112; 129n.135,
145, 156-157; Rotes Tor 103n.61,
143, 154, 156; St. Anna 20, 64, 69;
St. Leonhard 156-157; St. Moritz 41, 42n.79, 49, 57, 68, 102n.56;
St. Peter 47; Sts. Ulrich and
Afra 46, 68n.149
Austria 70, 133

Baden 69n.151
Basel 108, 152
Bavaria 3, 44, 70, 135, 148, 153n.69,
158, 164, 165n.123, 174, 178, 184-
185, 189, 194, 202-203, 206n.83,
220, 233, 235
Berlin 64n.133, 71
Bohemia 116, 119, 135, 156
Bologna 141, 162, 170, 173, 202
Brandenburg 148, 154-155, 166, 174
Braunschweig 71
Brescia 117-118
Bruges 29, 108, 152, 162
Brussels 108
Budapest 64n.133, 71
Burgundy 90

Cannae 181n.8, 187, 232

Carthage 217
Cologne 148, 155-156, 175
Constance 65

Denmark 189
Dresden 71

England 152n.64, 163, 188
Europe 182, 218

Flanders 152n.64
Florence 88-89, 96-97, 190, 227
France 93, 117, 133, 135, 141,
151n.58, 152n.64, 188

Germany 1-2, 4, 6-9, 10n.11-12, 62,
94, 113, 128, 133, 147, 178, 184,
201-203, 205, 208, 225, 234-236
Gotha 10
Greece 203, 205

Hall in Tyrolia 82
Hersfeld 201
Hessen 154, 164-165
Hungary 116, 189

Ingolstadt 181, 206n.84
Innsbruck 84, 110-111, 152n.64,
153n.70
Issus 186-187, 233
Italy 9, 63n.132, 82-84, 116-117, 128,
133, 141, 190, 193, 201, 204, 208,
217

Jerusalem 150, 163n.115

Koblenz 64,70

Lederer 136n.158
Legnaia 183
Leipzig 201
Lermos 2, 70, 85n.13, 102n.56
Lombardy 117
London 96n.44, 131n.142
Louvain 92, 108
Lucca 96-97

SUBJECTS

STUDIES IN MEDIEVAL
AND REFORMATION THOUGHT

EDITED BY HEIKO A. OBERMAN

1. DOUGLASS, E. J. D. *Justification in Late Medieval Preaching.* 2nd ed. 1989
2. WILLIS, E. D. *Calvin's Catholic Christology.* 1966 *out of print*
3. POST, R. R. *The Modern Devotion.* 1968 *out of print*
4. STEINMETZ, D. C. *Misericordia Dei.* The Theology of Johannes von Staupitz. 1968 *out of print*
5. O'MALLEY, J. W. *Giles of Viterbo on Church and Reform.* 1968 *out of print*
6. OZMENT, S. E. *Homo Spiritualis.* The Anthropology of Tauler, Gerson and Luther. 1969
7. PASCOE, L. B. *Jean Gerson: Principles of Church Reform.* 1973 *out of print*
8. HENDRIX, S. H. *Ecclesia in Via.* Medieval Psalms Exegesis and the *Dictata super Psalterium* (1513-1515) of Martin Luther. 1974
9. TREXLER, R. C. *The Spiritual Power.* Republican Florence under Interdict. 1974
10. TRINKAUS, Ch. with OBERMAN, H. A. (eds.). *The Pursuit of Holiness.* 1974 *out of print*
11. SIDER, R. J. *Andreas Bodenstein von Karlstadt.* 1974
12. HAGEN, K. *A Theology of Testament in the Young Luther.* 1974
13. MOORE, Jr., W. L. *Annotatiunculae D. Iohanne Eckio Praelectore.* 1976
14. OBERMAN, H. A. with BRADY, Jr., Th. A. (eds.). *Itinerarium Italicum.* Dedicated to Paul Oskar Kristeller. 1975
15. KEMPFF, D. *A Bibliography of Calviniana.* 1959-1974. 1975 *out of print*
16. WINDHORST, C. *Täuferisches Taufverständnis.* 1976
17. KITTELSON, J. M. *Wolfgang Capito.* 1975
18. DONNELLY, J. P. *Calvinism and Scholasticism in Vermigli's Doctrine of Man and Grace.* 1976
19. LAMPING, A. J. *Ulrichus Velenus (Oldřich Velenský) and his Treatise against the Papacy.* 1976
20. BAYLOR, M. G. *Action and Person.* Conscience in Late Scholasticism and the Young Luther. 1977
21. COURTENAY, W. J. *Adam Wodeham.* 1978
22. BRADY, Jr., Th. A. *Ruling Class, Regime and Reformation at Strasbourg, 1520-1555.* 1978
23. KLAASSEN, W. *Michael Gaismair.* 1978
24. BERNSTEIN, A. E. *Pierre d'Ailly and the Blanchard Affair.* 1978
25. BUCER, Martin. *Correspondance.* Tome I (Jusqu'en 1524). Publié par J. Rott. 1979
26. POSTHUMUS MEYJES, G. H. M. *Jean Gerson et l'Assemblée de Vincennes (1329).* 1978
27. VIVES, Juan Luis. *In Pseudodialecticos.* Ed. by Ch. Fantazzi. 1979
28. BORNERT, R. *La Réforme Protestante du Culte à Strasbourg au XVIe siècle (1523-1598).* 1981
29. SEBASTIAN CASTELLIO. *De Arte Dubitandi.* Ed. by E. Feist Hirsch. 1981
30. BUCER, Martin. *Opera Latina.* Vol I. Publié par C. Augustijn, P. Fraenkel, M. Lienhard. 1982
31. BÜSSER, F. *Wurzeln der Reformation in Zürich.* 1985 *out of print*
32. FARGE, J. K. *Orthodoxy and Reform in Early Reformation France.* 1985
33, 34. BUCER, Martin. *Etudes sur les relations de Bucer avec les Pays-Bas.* I. Etudes; II. Documents. Par J. V. Pollet. 1985
35. HELLER, H. *The Conquest of Poverty.* The Calvinist Revolt in Sixteenth Century France. 1986
36. MEERHOFF, K. *Rhétorique et poétique au XVIe siècle en France.* 1986
37. GERRITS, G. H. *Inter timorem et spem.* Gerard Zerbolt of Zutphen. 1986
38. ANGELO POLIZIANO. *Lamia.* Ed. by A. Wesseling. 1986
39. BRAW, C. *Bücher im Staube.* Die Theologie Johann Arndts in ihrem Verhältnis zur Mystik. 1986

40. BUCER, Martin. *Opera Latina.* Vol. II. Enarratio in Evangelion Iohannis (1528, 1530, 1536). Publié par I. Backus. 1988
41. BUCER, Martin. *Opera Latina.* Vol. III. Martin Bucer and Matthew Parker: Florilegium Patristicum. Edition critique. Publié par P. Fraenkel. 1988
42. BUCER, Martin. *Opera Latina.* Vol. IV. Consilium Theologicum Privatim Conscriptum. Publié par P. Fraenkel. 1988
43. BUCER, Martin. *Correspondance.* Tome II (1524-1526). Publié par J. Rott. 1989
44. RASMUSSEN, T. *Inimici Ecclesiae.* Das ekklesiologische Feindbild in Luthers "Dictata super Psalterium" (1513-1515) im Horizont der theologischen Tradition. 1989
45. POLLET, J. *Julius Pflug et la crise religieuse dans l'Allemagne du XVIe siècle.* Essai de synthèse biographique et théologique. 1990
46. BUBENHEIMER, U. *Thomas Müntzer.* Herkunft und Bildung. 1989
47. BAUMAN, C. *The Spiritual Legacy of Hans Denck.* Interpretation and Translation of Key Texts. 1991
48. OBERMAN, H. A. and JAMES, F. A., III (eds.). in cooperation with SAAK, E. L. *Via Augustini.* Augustine in the Later Middle Ages, Renaissance and Reformation: Essays in Honor of Damasus Trapp. 1991 *out of print*
49. SEIDEL MENCHI, S. *Erasmus als Ketzer.* Reformation und Inquisition im Italien des 16. Jahrhunderts. 1993
50. SCHILLING, H. *Religion, Political Culture, and the Emergence of Early Modern Society.* Essays in German and Dutch History. 1992
51. DYKEMA, P. A. and OBERMAN, H. A. (eds.). *Anticlericalism in Late Medieval and Early Modern Europe.* 2nd ed. 1994
52, 53. KRIEGER, Chr. and LIENHARD, M. (eds.). *Martin Bucer and Sixteenth Century Europe.* Actes du colloque de Strasbourg (28-31 août 1991). 1993
54. SCREECH, M. A. *Clément Marot: A Renaissance Poet discovers the World.* Lutheranism, Fabrism and Calvinism in the Royal Courts of France and of Navarre and in the Ducal Court of Ferrara. 1994
55. GOW, A. C. *The Red Jews: Antisemitism in an Apocalyptic Age, 1200-1600.* 1995
56. BUCER, Martin. *Correspondance.* Tome III (1527-1529). Publié par Chr. Krieger et J. Rott. 1989
57. SPIJKER, W. VAN 'T. *The Ecclesiastical Offices in the Thought of Martin Bucer.* Trans-lated by J. Vriend (text) and L.D. Bierma (notes). 1996
58. GRAHAM, M.F. *The Uses of Reform.* 'Godly Discipline' and Popular Behavior in Scotland and Beyond, 1560-1610. 1996
59. AUGUSTIJN, C. *Erasmus. Der Humanist als Theologe und Kirchenreformer.* 1996
60. McCOOG S J, T. M. *The Society of Jesus in Ireland, Scotland, and England 1541-1588.* 'Our Way of Proceeding?' 1996
61. FISCHER, N. und KOBELT-GROCH, M. (Hrsg.). *Außenseiter zwischen Mittelalter und Neuzeit.* Festschrift für Hans-Jürgen Goertz zum 60. Geburtstag. 1997
62. NIEDEN, M. *Organum Deitatis.* Die Christologie des Thomas de Vio Cajetan. 1997
63. BAST, R.J. *Honor Your Fathers.* Catechisms and the Emergence of a Patriarchal Ideology in Germany, 1400-1600. 1997
64. ROBBINS, K.C. *City on the Ocean Sea: La Rochelle, 1530-1650.* Urban Society, Religion, and Politics on the French Atlantic Frontier. 1997
65. BLICKLE, P. *From the Communal Reformation to the Revolution of the Common Man.* 1998
66. FELMBERG, B. A. R. *Die Ablaßtheorie Kardinal Cajetans (1469-1534).* 1998
67. CUNEO, P. F. *Art and Politics in Early Modern Germany.* Jörg Breu the Elder and the Fashioning of Political Identity, ca. 1475-1536. 1998
68. BRADY, Jr., Th. A. *Communities, Politics, and Reformation in Early Modern Europe.* 1998
69. McKEE, E. A. *The Writings of Katharina Schütz Zell.* 1. The Life and Thought of a Sixteenth-Century Reformer. 2. A Critical Edition. 1998
70. BOSTICK, C. V. *The Antichrist and the Lollards.* Apocalyticism in Late Medieval and Reformation England. 1998
71. BOYLE, M. O'ROURKE. *Senses of Touch.* Human Dignity and Deformity from Michel-angelo to Calvin. 1998

Prospectus available on request
BRILL — P.O.B. 9000 — 2300 PA LEIDEN — THE NETHERLANDS